Contents

Introduction to Our Stories in Our Voices

Dale Allender

> **This book**
> **is**
> **from**
> **you**
> **to**
> **you**
> **and this book is about you.**

Youth voices continue demanding Ethnic Studies classes from California to Minnesota. In Sacramento, youth voices also wanted their teachers to be taught how to teach Ethnic Studies classes. And, students in Sacramento wanted books that explored their past and present, while inspiring their future.

Thank you to Bridget Martinez and your two pilot Ethnic Studies program students for reviewing our first edition and helping us re-vision this new edition.

What is Ethnic Studies?

Ethnic Studies is the critical and interdisciplinary study of race, ethnicity, and indigeneity, with a focus on the experiences and perspectives of people of color within and beyond the Unites States.

—University of California (UC) Berkeley College of Ethnic Studies Web Site

Youth who are calling out for Ethnic Studies classes today are inspired by activism for Ethnic Studies classes enacted decades ago. In 1968 and 1969, Students and faculty from both University of California, (UC) Berkeley and San Francisco State University (SFSU) protested to have their stories told in formal learning spaces—schools and universities. The students held sit-ins in campus buildings, and held rallies to give speeches to other students, administrators, and campus security about the need for UC Berkeley and SFSU to change their curriculum to include classes in African American, Asian American, Native American, and Chicano studies. Dr. Gregory Yee Marks describes his participation in those events in his chapter describing the birth of Asian American Studies. Ultimately, the students' voices were heard and an Ethnic Studies department was established at UC Berkeley and an Ethnic Studies College was established at SFSU. Overtime, all UC and California State University (CSU) campuses would offer some form of Ethnic Studies classes.

However, even after students and faculty from UC Berkeley and SFSU were able to establish Ethnic Studies Departments on their campuses, students at SFSU continue to press administrators to keep offering Ethnic Studies courses. And, many communities have resisted similar efforts by students to open Ethnic Studies classes at other schools and universities. I became a high school teacher a generation later in 1995, but I still faced stiff challenges when I introduced diverse books in my classroom. Teachers, administrators, and some parents and students wondered why we read about the life histories and interpretive experiences of so many different ethnic and racial communities in my class. They wanted me to focus solely on European and White American events and individuals. African American, Puerto Rican, and Korean American students in my classes cried out to learn more about themselves and others. The experience became extreme when someone sent death threats to me at the school in an effort to prevent me from addressing all of my students' desires and need to grow in their understanding of self, history, location, and others. I was intrigued when I read that more than 10 years after my experience, administrators in Arizona shut down an Ethnic Studies class at a Tucson high school. Many students in Tucson are still fighting to have that class reinstated.

What is Ethnic Studies?

Ethnic Studies provides safe academic spaces for all to learn the histories, cultures, and academic traditions of Native Peoples and communities of color in the U.S. in the first person and also practice theories of resistance and liberation to eliminate racism and other forms of oppression.

—San Francisco State University (SFSU) Ethnic Studies Department

Photo by Arya Allender-West.

High school teacher Dominique Williams and Dr. Margarita Berta-Avila of Ethnic Studies Now-Sacramento.

After the state of Arizona shut down the Ethnic Studies Class in Tucson, California High School students and teachers, and CSU faculty took up the call for Ethnic Studies classes in high schools all over the state. In Sacramento, teachers, community members, and university professors joined together to support the Student Advisory Committee's effort to establish an Ethnic Studies course by gathering community support, helping write a school board resolution, and developing this textbook.

The Four Units

This book *Our Stories in Our Voices* explores local, national, and international settings and events, exploring past and present times. The four sections are intended to be units of study, exploring four philosophical questions through a multiethnic lens.

Read the titles and short summaries below to get a quick idea about the content of each unit. These summaries also appear later in the book in the introduction to each unit. Read the summaries again when you get to each unit to reinforce your learning and help you remember what you are reading about.

After this short introduction to the layout of the book, two essays exploring **the discipline** of Ethnic Studies follow: As mentioned above, Gregory Yee Mark talks about the origin of Asian American studies arising from the Third World Strike and Rosana Chavez shares how important Ethnic Studies was for her educational experiences.

Unit I: Inventing Images, Representing Otherness

Unit I explores the question "Who am I?" The concept of **Indigeneity** is a recurring theme throughout the book, but especially in the first unit, partly through a chapter outlining spiritual, social, historic, economic, and political worldviews of California Indians of the Sacramento region, written by Rose Borunda and Crystal Arlie-Martinez. The unit also explores how people come together and make new **identities** in essays about migration, spirituality, language, intermarriage and parenting. Chapter 4 in the unit, written by Brian Baker discusses indigenous identity, as it is self-constructed and constructed by others.

After reading this Unit and working through the workbook, we hope you will be able to

- Describe the Ethnic Studies Discipline.
- Explain the concept of Indigeneity.
- Write about and discuss the influence of language, spirituality, history, or other factors on your identity development with friends and classmates.

Unit II: Ghosts of the Past

Unit II takes on the question: "Where do I come from?" Coming from one place suggests that someone is going to another place. This unit describes **migrations**. Several chapters explore individual and family stories from Mexican American, Filipino, and Hmong communities migrating to the United States and California, in particular. For example, Julie and Macedonio Figueroa write about a father and daughter telling tales of migrating through Central California as part of the Bracero program; Chao Vang shares his family's experiences leaving their homeland in rural Asia and coming to the United States with other Hmong after the Vietnam War. These stories highlight ethnic specific histories and collective experiences as different ethnic groups come together and interact with each other. The chapters written by Vanessa Esquivido-Meza, Sohnya Castorena, and the photo essay from Arya Allender-West explore how indigeneity comes to contemporary American society.

After reading this Unit and working through the workbook, we hope you will be able to

- Describe or Explain two or more historical events important to different Ethnic communities living in the United States.
- Write about, discuss, or draw how different ethnic communities and individuals connect with their indigeneity.
- Compare one or more events described in the unit to one or more current events you have heard about from your family, on the internet, or on the news.

Unit III: A Glimpse of California

Unit III of *Our Stories in Our Voices* addresses "Where am I?" The chapters in this unit explore relationships and experiences of different ethnic and racial communities in different parts of the state. For example, the unit begins with Damany Fisher writing about early African American migration into the area, and efforts to establish community against a backdrop of housing segregation and racially motivated legal restrictions. Toni Tinker's narrative returns to mixed race identity themes discussed in the first unit by Darryl Freeman, but situating her experiences in a personal narrative in specific Sacramento neighborhoods. Mas Hatano's reflection of his experiences of Internment during World War II similarly focuses on a specific camp in the region where he and his family were held.

Although these essays explore events and experiences in specific places in California, they cover issues that have occurred in other locations as well.

After reading this Unit and working through the workbook, we hope you will be able to

- Identify and label agencies, organizations, institutions, policies, or practices that restrict movement.
- Describe different ways individuals and organizations resisted being controlled by others.
- Brainstorm creative ways to stand up against being controlled by others.

Unit IV: Solidarity

Unit IV considers the question "Where am I going?" by exploring coalition politics for establishing a better community and a better world for all. Chapter 20 on the Black Panther Party written by Dr. Dale Allender makes an effort to minimize the role of armed resistance for which the Panthers are well known, while emphasizing their work to address the health, education, and nutrition needs of African Americans and other oppressed communities. Rhonda Rios Kravitz and her coauthors demonstrate efforts to address unfair treatment in education, law, and citizenship across racial and ethnic borders within the United States.

After reading this Unit and working through the workbook, we hope you will be able to

- Identify and describe different social movements involving multiple groups coming together to counter oppression.
- Describe how different communities establish solidarity between their past and present to struggle for a harmonious future.

The Glossary

Most chapters begin with a list of important words and concepts found in that chapter. Most of the chapters also include those words highlighted in red throughout the chapter. Some of the words are defined within the chapter in text boxes. All of the Important Words and Concepts are defined in a glossary at the end of the book.

Conclusion

Ultimately, each chapter is about personal and social healing and learning to thrive by oneself and with others who are similar to and different from each of us. We hope these stories will inspire you to self-discovery and outward exploration of the world around us. We hope it will inspire you to act as well.

Photo by Arya Allender West

Igniting Critical Hope.

Introduction to the Ethnic Studies Discipline

"We're Going Out. Are You With Us?" The Origins of Asian American Studies

Gregory Yee Mark

Introduction

Scholars trace back the beginning of Ethnic Studies in the United States to the student-led strikes at San Francisco State College, now San Francisco State University (November 1968), and University of California, Berkeley ("Berkeley") (January 1969). At most universities and colleges, Asian American Studies (AAS) is one of the major components of Ethnic Studies. I grew up in Berkeley and Oakland, California, and the beginning for me was the summer of 1968. I was a student at UC Berkeley and majored in Criminology. Earlier that year, I had transferred from Merritt Community College, which was on Grove Street (now Martin Luther King, Jr. Way) in Oakland. Three events that summer played key roles in creating and defining the Asian American Movement and my own lifelong interest and commitment to Ethnic Studies.

The first was a family journey that I still travel today. From age 6 to 19, I lived in Berkeley and my grandparents lived two blocks away on California Street. One day, in June 1968, my grandmother, Violet Wong, asked me to go downstairs with her to the basement and she pulled out an old film canister, which contained three reels of a 35-mm film. As she was pointing to the canister, grandmother told me "Gregory, you do something with this." I took the film to Palmer's Camera Shop in downtown Berkeley to a childhood friend who worked there. From the decaying reels, he saved 30 minutes of film and transferred it to 16-mm film. Five years later, at our 1973 family Christmas party, 60 family members viewed a screening/showing of the 1916 silent movie *The Curse of Quon Gwon*, the very first Asian American film. Grandmother starred in the black/ white film, which costarred her sister-in-law, Marion Wong. Marion played the villainess but, most importantly, *The Curse of Quon Gwon* was her creation. A unique aspect about this motion picture is that the key actors and people behind the scenes were Chinese American women. In fact, three generations of women in my family are in this pioneering film. Marion conceived the idea, raised the money, wrote the script, and directed the film. Today, I am still "doing something with it." In 2006, *The Curse of Quon Gwon* was selected to the Library of Congress' National Film Registry. I continue doing research on this motion picture, and I hope to transform the remnants of the film into an educational tool to examine the early Asian American community via film.

The second historical event was the founding of the Asian American Political Alliance (AAPA) in Berkeley by Yuji Ichioka and Emma Gee. I attended AAPA meetings and activities and considered myself a fringe member. The AAPA became the major political organizing arm of a large contingent of UC Berkeley's Asian American students and represented these students in the Third World Liberation Front coalition. AAPA played a key role on campus in Asian American student visibility and leadership.

The third historical event was the August 17, 1968 demonstration in San Francisco Chinatown (Umemoto, 2007, p. 33). The purpose of this demonstration, which was my first protest, was to bring attention to the numerous social problems that plagued San Francisco Chinatown. We wanted to push the Chinatown establishment to take action and make the public, especially government agencies, aware of these hidden social issues. I remember the sign that I held; it said, "Look around You, Chinatown is a **GHETTO**." This peaceful demonstration was especially important because it brought together community folks, university students (primarily from UC Berkeley and San Francisco State College), and even AAPA members.

The 1968 San Francisco Chinatown demonstration for the first time brought together Asian American community members and student activists advocating for their communities. Many of these students later became leaders in community mobilization efforts such as the International Hotel (I-Hotel) Struggle, Oakland Chinatown youth organizations, and Japanese American senior citizen programs in the cities of Berkeley and San Francisco. These community service projects have left their legacies through an extensive network of community-based organizations and created a pipeline for young Asian Americans to become involved in today's social justice issues and social services. For example, the multiservice Asian Health Services in Oakland Chinatown can trace its origins to 1970 and young Asian American activists.

The Asian Experience in America: Yellow Identity Symposium

In November 1968, 3 months after the San Francisco Chinatown demonstration, I was talking with five other Asian American students in the Chinese Students Club (CSC) office, on campus in Eshleman Hall. At that time, I was President of the CSC. In 1968–1969, Asian American students made up 10% of UC Berkeley's student population. There were four major Asian American student organizations: the CSC (primarily American born Chinese members); the Chinese Students Association (CSA; primarily Chinese Foreign born and immigrant students); the Nisei Students Club (NSC; Japanese American students); and Pi Alpha Phi (the Asian American fraternity). The first three organizations had offices on the fifth floor of Eshleman Hall.

On that November Friday afternoon, six male members from CSC, CSA, and NSC were talking about campus life. We started to talk about dating and one of the men, Gary, talked about a beautiful Asian American woman on campus who was from Sacramento.

All the men knew who she was because she truly stood out on campus. In a dejected fashion, Gary told us that he had asked her out but she firmly said, "no." He then asked her why she wouldn't go out with him. Gary said that she told him, "I only go out with White men." Then, the six men let out a spontaneous groan. For the next 2 hours, I led my first discussion dealing with Asian American men and their relationships with Asian American women. A significant part of our discussion was about a topic, which later became known as "Asian American Identity." After our impromptu discussion, Gary and another friend said that they really enjoyed the discussion and gained a lot from it. As I was going down the elevator, I thought to myself, "Why not expand the discussion beyond the six of us?"

As President of the CSC, I called together a cabinet meeting and asked the members what they thought about the Club organizing a conference about Asian Americans. No one wanted to take the lead. At the first planning meeting, about 10 people attended; the next meeting, about twenty, and by December 1968, there were 60 people on the conference planning/implementation committee.

On January 11, 1969, CSC and some of the other Asian American clubs hosted the "Asian Experience in America: Yellow Identity Symposium" which was attended by 800 Asian Americans from around the United States, but mainly from California. This meeting was the first national conference that was organized by Asian Americans, about Asian Americans, and was for Asian Americans. I served as the emcee and we had three keynote speakers. They were Dr. Paul Takagi, Isao Fujimoto, and Dr. Stanford Lyman. The topics ranged from Asian American history to the socioeconomic political status of Asian Americans. Many of the Asian Americans who helped plan the conference and attended the meeting, later also participated in the Berkeley Third World Strike.

From that Friday afternoon in November to the day of the conference, I knew the conference was going to be very important. I just did not realize how important. Nor did I comprehend its long-term importance. In fact, noted criminologist and Asian American scholar-activist Dr. Takagi, the symposium's lead keynote speaker, often laughed years later with the remark, "Can you believe that?" regarding the "boldness" in using the term "Yellow" for "Asian Americans," since it was not commonly used at the time. When Dr. Takagi was asked in May 2011 to reflect on his life's work, he wrote, "Perhaps Greg Mark asking me to keynote an event that he titled, The Yellow Symposium, was the beginning of my career!" (Takagi & Shank, 2012, p. 38). Here, Takagi was referring to his criminology career that took a significant turn from traditional and radical criminology to AAS scholarly activism. To Dr. Takagi, the Yellow Identity Symposium was so significant, that he stated, "That symposium was the true beginning of Asian American Studies" (Takagi & Shank, 2012, p. 39). By this, he meant the symposium was one of the primary catalysts in initiating the formation of the field of AAS.

The noted "Dean" of Chinese American Studies, historian Him Mark Lai, also attended. Just before he passed away in May 2009, in conversation at his home with the author of this chapter, Him Mark proclaimed this first-ever Asian American conference's historical significance when he said, "It was an awakening."

Courtesy of Gregory Mark

asian experience / yellow identity

From: Asian Students of Chinese Students Club and Nisei Students Club 509-600 Eshleman Hall, University of California, Berkeley, 94720, 642-4216

Bring this, your invitation, to the 1st Asian Experience in America, Sat. Jan. 11, 1969, 9:00am-4:30pm Pauley Ballroom, ASUC Building UC Berkeley.

Asian Experience in America/Yellow Identity Symposium Program Heading, University of California, Berkeley, January 11, 1969

The Sacramento Connection

Another Asian American activist who attended the "Yellow Identity Symposium" was California State University, Sacramento (Sac State) student Wayne Maeda. In May 2011, Maeda wrote

Sac State 42 years ago was a place that had its political awareness shaped by the Civil Rights Movement, the war in Vietnam and the Black Power movement. It was, after all, in Sacramento in 1967, that Black Panthers carried guns into the Capitol. However, it was events in 1968 that shaped many of us who were just students then. 1968 began with the Tet offensive where the Viet Cong attacked across Vietnam with impunity, followed by revelation of Mai Lai massacre cover up, assassinations of Martin Luther King and Robert Kennedy, Mayor Daly's thugs turned loose at the Democratic conventions in Chicago and San Francisco State and UC Berkeley campuses shut down in a push for Ethnic Studies. So there was a core of us becoming politically aware of issues of social justice and inequalities. But it was not until the 'Asian American Experience: Yellow Identity Symposium' held in January 1969 that we began to think in terms of Asians in American and our identity. A number of us came back from this first ever conference on Asian Americans even more focused and dedicated to push for Ethnic Studies at Sac State. We consolidated a coalition of Black, Chicano, Native American and white radical students to push for hiring minority and women faculty, and fundamental change in curriculum.

The timing of the "Yellow Identity Symposium" was significant for another reason. During the symposium's lunch break, my fellow classmate in Criminology, Maurice Williams, came by to see me. Maurice was a good friend who took me to African American parties and restaurants, and likewise, I took him to Asian American parties and restaurants. Originally, he was a student athlete recruited to play football at Cal (UC Berkeley). Maurice was the Black Student Union (BSU) liaison with other student groups. So Maurice told me that at last night's (Friday, January 10, 1969) BSU meeting, **"We met last night and decided that we are going out. Are you with us?"** I told Maurice, "Yes, we are with you." In other words, I was telling him that the Asian Americans students would be part of the Strike, too. On January 19, 1969 the Third World Liberation Front began the Third World Strike at the University of California, Berkeley.

The Fight for Ethnic Studies: The Third World Liberation Front

The Third World Liberation Front (TWLF) student coalition went on strike for the creation of a Third World College that would incorporate four programs: AAS, Black Studies, Chicano Studies, and Native American Studies. A significant part of the strike agenda was to achieve individual and community self-determination, social justice, service to the community, and to end racism. Third World (TW) was a term adopted from Frantz Fanon's (2004) book, *The Wretched of the Earth*. To the strikers, TW meant not only the underdeveloped countries of the world but also the U.S. working class people of color.

In the first 2 weeks of the Strike, it was exciting: peaceful picketing, marching around campus, listening to speeches from community folks and older student leaders, and handing out leaflets in front of classroom and administrative buildings. We had to have moving picket lines and not block the entrance to any buildings. We held our signs up proudly and over and over again shouted, "On Strike, Shut It Down, On Strike, Shut It Down!" and "Power to the People!" I remember the Asian American contingent holding long planning meetings to plan for the next days' strike events. Meetings sometimes lasted virtually the whole night. Our representatives also met with the other Coalition members to agree on the day's and even the week's strategies.

As the Strike progressed, there was an increasing law enforcement presence. In the first week or so, it was the campus police and folks from the Dean of Students Office who monitored our activities. Next came the City of Berkeley Police Department, then a consortium of local police departments to augment the Berkeley Police Department, such as departments from Oakland and San Leandro, and then the California Highway Patrol joined them. Then the TWLF strategy changed from moving picket lines to what we called the "snake" which consisted of strikers moving around campus, making noise, and disrupting classes that still met. As the number of student strikers declined from the daily grind and stress, the "snake" tried to avoid law enforcement and be moving targets. As the Strike progressed, the Alameda County Sheriffs or the "Blue Meanies" escalated the tension and violence even more. By the last few weeks of the Third World Strike, the National Guard was brought in with fixed bayonets attached to their rifles, and physical, violent confrontation became the daily standard mode of operation. They used tear gas and even brought in helicopters to tear gas us. Of course, tear gas did not know the difference between a striker and a student going to class. The end result was the campus was shut

Riot police attempting to move protesters from the administration building, Sproul Hall, plaza, U.C. Berkeley Third World Liberation Front Strike, near Sather Gate. Circa: March 1969.

Photo: © Ilka Hartmann

xx   "We're Going Out. Are You With Us?"

Photo: © Ilka Hartmann

Asian American student walking past riot police along Oxford Street near the west entrance of the campus, UC Berkeley Third World Liberation Front Strike, circa February 1969.

down because of the increasingly heavy-handed law enforcement presence.

For the students the strike was very trying. In week six, I remember going to Cowell Hospital, the University student hospital, for treatment and the waiting area was filled with strikers. Everyone was just so tired, run down, and suffered from a lack of sleep and fatigue.

Around this time, I remember several personal low points in the strike. The first low point was the increasing violence. I personally believed in nonviolence and I still do. However, the Strike was becoming increasingly more violent. Two major contributors were the Alameda County Sheriffs or the "Blue Meanies" and the National Guard. One day, from the fifth floor of Eshleman Hall, I looked down from the outdoor stairways balcony at the role of baton-carrying Sheriffs and fixed bayonets Guards trying to stare down protesters on the other side of Bancroft Ave. For some reason, one of the Sheriffs looked up and fired what I thought was a tear gas canister at me. I was not doing anything wrong or illegal, yet this man—this stranger—felt that he had the right to take a shot at me. It took all my self-control not to throw a chair down at him.

The second low point was a rumor that the strike was going to end . . . that the University Administration was going to meet our demands. One of the members of the Black Student Union, Charles wanted to celebrate on the steps of Sproul Hall (the Administration Building). He brought some watermelon and then he asked me if I had any opium. (And no, he wasn't joking about stereotypes of Blacks and Asian Americans.) I was so disappointed in Charles that he, a fellow striker, negatively stereotyped me with the old images of Chinese Americans as opium addicts and dealers. He thought that because I was Chinese American that I had access to opium. During the Nineteen century, the early Chinese pioneers to the United States were frequently accused of smuggling opium into the United States, operating opium dens and exposing/polluting White Americans to the drug.

Actually, in the late 1700s, the British, French, Americans, and most of the European powers smuggled opium into China, and by 1900, essentially, 27% of China's adult male population were opium addicts. So, when Charles asked me if I had any opium, I was really disappointed in him.

By week eight of the strike, the end of the Winter 1969 quarter, on March 15, 1969, the UC Berkeley Third World Strike ended. The TWLF and the University negotiated a compromise. The main demand was the creation of a Third World College. Instead, we ended up with four separate Ethnic Studies programs, which combined to become one department. Somehow, Black Studies worked out an independent arrangement with the administration and they became a separate Black Studies Program. I could not believe this—after this intense Strike, a significant component of Ethnic Studies went off on its own.

By the end of the Strike, I was getting tired from the daily demands to sustain the strike but also I was getting upset with outside elements in the Berkeley street community. As the Strike progressed, they felt entitled to become involved with the TWLF strike. In the Strike's last month, they used it as an excuse for violence and trashing the University. I felt that this outside element and law enforcement moved the Strike more towards the confrontation mode than the Strikers. Here, I learned a valuable lesson. Six years later, at San Jose State University, I was the Director of the AAS Program. I led a takeo-

Asian American Studies, Fall 1972 Schedule of Classes, Sacramento State University.

ver of President John Bunzel's office because he was threatening to take away some of the meager resources from AAS. During the takeover, in the late afternoon, non-Asian Americans came to me and one of them said, "Let's break some windows and trash the administration building." I told them something to the effect of, "You don't tell us Asian Americans what to do. We determine our own strategies and our own destiny, and if you want, you can support us, but you don't tell us what to do." I never saw him or his friends again.

Sacramento State University was highly impacted by the two Third World Strikes. Professor Wayne Maeda recalled that

> *Beginning an Ethnic Studies program, hiring faculty, developing curriculum, and the general demand for fundamental change at the campus level was made infinitely less confrontational by enormous sacrifices of students and faculty at both SF State and UC Berkeley. Moreover, they provided us models for classes, curriculum, and they even came to Sac State to provide guidance and inspiration to us. Thus, we were able to institute the first Asian American course in the Fall 1970, which was team-taught.*

The Very First AAS Course in the United States

During the first week of the Winter 1969 quarter, we went "On Strike" and on Wednesday nights, the first ever AAS course,

AAS 100X, met. Since we were "On Strike," we had to meet in one of the off-campus university's residence halls. Of course, we could not violate our own Strike by going to class on campus. There were 150 students enrolled in the class—and I was one of them.

Professor Paul Takagi was the instructor of record. However, it was a team-taught class in which the team included graduate students such as Floyd Huen, Ling-Chi Wang, Bing Tom, Alan Fong, and Richard Aoki. Class meetings were electric. There was this positive tension in the air that for the first time we were all meeting to learn about ourselves. Most students had attended Asian American weddings, baby parties, dances, and even funerals but now we were studying "Our History, Our Way" (the slogan of the University of Hawai'i at Manoa Ethnic Studies Department).

We students networked, studied, and discussed issues/topics that were relevant to our lives, and were simply awed by having the opportunity to validate our own and our family's lives. Since this was the first AAS class ever, there were no textbooks. Therefore, each week, we had lectures and frequently guest speakers were brought in such as Edison Uno who talked about the World War II Internment of Japanese Americans. Another time, a European American Anthropologist, George DeVos, spoke to the class. He came in with an arrogant attitude and was challenged by several students. The students questioned him regarding what gave him the right to tell us who we were. One of these students, Danny Li, is one of my close friends. He objected to the lecturer's "holier than-thou" tone and questioned "whether a non-Asian would have the insights of people of color who had experienced racial discrimination firsthand."

Danny later moved to Hawai'i in the fall of 1971 to continue graduate studies in Chinese History and he was involved in community-based organizations in Honolulu's Chinatown. These multiethnic residents were also facing "urban development" relocations, just like elderly Chinese American and Filipino American residents in the International Hotel (I-Hotel) in San Francisco's Chinatown. As with other involved Asian Americans, the Strike and the Movement provided Danny and many others a beginning of a lifelong commitment to end racism, fight for social injustice, and improve society.

Another person who was involved in the Strike and AAS 100X was my childhood friend, Floyd Huen. Floyd was one of the early leaders for AAS. He wrote the first proposal for AAS and represented AAPA on the TWLF Central Strike Committee. This Committee made the long- and short-run decisions for the Strikers and negotiated with the university administration. After AAS became a program at UC Berkeley, Floyd became its first program administrator (1969–70).

Floyd had been one of the hardest working members of the Asian American student contingent. Prior to the TWLF Strike, Floyd fell in love with another student activist who was deeply involved in the Strike, AAS 100X, and in general involved in the creation of AAS. Her name was Jean Quan. Jean was an undergraduate student in charge of communications during the Strike. At UC Berkeley, she cotaught the first Asian American Women's course with Emma Gee and edited and wrote the Asian Women's Journal. Later, in the mid-1980s, Quan was the Western Regional Coordinator of the Justice for Vincent Chin campaign. In 2011, Jean Quan became Mayor of Oakland.

January 1969 was truly a highpoint for me personally and for the Asian American Movement. "The Asian Experience in America: Yellow Identity Symposium" was not only successful, but also the first national Asian American conference ever. AAS 100X was an amazing experience—it was very dynamic, exciting, and historical because it was the nation's first AAS class. I served as a volunteer Teaching Assistant (TA) for AAS 100X. In my section, I had 30 students. A group of the students and I compiled a resource directory, conducted an informal needs assessment survey, and started to network with individuals and organizations in Oakland Chinatown.

Service to the Community: Oakland Chinatown

During the middle of the Strike, around February 1969, I started to reflect more about the roles that we, as Asian American students, should play to improve the quality of life in our communities. I thought about the needs in my own community—the community that had been a major part of my life—and what I could do as "an insider" to work on behalf of my own community. As a result, I started community service projects in the Oakland Asian American community, or specifically in the City's Chinatown.

I was born in Oakland and raised in both the cities of Oakland and Berkeley. As a child and young adult, my father frequently took me to Chinatown to visit with friends, eat Chinese food, and visit Chinese societies such as the Suey Sing Tong. As a young boy, I got haircuts from the barber on eighth Street, and this elderly Chinese woman barber gave children lollipops. I remember the corner grocery store at eighth and Webster. Its owners, Mr. and Mrs. Gee, frequently treated me to soda and salty plum crack seed.

As a part of the Asian American Movement, I felt that I could use my education to better serve my community. In fact, at this time, I decided to apply to the School of Criminology graduate program because I thought that I could be more effective in my community work with an advanced degree.

In 1965, Oakland began to experience what other major U.S. cities experienced as a result of the change in U.S. immigration policy created by the Civil Right movement inspired 1965 Immigration Reform Act. This dramatic increase in the Asian American population, in particular, initially impacted the Chinese American and Filipino American populations. As a result, by 1969, Oakland's Asian American community was undergoing a dramatic transition. Many new immigrants, especially Chinese, were moving into the Bay Area.

Oakland Chinatown attracted many newcomers, as demonstrated in the three Chinatown-serving neighborhood schools: Lincoln Elementary School, Westlake Junior High School, and Oakland Technical High School. As with San Francisco Chinatown, there was a critical need for bilingual education, job training, and bilingual services such as in health, affordable housing, and youth programs. Inspired by the Civil Rights movement, the Asian American Movement and the Third World Strike, community-based organizations were created as early as the mid-1960s to address these needs.

During the last month of the Strike, I networked with Oakland Chinatown organizations such as the Chinese Presbyterian Church. I also attended board meetings of the Oakland Chinese Community Council (OCCC), which at that time was the primary social service organization in Chinatown, and I served as their youth representative.

Lincoln's principal, Mr. Moynihan, was on the OCCC board. At that time, two-thirds of Lincoln School students were Asian Americans, primarily Chinese Americans, many of whom were immigrants. At board meetings, Moynihan expressed his concern regarding the difficulties faced by these non-English speaking, new arrivals from Asia, and how these students needed special assistance. I volunteered to help, thinking of the many Asian American students involved in the emerging Asian American Movement who would likely answer to such a call for service.

In AAS 100X, I had worked with a small group of students. These students and I did a preliminary needs inventory of Oakland Chinatown. One of the greatest concerns was for the community's youth. The three primary public schools serving Chinatown expressed their concern for their recent Asian American immigrant students, and there was a growing youth violence and gang problem in this community.

In the spring 1969 quarter, three new additional AAS courses were offered. One of the courses was the "Asian American Communities" course, which was also referred to as the "Asian American Field Work" class. I was a TA for one of the sections, which was called the "Oakland Chinatown" section. There were 40 students in my section. In this course, we studied Oakland Chinatown needs, the community's history, and started a community service project. It was clear that one of the community's greatest needs was to expand social services for young people.

Considering the research findings coupled with Moynihan's appeal for help at Lincoln, I recruited students from the AAS Field Work course to tutor at Lincoln. As a result, the Lincoln Elementary School Tutorial Program was born.

The Program was geared toward all Lincoln students, and its goals included improving reading and writing proficiency. However, for those students with limited English speaking abilities (primarily Asian American immigrant children), the program also aimed to improve their English verbal skills. In this way, the AAS Field Work course served as a direct pipeline to the Lincoln School Tutorial Program. My section of the Field Work course supplied the majority of the 35 tutors in the program.

The Tutorial Program was a success and continued for 4 more years. According to Moynihan, the immigrant children's English proficiency scores dramatically improved. Furthermore, this project was a manifestation of one of the first times an AAS course was directly involved with local Asian American communities. It literally applied theory and research to direct practice. In addition, it helped to jumpstart a new community-based organization, which focused on Oakland Asian American youth.

In August 1969, I founded the East Bay Chinese Youth Council, (EBCYC) Inc. This wouldn't have been possible without my roots in this community, the partnerships that I had developed with youth in the community, and with the support from Reverend Frank Mar of the Oakland Chinese Presbyterian Church.

The East Bay Chinese Youth Council, Inc.

The EBCYC was formed to improve the quality of education, provide employment training and opportunities, prevent youth violence, and provide recreational activities for Asian American youth in the East Bay. From 1969–1973, it ran an impressive array of youth programs and simultaneously sought to empower these Asian American youth. We were able to obtain funding from car washes, dances, and via the Neighborhood Youth Corps (NYC) subgrants from the Oakland Model Cities Program and the Oakland Unified School District.

One of EBCYC's nine programs was the summer NYC project that in 1970 and 1971 employed 133 and 230 Asian American youth, respectively between the ages of 14 and 18. Some of these programs were a community school for immigrant youth, community celebrations, film festivals, general community outreach, and the medical service outreach program.

In 1973, the Youth Council changed its location and name but continued many of the initial programs. The name changed to East Bay Asians for Community Action (EBACA). EBACA continued its health committee. In 1974, the health committee became Asian Health Services, which started as a one-room clinic. Asian Health Services has now become a multilingual, multispecialty community health center. Many consider it one of the nation's top community health centers/clinics. It offers health, social, and advocacy services. It is an ever-expanding center, which annually offers primary health care services including medical care, dental care, and mental health services to 27,000 adults and children, and services to over 101,000 patients. Occupying two three-story building in the heart of Oakland Chinatown, AHS has 36 exam rooms and a dental clinic with seven chairs. Its staff is fluent in English and 12 Asian languages (Cantonese, Vietnamese, Mandarin, Korean, Khmer Cambodian, Mien, Mongolian, Tagalog, Karen, Karenni, Burmese, and Lao) (*http:// asianhealthservices.org/*: 2015)

The I-Hotel

One of the founding principles of Ethnic Studies was a commitment to service to our communities and "to do community work," which later became known as "community service." For the past 25 years, this model of bridging the community with mainly higher education has been more popularly called Service-Learning. Yet little acknowledgment is given to the contributions of Ethnic Studies to the development of the Service-Learning paradigm. In its purest form—community service—was actually a critical part of the original mission of Ethnic Studies and was in fact practiced as early as 1969 with the formation of Ethnic Studies.

The UC Berkeley AAS students focused their community work (service) on five projects in Berkeley, Oakland, and San Francisco. In Berkeley, the project centered upon the Issei (first generation Japanese Americans). In San Francisco, students worked with Issei in Japantown (J-Town), Chinatown with garment workers, a bookstore, and the International Hotel.

Courtesy of *Yellow Visions*, the Asian Americana collection of Christina Fa Mark

"Fight for the International Hotel" linocut with rubilith color overlay. Featured are I-Hotel tenants (left to right) Wahat Tampoa, Felix Ayson, and Mrs. Auguila. Slogan from a community-organized effort of supporters of the I-Hotel under the leadership of the tenants' association. Circa 1976. Artist: Rachael Romero, SF Poster Brigade.

The most immediate and high impact project was "Save the I-Hotel." In 1969, the Hotel was home to manongs (first generation Filipino American farmworkers) and elderly Chinese. One of the leaders to emerge from the struggle to save the I-Hotel and also, a key participant in the Berkeley Third World Strike, was Emil DeGuzman. He was born and raised in San Francisco. In April 2011, he said

My father would take me down to Kearny Street as a little kid along with my younger brother. I had a godfather who had his photography shop under the Palm Hotel near Washington and Kearny Street. The Palm went down in 1968 and the I-Hotel was next. So I was very familiar with Manilatown growing up. When the fire happened that killed three manongs in March 1969, the Third World strike had just concluded … and we had fought so hard and learned so much, we were ripe to battle in the community.… Fortunately, my roommate Dwight Scott and myself organized students both from the strike and non-strikers who were anxious to be active to make a difference in the lives of their people. We did community work but it allowed us to join with the United Filipino Association representing the tenants to fight the owners. The success of the struggle which is true even today is the intergenerational unity where the young people unite with the elderly was the winning combination that drove the fight for eight years to stop eviction of the tenants at the I-Hotel…

It was the one of the best times in my early student years because the summer was hot and the campus was bustling with activity. The Third World Strike had ended after the Winter of 1969. This long fought struggle opened doors for minority students in the university. The victory to open an Ethnic Studies department was a major concession from the University Of California Board Of Regents. The TWLF movement had achieved new respect in the fight for the principle of self-determination in higher education.

In 1969, the Asian American population was 3,089,932 (U.S. Department of Commerce, 1973). This represented a significant increase from the previous decade. The three major Asian American groups were Japanese (591,290), Chinese (435,062), and Filipino (343,060).

The war in Southeast Asia was reaching a peak with the Tet Offensive just the year before. The Asian American Anti-War Movement was just beginning to take form and become visible in certain cities and campuses. This movement peaked a year later in April 1970 with the United States invasion of Cambodia and the increased intensity of the larger Anti-War Movement. At UC Berkeley, Asian Americans as a united group were highly visible in the Anti-War demonstrations and marches.

I remember at a planning meeting (April 1970) at the YMCA on Bancroft Avenue for one of the marches, there was a childhood friend who was attending this meeting. Ron, a Japanese American, was a Black Belt in Karate and a City of Berkeley Police Officer. I asked Ron, "Are you working now?" He embarrassedly said that he was working. We kind of laughed because it was obvious that he was working undercover to gather intelligence information on the pending march.

The summer of 1969 symbolized a critical time for the United Farm Workers Union (UFW) and their link to the Asian American Movement. Early Union leaders such as Larry Itliong, the original organizer and leader of the Delano Grape Strike, Philip Vera

Cruz, and Cesar Chavez were utilizing Mahatma Gandhi's tactics of nonviolent protesting. Itliong and Vera Cruz, both Filipino Americans, also represented an important part of the 1969 Asian American population: the manongs. Many were retired farmworkers who worked in the fields with their Chicano counterparts. In order to improve farmworkers' wages and work conditions, the UFW utilized numerous nonviolent methods to achieve their goals such as strikes against nonunion farms, boycotts of supermarkets such as Safeway that sold grapes and lettuce from nonunion growers, a march to Sacramento, and Chavez's well-known hunger strikes.

A short time after the TWLF Strike, Professor Takagi organized a car caravan of Berkeley Asian American students and farmworker supporters to go to the UFW headquarters in Delano to show our support for the Union and delivered carloads of bags of rice. I remember arriving in Delano and going with Professor Takagi and a small group of students into the UFW headquarters. We walked into a back room and in a hospital bed was Cesar Chavez. He waved to us to come closer to him. My impressions for those 5 minutes were how kind he was, passionate about his cause, humble, and angelical. Although Chavez was weak and in poor health from his hunger strike, there was a peacefulness about this experience that I will never forget. This experience has left a lasting impression on me. To move people, to move mountains, one can do it with the positive, unflinching attitude of "Si, se puede (Yes, we can)."

The Third World Strike to establish Ethnic Studies at UC Berkeley was a hard-fought battle to establish a new discipline in higher education, but also in K-12. The College of Ethnic Studies was established at San Francisco State University and the Ethnic Studies Departments and Programs flourished at universities such as Sacramento State and the University of Hawai'i at Manoa. Ethnic Studies and related race and ethnicity courses sprang up all over the United States. Just as important was a new generation of community organizers and community-based organizations that for the past 48 years have truly impacted the communities they were meant to serve.

Photo: © Christina Fa Mark

Concluding Thoughts

After Dr. Paul Takagi retired, he continued to actively write about, reflect on, and was a strong advocate for social justice. For over 47 years, he had been my mentor and friend. Paul passed away on September 13, 2015.

Dr. Paul Takagi and Dr. Greg Mark (left to right) at the Founding Meeting of the UC Berkeley Asian Pacific American Alumni Chapter, when Professor Takagi, Professor Emeritus of Criminology, was honored "for his pioneering role in helping create Asian American Studies...," October 11, 2008, Alumni House, UC Berkeley.

Him Mark Lai passed away May 2009. His research, publications, and mentoring of students about Chinese American history lives on.

Danny Li is semi-retired on the Big Island of Hawai'i. He continues to fight for social justice and equal rights for all.

Floyd Huen, M.D. was recently Medical Director at Lifelong Medical Care and Over Sixties Health Center in Berkeley and Oakland. He continues to organize communities for social justice and equal rights.

Jean Quan is the immediate past Mayor of the City of Oakland. She was the City's first woman mayor and its first Asian American mayor, along with the first Asian American woman mayor of a major U.S. city. Mayor Quan brought her decades of training in the Civil Rights Movement to her public service positions on the Oakland School Board, Oakland City Council and as the Oakland City mayor.

Emil DeGuzman was a member of the City and County of San Francisco Human Rights Commission. He has also been a Fair Housing & Public Accommodations Investigator/Mediator. He continues to fight for social justice and is an activist in the Filipino American community.

Dwight Scott passed away November 2008. I have never forgotten his commitment, strength on the basketball court, and friendship.

Sac State had been very fortunate to have Wayne Maeda teach for 43 years in the Ethnic Studies Department. Since its inception, Wayne had been the foundation for AAS at Sacramento State Brah, RIP.

I am now a Professor of Ethnic Studies and the Director of AAS at California State University, Sacramento. My community service work in Oakland was followed by decades of service in Honolulu, and, even today, I'm engaged in community service programs that I have created in Sacramento. I continue to work for a more just and fair society for all.

Photo: © Christina Fa Mark

Gregory Mark, left, holding photo of Oakland Suey Sing Tong members in 1970, which included his father, then Oakland Suey Sing Tong President Byron Yee Mark. Standing on the right is Yi Ling Tsao, Oakland Suey Sing Tong President at the time of the photo. Taken during a presentation by Dr. Mark about Oakland's Suey Sing Tong to students at an Asian American Studies field trip from Sac State to Oakland Chinatown, November 2013.

References

Asian Health Services. (2015). Retrieved from http://asianhealthservices.org/, 2011 and 2015.

Fanon, F. (2004). *The Wretched of the Earth*, Grove Press.

Umemoto, K. (2007). 'On Strike!' San Francisco State College Strike, 1968-1969: The Role of Asian American Students. In Zhou & Gatewood (Eds.), *Contemporary Asian America* (2nd ed.). New York, NY: University Press: 2007.

U.S. Department of Commerce. (1973, July). *Japanese, Chinese, and Filipinos in the United States: 1970 census of population*. Washington DC: A United States Department of Commerce Publication.

Takagi, P., & G. Shank. (2012) *PAUL T. TAKAGI: Recollections and writings*. San Francisco, CA: Crime and Social Justice Association.

Wei, W. (1993). *The Asian American movement*. Philadelphia, PA: Temple University Press.

Interviews

DeGuzman, Emil, prilA 2011. Huen, Floyd, April 2011. Lai, Him Mark, May 2009. Li, Danny, August 2010. Maeda, Wayne, May 2011.

Takagi, Paul, March 2011 and April 2011.

Why Ethnic Studies Was Meant for Me

Rosana Chavez-Hernandez

Important Words and Concepts

Chicano gente
Chicano Movement
Cesar Chavez
MEChA
Empowering
Consciousness
La Mujer Chicana
Chicana

My Golden Moment

I remember my graduation as if it were yesterday. Stepping foot into this huge stadium where the lights were so bright, all I could hear was the roaring crowd. I was instructed to move forward to take my photo, and then was hooded. I find myself standing next to these strong bronze women sharing this celebratory moment together. Everything is happening so fast and it's all just a huge blur. Then I hear my name being called into the microphone "Rosaaannna Chaveeeez". What! They said my name correctly! This was the first thought that rushed into my head. My goodness they actually said my God-given name the way it was meant to be pronounced. I shook the hand of the Dean of the College of Education and my paper diploma was handed to me. This is it? I thought to myself out loud. This is truly it. I did it! I felt this huge sense of accomplishment take over my entire body. I felt as if I could fly and a huge weight had been lifted from me. Tears rolled down my cheeks as I looked for my family in the sea of people. With my diploma in hand, I waved it in the direction of my family. I yelled to my family, "This is for you!" This was my golden moment that I owned and that no one could take from

Couresty of Manuel Pacheco

me. I worked for the past seven years beginning with my undergraduate and ending with my graduate degree with fierce determination. Logistically, I earned a piece of paper that the University likes to call a Master's degree. But, it was more than just a piece of paper with fancy writing. This was a piece of paper that symbolized much more.

Receiving this diploma embodied all of my and my family's hard work. Receiving this diploma represented overcoming many struggles and barriers that I had faced in addition to those that my family had endured. This piece of paper represented the blood and sweat of my Chicano gente involved in the Chicano Movement and the many educational struggles it took before my time for me to be able to experience my golden moment. This piece of paper represented far more than what words can express. Receiving this diploma symbolized my new beginning as a first generation college graduate. I became the first woman in my entire family to earn a master's of science degree. I reflect on my degree hanging in my bedroom wall and relive the moment as much as possible. I relieve them to appreciate the past and present efforts to make education accessible. Sharing the graduation experience serves as a benchmark to remember that moment strongly influenced by my decision to major in Ethnic Studies as an undergraduate. Selecting the right major as an undergraduate is never an easy process, especially a major few people generally understand. Just the fact that people did not understand Ethnic Studies as a discipline did not deter me. In fact, the more I took courses in Ethnic Studies, the more I recognized its universal applied value. I want to share my proud experiences for the sole purpose of educating those who are considering majoring in Ethnic Studies. However, my positive feelings about being an Ethnic Studies major also meant confronting many hurdles in order to experience academic success. But, in order to understand my reflections I must first share what life was like before my college journey began.

Where My Journey Began

What do you want to be when you grow up is a common question that many children have been asked while in grade school. Some might respond with wanting to be a doctor, a lawyer, an astronaut or even a teacher. As very young children, our range of career choices are framed by the exposure we receive through school, in our home or even through media. Although we might not realize at the time, we are asked such questions as children, but those messages are informing part of our career development process. I am sure no child would answer (at least that I am aware of) that they want to major in Ethnic Studies and study social justice in a modern day society. As a child, I was definitely not the exception. However, I will tell you this: ever since I can remember, I wondered why history books presented in classes always seemed to cover the same topics over and over again and at the same time could never seem to locate my cultural history or see people who looked like me, represented in my history books. As this learning experience continued, I became more eager and curious to learn and discover what was being hidden from me and why.

> Just because people did not understand Ethnic Studies as a discipline did not deter me. In fact, the more I took courses in Ethnic Studies, the more I recognized its universal applied value.

As an adult, I remember being in the second grade and the first book I checked out from my school's library was a book titled, Cesar Chavez. I did not know who he was or the history of the United Farm Workers Movement at age eight, but I choose this book because I read my last name "Chavez" on the front cover. I was so excited because my very own last name was written on a book. Now was this a coincidence? Or, was I actually beginning the planning of my future major in Ethnic Studies? Reflecting on this experience helps me to reinforce that even as a child, I was eager to learn about sociocultural history. I was captivated by the title of this book simply because I could relate. These feelings I was exposed to at such a young age were the same feelings I felt as I discovered Ethnic Studies as a major.

My curiosity of my culture did not end in elementary school, but it definitely transferred into my high school years. I was a sophomore and I attended my first MEChA (Movimiento Estudiantil Chicano de Aztlan) Youth Conference at Sacramento State. This was my first time stepping foot on to a college campus and I instantly fell in love. The campus felt welcoming and it was covered with many trees and buildings. There were many people walking from class to class and I remember seeing all the diverse faces. It was such a foreign world to me but I wanted to be part of it. This is when I first set the goal of graduating from high school and making college a part of my future plans. I did my research; I spoke with advisors and did everything possible in my power to make sure that I was eligible to apply for college. I was determined to attend Sacramento State even though my high school counselors told me that I was not university bound.

College Can Come True

In the fall semester of 2001, my dream became a reality when I began my college career at Sacramento State. I was a first time freshman and scared out of my mind. I moved from a small local high school to this city size campus of 28,000 people overnight. I only knew one person from my high school that also began that same semester. Not knowing many people at the university was scary and I felt alone. I needed to make connections with students and the best way to do so was through my major. Initially I was majoring in apparel marketing and design. I wanted to be a fashion designer which in my mind translated into becoming rich and famous just like on television. This is what sounded good to me at the time because I had no other perception of what else was out there. I took classes in this major but did not find a personal connection. Before I discovered Ethnic Studies as a major, I felt this huge emptiness and confusion about who I was as a person of color and where I was going with my life. I needed to find a major that matched my intellectual talents with my personal values and beliefs.

A connection similar to the one I experienced as a child when I read my first book on Cesar Chavez. I knew that I had some type of purpose and mission to fulfill, but at the moment I was lost like many college students can be throughout their college experience. What am I going to do with my life? I put this huge pressure on myself because it took so long for me to get into college and now I had no plan.

> **I knew that I had some type of purpose and mission to fulfill.**

It was not until my beginnings of junior year at Sac State that I decided to take a class called Ethnic America with Professor Wayne Maeda. I chose this class because the description spoke to me. Achieving my educational goal of beginning college also meant I could further educate myself on my culture, and I felt this class was my opportunity to do so. Since my ideas about having a career in fashion was steadily becoming uninteresting, I figured I had nothing to lose by exploring my personal interest. Little did I know that making this one simple decision, I was about to embark on a life-changing experience that would impact my life forever.

I still remember my first day of class. I couldn't find the building, I was late. I had to beg Professor Maeda to add me into his section. Luckily he did! Taking this course made me feel as if I was opening my eyes for the first time. Professor Maeda kept true to the description of the course. Learning about racism, oppression, and the various social justice movements of the four ethnic groups was empowering. Empowering in that I was learning about how and why these terms came into existence. My consciousness was being expanded. I stepped foot into this course that I was able to grasp an intellectual understanding and put into context how my own socially lived experiences related to my history in the United States. My life began to make sense. Hearing what I like to call the other half of history made me feel complete. As Professor Maeda would say "I was given a new pair of lenses to see the world through." This statement carries so much meaning. Taking this course was like having a new pair of eyes and I could see life so clearly. My experiences as a woman of color began to make more sense to me. During that class, Professor Maeda became a great mentor and actually convinced me in changing my major to Ethnic Studies. That is exactly what I did.

In the Process

Changing your major is not always the easiest process. Sure, all it takes is a piece of paper with a few signatures, but there are social obligations and responsibilities that come along with receiving an education. Even though I found my calling and I knew Ethnic Studies was for me, I now had the duty to explain to my family and my peers what this major entailed. When asked what my major was going to be, my family and peers always responded with "What are you going to do with that major?" Sounds familiar? At the moment, I could honestly say I did not know how to answer that question. Or, what was to become of me majoring in this field, but all I knew was that it felt right. With this deep-seated conviction, all I needed to know was to keep moving forward without regret or doubt. I remember when I told my dad what I was studying he responded "Que es eso?" ("What is that)? I slowly explained Ethnic Studies, but all he would ask was if I was going to make good money and if I was going to graduate fast. My mother, on the other hand, did not question me at all, she was just happy to see her daughter follow her path. My parents never really knew what this major was about, and I am not too sure if they still fully understand, but they were definitely proud of my renewed confidence as a student and daughter. My parents realized that selecting a major with this much enthusiasm meant I had direction to accomplish not just graduating from college but obtain a career that was personally and professionally fulfilling.

My Experience Matters

Ethnic Studies has built a strong foundation for my career and my everyday life. Learning about my cultural background in the classroom has been empowering to me. It was not until I stepped foot into an Ethnic Studies classroom that I was told my experience matters. One course in particular helped me conceptualize what it meant to be a woman of color and has facilitated my understanding of my different life roles. The course titled La Mujer Chicana (The Chicana Woman) taught by Dr. Julie Figueroa was a course where I literally studied and was invited to reflect on myself and the life I was living. This is a course where the bar was consistently set to a high standard. Some of the most sensitive culturally taboo topics were addressed, and it brought me out of my comfort zone. Topics included identity, feminism, sexuality, cultural tradition, language, religion, and art—just to name a few. Studying these types of topics in a classroom setting was mind blowing. It was through this course that I was able to ethnically identify myself through studying my own identity. I was never too sure how to ethnically define myself on campus until I met Dr. Figueroa. I knew that I was a mixture of different cultures and that I was more than a person who was born in the United States, of Mexican descent. Like many first generation college students, I struggled to understand my identity on a college campus and in my home. At home, I was Mexicana, even though my aunt from Mexico begged to differ. She said I was a pocha with Mexican parents. On campus I did not identify as an American because this term did not embrace the whole me. This is when I decided that I was to reject the predetermined labels that were given to me and that I was going to take charge on how to ethnically identify myself. I was then able to link my two worlds and make it into my one entity. I identify as a Chicana woman because it personifies the full me and it represents my experience best in the United States. Overall, this course supported my critical thinking skills and challenged what I thought I knew about myself and has taught me what I needed to know. More importantly, it helped me understand where I wanted to go in life and how I was going to get there. Dr. Figueroa constantly pushed me towards academic success and she succeeded as a professor. My experience truly matters and I do have something worth sharing. Just as you do too.

My experiences with Dr. Maeda and Dr. Figueroa's courses have demonstrated how Ethnic Studies has supported my critical thinking skills. I was able to develop this new-found consciousness and understanding of who I am as a Chicana woman. In respects to learning about myself, I also became aware of the diverse cultural backgrounds that surround me. I experienced various courses that shared the social lived experiences of a wide range of ethnic groups. Learning about social justice made me aware that different ethnic groups share a commonality with one another. We have all faced and continue to face different oppressive social issues and struggles. Learning that when we unite as a people, we can overcome hardships that cross our paths. This has enlightened me. More importantly, it has taught me the importance of celebrating diversity and as humans, we actually have a lot more in common than what we think. Ethnic Studies has humbled me to appreciate not only myself, but the experiences of others. This is what Ethnic Studies can offer you.

> ...refuse what society has made of us and become trend-setters within your families and communities. In doing so, you will find your purpose in life through fulfilling their own dreams.

Lessons Learned

I currently work as a full-time Counselor/Sophomore & Career Success Coordinator for the Educational Opportunity Program (EOP) at Sacramento State. I serve first generation college students from year one to graduation. Having Ethnic Studies as my foundation has not only allowed me to understand my student's sociocultural backgrounds; I am also able to share and relate my own experiences with them. As my students are going through their own self-exploration process, I teach them to refuse what society has made of us and to become trend-setters within their families and communities. In doing so, they will find their purpose in life through fulfilling their own dreams. There are many lessons that I learned while going through my college journey. They are the same lessons I pass down to my own students and that I will like to pass on to you. Lesson number one: follow your heart. Nowadays people seem to focus too much on their external influences and forget to give themselves permission to explore their likes and interest. It is through exploring yourself that you will find what is meant for you. Even though you may not know your calling, it will shine through if you accept the exploration process. Lesson number two: trust yourself. It is completely natural to experience self-doubt and ask what I am doing? However, sometimes it takes this self-doubt to help you open your eyes and see what is truly right for you. Embrace this self-doubt and redirect those emotions as a motivation to do some of your own research as you are shopping for a major.

Trust this process. Lesson number three: never settle for less. Don't go for the major that you randomly select with closed eyes or the major your family and peers tell you to follow. Don't settle for what you think will be the easiest. You will not be fully satisfied with your career in the long run if you opt to take a short cut. Lesson number four: discover who you are through understanding where you come from. This helps keep you focused and humble. It will help you keep your priorities lined up and it will remind you why you are here in the first place? Coming to your realization and following these lessons will help you achieve academic and career success at Sacramento State.

The Journey Continues

As a counselor, I enjoy working with my students and being part of their exploration process. I am happy to give back and share what Ethnic Studies has given me. Over the years, I have refused to be another negative statistic and decided to become a trend-setter for my family and my community. I decided to follow my dreams which created my path of success. I continue to give myself permission to explore, for this process does not necessarily end once you graduate. I challenge you all to make similar efforts and create your path towards success. Fulfill your life destinies so you too can experience your own golden moment. When in doubt follow your heart and your instincts and you will find that things will naturally unfold. Remember your experience does matter and you have a lot to share. You will come across your own lessons learned in your college careers that you too can share with future generations. Remember, the journey still continues after you graduate, but it is up to you how you decide to navigate it. If you are deciding to purse Ethnic Studies and the next time someone asks you what can you do with that major, I would like for you all to please respond "What can you NOT do with that major" Now give yourself permission and go explore!

¿Quién soy? ¿Quién soy? ¿Quién soy?
¿Quién soy? ¿Quién soy? ¿Quién soy?
¿Quién soy? ¿Quién soy? ¿Quién soy?
¿Quién soy? ¿Quién soy? ¿Quién soy?
¿Quién soy? ¿Quién soy? ¿Quién soy?
¿Quién soy? ¿Quién soy? ¿Quién soy?
¿Quién soy? ¿Quién soy? ¿Quién soy?
¿Quién soy? ¿Quién soy? ¿Quién soy?
¿Quién soy? ¿Quién soy? ¿Quién soy?
¿Quién soy? ¿Quién soy? ¿Quién soy?
¿Quién soy? ¿Quién soy? **Who am I?**
¿Quién soy? ¿Quién soy? ¿Quién soy?
¿Quién soy? ¿Quién soy? ¿Quién soy?
¿Quién soy? ¿Quién soy? ¿Quién soy?
¿Quién soy? ¿Quién soy? ¿Quién soy?
¿Quién soy? ¿Quién soy? ¿Quién soy?
¿Quién soy? ¿Quién soy? ¿Quién soy?
Who am I? ¿Quién soy? ¿Quién soy?
¿Quién soy? ¿Quién soy? ¿Quién soy?
¿Quién soy? ¿Quién soy? ¿Quién soy?
¿Quién soy? ¿Quién soy? ¿Quién soy?
¿Quién soy? ¿Quién soy? ¿Quién soy?
¿Quién soy? ¿Quién soy? ¿Quién soy?
¿Quién soy? ¿Quién soy? ¿Quién soy?
Kuv yog leej twg? ¿Quién soy?

Unit I

Inventing Images, Representing Otherness

Chapter 1

California History: Depth and Breadth From Original American Indian Tribal Nations: Beyond a Mere 250 Years

Crystal Martinez-Alire and Rose Borunda With Susan Olsen

The most important thing that people need to know about the Nisenan people is that we are still here. The other thing that needs to be known is that we need to correct the history books. The history books have it wrong.

Richard B. Johnson, Tribal Chair of Nevada City Rancheria

Important Words and Concepts in This Chapter

There are several important words and concepts throughout the upcoming chapter. The words appear several times in different places in order to help you remember the words and understand the chapter. The words are defined several times.

- Immediately below right before the chapter begins
- In text boxes throughout the chapter
- In red and boldfaced within the chapter
- In a glossary in expanded form at the end of the units

Some of the words also appear in other chapters. Talk about the words with other students, teachers, friends, and family members before you read, while reading the chapter, and after you have read the chapter.

Contributed by Crystal Martinez-Alire and Rose Borunda. © Kendall Hunt Publishing Company.

Original Nation

A name for indigenous people, sometimes referred to as First Nation, Native American, or American Indian. These terms refer to many different ethnic groups (e.g., Cheyenne, Lakota, Maidu, Miwok, Mohawk, and Cherokee) all at once so they are not specific and may not be the way to refer to themselves.

Place Names

The name given to geographical location, such as a town or street. Often place names originate from indigenous names.

Sacred Narratives

Myths. Stories about how the world was created, and humans' role in it.

Indigenous Cultures

The practices and beliefs of people whose family and ethnic group lived in a particular land first. Some of these practices and beliefs change over time and some of them stay the same for many years.

Indigenous Spiritual Belief Systems

Ideas form people whose family and ethnic group lived in a particular land first about how the world was created; where people came from and where we will go when we die; also how we should treat our families and other people living or dead.

Ethnobotanist

Someone who studies the stories, beliefs, and agricultural practices of an ethnic community.

Cultural Proscriptions

A restraint or restriction from doing or saying some things based on cultural heritage.

Sociopolitical

Of or relating to both social and political factors.

Genocide

The systematic killing of an entire ethnic community.

Cultural Genocide (Culturcide)

Comes from the word "gens," meaning a clan or community of people related by common descent. The idea of cultural genocide implies the process of undermining, suppressing, and ultimately eliminating native cultures.

Cosmology

Cosmology explores how and why the universe works. Cosmology involves the philosophy and the scientific study of the large-scale properties of the universe as a whole. It endeavors to use the scientific method to understand the origin, evolution, and ultimate fate of the entire universe. Like any field of science, cosmology involves the formation of theories or hypotheses about the universe which make specific predictions for phenomena that can be tested with observations.

Federally Recognized Tribes

Federally recognized Indian tribes or groups are eligible for funding and services from the Bureau of Indian Affairs (BIA). There are currently 566 federally recognized tribes throughout the United States. This is an important political and legal category, as there are also "state recognized tribes" and "unrecognized tribes" which are not officially recognized by the U.S. government.

Sovereignty

The authority possessed by the governing individual or institution of a society. Sovereign authority is distinct in that it is unrestricted by legal regulation since the sovereign authority is itself the source of all law.

Elders

An influential member of a tribe, community, or family—often considered wise.

Sacred Geography

There are many different types of sacred geography. Some examples include the following:

1. Shrines, vision quest sites, altars, and sweat bath sites that serve as ritual settings.
2. Monumental geographical features that have mythic significance in a group's origins or history. Included are mountains, waterfalls, and unusual geographical formations such as Pilot Knob, Kootenai Falls, Celilo Falls, and Mount Adams.
3. Rock art sites such as pictograph and petroglyph panels.
4. Burial sites and cemeteries.
5. Areas where plants, stones, earth, animals, and other sacred objects are gathered for ritual purposes or where sacred vegetation such as medicine trees serve as objects or center of ritual.
6. Sites of major historical events such as battlefields where group members died.
7. Sites where groups are thought to have originated, emerged, or been created.
8. Pilgrimage or mythic pathways where groups or individuals retrace the journeys and reenact events described in myths and in the lives of mythic and other figures.
9. Lakes, rivers, springs, and water associated with life and the vital forces that sustain it.
10. Areas or sites associated with prophets and teachers like Smohalla, Handsome Lake, Sweet Medicine, and others.

Tribal Governments and Councils

The term "tribal government" is defined as any Indian tribe, band, nation, or other organized group or community, including any Alaska Native village or regional or village corporation as defined in or established pursuant to the Alaska Native Claims Settlement Act (85 Stat. 688; 43 U.S.C. 1601 et seq.), which is recognized as eligible for the special programs and services provided by the United States to Indians because of their special status as Indians. The tribes have their own laws and governments.

Horticulture Techniques

The scientific and artistic practices of growing fruits, vegetables, flowers, or ornamental plants. These practices are influenced by culture.

Government-to-Government Relations

November 6, 2000, with Executive Order 13175, the United States in consultation with Native American tribes codified their government-to-government consultation policy. The government-to-government relationship is not new, but has strong roots that took hold with the very earliest contact between the American Indians and the first European settlers. The settlers and the tribal leaders dealt with each other as separate sovereigns and that relationship is the foundation of all dealings that have taken place between the United States and Indian tribes throughout the history of the nation. This Indian policy has found its way into federal statutes and case law and into executive orders. As nations separate from the United States, the internal affairs of tribes are the responsibility of the tribal entity and are not to be tampered or interfered with by the United States.

Symbiotic Connection

Usually a close connection over a period of time between two different specious—or communities that enjoy a mutual benefit by connecting.

Primary Source Data

In research activities, *primary source* refers to information collected firsthand from such sources as historical documents, literary texts, artistic works, experiments, surveys, and interviews. Also called *primary data.*

Servant Leadership

Someone who leads by serving others. In other words, servant leaders place the interests and needs of their followers ahead of their own self-interests and needs. Generally, they value the development of their followers, building their communities, acting authentically, and sharing power.

Encomienda System

A system that was created by the Spanish to control and regulate American Indian labor and behavior during the colonization of the Americas.

Great Law of Peace

The Great Law of Peace is the name given to the constitution of the Iroquois Confederacy, a union of Native American tribes centered south of Lake Ontario that thrived for 600 years up to the formation of the United States. The U.S. Constitution is based on the Great Law of Peace.

Dawes General Allotment Act

This law was named after Senator Henry Dawes of Massachusetts who was main person who authored and introduced this act to Congress in 1887. The law allowed for the president to break up reservation land, which was held in common by the members of a tribe, into smaller allotments that were parceled out and assigned to individual tribal members as heads of households, generally in 160-acre allotments. After reservation land was allotted to tribal members, remaining land was deemed to be excess land and then sold to non-Indians. While in effect, the overall land based for Native Americans decreased from 138,000,000 in 1887 to 48,000,000 in 1934. The legacy and negative effects of the allotment policy continue to play out on many Indian reservations today.

Unratified Treaty

A treaty that has not been confirmed, signed, or acted upon. This term is often used with regard to Native Americans where the ungratified treaty has resulted in a loss of land.

Missions

A ministry commissioned by a religious organization to propagate its faith. Religious missions, such as Spain's Missions in California, are often one factor in the colonization of an indigenous community's land and resources.

Storytelling

The act of sharing an event, incident, or sacred narrative for entertainment, social cohesion, spiritual insight, and so on.

Important Words and Concepts in This Section

Genocide
Original Nations
Primary Source Data
Place Names

If it were not for the resilience and persistence of American Indians, we would not know that they lived in greater numbers, across the Americas on the land now called the United States. Although there is a larger story to be told about the American Indian experience, this chapter focuses on the multiple and diverse California Indian communities living in the greater Sacramento region. Evident today is the fact that despite relentless genocide and culturcide enacted upon these communities, their languages, traditions, practices, and beliefs that comprise the identity of a people have endured, survived, and are being actively revitalized. With the intention of "correct(ing) the history books," the content of this chapter provides first-hand testimony from members of California Indian communities. This type of testimony is referred to as Primary Source Data in which we learn about a people from the people themselves. In doing so, we will gain knowledge about their contributions, sources of strength and perseverance, knowledge, and wisdom that span thousands of years on the land now called the Americas. While the terms Native American, American Indian, Indigenous, and First or Original Nations are often used interchangeably, this chapter most often uses the term, Original Nations.

The Original American Indian Tribal Nations of the Sacramento region include the Sierra Miwok, the Nisenan, the Patwin, and Northern Valley Yokuts. Since intertribal networks extend beyond the Sacramento region, there can also be references to the Konkow, Maidu, Nomlaki, and Wintu who live to the north of the Sacramento region; the Lake Miwok, the Pomo, the Wappo, Coast Miwok, and Castanoan to the west; and the Washoe and Paiute to the east. This chapter follows a curriculum framework that touches upon 10 historical and cultural themes: origins, religious systems, language, sociopolitical systems and networks, economic systems, interactions with place, material culture, life cycle, colonialism, and native peoples and communities today. Each theme explores various subcategories, which are identified in *italics*, as you are introduced to the richness of each community.

Original Nation contributions can be found in our vocabulary. Place Names reflect of our ecological diversity and were given by people who lived in direct relation to the land.

While the terms:

- **Native American**
- **American Indian**
- **Indigenous**
- **First Nations or Original Nations are often used interchangeably, this chapter most often uses the term, Original Nations.**

These names reflect the ecological diversity of our region. To illustrate this point, "Umne" means "people of," Moke means "fishnet," and "Kosum" means "Salmon." Whenever we say Cosumnes and Mokelumne as in two major rivers that flow through the Sacramento region, we are using the Miwok language. Tahoe, as in Lake Tahoe, is a word from the Washoe tribe and means "big water." These examples enhance our awareness of Original Nation contributions to our own cultural landscape while heightening our understanding of the history and perspective of the people who have called this land home for thousands of years. While only so much can be addressed within the scope of this contribution, the questions at the end of this chapter guide your inquiry and perhaps encourage you to ask why these voices, experiences, and perspectives have not been included in mainstream education.

Origins

Important Words and Concepts in This Section

Cosmology
Sacred Narratives
Sacred Geography

Cosmology, the science of the origin and development of the universe, is contained in the oral tradition of indigenous cultures. **Sacred Narratives**, the histories of a people, are retold, generation after generation, and convey not only the origins of a people but also transmit valuable information about what transpired over the course of thousands of years. When communities have strong intergenerational systems in which knowledge is passed on from one generation to the next, then, we can learn vast information about historic climatic shifts and how people responded to and related to their universe.

To this point, the Sierra Miwok had circular assembly houses, similar to the active Round House in use at Indian Grinding Rock State Park in Pine Grove. Selected men, known as an Utentbe, would travel to the various villages and tell the stories at night in such gathering places. The storyteller was supported by the communities who paid him with baskets, beads, furs, and food. This was a form of *currency*. Thomas Williams, a former Miwok Utentbe, said that the telling of a myth often took all night. Not infrequently the myth was chanted. Each myth, whether chanted or told in ordinary prose, was accompanied by the songs of the various characters. For example, with the story of Prairie Falcon's marriage belong three songs, one sung by Prairie Falcon, one by his wife, and one by his father. Williams related 11 stories that were secured in 1913 and 1914. These stories were originally recorded in Miwok and translated, word for word, into English. The following Miwok story entitled "How Kah'-Kah-Loo the Ravens Became People" speaks to a cataclysmic flood which was followed by the repopulation of the world after the water receded.

Ten historical and cultural themes:

1. **Origins**
2. **Religious systems**
3. **Language**
4. **Sociopolitical systems and networks**
5. **Economic systems**
6. **Interactions with place**
7. **Material culture**
8. **Life cycle**
9. **Colonialism**
10. **Native peoples and Communities Today**

When water covered the world only the top of the highest mountain rose above it. The people had climbed up on this mountain, but could find no food and were starving. They wanted to go off and get something to eat. When the water went down all the ground was soft mud. After a while the people rolled rocks down to see if the mud were hard enough to hold them. When the rocks stayed on top, the people went down to search for food. But the mud was not hard enough to hold them and they sank out of sight, leaving deep holes where they had gone down. Then Kah'-kah-loo, the Ravens, came and stood at the holes, one at each hole where a man had gone down. After a while, when the ground hardened, the Ravens turned into people. That is the reason the Mewuk are so dark. (Merriam, 1993, p. 101)

From such stories, a community learns "value systems, patterns of thinking, kinship systems, philosophies of life, and adjustment" (Masson, 1966, p. iv). This story provides insight to a historical and catastrophic event in which people were forced to higher ground due to rising waters. The displaced people were left with no resources yet responded collectively (consistent references to "people" rather to one individual alone), strategized and worked together in order to determine the safety of their environment. Also, the role of the Ravens in the story indicates how important animals are and that by observing their behavior, in this case, led to people being able to safely come down from high places and repopulate the world.

Significant locations referred to in such stories speak to a Sacred Geography in which indigenous people have historical *and* spiritual connection. Cultures that embrace the belief that human existence is dependent on living in balance with all living things require reverence for life. This includes the earth and all living entities on it. Subsequently, places in our region may hold special meaning as they may be places of historical and/or spiritual significance. In this case, these places should be given the same respect as given to places of worship such as churches, synagogues, mosques, and other places where people come together under a faith system.

> The displaced people were left with no resources yet responded collectively (consistent references to "people" rather to one individual alone), strategized and worked together in order to determine the safety of their environment.

Religious Systems

Important Words and Concepts in This Section

Indigenous Cultures
Indigenous Spiritual Beliefs
Cultural Proscriptions

The three destructions of the earth is a common theme in many indigenous cultures. One such story is related by Laktcharas Tauhindauli (1873–1963). A direct descendant of two Wintu Headmen, Tauhindauli was told and became bearer of the stories of his people. In one story, he relates how Olelbes (one who is up above) created this earth. Similar to indigenous spiritual beliefs across the Americas is the belief in one higher power. An erroneous misinterpretation of indigenous belief systems is that there are multiple deities. This misperception comes from the observance of how a name or acknowledgment might be given to the element or life force within all living things. For example, Sage La Pena (2016) speaks to the danger of commercializing plants when plants have been given to us freely. She communicates the importance of these gifts when she states, "All these plants were given to us by Mother Earth as all of them being holy and *sacred medicines*. Given to us as gifts. For our own existence and to help each other." Plants were utilized for *doctoring* as people within tribal communities were taught the medicinal properties of the plants in their region. This belief system extends "holiness" and "sacredness" to plants which, as previously noted, are life forms to be respected.

Sage LaPena, Clinical Herbalist, ethnobotanist, lecturer, teacher, and gardener specializing in both Native American and Western herbal traditions.

Photo Courtesy of Sage LaPena.

Cultural proscriptions, *rules and laws*, when not adhered to, can at the most extreme end even bring destruction to the earth. These guidelines for living were passed down from one generation to the next. Tauhindauli told how ". . . the human people multiplying in great numbers were fighting among themselves too, like the animals did before them. But Olelbes looked on and didn't bother them." Olelbes' tolerance for the "fighting" only lasted so long because what was then related in Tauhindauli's writings was, "It is said that earth was destroyed three times" (Masson, 1966, p. 26). This destruction as told by Tauhindauli, from the Wintu Nation, sounds similar to the story shared by Utenbu Thomas Williams of the Sierra Miwok.

Now the rain was coming down so much that the water sprouted out of the ground everywhere all around the lowland filling up creeks and rivers very fast. The people that knew where there was a cave way up on some high mountains, those went there and were save(d) from drowning, but those that stayed back and tried to save themselves on rafts and canoes were all drowned. Some animals saved themselves by going upon high mountains too. (Masson, 1966, p. 32)

Sociopolitical Systems and Networks

Important Words and Concepts in This Section

Elders
Federally Recognized
Storytelling
Tribal Governments and Councils

Foundational to the community are the cross-generational relationships that form the basis for regeneration of knowledge and values. Sage La Pena, noted Clinical Herbalist and a member of the Nomtipon Wintu, reflects on the value of **Elders** and children in the community.

> One thing is listening to your elders because they have experience. They have the know-how that you don't have. If you're younger then they know more than you, period. And it's not always necessarily positive knowledge that they know, but there is a value in listening to them even if it's for kick of that value. The value is that you are able to give back to them by listening to them, and showing respect to that elder's voice rather positive or negative. The elder's use their voices to speak to the rest of the tribal community therefore, listening to your elders is a multi-fold value and then again everyone has a voice. People who are in those tribal council meetings like children also have something to say, and a lot of times the value in that is overlooked, but in our traditional value a lot of information comes from children. (Martinez-Alire, 2013, p. 105)

The respect for and value of all people in the community is transferred through a range of interactions. From birth, a child attends and participates in ceremonies and in the various traditions that maintain the culture such as learning how to make the regalia, the ceremonial attire worn during ceremonies. They watch, listen, and learn how to participate so they grow up to become bearers of the culture.

The intergenerational process of transmitting this knowledge is dependent on the ongoing contact between a multigenerational family system which is why "elders are libraries of Indian knowledge, history, and tradition" (Clark & Sherman, 2011, p. 14).

The **elders** within the Native American community play a critical role in guidance and have a significant role in **story telling** as they help to pass along certain traditions and knowledge. In many local tribes, **elders** share precious memories and meanings to certain songs, dances, and language that otherwise would be difficult to learn. According to Clark and Sherman (2011), within the Native American community, there is a tradition of respect for the importance of honoring elders and family. This is fairly common among many **Original Nations.**

> **Storytelling:** sharing events to help pass along traditions, knowledge, precious memories and meanings of songs, dances and language.

Photo Courtesy of Crystal Martinez-Alire

Coauthor Martinez-Alire and daughter, Mariah.

Photo Courtesy of Crystal Martinez-Alire

Dr. Crystal Martinez-Alire, Tribal Chair of the Ione Band of Miwok Indians.

Martinez-Alire, one of the coauthors, a member and tribal chair of a **federally recognized** Miwok tribe in California, can relate to this value. She notes that it is important to honor the elders and give thanks to them because many times the road would not have been possible without the ancestors who walked and endured the struggle of the people. A regular routine community event that takes place annually to honor Native elders occurs every June at the State Indian museum in Sacramento, California. This is a time for the community to recognize those elders that are part of the community and is a day to celebrate with many dancers and blessings. The elders are looked upon as having strength and wisdom.

According to Wallis (1996) in the story of "Two Old Woman," the author gives a full on description of what many elders had to endure during difficult seasons. The book describes how the women were able to become self-sufficient even when they were left behind by their tribal people. This book is another example of the journey, recognition, and roles that elder's often play in Native American society. Additionally, many elders have a role in tribal governance that will be discussed next. **Tribal governments and councils** often have elders who help with the leadership of the community.

Governance

Important Words and Concepts in This Section

Sovereignty
Government-to-Government Relationship
Dawes Allotment Act
The Great Law of Peace
Federally Recognized Tribes

When discussing tribal leadership and governance, we need to examine what inherent sovereignty means and how important the government-to-government relationship is between Native American tribes and the U.S. government. In essence, though Native American federally recognized tribes exist within the United States, they are separate countries and have their own forms of government. According to O'Brien (1989), sovereignty is supreme in power or authority. This is important to leadership as seen today as most Native American tribes have a governing council and are organized under constitutions in which they exercise executive, legislative, and judicial functions (O'Brien, 1989). Oftentimes, tribes help to educate others about their government status and governing laws. Most tribal councils are elected. The role

> **Sovereignty:** Supreme power, especially politically; without external control.

of a council member is very significant as the members make decisions on behalf of the entire community. The leader is openly selected and placed in the role of authority through the consent of the people and many years ago the leaders were from families that held leadership positions. There were many leadership roles and responsibilities and a common form of leadership was shared and servant leadership. This approach incorporated the tribal traditions and values, such as working collaboratively and leading with a long-term vision and also serving the needs of others before your own. Some tribal leaders today still operate in that fashion and many tribes work together, when possible, to share resources.

> **This approach incorporated the tribal traditions and values, such as working collaboratively and leading with a long-term vision and also serving the needs of others before your own.**

In order to discuss leadership, one must first understand the concepts of *ownership/property rights*. There was tremendous impact on Native American land due to the Gold Rush era in California in which many of the habitats and original land bases were taken away and destroyed. From history, we can see how certain governmental policies impacted tribes and created barriers for tribes to live on their natural land. According to O'Brien (1989), Congress passed its most assimilative law in 1887 which was the Dawes Allotment Act. This act essentially allotted reservation lands as they were divided up and separated for farming. This Act provided for the federal government to purchase land left over after the allotment process and the surplus land was then sold to setters. If you can imagine, many of the lands that native tribes once called home were sold under this policy. This act was driven by an individualistic and separation orientation that went against tribal collectivistic cultural values.

> **The distinction of being "stewards" rather than "owners" of the earth suggests a conscious and reciprocal relationship with the land, the water, the air we breathe, and all the animals that swim, walk, and fly.**

This policy was one of many that had direct impact on Original American Indian Tribal Nations. The Termination Era which was introduced in the late 1940s and 1950s aimed to terminate government responsibilities to tribes and to integrate Indians into white communities (O'Brien, 1989). The historical record attests to many broken promises and pain inflicted on Native tribes that have a lasting effect on tribal nations today. Nonetheless, in order to understand our present, we must look to the past and also acknowledge the early forms of tribal leadership in which the U.S. constitution has been modeled after such as the Iroquois Nation.

The Iroquois political structure of leadership was regulated by **The Great Law of Peace**, and is passed down from one generation to the next. The foundation outlined a complex system of checks and balances between nations and genders (Grinde & Johansen, 1991). The written document was an early representation of tribal leadership examined by the U.S. government system to help structure the U.S. constitution. This was an early form of leadership prior to European contact and is a prime example of how tribes governed in the past. From these examples, we are able to gain a greater understanding and appreciation of Native tribes and people of today.

Interactions With Place

Important Words and Concepts in This Section

Horticultural Techniques
Symbiotic Connection

Traditional Ecological Knowledge (Land Management)

Native peoples lived *with* rather than *on* the land. They actively managed the landscape using **horticultural techniques** that increased the health, vitality, and numbers of the plants upon which they relied. This, in turn, increased the health, well-being, and the numbers of the animals on which they relied (Ortiz, 2015, p. 1).

The distinction of being "stewards" rather than "owners" of the earth suggests a conscious and reciprocal relationship with the land, the water, the air we breathe, and all the animals that swim, walk, and fly. In essence, it is about human beings living responsibly so as to ensure the survival of not only those who exist now but to safeguard the habitat for future generations. This mindful relationship with the earth and all life forms reflects an

Respect for All life is vital in the web of relations. For example, one would not take the life of an animal just to kill. Deer and other abundant animals were *hunted* to feed the community . . .

orientation inherent to California Indian culture and way of life. An intimate knowledge of the *geology* of the region is often reflected in the stories passed from one generation to the next and speaks to a symbiotic connection to the land. This reciprocal relationship with the earth is discussed by Mr. Richard Johnson, Tribal Chair of the Nevada City Rancheria, home of the Nisenan Tribe.

> **Symbiotic Connection:** a close relationship between people, or between a person and a natural environment where both the person and the environment take care of each other.

> Life before the gold rush was basically . . . considered a paradise. Our people did not need to travel very far. We did not need a great deal of land. 20 to 40 to 80 square miles would have taken care of a large number of people. We changed the environment of our living area through *burning* and *pruning* of nature. We discovered long ago we could plant the oak trees in groves. Forestry people have discovered that when they look at the old groves and some of the old forest that they can find perfectly square oak groves from long ago. Also, most the vegetation around here was gone. We burned it for grass fields. Grass seeds was one of our main staples as well as acorn. So we nurtured nature and lived with nature and everything came from nature. All we needed to do was find water. Water was plentiful around here. We had Deer Creek here. Also supporting Deer Creek were all the main springs that come off the hillsides which is where all the main villages were. They sought out the springs on the bluff with southern exposure because of the warmth so that is where you would find most of the habitat.*

Respect for All life is vital in the web of relations. For example, one would not take the life of an animal just to kill. Deer and other abundant animals were *hunted* to feed the community and every part of the animal such as the antlers and the hide was utilized for making *tools* and coverings. Communities were strategically situated near streams which allowed easy access for *fishing*. Oak trees provided acorns, a staple of the diet, which were then grounded into a mush. *Digging* was a form of *cultivation*, as people knew the edible roots that diversified their diet and source of nourishment. Knowing the *seasonality* of the earth ensured a year round range of *food sources*.

In review of other *Horticultural Techniques* and *Plant Gathering and Processing* methods, the teachings of Elders from one generation to the next guaranteed that knowledge and wisdom of plants conveyed what was edible as well as which contain medicinal purposes. La Pena addresses this cross-generational instruction that led her to become an imminent authority in plant medicine. At the early age of 7, she was instructed to spend time with Mabel McKay, a descendent of the Pomo and Wintu communities who was a noted Dreamer, Weaver, and Doctor. La Pena explains:

> We would help her gather plant medicine . . . she would constantly tell me about what I was seeing. We would do harvesting. She would tell me why certain plants live together. Who interacts with whom. Why they do those things. And then as I grew I didn't understand that I was being groomed or taught to be anything. It was not

* Contributed by Richard B. Johnson. © Kendall Hunt Publishing Company.

until I worked at a California Native plant nursery in my 20's that someone told me I was an herbalist and I had been trained to be one. I didn't know what that meant because it is just something we do. It didn't have a name. I didn't know what mosaics were . . . bioregions . . . and people would say how do you know all those plants live together? I would tell them because I grew up living with them. They are people, just like we are. Their legs move a lot slower and they move down but they still move out. (Finerman, 2016)

The multiple uses of plants such as the Elderberry indicates a depth of knowledge in the reciprocity of respectful relations with nature which was not considered "wilderness" as it is often referred to but more so as the source that sustains life. La Pena decries the overharvesting and corporate monopolizing of plants that further removes these gifts from humanity. She reminds us that, "Previous to the introduction of lawns in America, your village where you lived, your medicines were all around you and medicine that didn't grow right in the village was brought to the village to grow. I just want to remind people that they have the knowledge and to utilize their rights to take out their lawn and grow food . . ." She expresses concern over how far from the earth's gifts people have become when she communicates, "We abuse our plant allies in the name of economic venture and all of us suffer because of it."

La Pena encourages people to grow their own food. She informs us, however, that the sustainability of future generations is compromised by the mass production of plants that produce sterile seeds and thereby interrupting the capacity to regenerate more food sources. The consideration for what is best for humanity in the future, and not just for the present, is a cultural value in how we relate to one another and all gifts in the world. This worldview promotes stewardship in the present in order to ensure a future.

Material Culture

Structures were varied and dependent on what the earth provided so that *homes* were made with natural materials found in the region. For example, the Yokuts, estimated to have numbered up to 70,000, lived in relation to Tulare Lake and made *their homes, shelters, and watercraft* from the abundant reeds surrounding the Lake. At one time, this lake was twice the size of Lake Tahoe. Access to this Lake ensured access to food and habitat.

> **The consideration for what is best for humanity in the future, and not just for the present, is a cultural value in how we relate to one another and all gifts in the world.**

In contrast, the Sierra Miwok utilized cedar bark for constructing their *homes*. These are called u'macha's. Given the vast number of oak trees in the Sierra Foothills, the sturdy wood from these trees plays prominent in the construction of the Sierra Miwok *Ceremonial* Roundhouse which serves as a social and religious center. It is a place of worship. An active Roundhouse and reconstructed village which includes u'macha's and *granaries* can be found at Indian Grinding Rock State Historic Park in Pine Grove. This park is known to the Original Nation of this area, the Miwok, as Chaw'se which means grinding rock. For thousands of years, the Miwok people ground acorns and other seeds into meal upon a slab of stone. Years of use slowly formed cup-shaped depressions in the stone. Still visible on the slab are decorative carvings that are considered unique to California.

Colonialism

> ## Important Words and Concepts in This Section
>
> **Encomienda System**
> **Colonization**
> **Culturicide**
> **Missions**
> **Unratified Treaty**

During the sixteenth and seventeenth centuries, Spain set out to conquer what is now called Mexico and all the land south of Mexico. Feeling threatened by Russia who wanted to explore and possibly settle in California, Spain wanted to secure lands north of Mexico and deter the threat of Russian expansion. Spain had already created in Mexico the encomienda system in which indigenous people were subjected to cruel enforced labor by the Spanish colonists. Subsequently, the King of Spain designed a plan that expanded the encomienda system in which "*presidios* (forts), missions, and settlements would be established along the Alta California coastline" (Castillo, 2015, p. 32).

José de Gálvez, the Visitor General of New Spain, was charged with carrying out King Carlos III's plan and choose "Franciscan missionaries who were close at hand, readily available and experienced in controlling Indians at little expense" (p. 33). The padre president, Junipero Serra, would lead the expedition into Alta California. This marked the beginning of a series of attacks on California Indians by seizure of their lands, disruption of their way of life, and concerted efforts to enslave, and later annihilate the entire population.

> **Encomienda System:** A system similar to slavery whereby the Spanish government allowed conquerors of new territories to force Native Americans to force them to work or pay them gold, silver, or other goods.

Indoctrinated with the belief that the spiritual beliefs of indigenous people needed to be replaced with Catholicism, Serra was "blind to granting any human rights to the Indians" (p. 64). His single-minded purpose of "saving souls" led him "to establish a policy of packing each mission with as many Native Americans as he could, heedless of the quality of life within those compounds" (p. 74). By force or by coercion, Serra captured and enslaved California Indians who were forced to work in order to supply the soldiers at the presidios and the priests at the missions. Subhuman living conditions, forced attendance of daily mass, separation of boys and men from girls and women, and punishment by whip, shackles, and imprisonment was meted out to anyone who disobeyed or who dared to run away (Castillo, 2015). Junipero Serra and his fellow Franciscans believed that:

> Indians were to be treated more like mere chattel. They were to be fed, encouraged to marry and reproduce, kept free of sin, provide forced labor, and ultimately give up their souls to God. Serra's and the friar's lack of compassion for the Indians stemmed from their minds being mired in the dark ages, suffused with the attitude that Spanish Catholicism was to be rigidly followed and that Spaniards were members of a master race—all others and non-Catholics were beneath them. (p. 5)

Spanning from the founding of the first Mission site in San Diego in 1769 to the last site in Sonoma in 1823, California Indians were forced or coerced into the mission life. Not a docile people, within their hearts and minds was not the mythical and romanticized version of devotion to Serra and the Christian faith, instead there was resentment and disdain for their colonizers. Subsequently, California Indian resistance was evident throughout California as they banded together to destroy the development of the Missions and put an end to the cruelty inflicted upon their people.

Mission San Diego de Alcala, Misson Valley Road, San Diego. Historic American Buildings Survey Photographed by Henry F. Withey, December 1936 SOUTH FACADE TOWARD WEST. Source: Library of Congress

One of the many uprisings was at the very first Mission site, San Diego, where members of the Kumeyaay tribe burned the buildings and beat Friar Luis Jayme to death. Additionally, "Indians killed 110 Spaniards, including four Franciscan friars, thirty-one soldiers, and took seventy-two prisoners" (p. 174). At Mission San Miguel, three friars were believed to be poisoned to death. This also took place at Mission San Diego when Friar José Pedro Panto's cook, Nazario, admitted to trying to poison him to death in retaliation "after having suffered whippings of fifty, twenty-five, twenty-four, and twenty-five lashes in succession" (p. 175).

Escape often resulted in being hunted down by soldiers. If an Indian community was caught giving sanctuary and aiding a fellow California Indian, they risked being killed on site or possibly captured and forced to replace the dying numbers of captives within Mission walls. If escapees were caught, they were subjected to the floggings given to mission Indians which was justified by Junipero Serra when he stated to Governor Felipe de Neve, "That the spiritual fathers should punish their sons, the Indians, by blows appears to be as old as the conquest of these kingdoms" (p. 54). This was the policy and practice enacted upon indigenous people by Spain in the act of conquest and colonization.

The mistreatment upon California Indians during *Spanish era* intrusion was also evident in Mexico where the people rebelled and united to expel the Spaniards. Although there were multiple acts of resistance by California Indians to Spanish presence, many of the coastal communities were left decimated and their way of life disrupted by the establishment of the Spanish Missions. It is estimated that there were 300,000 coastal Indians in 1769 whose numbers dwindled to 16,624 in 1890. Once Mexico gained its independence from Spain in 1821, there was a brief *Mexican era* (1821–1848) in California that lasted until Mexico lost the land to the United States in the Mexican–U.S. War. Intent on eliminating slavery from all previously Spanish held lands, Mexico secularized the Missions which meant the Church no longer had control of the land, and more so, of the California Indians within the Missions. The land instead of being returned to the original people of California was handed over to well-connected families who established *Ranchos* where California Indians were employed in standards often regarded as peonage. One well-known individual who was granted land during this era is John Sutter. His relationship to the Nisenan is well documented and remembered by Tribal Chair Johnson.

> Sutter's Fort was built by Nisenan Indians and others. He would bring his militia up to the Foothills and capture whole villages and then take the whole village down there and cage the children in order to keep the adults there. The leader of the tribe— his head would be severed and hung from the gate post at the entrance, so all the people would know the power of the white person because their leader's head is hung and rotting at the main entrance of Sutter's Fort. History is not told. It is just not told. What happened to our people but it is there and we are trying to get some of this word out and this is what we have been hoping to do. We have been quiet for too long. *

This state of subsistence on Ranchos and resistance from terrorizing exploitation continued and accelerated the word "Gold" traveled across the world.

American Era

> A War of Extermination will continue to be waged between the two races until the Indian race becomes extinct.
>
> *Peter H. Burnett, Governor of California, December 1849 to January 1851.*

California Indians struggled to survive the Missions, the Mexican era, the disease brought by Russian fur traders, and then, the overwhelming intrusion of people from all over the world who came to California for first, gold, and then land. The figures speak for themselves as in the year 1848, it is estimated that the California's native population was at 150,000 with a nonnative population of 15,000. In just a little over 60 years, by 1910, the California native population dwindled to 16,371 and the nonnative population exploded to 2,377,549 (Lindsay, 2012).

---

* Contributed by Richard B. Johnson. © Kendall Hunt Publishing Company.

Portsmouth Square near harbor in 1851—San Francisco during the Gold Rush. Source: Library of Congress

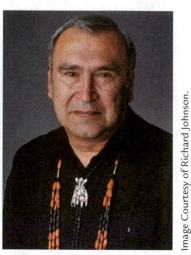

Image Courtesy of Richard Johnson.

Richard Johnson, Tribal Council Chairman, Nevada City Rancheria Nisenan Tribe.

Tribal Chair Johnson provides insight to the impact of the *Gold Rush* on the Nisenan.

We estimate by going back in the census that there were conservatively over 7,000 people living in our territory. Two years after the *Gold Rush*, this number dropped to 3,400 people. By 1867, there was only 500 natives left. By the census of 1905, there was only 84 natives that could be located. By 1934, when the Native reorganization act took affect, there was only 18. This is one of the reasons . . . why people everyone thinks the Nisenan Nation was extinct is basically because there were very few left. Nevada City Rancheria was the very last in our territory, the last location. All the villages around as time went on after the Gold Seekers and newcomers arrived they started condensing into other villages because of the fast population decrease.*

Richard Johnson, Nisenan

The rapid population decrease of American Indians across the continent speaks to a concerted effort to subdue and enslave when possible or, otherwise, annihilate. In California, the various stages of colonialism that started with the Spanish intrusion, followed by the brief Mexican era, and then the American era that brought massive destruction to the California communities living in the Sacramento region. Nisenan Tribal Chair Johnson expands on the major factors contributing to the near annihilation of California's Original Nations:

Pure Slaughter. . . . The native people were basically considered as vermin and they actually placed bounty's on them in the 1850's . . . our first governor called for the extinction of the red race in California . . . you could get as much as $5 for the head or the scalp of any Indian. This really came into swing right after the gold rush because the easy gold was already gone. People who came in the thousands and thousands and thousands still needed an income. Some of these people who were quite ruthless

* Contributed by Richard B. Johnson. © Kendall Hunt Publishing Company.

took up the career of Indian hunting to make a living. Also, some of the laws changed where they created indenturement . . . a nice term for slavery. Those people went out from the valleys and the cities that were in the valley and came up to our country in the foothills and find villages with lots of children and they would slaughter all the adults, the men, women, & the grandparents just to capture all the children to take them into the valley or the mining camps and sell them. They could get up to $60 for a boy or up to $200 for a girl . . . up until the 1870's. The other thing that affected our population was disease. We had no immunities; you could go back further when malaria came up in the 1830's from the traders who came up the rivers. Reports are as the boats came . . . total death; skeletons leaning up against trees. During the Gold rush, we weren't as affected too much by the malaria as that was down below. The other thing was starvation; you'll see at the early portraits of Grass Valley and Nevada City you will see as far as the eye can see that there was not a tree existing. While Oak Trees and Pine Trees were our food source. They used them to build the communities . . . to make the mines. These were our main staples so our food sources were gone. They also brought up foreign grasses for their livestock that took over our food sources. Hydraulic Mining started . . . just a handful of men were able to take away the guts right out of the mountain. All that (muddy) water ended up going down the Yuba River. With the muddy waters the salmon didn't return. This caused the starvation. Another disease was small pox. Our people did not have immunity. It literally decimated whole villages. When a village was hit, it generally killed all the children first, then started killing the younger and the older people. The people would move and abandon that village because it was such a small population they would have to join with larger villages. That is why villages kept combining and combining until we ended up just with Nevada City Rancheria.*

Laws were created that ultimately served those who sought to obliterate California Indians and dispossess them from a way of life that had been intact for thousands of years. Such laws marginalized California Indians at every turn as they could not even testify in a court of law against a white person regardless of the crime committed against them. Additionally, treaty after treaty meant nothing when colonizer's economic interests resulted in either breaking existing treaties or just not ratifying the ones already made. The Yokut, having lived on the shores of Tulare Lake for centuries, agreed upon a treaty to be placed in a government protected reservation. This was never honored. It was an example of another unratified treaty. Instead, the Yokuts were split apart and sent to different parts of the state of California. This was one of the tactics used by which to clear indigenous people of the land they had lived on for thousands of years to make way for people wanting the land for themselves. As stated by Lindsay (2012), the desire for land replaced the quest for gold which forced a series of laws and policies that promoted acts of genocide. Subsequently, the Yokuts from the San Joaquin Valley were forcibly moved to Coalinga and made the 50–60-mile trek, by foot. Once oil was discovered here, the people were, once again, forced off to another desolate piece of land 40 miles away that no one wanted (Tachi Yokut Website).

* Contributed by Richard B. Johnson. © Kendall Hunt Publishing Company.

The Citizenship Act of 1924 granted Native Americans U.S. Citizenship and allowed them to retain tribal citizenship as well. The implementation did not go well for Native Americans as this started efforts to assimilate indigenous people to U.S. customs. This meant that children were forcibly removed from their families and sent to live at Boarding Schools. When this direct connection of children to their families is broken, the means by which to teach the next generation their rich heritage is interrupted. This, in turn, leads to termination of cultural practices, a form of culturcide. Additionally, Original Nations were not allowed to openly celebrate spiritual practices. Teaching of language and culture was forbidden. Not until 1978, were spiritual practices that had gone underground, allowed to return to the open.

> **Tribal communities are preserving their cultural heritage through *Ceremony*, song, dance, and stories in addition to creating their own educational centers in which language and cultural practices are valued and taught.**

Native Peoples and Communities Today

Many communities have taken critical steps in enhancing their own *economic development* which, in turn, promotes the self-sufficiency of tribal members. From these ventures, the larger community has benefitted in that jobs, educational opportunities, and the uplift of the tribal communities also extend to others. Donations, a practice stemming from the collectivist-centered cultural values, and grants promote the vitality of all.

Tribal communities are preserving their cultural heritage through *Ceremony*, song, dance, and stories in addition to creating their own educational centers in which language and cultural practices are valued and taught. The protection of sacred places is key to respecting Original Nation's places of connection with the earth and with one another. The revitalization of language is also of major concern for Original American Indian Tribal Nations as efforts are being made at institutions such as UC Berkeley to ensure that languages are not lost due to the violent interruption of intergenerational cultural systems.

Of value, today is to recognize that Original Nations are still here. There is much to learn from a way of life that values being *in relation* with one another, with the earth, and the gifts we have been granted. With the questions that follow, our hope is that you come to perhaps not just understand but to value an orientation that exists today and survives and celebrates in our midst.

Acknowledgments

All our contributors, elders, and mentors.

References

Castillo, E. (2015). *A cross of thorns*. Fresno, CA: Craven Street Books.

Clark, P., & Sherman, N. (2011). *The importance of elders and family in Native American culture*. Retrieved from http://blog.nrcprograms.org/wp-content/uploads/2011/05/importance1.pdf

Grinde, D., & Johansen, B. (1991). *Exemplar of liberty: Native America and the evolution of democracy*. Los Angeles, CA: The Regents of the University of California.

Lindsay, B. (2012). *Murder state. California's Native American genocide, 1846–1873*. Lincoln, NE: University of Nebraska Press.

Masson, M. (1966). *A bag of bones. The Wintu myths of a Trinity River Indian*. Happy Camp, CA: Naturegraph Press.

Merriam, C. H. (1993). *The dawn of the world*. Lincoln, NE: University of Nebraska Press.

Martinez-Alire. (2013). *The perceptions of tribal leadership and the impact of education and cultural knowledge: Examining tribal leadership and education within California Native American communities* (Doctoral dissertation). Retrieved from http://csus-dspace.calstate.edu/handle/10211.9/2069 Scholarworks. (10211.9/2069).

O'Brien, S. (1989). *American Indian tribal governments*. Norman, OK: University of Oklahoma Press.

Ortiz, B. (2015). *Ohlone curriculum*. Oakland, CA: East Bay Regional Park District.

Finerman, L. (January 6, 2016) *Women rising radio XXVIIII: food sovereignty. Sage La Pena radio interview* Retrieved from http://www.womenrisingradio.com/, http://www.womenrisingradio.com/2016/01/06/women-rising-xxviiii-food-sovereignty/, and http://www.parks.ca.gov/?page_id=935

Wallis, V. (1996). *Two old women*. New York, NY: Epicenter Press.

Chapter 2

Mixed-Race Individuals: A Solution for Race Relations in America?

Darryl Omar Freeman

Important Words and Concepts in This Chapter

There are several important words and concepts throughout the upcoming chapter. The words appear several times in different places in order to help you remember the words and understand the chapter. The words are defined several times:

- Immediately below right before the chapter begins
- In text boxes throughout the chapter
- In red and boldfaced within the chapter
- In a glossary in expanded form at the end of the units

Some of the words also appear in other chapters. Talk about the words with other students, teachers, friends, and family members before you read, while reading the chapter, and after you have read the chapter.

Race

A classification of human beings into different categories on the basis of the way we look, for example, our skin color, head shape, eye color and shape, nose size and shape, and so on.

Contributed by Darryl Omar Freeman. © Kendall Hunt Publishing Company.

Ethnicity

Membership or affiliation in a particular ethnic group.

Ethnic Stereotyping

To stereotype is to apply a gross generalization, to people from a specific ethnic group rather than seeing the individual variation.

Bias

An inclination or outlook; *especially* a personal and sometimes unreasonable judgment; prejudice or an instance of an instance of such prejudice.

Phenotype

1. The <u>physical</u> <u>appearance</u> or <u>biochemical</u> <u>characteristic</u> of an <u>organism</u> as a result of the <u>interaction</u> of its <u>genotype</u> and the <u>environment.</u>
2. The <u>expression</u> of a particular <u>trait</u>, for example, <u>skin</u> color, <u>height</u>, <u>behavior</u>, and so on, according to the individual's <u>genetic</u> makeup and <u>environment.</u>

Genotype

1. (<u>genetics</u>) The entire set of <u>genes</u> in an <u>organism.</u>
2. (<u>genetics</u>) A set of <u>alleles</u> that determines the expression of a particular characteristic or <u>trait</u> (<u>phenotype</u>).

DNA

Various nucleic acids that are usually the molecular basis of heredity.

Social Construction

A theoretical approach which regard certain aspects of human experience and knowledge as originating within and cultivated by society or a particular social group, rather than existing inherently or naturally.

Social Scientists

A scientist who studies society and human behavior, such as a historian, economist, or sociologist.

Racial Identity Dilemma

Racial Identity Dilemma concerns a person's inability to experience Immersion, Internalization, or Commitment to a racial identity. Rather than experience comfort, realization, and positive sense of one's race, the individual is stuck at a preencounter or an encounter stage where there is a general lack of awareness of the impact of race or an ever-new sense of racial discovery. For nondominant racial groups, the encounter stage is sometimes very negative or hurtful.

European American

Americans with ancestry from Europe, such as Germany, Italy, England, Austria, and so on.

Introduction

Have you or any of your friends who identify as mixed race ever felt that there are challenges in developing an individual identity that are different from those who identify themselves as a single race? Do you think that the general population in the United States thinks about mixed-race individuals in the same manner as they view single-race people in terms of social matters such as friendship and marriage? Are public policy laws designed to prevent discrimination in the public sphere applied equally to mixed-race people? This chapter explores these and other issues regarding the different identity challenges and experiences of mixed-race individuals navigating life in this society of the United States.

Race: A classification of human beings into different categories on the basis of the way we look, for example, our skin color, head shape, eye color and shape, nose size and shape, and so on.

A recent U.S. Census Report reveals that the total population of Americans who identify as mixed race is about nine million people or a little over 3% of the total U.S. population.[1] As small a number as this may seem, it has been increasing at a rate three times faster than those who identify as single race in the United States.[2] California is the fourth highest state in the country with residents who report being of more than one race. As the number of individuals who identify as mixed race increases, could this phenomena be the solution to the continuing racial, social, and political conflicts in this country? After all, how can racism or ethnic stereotyping continue to flourish as our population becomes more mixed? From initial physical appearance, it will become more difficult for people to make

---

1 U.S. Census Bureau Report, U.S. Department of Congress, News Room Archives, September 27, 2012.
2 *Mixed Race America.*

stereotypical judgments about people they meet. This chapter explores the identity challenges of mixed-race/ethnicity individuals from a personal, social, and public institutions' perspective. We examine issues such as how do "mixed-race" individuals see themselves in relationship to how others see them? How do they navigate living in this diverse American society? Additionally, this chapter explores the impact of the increase in the number of mixed-race/ethnicity individuals on the social attitudes of the general population and the political atmosphere in this country.

Race a Social Construction

Before we delve into the challenges of the racial identity of mixed-raced individuals, it is valuable for us to understand more about this identity notion we call "race." You may have heard your teachers, commentators on the news, or Internet bloggers refer to this idea of race as a social construction. What we mean by that definition is that there is no scientifically consistent identifiable evidence that reliably distinguishes one so-called race of people from another. We are often misled by superficial physical traits such as skin color, hair texture, eye shape, and other body features that lead us to believe that we can in fact identify one race from another. Modern science, through DNA sampling and other biological and genetic examinations, establishes that, beyond all of the phenotype understandings we have about race, we are all virtually the same in terms of body organs, including the brain. DNA evidence, for example, challenges the notion of genetic racial difference by demonstrating that there are more likely differences in DNA make up between individuals within a so-called racial group than there are between individuals of different racial groups.[3] What then is the explanation of why we in the United States as well as other countries use race as a personal, social, and often political determinant as to how we relate to each other as human beings?

> **Social Construction:** understanding human experience and knowledge as originating within and cultivated by society or a particular social group, rather than existing naturally

> **Phenotype:** A person's physical appearance based on unique genetic code.

The population of the United States is often referred to as a "melting pot" or "salad bowl." Both of these terms acknowledge the general understanding of people that this country is a diverse society consisting of many different races and ethnicities. The recognition of this diversity suggests that we define our society in terms of racial/ethnic categories. Classification of people can be meant to group people together. However, this social construction grouping of people can also result in ranking or discrimination of groups of people. Social scientists have produced evidence that demonstrates that there

---

3 For a more detailed explanation of the social construction of race, view the video *Race—the power of an illusion*. Retrieved from https://www.youtube.com/watch?v=Y8MS6zubIaQ&list=PLt6nX4f8WjdW-geomQQ3oLzVH5EoahlcQB.

is perhaps a universal human need or trait to identify and classify other humans to create order in one's world. This characteristic of human nature is exemplified, for example, in the practice of almost every country in the world conducting a periodic census of the county's population often identifying the number and percentage of the population by race or ethnicity.[4] Acceptance of the grouping of people promotes the stereotyping and subsequent discrimination of individuals within groups based on changing social and political attitudes of a population. This behavior is problematic for those who identify themselves as single race. However, the ramifications of this propensity by society to validate people by race become even more problematic for mixed-race individuals.

Identity Development and Mixed-Race Individuals

Social scientists Omi and Winant (1994) have demonstrated through extensive research that when humans first meet someone, we automatically assign them to a racial category based often on physical features such as skin color or hair texture. Once placed in that category, we subconsciously possess a set of stereotypical characteristics and behavior that we expect this person to exhibit. (The theory in its entirety can be found

> **Both sides of the family desire to be included equally as a part of the identity heritage of a mixed-race child.**

in their book *Racial Formation in the United States.*) When someone we meet does not fit into any certain racial category, it may cause some sense of discomfort, especially when the person is perceived to be of mixed-racial heritage. Those people who identify with a single race are often somewhat perplexed as to how to relate to a mixed-race individual. Many questions occur in the single-race person's mind about the mixed race individual, such as where are they from? What percentage mixed are they?, and what race are their parents? This verbalized questioning by single-race individuals can cause a sense of insecurity or identity challenges to a mixed-race person who just wants to be accepted and treated as an individual human being.[5]

Since most people identify and profess to belong to a particular racial group, racial identity can be a quandary for mixed-race individuals. A mixed-race individual who cannot figure out where they "belong" may become preoccupied with an identity crisis. In cases where there is a stark difference of physical appearance such as skin color between the different racial heritages of a person's parents, a **dilemma of racial identity**

---

4   The chapter by Asher contains a detailed explanation of this categorization phenomenon with related examples specifically as they are applied to Asian Americans.

5   The YouTube videos *what mixed race people hear* and *6 rules with mixed race* are excellent examples of the identity challenges mixed-race people face on a regular basis. They can be found at http://www. youtube.com/watch?v=90gt3y32q_A and http://www.youtube.com/watch?v=KxKn4MuGHos.

may present itself. Both sides of the family desire to be included equally as a part of the identity heritage of a mixed-race child. However, due to dominant features such as skin color, the outside world may view and subsequently treat a mixed-race person in a single-race stereotypical manner. Other factors such as language and religion can also play a major role in the identity development of a young person. These conflicting forces may cause a mixed-race individual to deny or reject one side of family heritage in order to obtain some sense of identity security. This decision can cause considerable anguish not only with the rejected family members, but also with the mixed-race person. After making this decision, the mixed-race individual may still feel unfulfilled in terms of racial identity.

Sometimes, the social pressures of needing to have racial group acceptance are so intense, at least in the mind of mixed-raced individuals, that they feel compelled to adopt a racial identity that is really only part of who they are in terms of heritage and life experience. While this identity compromise initially pacifies their social identity crisis, the void of connection with their complete family heritage can often cause psychological pain later in adult life. The supporting video identified in the following tells the story of a biracial woman who was forced to adopt the European heritage part of her identity and totally disregard her African American heritage. As an adult, she completely immersed herself in the European heritage identity to the point where her husband and closest friends did not know she was actually mixed race. "Passing" had served the purpose as purported by her mother, for a comfortable life of financial success and social acceptance. However, estranging herself from the African American side of her heritage came at a price. When she received word that her African American father, whom she had not seen or communicated with for years, was dying, she could not go to see him to prevent exposing to her "passing" life that she was in fact biracial.[6] While this anecdotal story is certainly an extreme example of the identity challenges of mixed-race individuals, it is illustrative of the emotional dilemma many mixed-race individuals face while developing a strategy for navigating life in the society of the United States.

Social Identity and Mixed-Race Individuals

The attitude of the general population of the United States has grown and become more accepting of the idea of mixed-raced individuals on an equal status as any other single-race/ethnicity person. That has not always been the case. Just 50 years ago (your parent's generation), there were numerous laws throughout the United States that prohibited and even criminalized marriage between individuals of a different race. The thinking of society at that time was that the strength and purity of genetic heritage would be seriously threatened by the mixing of races. These public policies and general public attitude existed, even though historically as far back as early colonization

---

6   For the complete TED talk presentation, view the video. Retrieved from https://www.youtube.com/watch?v=CIulfoJPnq0.

of this country, **European Americans** intermarried with American Indians, enslaved African Americans and other different racial groups immigrating to this country. It took a U.S. Supreme Court decision to finally mark the beginning of a dramatic change in the public attitude and subsequent public policy change in the treatment of the mixing of races.[7] The court found a law forbidding interracial marriage in Virginia unconstitutional. You can imagine to some extent the feelings of isolation and second-class status people of mixed-race heritage must have felt during this time.

> **European Americans:** American citizens whose parent, grandparents, or ancestors are from one or more countries in Europe, such as Germany, Norway, Ireland, and so on; often referred to as White Americans, or White.

Of course, changes in public policy do not insure instantaneous change in the minds and hearts of the general public. The long history of **bias** by generations of people against interracial marriage and subsequent

> **Bias:** a personal and sometimes unreasonable judgment or prejudice.

mixed-race offspring is difficult to adjust to in terms of individual and family perspectives. Even in contemporary times, conflicts may arise when a member of the family violates the unwritten "rule" of marrying within the chosen racial identity of the family heritage.[8] The video identified in the following footnote highlights the adversity that mixed-race couples may encounter from otherwise loving family members due to choosing love over out-dated social tradition.

The impact and influence of this bias is not relegated only to adult identity formation. Even elementary school-aged children are affected by the racially biased conduct of their classmates. During the early age of identity development of young children, acceptance by their peers is an important element in feeling secure and confident in navigating life outside of the home. Mixed-race children often find themselves isolated from children who identify as single race and have "bought in" to this notion of racial grouping. The mixed-race little girl in the video footnoted in the following expresses a distressed feeling of being invisible. Her African American classmates say she is not "Black" enough and her European American friends insinuate that she is not "White" enough. Mariah Carey, a mixed-race person, joins in the discussion about the trials and tribulation of growing up mixed race.[9]

Identity formation becomes even more complex for mixed-race children. Adults can complicate matters by introducing language and ethnicity requirements to the determination of who belongs to a particular social group. There have been numerous conflicts between members of several of the American Indian Nations in this country over the citizenship of mixed-race Indians. In the article, with video insert footnoted in the

---

7   View this short video highlighting with actual photographs of the interracial couple who dared to defy the biased public policy in the name of love and marry in another state only to be prosecuted in their home state of Virginia. https://www.youtube.com/watch?v=0Q8feg_Wg6U.

8   This video entitled *Mixed marriages in the south* is a classic example of the struggle some family members have accepting the new morals of society and the courage it takes for individuals to venture into a mixed-race relationship even in contemporary times. https://www.youtube.com/watch?v=uKkpEcrwV94.

9   The Oprah video *White looking black people*. https://www.youtube.com/watch?v=v19Pmgjj894.

following, a dark-skinned child beauty pageant contestant found herself the center of a racial ethnic controversy. She identifies as Hispanic via her mother's Spanish speaking Dominican Republic heritage. Shortly after she won the Miss Hispanic Beauty Contest in Delaware, members of the Latino community protested her crowning because, in their opinion, she was not "Latina enough." The phenotype implications were clear that many in the community had succumbed to the historic stereotype of the light-skinned Latina beauty.[10] This shameful behavior by adults regarding a beauty pageant for 7-year olds is evidence that our society has not evolved as much as we might think in terms of race relations, even within racial minority communities.

These anecdotal narratives are just a sampling of the complex issues regarding mixed-race relations and that still exist in this society. We have seen that mixed-race individuals are often forced to contend with dual-race identity issues at a young age where group acceptance is important in personality development. Additionally, we have seen an example how older generational racial perspectives within families conflict with the contemporary understanding of a younger generation. And finally, we have seen how group race formation mind-set can impede race relations progress even within minority racial/ethnic groups.

Governmental and Institutional Bias and Mixed-Race Identity

Government and educational institutions could be considered complicit in the arguably snail-paced development of race neutral relations in our society. Application forms from driver's licenses to college applications usually request single-race or ethnicity identification. At the moment, few of these forms identify a category of "Mixed-race." What is a mixed-race person to do in order to comply with the laws of the land, check every box that applies? The most recent U.S. Census form took some steps toward addressing these issues by offering a blank for "Other" on some Census forms. Hopefully, with the advances in super computing power, perhaps the next Census forms may allow individuals to just "self-identify." Computers can then calculate all of the different racial mixes in this country.

> Hopefully, with the advances in super computing power, perhaps the next Census forms may allow individuals to just "self-identify." Computers can then calculate all of the different racial mixes in this country.

Meanwhile, even in the U.S. "halls of justice," mixed-race issues seem to be perplexing to even our most learned judicial scholars. In April 2014, a case was brought before the U.S. Supreme Court regarding an amendment to the State of Michigan's Constitution eliminating race-based affirmative action programs in the application process of state-run universities.

---

10 *Little Miss Hispanic Delaware.* http://nbclatino.com/2013/09/26/little-miss-hispanic-delaware-stripped-of-her-crown-for-not-being-latina-enough/.

The Supreme Court had an opportunity to determine whether a state violates the Equal Protection Clause by amending its constitution to prohibit race- and sex-based discrimination or preferential treatment in the admissions decisions of public universities. In upholding the State of Michigan ban on affirmative action programs in public universities, the majority of Justices seem to hold "mixed-race" individuals as culprits in arriving at their decision. Justice Kennedy wrote for the majority that mixed-race people confound the court's capacity to "define individuals according to race." He continued, "In a society in which those lines are becoming more blurred, the attempt to define race-based categories also raises serious questions of its own."[11] This decision appears to discount mixed-race individuals for consideration in public policies regarding race relations because they are too difficult to classify. Throughout this chapter, we have seen examples of identity conflicts between mixed-raced individuals with single-race individuals, mixed-race conflict within families, and mixed-race issues within the general public even within racial minority groups. Now we have seen how even public institutions grapple with issues of mixed-race identity. It is no wonder that many mixed-race folks often feel estranged from the mainstream of American society.

The Entertainment Industry, Corporate America, and Mixed-Race Relations

Is there any sector of American society that is making progress in addressing issues of identity and social acceptance confronting mixed-race individuals? Perhaps the entertainment industry and corporate America are slowly making inroads with the attitude of the general public regarding the recognition of mixed-race people in the country. In the past, commercial interests have created and perpetuated racial stereotypes of minorities with images of Aunt Jemima (a scarf wrapped head enslaved African American character) on baking mix boxes and Mexican banditos (big mustached, sombrero wearing, six gun toting Mexican characters) on potato chip products.[12] The entertainment industry was also complicit in segregating African American musicians and audiences from mainstream European heritage music and audiences.

However, in recent times, the music industry has deemphasized the "soul music" category of contemporary entertainers of African American heritage and has presented mixed-race artists such as Maria Carey, Alicia Keys, Dwayne "The Rock" Johnson, and Prince in a race neutral manner. Even major corporations such as General Mills and Old Navy have created advertisements depicting mixed-race couples and mixed-raced children. In an indication of how far our society still has to go in terms of mixed-race identity attitudes of the general public, both corporations encountered considerable criticism from bloggers who

---

11   A detailed summary of mixed-race public policy history and details on this Supreme Court's decision can be found at http://www.cnn.com/2014/04/24/living/scotus-mixed-race-identity/index.html?sr=sharebar_facebook.

12   See public domain images.

still hold negative racial beliefs and are not afraid to voice their displeasure regarding what they perceive as corporate promotion of undesired human interaction.[13]

Observations

Taking into consideration, the evidence of the increase in individuals identifying as mixed race, the chapter example of a young mixed-race couple having the courage to marry and have children and the willingness of the entertainment industry and major corporations to venture into the recognition of mixed-raced people on an equal status with those who identify as single race, perhaps we are seeing the beginning of a new consciousness by the public sphere toward mixed-race individuals. There is glaring evidence that societal attitudes are still struggling with the acceptance of categorizing mixed-race individuals when public figures like President Obama and pro golfer Tiger Woods are still referred to as African American, when they are in fact equally mixed with another racial heritage. Cameron Diaz is of Cuban, English, Filipino, and Cherokee heritage. However, many Latino heritage people think she is not Latina because of her blonde hair and blue eyes. News anchor Ann Curry is Japanese, French, Irish, and Dutch heritage recently remarked how hard it is to embrace being mixed race when so many people from a different race think she is part of their group.

References

Asher, N. (2010). Checking the box: The label model minority. In H. Dalmage & B. K. Rothman (Eds.) *Race in the era of change: A reader*. New York, NY: Oxford University Press.

Mixed Race America. *New York Times article*. Retrieved from http://economix.blogs.nytimes.com/2012/09/27/mixed-race-america/?_php=true&_type=blogs&_php=true&_type=blogs&_r=1

Omi, M., & Winant, H. (1994). *Racial formation in the United States*. New York, NY: Routledge.

---

13   See the Internet blogging reaction to the mixed-race Cheerio's advertisement available at https://www.youtube.com/watch?v=KZT-qf3N7o4.

Chapter **3**

Californios: Beyond What We Learned in Fourth Grade

Mimi Coughlin

Important Words and Concepts in This Chapter

There are several important words and concepts throughout the upcoming chapter. The words appear several times in different places in order to help you remember the words and understand the chapter. The words are defined several times:

- Immediately below right before the chapter begins
- In text boxes throughout the chapter
- In red and boldfaced within the chapter
- In a glossary in expanded form at the end of the units

Some of the words also appear in other chapters. Talk about the words with other students, teachers, friends, and family members before you read, while reading the chapter, and after you have read the chapter.

Precontact

Of or relating to the period before contact of an indigenous people with an outside, often industrialized culture.

Contact

Of or relating to the period of contact between an indigenous people and an outside, often industrialized culture.

Castas System

In effort to legally divide and label the racial diversity of colonial society, Spain developed the castas system which spelled out 16 different categories of people produced through various intermarriages between Spanish, Indian, and African men and women. The castas used race and place of birth to rank people, with the highest status being reserved for "pure blood" Spanish and the lowest status being assigned to Africans.

Californio Era

The Californio era spans approximately 80 years (1769–1848), during which the Californios navigated life under three different political systems, Spanish (1769–1821), Mexican (1821–1848), and American (1848 to present).

If you went to elementary school in California (*and* you were offered a robust history–social science curriculum), you learned about the Native Americans who are the first people to call this region home. You also learned about the Spanish Mission System and the Gold Rush. However, you are probably not sure if you learned about the Californios because you can't remember who they were. Learning more about these people of mixed Spanish, Indian, and African decent, and how and why they came to California will help you to understand the deep and long-standing cultural connections and tensions between Mexico and California. I hope it will also help you to ask new questions about how history represents/misrepresents the people and events from the past. Perhaps, most importantly, this will help you to consider how the Californio's multicultural legacy impacts the present.

Precontact

It is essential to recall that the people we call Californios enter a geographic stage already set with thousands of people with a very long history. For thousands of years, a large and diverse population of California Indians thrived, supporting over 500 distinct tribes. These communities built trading economies that used the rich natural resources of plants and animals to sustain a high quality of life. It is estimated that the population of this region before 1492 (this date marks European "discovery" of the Americas also referred to as contact) was over 300,000. This means that precontact California was the most densely populated region in all of North America. Today, California still has the largest Native American population of any state and the greatest number of distinct tribes (100 + recognized tribes).

Contact and Spanish Empire Building

In the early 1500s, Europeans began to aggressively discover, conquer, colonize, and otherwise exploit the people and the resources of the Western Hemisphere. Forces lead by Hernan Cortes defeated the leadership of the Aztec Empire in 1521, allowing Spain to essentially take over their existing empire. The Spanish built their colonial capital, Mexico City, on top of the urban infrastructure of Tenochtitlan that had been the center of the Aztec Empire. Clearly indicating the purposes of their conquest, this territory was named "New Spain" and encompassed large areas of South, Central, and North America. The areas we know today as Mexico and California were within the huge Spanish land claims. To help you keep track of the changing borders, territorial claims, and place names in this story, it will be helpful to have a historical atlas handy—or you can do an Internet search for the historical maps you would like to see.

In Mexico, the Spanish became rich off the forced labor of the Indians and Africans. Enslaved Africans were imported from the earliest days of Spanish colonization and became increasingly important labor source as the Indian population collapsed. It is estimated that by 1800, the Indian population of Mexico had been reduced by 95% as a result of exposure to diseases brought into the Western Hemisphere by the Europeans and Africans. Spanish mistreatment—especially in the lucrative gold and silver mines, also contributed to high numbers of Indian deaths.

Mestizo Culture

The Spanish empire builders and bureaucrats sent to Mexico to develop New Spain were often single men looking to acquire a family and fortune for themselves. Intermarriage with Indian women was common. Generations of intermarriages produced a "mixed race," or mestizo, society. Further adding to this hybrid culture were free Africans. Although brutal and dehumanizing, the Spanish slavery system was different than British system familiar to us in the United States. In North America, enslavement was a multigenerational and totalizing system. In Mexico, it was much more likely that an enslaved Africans would have some possibility of purchasing freedom for themselves or family members. By 1700, free Africans outnumbered enslaved Africans in colonial Mexico. Although these Afro-Latinos continued to face discrimination, they were integrated into social and economic life and are important contributors to mestizo culture.

In effort to legally divide and label the racial diversity of colonial society, Spanish developed the castas system which spelled out 16 different categories of people produced through various intermarriages between Spanish, Indian, and African men and women. The castas used race and place of birth to rank people, with the highest status being reserved for "pure blood" Spanish and the lowest status being assigned to Africans. In between were the various combinations that could be produced through intermarriage.

There were fewer restrictions on land ownership and job opportunities for people in the lower castas in communities further away from the administrative hub of Mexico City. Thus, moving north to the frontiers of New Spain for social, political, and economic opportunities became an established route of advancement.

Onward to Alta California: Missions, Presidios, and Pueblos

European colonization was a power game and by the mid-1700s, Spain began to feel threatened by the Russian and British colonies on the North American continent. Spain decided to expand New Spain into the strategically important coast of California. One of the biggest challenges was simply getting there. Google a good map and you will notice several geographic barriers to getting people and supplies from Mexico City to California. Mountains and deserts must be crossed as well as the Colorado River. Where the city of Yuma, Arizona is today was the best, but still a very unpredictable and difficult, place to cross the river.

Why not just sail to California? It is possible, but the prevailing wind and water currents flow south, making it dangerous and impractical to rely on sailing vessels for transportation.

Despite these difficulties, the Spanish were able to slowly build a series of outposts in Baja California (the peninsula south of San Diego) that gradually extended into Alta California, which was the name used for everything north of San Diego. Initially, Spanish efforts to colonize Alta California consisted of a system of missions and presidios. The mission system used religion and agriculture to "civilize" the Native Americans. The presidios were the military forts that provided protection for the Spanish and were used to suppress Indian rebellions, sabotage, and other acts of resistance.

Eventually, the Spanish decided that to further solidify and develop Alta California, settlers were needed. In 1775, Captain Juan Batista de Anza was commissioned to scout an overland migration from northern Mexico to Alta California. Relying on an Indian guide, Anza did find a way through the mountains, deserts, and across the rivers. He returned to Mexico and was given permission and financial support to recruit and lead a group of settlers and a large herd of livestock to Alta California. In 1776, the Anza expedition successfully made the 1800-mile trek. Many members of the Anza expedition saw California as an opportunity to gain status by putting the limitations of the castas system placed upon them. Do an Internet search for the members of the Anza expedition and you will learn many details about the names, castas, occupations, and family relationships of this diverse group.

The Emergence and Submergence of Californio Culture

The Californio era spans approximately 80 years (1769–1848), during which the Californios navigated life under three different political systems: Spanish (1769–1821), Mexican (1821–1848), and American (1848 to present).

California in the Spanish era is dominated by the Mission system. The Franciscan priests called the Indians they converted to Catholicism, neophytes. Neophytes built and maintained the churches, courtyards, vineyards, orchards, cemeteries, and everything else associated with the functions of the missions. If you were assigned a Mission project in fourth grade, then you and your classmates, just like the Indian neophytes, built the mission system. The Spanish crown had granted huge tracts of land to each of the 21 missions so almost all of Alta California was property of the Catholic Church.

When Mexico revolted and gained independence from Spain in 1821, Alta California entered the Mexican era. Franciscans withdrew from the missions and the new Mexican government secularized the mission lands claiming them as private property.

Half of the reclaimed lands were to be returned to the original Indian occupants. Because the mission system had been so destructive to local Indian communities, many were no longer intact. Secularization did free the "neophytes" from their labor bondage to the Mission and many used this freedom to move inland, where they joined into community with another tribe. Others remained working on the land as paid labor for the new rancho system.

The other half of the huge land holdings of the Mission was subdivided into more than 500 pieces and granted to prominent members of the Mexico's mestizo elite. Hand drawn maps, called diseños, used landmarks like rivers, valleys, rock formations, and even trees to indicate each grant's boundaries. The land grants were known as *ranchos* and were the center of Californio culture for prominent families.

Rancho Culture

Life under Mexican rule represented the height of Californio culture.

The cattle that ranged freely on these vast lands were the source of wealth that kept powerful ranch families and their homes outfitted in the finest goods from around the world.

How did rural California ranches connect with the world markets that supported their elaborate lifestyles? Although there was no market for beef, prior to the population boom brought on by the Gold Rush, there was loads of money to be made in the *hide* and *tallow* trade.

Remember the mestizo culture and interracial castas that emerged from Spanish colonization? These people and their descendants made the ranching possible and profitable. They worked as vaqueros (cowboys) herding and roping cattle, processing the animal skins (hides) and fat (tallow) to be transported to coastal ports and traded for goods from around the world. The hides typically went to Boston to be made into leather goods, and the tallow went to South America to be made into candles and soap. Other rancho workers tended to the gardens, vineyards, and orchards. Intermarriage continued to blur existing racial categories as European and American newcomers married into Californio families.

The Mexican era is considered by some to be the "halcyon" or golden days of Old California. This idyllic image is based on romantic depictions of this time period that emphasize the charm of rural life and the simple satisfactions of work and family. Californios were well known for their hospitality and informal parties called fandangos. Many occasions called for the festive atmosphere, music, and dancing of a fandango.

The Coming of the Americans and Other Foreigners

These halcyon days were short lived, however, as the Californio elite lost their land and social status with the coming of the Americans and others foreigners.

The United States had been eyeing California as a prize for "Go West" pioneers eager for their own chance to own land and build wealth. The vast agricultural potential of California's abundant lands was considered prime real estate. To gain these lands, the United States waged a lop-sided war against Mexico in 1848. When the United States took possession of Mexico's North American territories as a result of the Treaty of Guadalupe Hidalgo that ended the war, the race for California land was on.

With the discovery of gold in the foothills above Sacramento in 1849, the race to California to strike it rich quick in the gold fields was also on. The flood of new comers from the eastern United States were at odds with the multiracial, Spanish-speaking, Catholic, family dynasties they encountered. White Anglo-Saxon Protestants (WASPS) viewed the lifestyle of the rancho elite as lazy, frivolous, immoral, and corrupt—ultimately incapable of developing and ultimately unworthy of developing the vast resources of California. These nationalistic and racist attitudes were part of a larger ideology of Manifest Destiny that proclaimed that is was God's will for the United States to extend her empire across the continent from the Atlantic to the Pacific.

Remember the hand-drawn maps or diseños that were the legal basis of Mexican land grants? Forced to defend these claims in the American judicial system, while American squatters rapidly occupied them, bankrupted many Californio families. Most ultimately lost their lands and with it their lifestyle. New forms of exclusion like the "Mexican and Foreign Miners' Tax" defined third and fourth generation Californios as foreigners on what they claimed as their own land.

In the rapidly changing context of California statehood (1850), many old time Californios had no choice but to assimilate. The mestizo mix of Spanish, Indian, and African cultures that characterized California before statehood continues to be at the heart of California identity. In the 1920s, a wave of nostalgia and renewed pride in the Spanish and Catholic roots of the state lead fueled efforts to rebuild and restore Mission era buildings. Celebrating connections to this past was promoted partly because it is good for business. The missions continue to be the state's most popular tourist attractions and modern versions of Spanish style architecture are everywhere. Hollywood has also contributed to the mythologizing the Californio story. Romantic tales set on old time ranchos depicted love affairs between exotic maidens and brave vaqueros. These popular movies influenced both positive and negative images of California's Hispanic culture.

This chapter explores a specific time period from 1769 when the Spanish started to explore the coast of California to 1850 when California was admitted to the union and the 31st state of the United States. There are so many more interconnections between historic and contemporary Mexico and California. I hope this introductory overview of Californios gives you some new ways to understand this relationship and encourages you to do your own research to learn more.

Chapter 4

"Imaginary Indians" Are Not Real

Brian Baker

Important Words and Concepts in This Chapter

There are several important words and concepts throughout the upcoming chapter. The words appear several times in different places in order to help you remember the words and understand the chapter. The words are defined several times:

- Immediately below right before the chapter begins
- In text boxes throughout the chapter
- In red and boldfaced within the chapter
- In a glossary in expanded form at the end of the units

Some of the words also appear in other chapters. Talk about the words with other students, teachers, friends, and family members before you read, while reading the chapter, and after you have read the chapter.

Imaginary Indians

A concept used to emphasize the stereotypes and images related to and associated with Native Americans that appear in popular culture, especially through the mass media or typified by team names and mascots used in sports.

Contributed by Brian Baker. © Kendall Hunt Publishing Company.

Prejudice

To make a judgment about an individual or group of individuals on the basis of their social, physical, or cultural characteristics. Such judgments are usually negative, but prejudice can also be exercised to give undue favor and advantage to members of particular groups. Prejudice is often seen as the attitudinal component of discrimination.

Institutional Discrimination

Policies, rules, and practices created and followed by companies, agencies, and other government or nongovernment organizations favorable to a dominant group and unfavorable to another group that have existed for a long time, and that get repeated over and over.

California Racial Mascot Act Discrimination

Section 221.3 of this California law stipulates:

1. Beginning January 1, 2017, all public schools are prohibited from using the term Redskins for school or athletic team names, mascots, or nicknames.

Through this enactment of this law, California became the first state in the United States to ban the use of "Redskins" in public schools.

Indigenous

Those people whose family and ethnic group inhabiting a land before it was taken over (colonized) by another nation. Indigenous can also mean not only the first people on a land, but also still alive and (possibly) still inhabiting some part of that land to which that person's ancestors inhabited.

Bureau of Indian Affairs

Interior Department agency that serves as the principal link between federally recognized Native American populations (officially *American Indian tribes*) and the U.S. government.

Introduction

In this chapter, we explore expressions of imaginary Indians.[1] The expressions addressed have to do with ideas and images that are associated with and attributed to American Indians. The ideas and images related to imaginary Indians exist in popular culture in both an historical and contemporary context. For example, in terms of history, it was common for Americans to describe American Indians as *savages*. In the contemporary period, when we get into the idea of American Indians being used as mascots or names in sports, they are being imagined as *warriors*. For example, in high school or at colleges and universities in the United States, even including professional sports teams, fans attending games will engage in certain behaviors or practices such as the *tomahawk chop*. These examples illustrate the point that people act on ideas and behaviors in terms of how they *imagine* American Indians. This is what I call **imaginary Indians**, as people in general already have a set of ideas and images in their heads that they associate with and attribute to American Indians.

> **Imaginary Indians:** set of ideas and images in their heads that they associate with and attribute to American Indians.

In this discussion of **imaginary Indians**, I also introduce other important social science concepts such as **prejudice** and **institutional discrimination**, and how they are interrelated. I then introduce the problem of how *imaginary Indians* as a set of ideas that characterizes Americans Indians as *the other*. After a brief discussion of these concepts, we explore some themes and examples of *imaginary Indians* rooted in history, where the ideas and images are related to the inequality and injustice experienced by American Indians. Toward the end of this chapter, we explore contemporary examples of *imaginary Indians* as in the case of *mascots*. I conclude with a short discussion of the **"California Racial Mascot Act"** passed in 2015 as it relates to *redskins* and Indian mascots. Although it can be shown that *redskin* is a word and idea rooted in racism, some Americans continue in their efforts to normalize and validate the "r word" as socially and politically acceptable.

Prejudice, Institutional Discrimination, and "the Other"

It is the set of ideas and stereotypes that exist in popular culture that create *imaginary Indians*. They are not real and exist in the imaginations of people. While *imaginary Indians* are not real, they influenced the daily lives of American Indians in history and continue to do so in the twenty-first century. Social scientists who investigate racial and ethnic relations have often related the inequality and injustice experienced by racial and ethnic minority groups as an outcome of **prejudice** and *institutional discrimination*. These two are very basic and important concepts, and they are connected to each other.

> **Prejudice:** judgment about individuals or groups based on their social, physical, or cultural characteristics.

---

1 See Baker (2007).

First, *prejudice* refers to preconceived ideas and notions held by people toward other groups.[2] The forms of *prejudice* in general that are of most concern relate to race, ethnicity, gender, or ability. Often these ideas exist in popular culture, and it is possible for someone to already form an opinion about another group without having any direct knowledge or personal experience. For example, someone just posted pictures of t-shirts on my Facebook page. The t-shirts reflect the *alcoholic* aspect of *imaginary Indians:* one t-shirt stated *My Indian Name is "Drinks Like a Fish"* and another noted *My Indian Name is "Crawling Drunk."* Thus, prejudice relates to the ideas and images, especially those that are negative and harmful to the group who is the target or subject of the prejudice.

Second, **discrimination** refers to situations when people act on prejudice, where they treat members of one group differently than members of another group (Aguiree & Turner, 2004, p. 6).[3] Generally,

> **Discrimination:** Acting out prejudice.

discrimination is an action related to *prejudice*. While the t-shirts mentioned in the previous paragraph reflect an idea or image of *American Indians are alcoholics* the fact that the t-shirts were made and produced in large numbers to be sold in stores, that this is a form of **discrimination** related to race. To deny someone, a job based on their race, that is discrimination. Both of these examples are actions are forms to *racial discrimination*.

A larger and more complex form of **discrimination** is **institutional discrimination**, which occurs when society as a whole works to the advantage of some groups (*more powerful groups*) and to the disadvantage of other groups (*less powerful*) who are denied access to valued resources.[4] While there are many examples of laws passed by the U.S. government that limited the lived experiences of various **racial and ethnic groups**, an excellent example of *institutional discrimination* that occurred in the United States was the Jim Crow era of the American South. During that time, the idea of *separate but equal* defined the time period. Comparatively, the resources and opportunities available to Blacks were fewer and less valuable when compared to the resources and opportunities for Whites. The way society was structured worked to the disadvantage of African Americans, and the laws and norms of that time period operated in ways that normalized the everyday forms of inequality and injustice they experienced.

In recent years, scholars in the field of Ethnic Studies have used **the other** as a way to understand the experiences of racial and ethnic minorities in American society. In general, by using the term *minority groups*, we are referring to groups that are less powerful when compared to the *majority group* (Aguiree & Turner, 2004, p. 4).[5] Overall, historically and currently, racial and ethnic minority groups have been less powerful groups in society. In describing his own experience as a Mexican American individual, Arturo Madrid wrote about experiencing life as **the other** in American society.[6] A minority group is relegated to the status of *the other* when it is set apart from and distinguished by the majority as

---

2   See Aguiree and Turner (2004).
3   See Footnote 2, p. 6.
4   See Footnote 2, p. 10.
5   See Footnote 2, p. 4.
6   Madrid (1997).

being different. In addition, and this is very important, the racial and cultural differences being highlighted as different are also assumed to be inferior. Madrid shares important aspects of his biography in a time period before colleges and universities included larger numbers of racial and ethnic minorities as students. Given the time period when he was a university student, fellow students assumed he was a groundskeeper because there were not many Mexican American students on campus. Because the groundskeepers on campus tended to be Mexican Americans, students assumed that he was also a groundskeeper. Due to his racial-ethnic background, Arturo Madrid was socially isolated from the predominately White student population. Because the number of Mexican American students at the university was very low, he had a difficult time relating or being connected to an institution that did not value his racial-ethnic identity.

Historically, prejudice and discrimination affected the lives of American Indians, as law and policy emphasized their status as the other. I discuss some ways in which American Indians were imagined as *the other*. In doing so, I make a connection between historical images and ideas to a contemporary form of imaginary Indians. In discussing *Indians as mascots*, I place an emphasis on *redskins*. Although this is a term rooted in racism toward American Indians historically, its use in the contemporary period is an example of institutional discrimination. I close by presenting a short discussion of the California Racial Mascot Act, passed in 2015. With this law, California became the first state to outlaw *redskin* as a team name or mascot in public schools, and therefore, addressed the problem of institutional discrimination.

Roaming on the Land

Although it is possible to challenge dominant ideas related to *imaginary Indians*, it is difficult to change them after they have become deeply embedded in American popular culture. Basically, stereotypes related to *imaginary Indians* have been around for a couple of centuries or more. I remember a camping trip to Sequoia/Kings Canyon National Park in California. On this trip, and in the redwood forest, and based on my identity as American Indian, I experienced *institutional discrimination* in the twenty-first century. Traveling with a group of friends in late spring, we saw and participated in many activities that the national park had to offer, such as hiking, camping, and swimming. As American Indians (*Chippewa, Wintun, Abenaki*), we experienced something so powerful and striking that it stood out from everything else we experienced. We encountered something so simple and created by Americans and imposed over the landscape: words on a sign that communicated ideas related to *imaginary Indians*.

In the park, we went on the trail to Moro Rock. At the summit, we were struck by the view of the Great Western Divide, it was truly spectacular. We talked about the beauty of the landscape and admired it, and like many tourists, we took pictures to memorialize our adventure. It was after this that we noticed a sign designed for tourists. Created by the National Park Service, the sign outlined two brief histories of Moro Rock, one having to do with its geological history and the other having to do with the human history of the area. It was the official human history inscribed on the sign that shocked us. The human history of the area began with this *imaginary Indian* declaration: *Indians roamed here for several thousand years.* What? Who? Were they lost? Were they just ignorant savages who did not know where they were for thousands of years? As American Indians who happen to be teachers and professors, we were especially aware of the power of the misconception being communicated. First, and especially important, the word *Indians* is a term that erases the *Monache* from this specific place altogether. The *Monache* are the people indigenous to this area, not *Indians*. Because the *Monache* are not included in this official version of history, they are removed from it.

> **Indigenous:** inhabiting a land prior to colonization by another nation.

A second problem with this sign has to do with the idea of the *roaming* or *wandering Indian*, an important characteristic or quality of *imaginary Indians* created during Manifest Destiny. The idea of Indians *roaming* over the land is especially important and powerful: it validated the idea that Indians did not settle on the land because they simply roamed over it. In the colonial process, White American lawmakers and officials working in the Bureau of Indian Affairs exploited *roam* and *wander* in reference to American Indians in order to justify how the United States would deal with the Indian problem. Eventually, it became necessary to constrain the *roaming Indians* and to limit their human existence on the land by drawing reservation boundaries around them in order to enclose and isolate them from American society. Once relegated to an isolated and inhumane existence on reservations where it was not possible to support their families, the *roaming Indian* no longer existed as an obstacle to Americans who were provided with the opportunity to settle the land when American Indians were confined to reservations.

It was here, at this public place, that we experienced institutionalized racism toward us as Chippewa, Wintun, and Abenaki peoples. To include the idea that *Indians roamed here for thousands of years* in this history is a powerful action related to the invention of *imaginary Indians*. But, this seemingly innocent inscription was followed by yet another *imaginary Indian* invention: *Neither sign nor record indicates that they considered Moro Rock a special place.* What? Were those Indians blind too? Did they roam around Moro Rock for thousands of years and not realize that it was there? At the same time, the National Park Service has preserved a village site in this area, which is evidence that tells about their residence. In addition, because this is evidence about residence, this also indicates that they did consider the area to be a special place because this was their homeland. The fact that the *Monache* did not feel a need to post a sign nor leave a record on Moro Rock is only evidence that they had a different cultural understanding and awareness of the world.

In a very simple yet powerful way, the National Park Service inscription to Moro Rock reinforces dominant ideas and stereotypes about American Indians. Before leaving this place, and in front of the sign that represented imaginary Indians and institutional discrimination, as indigenous peoples we mimicked the idea of *roaming Indians* unaware of their surroundings. We took pictures to memorialize our own Indian ignorance.

> **…they did consider the area to be a special place because this was their homeland.**

Being Like Children

The Americans created many strategic images pertaining to American Indians to fuel the colonial machine driven by them across the land, and like bumps and potholes in the road, Americans understood that they had an endless Indian problem. Throughout the 1800s and mid-1900s, the fact that Americans viewed American Indians as *a problem* is important. To describe or view American Indians as *a problem* reflects their negative bias toward them, viewing American Indian as *the other*.

Indigenous People Highlighted in This Chapter

1. Chippewa
2. Abenaki
3. Wintun
4. Monache
5. Cherokee
6. Lakota
7. Illini
8. Cheyenne
9. Muskogee
10. Miwok

In the United States, Indigenous people are sometimes called Native Americans or American Indians. When discussing Native Americans, it is more clear to use the name of the specific indigenous group.

Because Americans viewed and understood them as *blood-thirsty savages* who were prone to *laziness*, Americans viewed them as being incapable of looking out for their own interests and needs. In fact, in the early nineteenth century, American political officials increasingly described Indians as *children*, sometimes even referring to them as *red children*. This idea, that *Indians are like children*, is embedded in the 1831 ruling made by the U.S. Supreme Court in the *Cherokee Nation v. Georgia*. This case is important because it established the precedent that the United States is like a "guardian" who cares for the Cherokee Nation as the "ward" of the U.S. government. Basically, this case is premised on the idea that American Indians are like *children*. Citizens of the Cherokee Nation who were bilingual (*who spoke English and Cherokee*), who were well educated and literate (*they published newspapers in the Cherokee language and had public schools*), and who were business owners were relegated to the status of being *wards* of the government because they were considered to be like *children*. Through its self-appointed position of *guardian* looking out for the *wards* under its care, the American government created the idea of the *Great Father* doing good things when caring for the *red children* who, due to their own cultural inferiority, required constant American paternalistic guidance.

The two pictures above portray American Indians in "Imaginary" ways by exaggerating stereotypes. The picture on the left shows an image of Uncle Sam spoon-feeding an American Indian presumable because they are not able to take care of themselves. Bottle photo is from the collection of Dr. Brian Baker.

Near the latter part of the 1800s, indigenous peoples who at one time possessed the ability and means to sustain their own livelihoods were now blamed for the fact that they could not even feed or clothe themselves. While they continued to possess a sense of being **indigenous** to the land, Americans began to understand the *red children* as indigents on the land. Therefore, it became necessary for the *Great Father* to feed them. In a picture taken on the Pine Ridge Indian Reservation in 1891, a photographer captured a number of **Lakota people** standing in line on *ration day*. Instead of paying attention to the political and cultural circumstances associated with their geographic isolation or American racism toward Indians as the more relevant factors which prevented the Lakota in the photograph from making a living on their own terms, the accepted stereotype of the time viewed them as *lazy*. Because the **Lakota** were *lazy* and were like *children*, they were responsible for their own poverty and starvation, and Americans had to feed them.

Popular culture accepted this view of American Indians, and this stereotype was captured in an ad for *Boston Baked Beans* in the early twentieth century. In this ad, we are confronted by a carefully designed Uncle Sam as a good guy spoon-feeding an Indian. The ad identifies the Indian pictured as being Sitting Bull, a famous and well-known Lakota leader who left his mark on American history. While Sitting Bull is a real person in history, Uncle Sam is a fictional character connected to American patriotism. In the ad, Sitting Bull is short and is wrapped in blanket, and his appearance is *savage* and *animal* like. The fact that Uncle Sam is much taller and is holding the spoon for a much shorter Sitting Bull invokes the basic idea of a parent spoon-feeding a young child. In this image, a strong and powerful leader like Sitting Bull in Native American history was portrayed akin to *red children* incapable of feeding himself.

> In terms of racism toward American Indians, *redskins* as a racially offensive term played a part in the history of violence and injustice experienced by American Indians.

Indians as Redskins, Warriors, and Mascots

During a time period when Americans imposed many constraints over Indians that prevented them from practicing their religions and speaking their languages, Americans became increasingly fascinated with *imaginary Indians*. For instance, during a time period when American Indian children were sent to Indian Boarding Schools run by the American government, where they were severely punished when they spoke their languages or practiced their religions, Americans began to *play Indian*. For example, fraternal organizations were founded by nonnative people, such as the *Order of Redmen*, and sports teams took on names associated with *imaginary Indians* as in *chiefs* or *warriors*, and they also created Indian mascots. It is important to point out that in a time period when there was extreme racism toward American Indians and they were set apart from society as *the other*, at a time when Indian children were brutalized for *being Indian*, non-Indians began to act as *imaginary Indians*. Today, *Chief Wahoo* of the Cleveland Indians and the *Washington Redskins* are examples of *institutional discrimination* in the contemporary period. The fact that Americans regarded and viewed Indians as *wahoos* and *redskins* affected the lives of American Indians.

> In Kelseyville, California, the local high school changed the name of its mascot from *Indians* to the *Knights* in 2008.

As a mascot or team name, the *imaginary Indian* in the world of sports has become an acceptable and common aspect of popular culture. Indian mascots are one of the most visible ways *imaginary Indians* exist in popular culture today. In this imaginary world, Indians are viewed as *fierce heathen warriors* inherently prone to being *cold blooded* and *cunning* in their ability to *fight* and *kill*. In recent decades and throughout the country, there have been a number of heated debates in sports at high schools, colleges, and universities, as well as professional sports related to Indian mascots. In Kelseyville, California, the local high school changed the name of its mascot from *Indians* to the *Knights* in 2008. The *imaginary Indian* at Kelseyville High School had nothing to do with the local indigenous people or history of the area. This *imaginary Indian* was successfully challenged by the local California Indian tribe, the *Habematolel Pomo of Upper Lake*.[7] At

---

7 See http://www.upperlakepomo.com/.

the University of Illinois, Chamagne-Urbana, *Chief Illiniwek* as the mascot had been a source of debate and controversy for decades. The name of the sports teams at UICU is the *Fighting Illini*, but the image itself has nothing to do with the history and culture of Illini Indians. While the UICU retained its team name, the mascot, *Chief Illiniwek*, was retired in 2007 and is no longer the official mascot of the university.[8]

The most obvious example of *institutional discrimination* has to do with the *Washington Redskins*. In terms of racism toward American Indians, *redskins* as a racially offensive term played a part in the history of violence and injustice experienced by American Indians. In 2013, Dallas Goldtooth (*Lakota*) posted a picture of an 1863 newspaper clipping from *The Daily Republican* on his Facebook page. This newspaper article from Minnesota shows us the racism toward American Indians in the nineteenth century by showing us that American citizens could receive a bounty for American Indian scalps: the article announced that the "reward for dead Indians has been increased to $200 for every redskin sent to Purgatory."[9] In posting a picture of the article from 1863, Goldtooth wrote:

> It was only 5 generations ago that a white man could get money for one of my grandfather's scalps.
> At the time . . . it was Redskin that was used to describe us.
> So those who fail to understand the significance of this whole debate, think deeper about the word legacy. Is the legacy of racism, death, and plunder worth keeping?

It is important to point out this is only one example of *redskin* in American history, where Indian scalps were sold like fur pelts for cash. This happened in many parts of the United States in the 1700s and 1800s. The reality here is that *redskin* is a demeaning word directly tied to racism and the extermination of American Indians. For example, the State of California paid $1,100,000 to militia groups who attacked and killed California Indians in 1852. Here, *redskin* is associated with the *bounty* that settlers and Americans received for the scalps of American Indians they killed, and these occurred in times where there was no warfare between Americans and American Indians.[10]

Many American Indians have questions about the team name of the *Washington Redskins*, and view it is an example of *institutional discrimination*. In 1992, Suzan Shown Harjo (*Cheyenne/Muskogee*) filed a case with U.S. Patent and Trademark Office challenging the *Washington Redskins*. The strategy here was that, if the *Washington Redskins* lost its protected trademark, the owners of the team would then change the name of the Washington team. While Harjo almost won, the ruling was overturned and the case was refiled by Amanda Blackhorse in 2014. The case was decided in favor of Blackhorse on

---

8   See *In Whose Honor?* New Day Films (1997). While this documentary is very effective in highlighting the problem of *Chief Illinwek*, it is outdated in the sense that it was released before the mascot was officially retired. For additional information, see *Chief Illiniwek: Beloved by Students, (Still) Banned by the University*. Article available online, Indian Country Today Media Network: *http://indiancountrytodaymedianetwork.com/2013/04/29/chief-illiniwek-beloved-students-still-banned-university-149098*.

9   http://indiancountrytodaymedianetwork.com/2013/11/13/dakota-man-exposes-vile-history-redskins-facebook-152241

10 For an historical analysis of violence toward native people in California, see Lindsey (2015).

the grounds that *redskins* is a word that is disparaging (*offensive*) to American Indians. The case is still not completely settled, and the owner of the *Washington Redskins* continues to assert that the team name "honors" American Indians.

The California Racial Mascot Act

On October 11, 2015, Governor Jerry Brown signed into law The California Racial Mascots Act (CRMA).[11] By doing so, California became the first state to ban the use *redskins* as a team name and/or mascot. The legislation clearly prohibits the use of "racially derogatory or discriminatory school or athletic team names" in California public schools.[12] A deadline of January 1, 2017 was established for schools to decide on a new mascot and they would also be provided with some financial assistance in doing so, as there will be a number of financial costs to schools to comply with the law (*logos on gymnasium floors, etc.*). This law affects four schools in California: Gustine High School, Calaveras High School, Chowchilla Union High School, and Tulare High School.

After the Governor Brown signed CRMA into law, one American Indian teenager from Jackson, California, Dahkota Kicking Bear Brown (*Miwok*), who was involved in this legislative initiative stated:

> I hope everyone can move forward positively and select a new mascot, inclusive of all students to represent their campus community.[13]

In fact, one California high school pursued this course of action in 2011. While this was before the actual law was signed into law, a discussion about *redskins* had already been happening in Colusa, California. Despite strong emotions and nostalgic connections to the *redskin's* mascot which had been an important part of the school's history and identity, members of the community and high school did the right thing. They opted to implement a change in their school as an institution in order to embrace a more positive and inclusive future. In changing their name and their identity from the *Redskins* to the *Redhawks*, Assistant Principal Mike West made the following point:

> Give them their identity and let them run with it . . . Let them go forward and develop new traditions for their mascot.[14]

---

11 On October 11, 2015, Governor Jerry Brown signed into law *The California Racial Mascots Act* (Assembly Bill No. 30). Introduced by Assemblyman Luis Alejo, this law prohibits public schools in California from using the term *redskins* beginning January 1, 2017. California became the first state to acknowledge *redskin* as a racial slur toward Native Americans. Visit the California State Legislature website at https://leginfo.legislature.ca.gov/faces/billNavClient.xhtml?bill_id=201520160AB30 for more information.

12 https://leginfo.legislature.ca.gov/faces/billNavClient.xhtml?bill_id=201520160AB30

13 http://edsource.org/2015/california-is-first-in-the-nation-to-ban-redskins-school-mascot/88948

14 Colusa prepares to say good-bye to redskins.

Conclusion

Unfortunately, prejudice and institutional discrimination have shaped the lives and experiences of racial and ethnic minority groups for quite some time. Although it is possible to challenge the *imaginary Indian* invented by Americans, it is extremely difficult to change those ideas as they have become so deeply embedded in American culture. Especially in the world of sports where Indians are made into mascots, these imaginary Indians have become effectively institutionalized. *Imaginary Indian* ideas remain visible in the world of sports, where Indians are reduced to mascots and team names. But, with respect to *redskins* as an obvious and negative aspect of the *imaginary Indian*, there seems to be some seeds for positive change. California law now requires public schools in the state to discontinue using *redskin* because it is a racially offensive term. When we look at American society and culture over time, we can identify changes in race and ethnic relations between an historical period (as in the 1850s, for example) and the contemporary period. By doing so, we understand how law has been an effective part of social change.

References

Aguiree, A., Jr., & Turner, J. (2004). Ethnicity and ethnic relations. In A. Aguire & J. Turner (Eds.), *American ethnicity: The dynamics and consequences of discrimination* (4th ed., pp. 1–24). New York, NY: McGraw Hill.

Baker, B. (2007). Imaginary Indians: Invoking invented ideas in popular and public culture. In J. L. Figueroa, B. Mosupyoe, & B. Baker (Eds.), *Introduction to ethnic studies* (pp. 261–275). Dubuque, IA: Kendall-Hunt.

Lindsey, B. (2015). *Murder state: California's native American genocide, 1846–1873*. University of Nebraska Press.

Madrid, A. (1997). Being "the other": Ethnic identity in a changing society. In J. Henslin (Ed.), *Down to earth sociology* (pp. 505–511). New York, NY: The Free Press.

Chapter 5

Implicit Bias: Schools Not Prisons!

Rita Cameron Wedding and Jon Wedding

Contributed by Arya Dawn Allender West. © Kendall Hunt Publishing Company.

Important Words and Concepts in This Chapter

There are several important words and concepts throughout the upcoming chapter. The words appear several times in different places in order to help you remember the words and understand the chapter. The words are defined several times:

- Immediately below right before the chapter begins
- In text boxes throughout the chapter
- In red and boldfaced within the chapter
- In a glossary in expanded form at the end of the units

Some of the words also appear in other chapters. Talk about the words with other students, teachers, friends, and family members before you read, while reading the chapter, and after you have read the chapter.

Microaggression

A comment or action that subtly and often unconsciously or unintentionally expresses a prejudiced attitude toward a member of a marginalized group (such as a racial minority).

Unconscious Bias

Unlike *explicit bias* (which rejects the attitudes or beliefs that one endorses at a conscious level), *implicit bias* is the bias in judgment and/or behavior that results from subtle cognitive processes (e.g., implicit attitudes and implicit stereotypes) that often operate at a level below conscious awareness and without intentional control.

Racial Discrimination

The unequal treatment of individuals on the basis of their race or perceived race. Discrimination usually refers to negative treatment, but discrimination in favor of particular groups can also occur.

Disproportionate

Too large or too small in comparison with something else.

*A*ll over California and across the nation you can see billboards going up that read "Schools Not Prisons." These campaigns are in response to the nation's growing awareness that school discipline such as suspensions and expulsions push youth of color out of school and into the criminal justice system. Trouble at school can lead to a student's first contact with law enforcement.

In 2014, the U.S. Departments of Justice and Education jointly issued a guidance letter advising schools that the disproportional application of discipline to certain groups of students might violate federal civil rights laws. The guidance letter stated, "In short, racial discrimination in school discipline is a real problem" (Frey, 2014). "Nationally black and Latino students are suspended and expelled at much higher rates than white students. Among middle school student's black youth are suspended nearly four times more often than white youth, and Latino youth are roughly twice as likely to be suspended or expelled than white youth" (Smith, 2007).

In 2016, the California Department of Education reported a decline in school suspensions 3 years in a row yet as indicated in the chart below, disparities persist for Black students.

Race/Ethnic Group	% Enrollment	% Suspensions
African American	6%	16.4%
White	24.6%	20.9%
Hispanic	53.9%	54%

According to Tom Torlakson, California's State Superintendent of Schools "removing children from schools and keeping them away from the educational environment can be very harmful" (Torlakson, 2016). *As a result of missing school, students fall behind academically. Kids suspended or expelled are two times more likely to drop out and five times more likely to commit a crime* (Siders, 2014). This chapter discusses how school suspensions and expulsions once seen as the solution to school discipline puts students at increased risk of school failure. Racial disparities in school discipline can be linked at least in part to implicit biases. Understanding implicit biases that inform individual and institutional practices offer the potential to improve educational outcomes and keep kids in school and out of prison.

The majority of suspensions are for code of conduct or willful defiance offenses that include nonviolent misconduct such as smoking tobacco, fighting, talking back, cursing, tardiness, and eye rolling. School discipline for such offenses is largely left to the discretion of school authorities, for example, teachers, administrators, or school resource officers. Because of the subjective nature of willful defiance offenses, these suspensions are not uniformly applied. Some students are suspended while the same offense committed by another student may be completely overlooked because identical behaviors are perceived and responded to differently depending upon the decision-maker's perceptions of the seriousness of the offense. The application and enforcement of discipline policies also vary by schools with some schools punishing misconduct more harshly than others.

In 2014, willful defiance was banned as grounds for school suspensions or expulsions except for grades kindergarten through third grade because such practices which are highly subjective in their implementation **disproportionately** discriminate against minority students. In 2012–2013, there were just over 60,000 students suspended, 43% of the suspensions were issued for defiance and 19% of suspensions involved Black students (Frey, 2014).

Implicit Bias: Decision-Making

According to Kimberly Papillon,

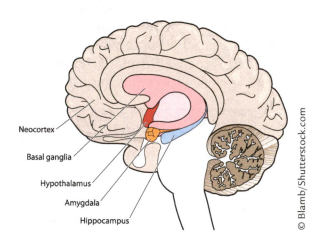

if scientists could scan our brains when we see spiders or snakes, they would see that the area or our brains that focuses on fear, threat, anxiety and distrust is triggered or, as neuroscientist say, "activates". Suppose scientists scanned the brains of people with unconscious or implicit bias toward African Americans. Would they also see that part of our brains activate? In short, yes. Studies have found that this same area of the brain activates more when they see pictures of African American faces than when they see pictures of Caucasian faces. What is truly remarkable is that many of the people who have this reaction state they have no conscious bias or prejudice towards others. (Kimberly Papillon, 2009)

While fear, anxiety, and response to threat involve many parts of the brain, the amygdala is central to this process.

So just as our brains react to our fear of things like spiders and snakes, our brains can respond to repetitive messages embedded in stereotypes that depict individuals as lazy, dangerous, terrorist, criminal, and so on. Though most people are aware that such stereotypes exist, they are often unaware of the influence these stereotypes have on their decision-making. Most people are unaware of any differences in their decision-making based on categories of race/ethnicity, gender, religion, or sexuality. They believe that their decisions are based on the facts and any disparities that might occur would be unintended because they do not harbor any conscious malice or ill will toward these groups. But, neither intention nor malice is prerequisite for bias.

> **Mindfulness practices can help weaken our implicit biases and increase healthy interactions. Mindfulness practices include deep breathing, jogging, progressive relaxation, martial arts, tai chi, and qi gong.**

Implicit biases cause people to make automatic associations between individuals and stereotypes based on images and information we are exposed to on a daily basis through repetitive direct and indirect messages, for example, cop shows and other TV shows in which Blacks and other people of color are repeatedly arrested for drug offenses and other criminal acts. Whites are also depicted negatively on these shows but such depictions do not produce stereotypes that stigmatize them as "criminals" because they are overwhelmingly depicted in all media as all-American citizens. On the other hand, stereotypes that link blacks to criminal behaviors have been so thoroughly imprinted on our thinking that it is no surprise that most people assume that black children sell more drugs. Contrary to this common belief, White children are one-third times more likely to sell drugs than Black children, but Black children are twice as likely to be arrested on charges of drug sales (Bernstein, 2014).

Stereotypes that link Black students to criminal like behaviors make it easier for decision-makers in all youth-serving systems (schools, after school programs, juvenile justice, etc.) to think that this is the group that would be in trouble.

Implicit biases informed by stereotypes can easily effect how decision-makers attribute guilt, innocence, or dangerousness to student behaviors. Because the student to whom negative characteristics such as "trouble-maker," "loud," "aggressive," or the subjective and powerful label of "willful defiance," are applied, will be punished more often and receive harsher consequences.

Law Enforcement in Schools

In recent years, law enforcement has had greater involvement in schools and therefore more contact with school children. Many schools use School Resource Officers for duties that were once the responsibility of school counselors. A once kid friendly, "kids-will-be-kids" approach to school discipline has been replaced in many schools by rigid discipline practices that in some school environments treat children more like criminals than students.

> Because there is often an officer present and available and criminal laws are so broad and vague, school discipline merges seamlessly into arrest. Having the police nearby transforms the daily school experience into a minefield of potential crimes: fighting in the hallway becomes a "battery" or even "aggravated battery"; swiping a classmates headphones can be classified as "theft" or "robbery" and talking back to an officer or teacher is "disorderly conduct." (Advancement Project, 2010)

Kindergarteners and the School-to-Prison Pipeline

Children as young as 4 and 5 years old are put on this school-to-prison pathway. Black children represent 18% of preschool enrollment and 48% of preschool children receiving more than one out-of-school suspension. White students represent 43% of preschool enrollment and 26% of children receiving more than one out-of-school suspension (Civil Rights Data Collection; Data Snapshot: School Discipline, 2014).

Avon Park, Florida—Police arrested a 6-year-old Florida girl and even handcuffed her when she acted out in class. Police officers said Desre'e Watson, a kindergarten student

Not all disciplinary actions lead to arrest but they do result in building a record of misconduct that is documented.

at Avon Elementary School in Highlands County, had a violent run-in with a teacher. "I was scared," the little girl said. Police claim the little girl got angry and began kicking and scratching. She even hit a teacher attempting to intervene in the disturbance.

"When there is an outburst of violence, we have a duty to protect and make that school a safe environment for the students, staff and faculty. That's why, at this point, the person was arrested regardless what the age," said Chief Frank Mercurio, Avon Park Police Department. The kindergartner was booked in the Highland County jail and was charged with a felony (battery of a school officer) and two misdemeanors (disruption of a school function and resisting law enforcement officers) (Herbert, 2007).

Not all disciplinary actions lead to arrest but they do result in building a record of misconduct that is documented in ways that can justify suspensions while similar or even identical behaviors of other students may result only in an informal verbal reprimand or no punishment at all.

Implicit Biases Do Not Make School Decision-Makers Bad People Since Bias According to the Research Is Normal and Inevitable.

The biggest problem with implicit bias is its influence school suspension and expulsion rates. Following are four examples of how implicit bias effects school discipline:

1. Implicit bias can cause decision-makers to perceive even the minor willful defiant offenses committed by students of color as more dangerous, disruptive, and more serious than those of white students.

2. Implicit biases are hard to notice because they are reflected in microaggressions not blatant acts of discrimination like racial slurs but *everyday verbal, nonverbal and environmental slights, snubs, insults, whether intentional or unintentional which communicate hostile, derogatory, or negative messages* (Sue, n.d.). Daily displays of microaggressions can have a detrimental effect on interactions throughout every aspect of a student's educational experience from the classroom to the cafeteria.

3. Implicit bias can influence the words decision-makers use to substantiate the offense, for example, aggressive, hostile, violent, volatile, or threatening when other less damaging words would be more accurate. Words such as these grossly exaggerate the seriousness of the incident. In the case of the 6-year old child who was arrested for behavior that most people would describe as a *tantrum* the chief of police described this child's behavior (even though there was no weapon involved) as an "outburst of violence." The words decision-makers use, for example, "outburst of violence" vs. tantrum, in reports can bias everyone who reads the report at every decision point. Daily displays of microaggressions can have a harmful

effect on interactions both academically and while applying school discipline. Microaggressions go undetected as school practices that promote biases. Simple statements or gestures can be seen as routine but in reality reinforce negative stereotypes about the students identified ethnic group. Many times these microaggressions began to display themselves during situations that involve the student not meeting behavior expectations in school. For example, when a student's behavior needs to be disciplined by someone other than the teacher, an e-mail is typically sent to notify the person who will address the behavior. In one such incident, a student did not return to class after leaving to use the restroom. In an attempt to ask for assistance in getting the student back to class, the teacher sent an e-mail describing the student as a "fugitive." Although the student should have returned to class, the student did not escape or make an attempt to avoid law enforcement. In this example, referring to the student as a "fugitive" implies something negative about the student. The negative effects of the label might be compounded by the fact that the student is Black. Of equal importance, the choice of this word could negatively bias the individual responsible for disciplining and result in harsher discipline. Words have power. They are easily converted to labels that once embedded in reports, files, affidavits, follow the students throughout their educational experiences. Biases in the choice of language will be used to justify more punitive decisions at subsequent decision points including law enforcement.

Implicit bias results in more bias. When a structured decision-making tool or school discipline matrix takes into account previous *run-ins* with law enforcement or even a previous suspension; even though these "priors" may have occurred due to bias they can still be used to justify the need for harsher discipline. Disparities in decision-making result in some students receiving verbal reprimands for the same offenses for which other students are suspended. Unlike informal verbal reprimands, formal disciplinary actions are documented and will remain in the student's permanent school record. For those schools that practice "three-strikes" discipline modeled after three-strike criminal

Do You Know How to Counter Microaggressions?
Give yourself and others affirmations and self-affirmations frequently! Affirmations are positive statements about someone or something for doing something specific; affirmations are compliments.

laws, this means that the students of color pay a discipline tax because they are more likely to be formally disciplined for nonserious offenses. Those students who are not labeled troublemaker or perceived as a threat based on the stereotypes, and receive only a verbal reprimand with no referral and no formal documentation for the exact same offense, essentially start with a clean slate. Each time they break a rule can be treated as the first.

What Effect Do Implicit Biases Have on Students?

While trying to understand the issues faced by students of color in education, Steele (1997) asks the following question: *what in the experience of these groups might frustrate their identification with all or certain aspects of school achievement?* (p. 613). Sustained academic achievement is heavily dependent upon the positive view of one's self in the classroom (Steele, 1997). For students of color to achieve positive results in education, they must feel they have the opportunities, the skills, and the resources to excel but more importantly they must feel a sense of acceptance in educational settings (Steele, 1997).

When existing in an environment where one is negatively viewed, it may be difficult to succeed in such a place even when the possibility of the stereotype has been removed (Aronson, 2002). This problem has definitely created a dire situation for African American students. Stereotype threat takes place throughout the educational experience of the black male, forever creating frustration and limited success even for those who possess the skills and ability to be highly successful in the classroom (Aronson, 2002). Oddly enough, the exposure to this threat comes not from their internal fears but from their own connection with the realm, in this case the classroom (Aronson, 2002). The collective effect of negative stereotypes begins to push students of color out of school even if they are not pushed out they most likely perform well below their abilities (Aronson, 2002). The reconceptualization of one's identity and values occurs because of this threat; the poor academic performance can be a protective strategy. This strategy creates a way for the member of the negatively stereotyped group to not care about the people or the place where they have been viewed negatively (Aronson, 2002). The effects of this are to push students further away from the classroom and potentially out of school all together (Osborne, 1997).

...REMEMBER THIS REMEMBER THIS REMEMBER THIS REMEMBER THIS...
You can fight Stereotype Threat by frequently remembering what you are good at, and the things you like to do, ESPECIALLY RIGHT BEFORE A TEST.
...REMEMBER THIS REMEMBER THIS REMEMBER THIS...

We all have unconscious biases that affect our perceptions and our decisions. Understanding implicit biases and their impact on school outcomes will improve the school environment and educational outcomes for all students.

References

Advancement Project. (2010, March 1). *Test, punish, and, push out: How "zero tolerance" and high-stakes testing funnel youth into the school-to-prison pipeline.* Retrieved from http://b.3cdn.net/advancement/d05cb2181a4545db07_r2im6caqe.pdf

Aronson, J. (2002). Stereotype threat: Contending and coping with unnerving expectation. In J. Aronson (Ed.), *Improving academic achievement: Impact of psychological factors on education* (pp. 279–301). New York, NY: Routledge.

Bernstein, N. (2014). *Burning down the house*. Retrieved from www.nellbernstein.com: http://www.nellbernstein.com/burning-down-the-house/

Civil Rights Data Collection; Data Snapshot: School Discipline. (2014, March). Retrieved from www.ed.gov: http://www2.ed.gov/about/offices/list/ocr/docs/crdc-discipline-snapshot.pdf

Frey, S. (2014, January 29). *New suspension data show drop in use of 'willful defiance,' but ethnic disparity remains*. Retrieved from www.edsource.org: http://edsource.org/2014/new-suspension-data-show-drop-in-use-of-willful-defiance-but-ethnic-disparity-remains/56925

Frey, S. (2014, September 28). *New law limits student discipline measure*. Retrieved from www.edsource.org: http://edsource.org/2014/new-law-limits-student-discipline-measure/67836

Herbert, B. (2007, April 9). *6 year olds under arrest*. Retrieved from nytimes.com: http://www.nytimes.com/2007/04/09/opinion/09herbert.html

Kimberly Papillon, E. (2009). *Implicit bias primer*. Retrieved from www.equaljusticesociety.org: https://equaljusticesociety.org/law/implicitbias/primer/

Osborne, J. (1997). Race and academic disidentification. *Journal of Educational Psychology, 89,* 728–735.

Siders, D. (2014, September 27). *Jerry Brown signs bill to ban school suspensions for 'willful defiance'*. Retrieved from www.sacbee.com: http://www.sacbee.com/news/politics-government/capitol-alert/article2613881.html

Smith, S. (2007, April 20). *Which side are you on? Zero tolerance means jail for minority youth*. Retrieved from socialistworker.org: http://socialistworker.org/2007-1/628/628_03_YouthJail.shtml

Steele, C. (1997). A threat in the air: How stereotypes shape intellectual indentity and performance. *American Psychologist, 52*(6), 613–629.

Sue, D. W. (n.d.). *Racial microaggresions in everyday life*. Retrieved from www.worldtrust.org: http://world-trust.org/wp-content/uploads/2011/05/7-Racial-Microaggressions-in-Everyday-Life.pdf

Torlakson, T. (2016, January 13). *State schools chief Tom Torlakson announces decline in suspensions and expulsions for third year in a row*. Retrieved from www.cde.ca.gov: http://www.cde.ca.gov/nr/ne/yr16/yr16rel5.asp

Chapter 6

Innocent American Life: My Experience as a Muslim Woman

Aaminah Norris

Important Words and Concepts in This Chapter

There are several important words and concepts throughout the upcoming chapter. The words appear several times in different places in order to help you remember the words and understand the chapter. The words are defined several times:

- Immediately below right before the chapter begins
- In text boxes throughout the chapter
- In red and boldfaced within the chapter
- In a glossary in expanded form at the end of the units

Some of the words also appear in other chapters. Talk about the words with other students, teachers, friends, and family members before you read, while reading the chapter, and after you have read the chapter.

Paradox

A person, group, or situation that appears to have contradictory qualities or experiences.

Contributed by Aaminah Norris. © Kendall Hunt Publishing Company.

Muslim

A follower of the religion known as Islam.

Hijab

The traditional covering for the hair and neck that is worn by Muslim women.

Ramadan

The 9th month of the Islamic year observed as sacred with fasting practiced daily from dawn to sunset.

American-ness

1. The quality of or relating to the United States of America or its people, language, or culture. Historically American-ness most often referred to White Americans of European Ancestry. However, the term can also mean the following:
2. The quality of or relating to North or South America, the West Indies, or the Western Hemisphere.
3. The quality of or relating to any of the Native American peoples.
4. Indigenous to North or South America.

Symbol

Something that represents something else by association, resemblance—a material object used to represent something invisible.

I recently watched a television news show where a military veteran and supporter of Donald Trump argued for registering Muslims in a database to track their movements and involvement in terrorist activities. He pointed out that he did not mind placing innocent Muslim lives at risk because Islamic culture is trying to destroy "our way of life." By using the pronoun "our," he was referencing white Christian Americans. While I watched him, I felt this peculiar sense of the familiar. My life as an African American Muslim woman is a paradox. The paradox lies in being an American citizen who is not viewed as an American because I am neither white nor

Courtesy of Aaminah Norris. © Kendall Hunt Publishing Company.

I continue to fight to preserve the freedom of religion in the United States of America, a right afforded to all American citizens by the constitution.

Christian. My fellow Americans do not believe that I should be afforded the same rights as they. Therefore, I continue to fight to preserve the freedom of religion in the United States, a right afforded to all American citizens by the constitution. My perseverance is not for me. It is for those who look like me. It is for those who will come after me. There are those that would have us believe that we are not valuable. However, I am empowered by those who have come before me, faced more harsh obstacles than I have and persevered. I realize that their perseverance was not for them, as many of them died along the way. It was for me and for others who look like me.

I wear hijab. This means that I cover myself including my hair out of respect for the tenets of my religion. I started practicing Islam about 20 years ago. It was Ramadan, 1996. Ramadan is a holy month for Muslims. It is the month that we believe the Quran was first revealed to Prophet Muhammad (may peace be upon him). During the month of Ramadan, Muslims fast every day from dawn until dusk. At the time, I was not a practicing Muslim. You might say that I was agnostic. I knew that I believed in God, but I was uncertain as to whether I should practice Christianity or Islam. I was introduced to both religions as a child and saw beauty in both of them. Since, I could not make up my mind, I was satisfied with believing in God. My older sister Jay called me on the phone. She said, "We should fast for Ramadan." My siblings and I were taught Islam by our father who is a practicing Muslim. When we were children, we would fast for Ramadan when we stayed with him. Therefore, my sister's call wasn't surprising, but still I was not convinced. "I don't do anything and you want me to start with the hardest thing they've got?" I joked. However, it did not take much urging. I fasted with my sister. Out of respect for the other Muslims, I started wearing the scarf to the mosque. When Ramadan ended, I was uncertain as to whether or not I should continue to wear hijab. I prayed for a sign. I was sitting in my car when in the rearview mirror, I saw an angel dressed in all white sitting behind me. This was the sign that I needed. I decided to don the scarf despite it being a symbol that causes Americans to view me as un-American. Although my initial intention was to wear the scarf for personal reasons, it now represents my resistance against the oppression of my faith in the United States.

Now that I am visibly Muslim, many no longer believe that I am an American citizen. Remarkably, my American-ness is called into question when I travel through the United States. I am aware of this, so I take extra time at the airport. I have been through the body scanner on numerous occasions. My scarf is often patted down along with my body parts. Security see me coming and ask extra questions as I fumble to take off my shoes and belt.

> **Hijab:** The traditional covering for the hair and neck that is worn by Muslim women

> **Ramadan:** The ninth month of the Islamic year observed as sacred with fasting practiced daily from dawn to sunset.

"I am American, I was born in New York and raised in California."

Once I make it through security, I am not free from examination. For example, while in the Boston airport waiting to take a return flight to San Francisco, I visited the Dunkin Donuts that was staffed by a Muslim sister working behind the counter.

"As Salaamu Alaykum (May peace be upon you)," I said.

"Wa laykum salaam (And upon you be peace), where are you from sister?" she asked as her coworker looked at us.

"California" I replied.

He interjected, "But originally?"

"I am American, I was born in New York and raised in California."

"What about your parents?" He continued.

His questions embarrassed the Muslim woman who had by then informed me that they were both Moroccan.

She asked, "Why do you keep asking her these things?"

"My mother is from New Jersey and my father is from Texas." I offered.

"New Jersey? You mean like here? The state of New Jersey?" He asked.

As Salaamu Alaykum (May peace be upon you)

"Yes." I responded.

And then he said, which would have been funny if it weren't the bane of my existence,

"Well yes, then you are American!"

"Yes, I know." I walked away as I continued to overhear the two of them argue back and forth about Americans. I couldn't really understand what was being said; However, I noticed that every other sentence was punctuated with "American!" It is exhausting proving that I am American. I often have to provide my pedigree. The truth is that I can trace my family back eight generations on my mother's side. When I sat down on the airplane, I cried in appreciation for the dedication and love of my ancestors who fought and died in the hope of a better tomorrow for me. I cried because I still need to prove myself worthy of their sacrifice.

Another time my American-ness became an issue was on a plane trip from Minneapolis, Minnesota to Columbus, Ohio. When I boarded the plane, I saw her, the flight attendant. A blonde woman with a

Courtesy of Aaminah Norris. © Kendall Hunt Publishing Company.

bouffant hairdo, fifty-something, and apparently pleasant to all of the other passengers who entered. "Welcome aboard" she offered as each one in the line passed her by. But, when she saw me, her demeanor changed. She maneuvered towards me gruffly. Before I could step foot on the flight she said, "you can't bring those bags in here. Put them back out with all of the other bags with orange tags." When I returned, she seemed irritated by my presence. Once I sat down, I witnessed this attendant as she spoke to the other individuals, "make sure your seat belt is securely fastened, keep your seat back and tray table in the full upright and locked position until the pilot turns off the fasten seat belt sign," she intoned. When she arrived at my seat, she leaned over and said, "Is this your assigned seat?"

"Yes it is," I replied as I motioned toward my ticket to prove that I was in the right place.

"Do you speak English?" she asked loudly.

"Do you?" I asked sarcastically.

She wasn't satisfied with two responses in English so she said, "Nooo, dooo, youuu?" As if she were speaking slowly because I didn't understand her. I glared at her and refused to answer her. It was obvious that I spoke English. The man behind me burst into laughter. Then she proceeded to tell me that she was only asking me if I spoke English because I was sitting in the emergency row and she planned to give the safety instructions in English. She needed to make sure I could understand her. I rolled my eyes and said. "Yeah, whatever." Now, as she pointed to the safety instructions I noticed that these were in large pictorials. I didn't even have to know how to read words on paper in any language to save my life and the life of others. In fact, the more pertinent question was, do you have a strong enough back to help load people onto the wing if we go down? Or do you give a damn? Because the answer to both of these would have been, "I do." Unfortunately, we never got around to those questions because she was blinded by my headscarf. My hijab rendered me mute. She could not hear the English that I spoke to her.

Being rendered mute and invalidated by others has become a common occurrence for me. My job has been to speak from behind the veil and to proclaim my citizenship and my right to be heard. Once, I went to Verizon to have my cell phone swapped out for one that worked. John, the guy behind the counter sheepishly asked me if I wore hijab. I smiled and nodded. At this point, I was unsure if he were Muslim and hinting to me because he was at work, or if he was proud that he knew an Arabic word. It turned out to be the latter.

He inquired, "If you don't mind me asking when did you become Muslim?"

"1996."

"Oh that was before everything happened."

I knew what he meant by "everything." He began to tell me that he took a course on Islam in America at UC Davis. He then said, "You know unfortunately many people who see you don't see anything but road side bombs."

"...my work is to ensure my voice is heard and I am seen."

Suddenly, we were no longer a white male veteran and an African American Muslim woman standing at the counter at Verizon, in Berkeley, California. His words transported us through space and time. All of a sudden, we were in Iraq. I was the enemy responsible for the death of innocents. The tragic irony is that he made me culpable while symbolically killing the American me. I told John that I remain a realist, and therefore I know that everyone is not able to see me. However, my work is to ensure my voice is heard and I am seen. I remain a threat to a way of life that renders me invisible. As an American, I **conscientiously object** to being registered, muted, and discriminated against.

Dr. Aaminah Norris and her daughters.

Chapter 7

Perspective

Abner Minor
Ms. Sims' Ethnic Studies Class

Well . . . I drew myself in a self-silhouette and I think I put a lot in it so you're probably wondering what it all means because we have different perspectives. I tried to put my perspective into it, I don't think I did it justice, though.
Let's start with my right arm
On the left you can see Aztec Sun Temple

A volcano, a river, a battle, with a fort, canons, and a boat, each of these represent stories my father told me about our history.

The Aztec Sun Temple that is in Mexico, is there as a reminder of an ancient civilization that rivaled the Egyptians and their pyramids. The Aztec and the Mayans were astronomers, architects, and warriors and that's something that I can be proud of.

A small volcano my father tells me he went inside.

The battle of Puebla when the French tried to take the city of Puebla, however, the natives use guerilla tactics to surprise the French invaders, it came to be known as the Cinco de Mayo.

The river is the Rio Grande, something my father mentioned on his trip to America, the "Nation of Dreams."

The chest area shows the flags which represent how I feel about my heritage. I'm Mexican and American . . . I mean, why can't I be both? I respect the ideals that were the building blocks for these great nations, why not have the best of both worlds? The N.J.G is abbreviation of our church, Apostle Naason and I find myself happy here with more than 50 nations around the world.

The buildings in my throat are called the beautiful province, in Mexico, Guadalajara. It used to be the place where people from my church congregated for the Holy Supper that I attended last year.

My creases on my hoodie are the border between the United States and Mexico.

My two eyes are different one is different colors representing that I try to look at everything throw different perspective or colors, the other eye is me trying to draw an ink drop test because whatever you see is what you make of it, whether I like it or not that always going to help make my perception of the world.

The thing in my ear is the negative emotion in me, I accept that it's part of me, but just because I accept it doesn't mean I'm going to let it control me or tell me what I am much less tell me what to do.

The plant on my arm is me in a way, as a child we grow by the values we were taught, the way we live, and what our moral compass (it's written on my hair) make of the world. We're almost like plants in that way, that's why there's a plant.

I drew a clock to represent the past which made me think about how to be better in the future, to learn from the past.

The sun rising, is my dream for a better tomorrow for everyone.

The heart represents my humanity and compassion in all of us, some less than other . . . yeah a lot less.

I tried to think what a soul looks like, I drew a blue orb floating. The double helix DNA is my past family members.

The last part is what I think people have done to the planet or what we will do, that's why I drew the planet on fire.

Anyways I think I covered it all, oh and the background means nothing, I'm just saying.

Chapter 8

Don't use that Tone with Me!
Intonation and Identity: An Interview

with
Dr. Nicole Holliday and Gretchen McCulloch

Important Words and Concepts in This Chapter

There are several important words and concepts throughout the upcoming chapter. The words appear several times in different places in order to help you remember the words and understand the chapter. The words are defined several times:

- Immediately below right before the chapter begins
- In text boxes throughout the chapter
- In red and boldfaced within the chapter
- In a glossary in expanded form at the end of the units

Some of the words also appear in other chapters. Talk about the words with other students, teachers, friends and family members before you read; while reading the chapter; and after you have read the chapter.

Linguistics

The study of human speech including the units, nature, structure, and modification of language.

Intonation

The manner of utterance; *specifically*, the rise and fall in pitch of the voice in speech.

Code Switching

The switching from the linguistic system of one language or dialect to that of another

Racial Identity

An individual's sense of having their identity defined by **belonging** to a particular race or **ethnic group**. The strength of such identity is dependent on how much he or she has processed and internalized the sociological, political and other contextual factors within that group.

Phonetics

1. the system of speech sounds of a language or group of languages.
2a. the study and systematic classification of the sounds made in spoken utterance.
2b. the practical application of this science to language study.

Sociophonetics

A branch of linguistics studying sociolinguistic aspects of speech sounds; the interaction between sociolinguistics and phonetics.

Vowels

1. The one most prominent sound in a syllable
2. a letter or other symbol representing a vowel —usually used in English *a, e, i, o, u*, and sometimes *y*.

Consonants

a speech sound produced by occluding with or without releasing (p, b; t, d; k, g), diverting (m, n, ng), obstructing (f, v; s, z, etc.) the flow of air from the lungs (opposed to a vowel).

Variation

A speaker's use of different linguistic forms on different occasions, and different speakers of a language expressing the same meanings as others using different forms. Most of this variation is highly systematic: speakers of a language make choices in pronunciation, morphology, word choice, and grammar depending on a number of non-linguistic factors, such as age, race and ethnicity, gender, geography etc.

This is a transcript for Lingthusiasm Episode 13: What Does it Mean to Sound Black? Intonation and Identity Interview with Nicole Holliday. The transcript has been edited for readability.

Gretchen: How did you get into linguistics?

Nicole: I went to college and was majoring in Spanish. I was a kid who was good at school but I didn't find the thing that I was super good at, like, other kids are really good at, like, math or something, and I just, I wasn't. Until we got to high school Spanish and it was like, no, this is my jam. Why haven't I been doing this my whole life? So, in college I was double majoring in Spanish and Arabic –

Gretchen: That's good. And how did you get into what your research topic is?

Nicole: Yeah, so, I study intonation, and my dissertation work was on black/white biracial men. I did my bachelor's at Ohio State University. And it was 2008, when I was a sophomore/junior, and I went to volunteer for the Obama campaign in Ohio, and I went into this campaign office and I saw this man on the phone trying to sweet-talk somebody out of money, right, he was, like, super hyper-standard, like, "Sir, Barack Obama could really use your support. . . ". And then he got off the phone, and then this guy – young black guy, from the neighborhood – came in and was like, "Yo, I wanna help out Obama," and he switched on a dime. He was like, "My brother, Barack Obama could really use your help, okay, when are you free? Can you bring your homies?"

Nicole: And so I ended up, you know, sort of being interested in this research question of people who are multiracial and code-switching and what it is that they change. And the more that I started to look into this, the more that I realized that I think what's going on is a lot of changes in the way that they use intonation: their tone and where their voice goes up and down. So that was the beginning of my love affair with intonation and racial identity.

Nicole: When I was at NYU trying to figure out what I was gonna do for my dissertation, and it took me a while to get to, like, what linguistic variables I was interested in? I knew that I liked phonetics, so sort of how we look at the physical properties of speech sounds, but it happened that there wasn't really anybody doing this intersection of social variation and phonetics, and particularly what voices sound like, what does it mean to sound black, or what does it mean to sound white? So this became my question, and I thought that a way to get at that would be to look at people who identified themselves as having more than one racial identity. So at first I thought, okay, I'll just get these people who have one black parent and one white parent, and I'll interview them talking to white friends and black friends, because surely they speak differently to their white friends and black friends.

Nicole: But I didn't really find that. It was true for some of the speakers, but the bigger difference in the participants, that I interviewed anyway, was they were more consistent, but it had to do with how they personally conceptualized themselves as biracial or black. So, the ones that saw themselves as more black did patterns that we would be more likely to associate with, I guess, traditional speakers of African-American language.

Nicole: And they sort of spread themselves out on this continuum from the ones who identified as very biracial to the ones who identified as very black. And this is an amazing finding because we're looking at tiny, tiny things about their tone of voice that are pretty much not at the level of conscious control.

Gretchen: And a lot of sociophonetics research is looking at like, okay, vowels – like what kinds of specific vowels are people doing? Or what kinds of, like, what is this "th" sound somewhere, or something like that. But this is looking at things at the level of the sentence, of the entire phrase, right?

Nicole: Right, of the phrase. So, how do you put it together to make something sound like a question? How do you put it together to make something sound like, "Oh, I'm not done talking, please let me hold the floor." Like, these kind of things. Where are the ups and downs in the voice? And we know that these are really salient, really obvious to not-linguists, but linguists haven't really jumped on this train and so. . .

We think about identity as something that is constructed and performed all the time. So it's not static, even in the example I was telling you with my dissertation participants, yeah, they're biracial, but some of them are more black more times than others, right, and they will tell you this if you bother to ask.

* * *

Nicole: a lot of people have shown that listeners very easily pick up on what's going on with a tone of voice, right, we can all tell when somebody is mumbling versus when they're excited. Like, we can tell things about their emotional state.

Nicole: You know, understanding the properties of vowels and consonants, this kind of thing is really important. Understanding a what phrase is, how it's different from a sentence, right, because you've got to be able to isolate the relevant units of measure. But truthfully, you can already hear where voices go up and down, and if you've got some analysis software, you can see where it goes up and down. . . mostly. . .

Nicole: the work that I am getting really interested into now is about the ways in which black people can be perceived as hostile or aggressive—all of these negative stereotypes that exist in our culture about black people I think are augmented by how people feel about African-American English.

Nicole: African- American English speakers don't tend to use hedges or up-talk – this thing where your voice rises at the very end, where everything sounds like a question. Not that no black speakers do it, some do, but it's not as common. And I think that, particularly for women, not using these strategies for politeness can be interpreted as rude or hostile.

Nicole: And then it ends up sort of feeding into negative stereotypes. So this is a project that I'm beginning now, I'm really interested in girls who are suspended, expelled from high school at higher rates – black girls – than ones who are not and comparing their baselines, patterns of these different intonational phenomena.

Gretchen: Oh, interesting. So if the teachers are, like, over-interpreting them as hostile

Nicole: Yep!

Gretchen: – because of their tone of voice and, like, "Oh, you sound defiant, so I'm gonna suspend you, or I'm gonna send you to the principal's office."

Nicole: Right! What politeness looks like is culturally specific, it's not the same, and so I really have thought for a while that this is what's going on. When I was a kid I got reprimanded, like, "Don't take that tone of voice with me".

Nicole: Don't change how you talk! But rather, the onus should be on the people whose job it is to educate these students to not let their prejudices have them enforce discipline unfairly, unequally.

Nicole: in 2015, I watched this video. . . Sandra Bland was a young woman who was driving through Texas because she got a new job, and she was stopped by a police officer for failure to signal a lane change, and the situation escalated to the point where he ended up dragging her out of her car, and then she was arrested and taken to jail, and she died under, you know, maybe mysterious circumstances. Her family settled a multimillion-dollar lawsuit with the police department because there was something very suspicious about everything that happened to her. Anyway. I'm of the opinion that was very clearly racial profiling. But anyway, back to the traffic stop, because there was a dash cam of the cop's video of all this. It seems like they're escalating sort of unequally. So, the analysis that we did basically says that the kind of contours that she's using, the kind of intonation that she is using, she's, you know, maybe at a level five irritation when he stops her, and he's at a one or two, I don't know. But it seems like, because he interprets her through his own lens –

So he hears her at a level ten when she's really at a level five, because if he were using that pattern of intonation, he would be at a level ten, because he's not a speaker of her variety of English. So they end up having this kind of emotional miscommunication, because they're actually speaking different varieties of English from each other. And I think what we came to is, she gets misinterpreted and this probably was one thing to contribute to the escalation of that traffic stop. So this is why this work is so important to me and why I'm really interested in girls who are being suspended and expelled. Like, this is not linguistics that we do for fun, just because we're curious about something. Like, this is people's, everyday experiences of even, you know, life and death in the case of Sandra Bland.

Gretchen: And if you can prevent some little girls from getting suspended or expelled and changing their whole futures, like, that's a big effect to have.

Nicole: Or even just some teachers who just don't do this anymore. Not that – I mean, I love teachers, like, y'all got a really hard job for no money. But a lot of times when people are participating in these things that are implicit bias, it's just because nobody ever pointed it out to them.

Gretchen: Yeah, yeah. Well, I think you told me about this like a year ago, and ever since then I've been noticing it in myself, being like, "Whoa! Like, I do think this person sounds angry." But if I can recast it in my mind as, like, energetic, you know, the same way when you have nerves when you're going on a stage or something and you're like, "Actually, I'm just excited!"

Gretchen: And then when you when you change that in your mind, you're like, okay, no, it's okay, like, I'm not nervous, I'm excited! And being like, oh no, she's just excited! Like, she's energetic. But I noticed it, like, after you said this to me, I was like, this is really interesting.

Nicole: So, George Zimmerman was the man who murdered Trayvon Martin, and this was sort of towards the beginning of what's now the Black Lives Matter movement But anyway, the last person that talked to Trayvon Martin alive was Rachel Jeantel, which was his friend. And she is this Haitian-American woman, she's 18, she had low literacy, she did not have a lot of success in school, and I suspect some of that is the stuff that we're talking about, this being, like, over-reprimanded.

Nicole: Rickford and King did this analysis of a number of features that she was using, features of African-American English, like G-dropping– saying something like "walkin'" versus "walking." And basically found that she was being misinterpreted, or or mischaracterized by the lawyers, on all sides of this, and the court reporters, and the jury, because people just literally did not speak the same language as her and they attached all of these negative stereotypes about like low literacy, like poor, like blackness. . .

Nicole: Yeah, and she was badgered, and she was young, right? And this was traumatic.

Nicole: So what Rickford and King do is they go through, piece by piece, different points of this testimony and highlight where it seems like whoever responded to her was not understanding what she was saying.

Gretchen: Wow.

Nicole: So there was one where the prosecutor, I think, asks her to pay attention, he assumes she's not paying attention. And she says, "I been payin' attention, sir." And what that means for speakers of African-American language is "I have been paying attention this entire time or for a long time."

Nicole: But he didn't interpret it that way.

Gretchen: So he interpreted it as something like, "I haven't been paying attention."

Nicole: Or, "I've just started paying attention." Yeah. So all of these little things – it's like death by a thousand paper cuts, right – add up to her being not painted as a credible witness and also her, you know, being kind of judged in the court of public opinion as well.

Gretchen: Yeah, and her testimony not being taken seriously as far as getting justice for Trayvon.

Nicole: Exactly.

Gretchen: And so that's an example of this work, another example of this work being very important, like, you know, all cops and juries and lawyers should be getting training in African-American English or in linguistics in general, sociolinguistics in general.

Nicole: In variation, right? Like, you can't assume that a jury and a courtroom and a judge and lawyers, a roomful of people who have only ever encountered people

who sound like them, are going to carry out justice evenly when they come across –
I mean and this is not just African-American English, it's people who speak **English as an L2**, right, people who are immigrants, and there's supposed to be provisions for people getting interpreters, but I've seen that not evenly implemented either.

Gretchen: Michel DeGraff is a prof at MIT who does a lot of work with Haitian **Creole** and trying to legitimize it in the school systems in Haiti as a language that can be used as a medium of instruction so kids can go to school in Haitian Creole, and they can learn stuff in there. Because at the moment, most kids in Haiti go to school in French, and so they're just taught in this language that they don't actually speak. So he's putting a lot of stuff into saying, look, you should teach people in the language they actually understand because, surprisingly, they'll learn better!

Nicole: 40% of the world's children are not educated in the language that they speak well, you know, speak fluently. And I'm 0% surprised, but, like, you know, you talked about in an earlier episode talking about **colonialism**, like, this is what happens! Like, we are so – when people talk about **institutionalized racism**, like this is it, right here, the fact that Rachel Jeantel was not treated fairly as a key witness in this trial because of all of these things about the way that she was educated, as well as people's ideologies about the way that she speaks.

Nicole: I also do work on Quechua languages in Peru and Bolivia. I was interviewing people who – indigenous people, right – who had grown up speaking in indigenous language, speaking Quechua, and then being educated in Spanish. And, especially the elderly people told me, they were beaten, they were physically beaten in school for speaking Quechua, like, for speaking their language, and it still goes on.

Nicole: Yeah, rural kids in Peru and Bolivia, who are expected to show up to school in Spanish, not speaking a word of Spanish.

Gretchen: Yeah, I think you got the same thing with **indigenous** people, residential schools here.

Gretchen: Or even, you know, African-American kids who're speaking African-American English at home and they come to schools and like, oh, now you're supposed to be learning to read and write in this variety,

Nicole: Right, and the teachers don't understand. So, that we don't teach kids or parents or teachers about what these differences are and about how to work with them – it's not a weakness to speak two varieties or to speak two languages, but we treat it as though it is.

Chapter 9

Learning Arabic

Dan West

Important Words and Concepts in This Chapter

There are several important words and concepts throughout the upcoming chapter. The words appear several times in different places in order to help you remember the words and understand the chapter. The words are defined several times:

- Immediately below right before the chapter begins
- In text boxes throughout the chapter
- In red and boldfaced within the chapter
- In a glossary in expanded form at the end of the units

Some of the words also appear in other chapters. Talk about the words with other students, teachers, friends, and family members before you read, while reading the chapter, and after you have read the chapter.

Defense Language Institute Foreign Language Center

The Defense Language Institute Foreign Language Center (DLIFLC) is regarded as one of the nest schools for foreign language instruction in the nation. As part of the Army Training and Doctrine Command, the institute provides resident instruction at the Presidio of Monterey in two dozen languages, 5 days a week, 7 hours per day, with 2–3 hours of homework each night. Courses last from 26 to 64 weeks, depending on the difficulty of the language.

The DLIFLC is a multiservice school for active and reserve components, foreign military students, and civilian personnel working in the federal government and various law enforcement agencies.

Contributed by Dan West. © Kendall Hunt Publishing Company.

Baghdad

Capital city of Iraq on the Tigris River *population* 3,841,268.

Mosul

A city on the Tigris River in northern Iraq; *population* 1,637,000. During the second Gulf War, the prison in this city was used as a U.S. Army interrogation and detention center. After the Gulf War the city was taken by the Islamic State of Iraq and Syria (ISIS). At the time of this writing, the Iraqi Army is advancing on Mosul and has nearly retaken this Iraqi city.

I learned two different types of Arabic. One was violent, a weapon to be used to "protect freedom" and "help the innocent." The other was peaceful and practical, for day-today interaction and conversation. In theory, the two would intersect eventually, but for me they rarely did. It seems silly and obvious to say it this outright, but there is a huge difference between learning a language in a combat zone and learning that same language in a classroom setting.

I joined the Army when I was 19 years old. I enlisted as an interrogator, or a Human Intelligence Collector after the Army rebranded us to make us not seem so aggressive. Part of my reason for choosing interrogation was that I thought I would be good at it. The other part was that I wanted to learn a language. Arabic and Korean were the two that stood out to me most. They eventually sent me to study Arabic in Monterey, California at the **Defense Language Institute (DLI)**, after deployments to **Mosul** and **Baghdad**, Iraq. DLI was my second teacher. Just so we're on the same page, I'll break it down a little further. The Army decided to teach me to speak Arabic after sending me to two different cities in Iraq. My job was to talk to people, and they didn't think I needed the language. So, I had to learn on the fly.

My first teacher was the country of Iraq. I had interpreters teach me basic numbers so I could ask pertinent questions ("How many bodyguards does he have?"), along with catch all terms for weapons and bombs to streamline questioning. Because I was young, I also learned the dirty words, and it gave me a thrill to see the look on someone's face when I told them in Arabic to "shut the hell up and stop lying." I didn't learn enough to hold a conversation, but I knew enough to use certain phrases. More importantly, I learned how the language sounds when spoken. I learned enough to cut someone off if they were getting off track, if they were veering off into professing their innocence rather than answering my questions.

I landed in California in the September of 2007 with a false sense of confidence. I assumed I would be fine; I already had a basic understanding of the language. I was wrong. I hadn't learned any grammar, I hadn't learned the written language, and I hadn't even learned the different letters. I struggled with every aspect of the class right alongside other students with no background in the language. I was left behind by some of them. I admit that part of it was the lack of urgency; I was sitting in a classroom 8 hours a day studying out of a book instead of sitting in a small room with a prisoner in a jumpsuit. It was hard to reconcile the importance of the task. But the location wasn't the only reason I had trouble recognizing the scope and importance of my task; it hurt that I wasn't learning combat applicable terms.

Our first two lessons were easy lessons that I picked up quickly: colors and numbers. These were lessons I knew from Iraq, they were just being applied differently and more thoroughly. I learned how to spell and write the colors, and how to form the numbers on paper. But after that we moved into foreign territory. We learned to describe food, vacation spots, holidays, and leisure activities. We played children's matching games and told each other about our families. And through all of it, I struggled.

It took me nearly 6 months to realize that I wasn't only struggling because it was such a different language from English, or because the scope of my learning had changed. I also struggled because I had to overcome the feeling that I was essentially learning from the "enemy." These were native Arabic speakers; one of my instructors was even from a small village outside of Mosul I had researched during a particularly difficult series of arrests and interrogations. I remember telling my classmates a joke I'd heard in Iraq. "Not all terrorists are Arabs, but all Arabs are terrorists." I didn't even think about how awful a statement that was until I saw how uncomfortable the other students were. That was a wake-up moment for me. I realized I was seeing my instructors

أ	ب	ت	ث	ج	ح	خ
alif	baa'	taa'	thaa'	jiim	h'aa'	kha'
د	ذ	ر	ز	س	ش	ص
daal	thaal	raa'	zaay	siin	shiin	saad
ض	ط	ظ	ع	غ	ف	ق
daad	Taa'	thaa	'ayn	ghayn	feh'	qaaf
ك	ل	م	ن	ه	و	ي
kaaf	laam	miim	nuun	haa	waaw	yaa'

arabic alphabet

Letters from the Arabic Alphabet.

as adversaries rather than people, and specifically people whose job it was to make me better able to do my job. It's a problem I fought against longer than I am proud of. I have always considered myself to be a very understanding and progressive person, but I fell for the accidental brainwashing. I say accidental because I have to hope it was inadvertent rather than by design.

The most important lesson I learned from DLI wasn't the Arabic language. It was that Arabic speakers aren't the kind of evil I believed. It took being immersed in the culture to recognize that, and I'm incredibly grateful for the experience.

Chapter 10

"Hyphiachi": Finding Inspiration In My Bay Area Blend of Cultures

By Michael Diaz

Growing up I was confused about of who I was. My family is from Mexico, but I didn't know much about my culture. I lived in a neighborhood in Oakland where I felt you were looked down upon if you spoke Spanish. It seemed to me that, if you were white, it was a safe place to live.

So I did my best to blend in.

At school, I was always a darker shade than other kids, so I felt extra pressure to "behave Caucasian" to make up for that. It didn't work. Kids would point out that I was "different." They'd count me out of games because and shout at me, "No this game is not for you." It made me felt all empty and bad inside. I didn't want to tell my parents because I was scared of how they would react.

Then, in 5th grade, I moved to a new school. For the first time, I was around other Mexican kids. On one level, I felt accepted. I didn't look different than the other kids. But other times, I felt like I wasn't Mexican enough. I was made fun of for not speaking Spanish and not putting hot sauce on my food.

It seemed like no matter where I was, I wasn't either not white enough or not Mexican enough, and that sucked. But I found my inspiration to pull through it all in an unexpected place. I was in 6th grade, listening to the radio on the drive home from school, and a song came on. I listened to the lyrics:

> *I'm not afraid*
> *To take a stand*
> *Everybody*
> *Come take my hand come*

"Hyphiachi": Finding Inspiration in My Bay Area Blend of Cultures, Youth Radio. Reprinted by permission.

We'll walk this road together, through the storm
Whatever weather, cold or warm
Just letting you know that, you're not alone
Holla if you feel like you've been down the same road

I found hope in these lyrics. I found out later the song was by Eminem, who was white but had been hated on for taking up rap, a so-called "black only" culture.

I figured that if he found his way, I could too. And I could do it with music.

Mariachi music is part of my culture and the Bay Area is the birthplace of hyphy music. In one beat I made I decided to mix the sounds together. I sampled mariachi music then pretty much just played out the individual trumpet sounds to get a nice sound. Then I hyphy-fide it with base and high hats.

My diverse background gives me the opportunity to create beats that not only represent me but others around me and allows me to grow as a music producer. Now, I have made over 100 beats in my free time so I can try new ideas and learn from my mistakes. I can also fill up pages with poems from my own creative mind. I have pushed myself to get to where I am today.

I plan to continue on this path so I can one day become a positive influence in the Bay Area. Rather than try to blend in, I'm creating art that celebrates how I stick out.

Chapter 11

That Special Relationship—Puerto Rico and the United States

Daisy Diaz-Granados

Important Words and Concepts in This Chapter

There are several important words and concepts throughout the upcoming chapter. The words appear several times in different places in order to help you remember the words and understand the chapter. The words are defined several times:

- Immediately below right before the chapter begins
- In text boxes throughout the chapter
- In red and boldfaced within the chapter
- In a glossary in expanded form at the end of the units

Some of the words also appear in other chapters. Talk about the words with other students, teachers, friends, and family members before you read, while reading the chapter, and after you have read the chapter.

Ethnocentrism

The tendency to view your own society or culture as superior and the standard by which other societies and cultures are judged.

Stereotypes

This term derives from the printing process and refers to a plate made by taking a cast or mold of a surface. A stereotype then is anything which lacks individual marks or identifiers, and instead appears as though made from a cast. In sociology, the stereotype (the plate or cast) is always a social construction, which may have some basis in reality but is a gross generalization (e.g., women like romance novels). To stereotype is to apply these casts, or gross generalization, to people or situations rather than seeing the individual variation.

Indigenous

Those people whose family and ethnic group inhabiting a land before it was taken over (colonized) by another nation. Indigenous can also mean not only the first people on a land, but also still alive and (possibly) still inhabiting some part of that land to which that person's ancestors inhabited.

Conquistadors

One of the Spanish conquerors of Mexico and Peru in the 16th century.

Genocide

The systematic killing of an entire ethnic community.

Manifest Destiny

A common belief in the 18th and 19th centuries that it was the destiny of the United States to expand its territory and extend its political, social, and economic influence over all of North America.

Colonialism

Political control of one nation over another that is institutionalized in direct political administration by the colonial power, control of all economic relationships and a systematic attempt to transform the culture of the subject nation. It usually involves extensive immigration from the colonial power into the colony and the immigrants taking on roles as landowners, business people, and professionals. Colonialism is a form of imperialism.

Commonwealth

A political unit having local autonomy but voluntarily united with the United States used officially of Puerto Rico and of the Northern Mariana Islands.

Foraker Act

The Foraker Act was signed on April 2, 1900, by U.S. President William McKinley to establish a civilian government in Puerto Rico. The purpose of the Foraker Act was to establish a limited government in the recently acquired territory of Puerto Rico.

Insular Cases

Following its victory in the Spanish–American War (1898), the United States acquired Hawaii, Puerto Rico, Guam, and the Philippines. In the Insular Cases (1901–1922), the U.S. Supreme Court determined the constitutional and political status of the new territories. In *De Lima v. Bidwell* (1901), a customs dispute, a 5-to-4 majority ruled that Puerto Rico was not a "foreign country" for tariff purposes. In subsequent cases, the court addressed the territories' relationship to the United States and whether "the Constitution follows the flag"; that is, whether and how constitutional provisions applied to these acquisitions.

Jones Act

On March 2, 1917, President Woodrow Wilson signed the Jones–Shafroth Act. This law gave Puerto Ricans U.S. citizenship. The Jones Act also established three branches of the Puerto Rican Government: Executive, Judicial, and Legislative

Plebiscite

A vote by which the people of an entire country or district express an opinion for or against a proposal especially on a choice of government or ruler.

Referendum

The submission of a proposed public measure or actual statute to a direct popular vote.

Nationalism

Devotion, especially excessive or undiscriminating devotion, to the interests or culture of a particular nation-state.

Self-Determination

1. Free choice of one's own acts or states without external compulsion
2. Determination by the people of a territorial unit of their own future political status

Diaspora

The voluntary or forcible movement of peoples from their homelands into new regions.

On May 7, 1998, a very popular American TV sitcom show called *Seinfeld* aired an episode entitled "The Puerto Rican Day." In the episode, the characters become frustrated as they try to get around traffic made difficult due to the fact that the annual Puerto Rican Day Parade is in progress. The episode was criticized for its negative portrayal of Puerto Rican parade goers who are depicted as an angry mob overturning a car with one of the characters exclaiming, "It's like this every day in Puerto Rico." This same character also accidentally burns and then stomps on the Puerto Rican flag in a scene that was an affront to Puerto Ricans. Flag-waving parade goers are featured as a character comments on the "hot, spicy flavor of it all" and remarks, "it's *caliente*," feeding

© spatuletail/Shutterstock.com

into the prevailing **stereotypes** that Puerto Ricans are loud, boisterous, and *muy caliente* (very hot). When the creators of the show were asked about the offensive stereotypes offered by the episode, their ethnocentrism was on full display; they trivialized and delegitimized the protests by Puerto Ricans explaining that everyone was "over sensitized" and that "they just didn't get the joke." Cultural misunderstandings abound when a dominant culture does not understand the particular practices of other cultures.

Cultural practices are often ways to commemorate significant events. For example, if the writers of this episode knew that in 1948, a gag law was passed in Puerto Rico, whereby any Puerto Rican who was found in possession of a Puerto Rican flag could be jailed for 10 years, and/or fined for $10,000, they might begin to understand the reverence that the Puerto Rican people have for their flag. This gag law was repealed in 1957 and the following year in 1958, the first Puerto Rican Day Parade was inaugurated with a sea of Puerto Rican flags flying freely for the first time in nearly a decade. The flag is sacred to Puerto Ricans as it represents a full expression of Puerto Rican nationalism and culture. The fact that Puerto Ricans would be offended to watch a TV show that shows a character burning and stomping on their flag is understood in this context. People are not "over-sensitive" and they do not need to "understand the joke." What is needed is an understanding of the unique cultures of the people which we encounter in our everyday lives. In this chapter, we will be looking at the unique history and culture of Puerto Ricans and the special relationship between the United States and Puerto Rico.

The island of Puerto Rico is located approximately 1,000 miles from Miami, Florida, in the north east section of the Caribbean. The island is approximately 100 miles long by 35

© Rawpixel/Shutterstock.com

miles wide with a varied terrain that contains hundreds of miles of sandy beaches, rainforests, deserts, caves, oceans and rivers, and a vast mountain range which takes up most of its interior. It is officially a commonwealth of the United States and its inhabitants are U.S. citizens and can travel freely throughout the United States. However, Puerto Ricans who reside on the island do not have representatives in the Senate or House of Representatives and do not get to vote for the President. Some of the details of the relationship between Puerto Rico and the United States can best be understood once the span of Puerto Rican history is examined more closely.

Early History—Tainos, Columbus, Spanish Imperial Rule, and Africans

For several centuries prior to the arrival of Christopher Columbus to the Caribbean, the Tainos/Arawaks flourished in Puerto Rico. The Tainos named the island *Borinquen* and today Puerto Ricans refer to themselves as *Borinquenos* or *Boricuas*. The Tainos lived in an organized, hierarchal society headed by *caciques* (chiefs). They secured a steady food supply through agricultural practices which yielded staples such as cassava, yams, corn, and beans which when added to protein from hunting and fishing rounded out their diet. They also had an elaborate system of religious beliefs and rituals centered on the worship of zemis, sculptural objects deemed to house deities and ancestral spirits; the zemi was understood to have concentrated powers related to social and political matters and to an individual's productivity and fertility. The Tainos were inventive people who, while never developing a written language, made exquisite and intricate pottery and wood and stone carvings. They had extensive knowledge about botany and natural medicinal cures, built large oceangoing canoes, and played games with a ball made of rubber. In short, the Tainos had a vibrant culture.

The Tainos were inventive people who, while never developing a written language, made exquisite and intricate pottery and wood and stone carvings. They had extensive knowledge about botany and natural medicinal cures, built large oceangoing canoes, and played games with a ball made of rubber. In short, the Tainos had a vibrant culture.

The Tainos were a very friendly, happy, and gentle people—traits that surely contributed to their demise. When Christopher Columbus and his sailors arrived, the Arawaks brought them food, water, and gifts, leading Columbus to interpret their kindness for weakness and to conclude that they would make fine servants who could easily be subjugated and made to do whatever the conquistadors wanted. Columbus' inability to appreciate non-European cultures and his lack of understanding of the Taino's complex spiritual life, led him to wrongfully conclude that Tainos were heathens, and that as people without religion they needed to be converted to Christianity. Misunderstandings abounded with **conquistadors** also believe that Tainos were cannibals. The dual fears of cannibalism and heathenism were used to fuel cruel prejudices and the dehumanization of the Tainos. The life that the Tainos enjoyed for centuries would be exterminated in a **genocide** perpetuated by the **conquistadors** and Spanish colonial rule. By the early 1500s, the Tainos had virtually vanished, wiped out by disease, malnutrition, and the cruel subjugation and abuse of the Spanish rulers. Interestingly, the Tainos had prophesized that the arrival of an invading force would overthrow their religious rites and ceremonies, lead to their enslavement and eventually their massacre. The Tainos as a distinct group vanished in Puerto Rico but their influences and legacy live on. The Taino culture became mixed with the African and Spanish cultures as these groups blended more freely on the island, often through marriage, creating a unique seamless blend with which Puerto Ricans strongly identify. In fact, this unique blending of Taino, African and Spanish blood occurred at the inception of Spanish colonization with the marriage of Pedro Mejias (who had arrived with Ponce de Leon and was of mixed race) to Luisa, a Taino cacica (chief).

By 1517, Spain began permitting the importation of slaves to Puerto Rico to work on gold mines, sugar plantations, and fortifications; the vast majority of these slaves were from the Yoruba, Bantu, and Igbo tribes of the Western Coast of Africa. As newly Christianized African slaves were absorbed into the culture, their own vigorous and deep culture was imitated by the Tainos with whom they created a deep bond. The Black population in Puerto Rico would increase significantly when in 1664, Spain issued an edict offering freedom and land to African people from other non-Spanish colonies in the Caribbean; these immigrating freemen would increase the population base to support

African influences in Puerto Rican culture are deep and broad and Puerto Rico's rich folkloric culture is steeped in African traditions.

the Spanish garrison and forts on the island. By the time slavery was outlawed in 1873, there were approximately six free non-White people for every slave on the island with a large portion of all Puerto Ricans at the time being non-White/mixed race.

African influences in Puerto Rican culture are deep and broad and Puerto Rico's rich folkloric culture is steeped in African traditions. For example, the Yoruba's religious practices including belief in the supernatural and ancestor worship were absorbed into Puerto Rican tradition most notably through the practice of *Santeria* (Afro-Caribbean religion based on Yoruba beliefs). Puerto Rican music, dance, language, and foods are also richly influenced by African elements. Folkloric musical traditions such as the percussion-driven bomba and plena forms which incorporated bongos, *la clave*, *timbales*, and *marimba* instruments, all of African origin, have long served as a vehicle for political and social expression. There is a profound African imprint on the Puerto Rican language beyond the incorporation of African words in everyday speech (which find a place alongside Taino words). Puerto Ricans have a way of dropping consonants or cutting off word endings when they speak, so that for example *"para nada"* (for nothing) becomes *pa'na* which is a typically African grammatical practice. The up-and-down speech intonations in Puerto Rican Spanish are also typically African (Tim). Finally in the political arena, prominent *Afro-Borincano* scholars and freedom fighters included Dr. Ramon Emeterio Betances (1827–1897), Arturo Alfonso Schomburg (1874–1938), and Pedro Albizu Campos (1891–1965).

End of Spanish Colonial Rule

In 1493, Christopher Columbus had claimed Puerto Rico for Spain. In 1508, Spanish colonization had begun with the appointment of Spanish explorer, Juan Ponce de Leon, as governor. Puerto Rico would remain a Spanish colony for nearly 400 years until it was ceded by the Spanish to the United States under the Treaty of Paris at the end of the Spanish–American War in 1898. Puerto Ricans lived under conditions of extreme poverty with illiteracy rates over 80% with no political or economic freedom; the fight against the exploitation of the Puerto Rican people by the Spanish colonial system was galvanized in 1867 under the leadership of Ramon Betances who led the first major uprising against Spanish rule, the Lares Rebellion. By 1897, Puerto Ricans were technically granted the right to self-government by Spain under the "Carta Autonomica" (constitutional autonomy) but this fact was overlooked in the aftermath of the Spanish–American War when the United States defeated Spain and took control of Puerto Rico, Cuba, and the Philippines as part of the Treaty of Paris of 1898.

American Imperial Rule

The end of the 19th century was the dawn of a new colonial era for America. The ideals of Manifest Destiny had led the nation to grow from the Atlantic to the Pacific Ocean and the nation looked overseas to find markets for excess manufactured goods, and strategic military outposts in the Caribbean and Pacific Oceans. America was ready to join the Imperialists Club and by defeating Spain in the Spanish–American War, the country was well on its way when Puerto Rico was ceded to the United States by Spain. As was the case with Cuba and the Philippines, the United States sought to limit self-rule in all of its new territories, including Puerto Rico, and exploit the natural resources and economic opportunities made available.

In 1900, U.S. President McKinley signed the Foraker Act, which established the new governing structure in Puerto Rico. There would be an American-appointed governor/executive leader of the island and a bicameral legislature with the lower house being popularly elected by Puerto Ricans and representatives to the upper chamber being selected in the United States. The first civil governor appointed by the United States under the Foraker Act was Charles H. Allen. The new governor moved quickly to exploit his powerful position in the new colony by raising taxes and withholding loans and financing for agriculture, education, and infrastructure. Allen instead worked on diverting funds to pay top salaries for new American bureaucrats imported to form part of Allen's ruling elite. This new ruling elite would focus on awarding lucrative contracts on the island to U.S. businessmen including Mr. Allen himself who resigned after only 17 months as governor to serve as president of both Morgan Trust Company and the Guaranty Trust Company of New York on Wall Street and to create the American Sugar Refining syndicate (today known as Domino sugar). By 1930, Allen and U.S. banking interests had converted 45% of all suitable land in Puerto Rico into sugar plantations and with less land available for agriculture, the Puerto Rican standard of living steadily declined.

In the early part of the 1900s, as America sought to define its relationship with Puerto Rico through a series of congressional acts and Supreme Court rulings, Puerto Ricans were relegated to a second-class status. In 1901, the Supreme Court issued a series of decisions in what became known as the Insular Cases, which established a unique position for Puerto Rico in relation to the United States; the court ruled that Puerto Rico was an unincorporated territory and that as such constitutional rights did not apply to the Puerto Rican people. Puerto Rico would instead be governed by federal territorial law (as defined by the Congress) outside of the constitution. However, the question of Puerto Rican citizenship was changed in 1917, when the U.S. Congress passed the Jones Act that created a territorial status for Puerto Rico, made Puerto Ricans citizens of the United States, and declared English the official language on the island. As citizens, over 20,000 Puerto Ricans would be drafted to serve in World War I. Nonetheless, Puerto Ricans would not enjoy full citizenship status and in 1922, the Supreme Court ruled in *Balzac v. Porto Rico* that Puerto Ricans were not entitled to certain rights contained in the constitution because Puerto Rico was an unincorporated territory. Jesus Balzac was a journalist in Puerto Rico who was charged with libel because he criticized the American appointed colonial governor and had been denied a trial by jury, a right guaranteed by the Sixth Amendment. The voice of Puerto Rican opposition to American colonial rule would continue to be silenced throughout the 20th century. Puerto Rico's relationship with the United States has remained complicated. In 1946, the United States appointed the first native Puerto Rican governor, Jesus T. Pinero. By 1947, partial self-government was granted to Puerto Rico and the first popularly elected governor, Luis Munoz Marin was elected. In 1950, President Truman signed the Puerto Rico Commonwealth Bill

Commonwealth:
A political unit having local autonomy but voluntarily united with the United States used officially of Puerto Rico and of the Northern Mariana Islands.

noting that Puerto Ricans were largely dissatisfied with the status quo and that different groups in Puerto Rico were debating between statehood, independence, or a commonwealth status with more local control. In 1951, The Puerto Rican Nationalist Party led by its president, Don Pedro Albizu Campos, led an unsuccessful armed insurrection against the United States with a series of uprisings in Puerto Rican towns and in the United States as part of the fight for Puerto Rican independence. An assassination attempt was made against President Truman and nationalist Lolita Lebron led an assault against the House of Representatives in Washington, DC, which resulted in the shooting of five congressmen. Despite the nationalistic fervor, in a referendum conducted in 1952, Puerto Ricans, given the option to vote for either a continuation of colonial status or the new commonwealth status, voted in favor of U.S. commonwealth status. Nationalists objected that neither the option of statehood nor outright independence was included in the referendum.

Over the years, as fiery debates over Puerto Rican self-determination have waged on, Puerto Ricans have remained divided over the question of their territorial status. A total of five plebiscites have taken place where the Puerto Rican people have voted on whether to remain a commonwealth, pursue statehood, or declare their independence. These plebiscites have been plagued with problems and have not pointed to a clear path for Puerto Rico. Today, the need for Puerto Rico to define its relationship with America has taken on some urgency as the island is facing an existential crisis. On September 20, 2017, Hurricane Maria decimated Puerto Rico resulting in loss of life, destruction of homes, bridges, roads, and loss of access to medical, educational, and other social services and the most basic necessities, including potable water and food. The Hurricane laid bare for the world to see an island reeling from a poorly developed infrastructure and the ravages of the intense poverty it had to show after a century of its special status as a U.S. commonwealth. Puerto Rico had been reeling from a recession that had been going on for over a decade with an unemployment rate over 10% and a dwindling tax base as the best-educated Puerto Ricans fled the island to pursue better opportunities on the mainland. The emigration from the island has increased dramatically after the hurricane adding to the Puerto Rican diaspora throughout the different states in America. Before the hurricane, Puerto Rico had sought to pursue bankruptcy stemming from its inability to repay over $100 billion debt. In June 2016, the U.S. Congress effectively placed the island's government under direct control of the U.S.

> Diaspora: the voluntary or forcible movement of peoples from their homelands into new regions.

Congress with the passage of the Puerto Rico Oversight, Management, and Economic Act (PROMESA), rendering Puerto Ricans powerless over their own financial matters. On the political front, in the most recent plebiscite (June 2017), 97% of voters chose statehood. However, voter turnout was abysmal with less than a quarter of all eligible voters participating. The fact is that in the event that Puerto Ricans could agree to statehood in a noncontested referendum, it would ultimately be up to the American Congress to decide if and when to admit the territory as the 51st state. In the meantime, it appears that the "special relationship" between Puerto Rico and the United States will continue.

SECRETARÍA DEL TRABAJO

DE LOS E. E. U. U.

998854 ☆

$\mathcal{P}$ongan todos atención a las siguientes palabras:

que el Sr. **FIGUEROA   CERVANTES MACEDONIO**
ha completado satisfactoriamente su Contrato de
Trabajo bajo el Convenio Migratorio de Trabajo

de 1951 bajo enmienda como bracero 312 20

El Gobierno de los Estados Unidos de América
presenta esta mención honorífica en apreciación
de la contribución prestada al aumento de la pro-
ducción de alimento y fibra necesarios para el
esfuerzo de defensa de la nación.

IMPRESIÓN DIGITAL
DEL ÍNDICE DERECHO

Fecha: OCT 2 5 1954

Secretario del Trabajo,
Estados Unidos de América.

C. H. Horden

Por

U. S. GOVERNMENT PRINTING OFFICE   16—65772-3

Kuv nyob qhov twg tuaj? Kuv nyob qhov twg tuaj?
Kuv nyob qhov twg tuaj? Kuv nyob qhov twg tuaj?
Kuv nyob qhov twg tuaj? Kuv nyob qhov twg tuaj?
Kuv nyob qhov twg tuaj? Kuv nyob qhov twg tuaj?
Kuv nyob qhov twg tuaj? Kuv nyob qhov twg tuaj?
Kuv nyob qhov twg tuaj? Kuv nyob qhov twg tuaj?
Kuv nyob qhov twg tuaj? Kuv nyob qhov twg tuaj?
Kuv nyob qhov twg tuaj? Kuv nyob qhov twg tuaj?
Kuv nyob qhov twg tuaj? Kuv nyob qhov twg tuaj?
Kuv nyob qhov twg tuaj? Kuv nyob qhov twg tuaj?
Kuv nyob qhov twg tuaj? Kuv nyob qhov twg tuaj?
Kuv nyob qhov twg tuaj? Kuv nyob qhov twg tuaj?
Kuv nyob qhov twg tuaj? **Where do I come from?**
Kuv nyob qhov twg tuaj? Kuv nyob qhov twg tuaj?
Kuv nyob qhov twg tuaj? **¿De donde vengo?**
Kuv nyob qhov twg tuaj? Kuv nyob qhov twg tuaj?
Kuv nyob qhov twg tuaj? Kuv nyob qhov twg tuaj?
Kuv nyob qhov twg tuaj? Kuv nyob qhov twg tuaj?
Kuv nyob qhov twg tuaj? Kuv nyob qhov twg tuaj?
Kuv nyob qhov twg tuaj? Kuv nyob qhov twg tuaj?
Kuv nyob qhov twg tuaj? Kuv nyob qhov twg tuaj?
Kuv nyob qhov twg tuaj? Kuv nyob qhov twg tuaj?
Kuv nyob qhov twg tuaj? Kuv nyob qhov twg tuaj?
Kuv nyob qhov twg tuaj? Kuv nyob qhov twg tuaj?
Kuv nyob qhov twg tuaj? Kuv nyob qhov twg tuaj?
Where do I come from? Kuv nyob qhov twg tuaj?
Kuv nyob qhov twg tuaj? Kuv nyob qhov twg tuaj?

Unit II

Ghosts of the Past

Chapter 12

My Father's Labor: An Unknown, but Valued History

Julie López Figueroa and Macedonio Figueroa

Important Words and Concepts in This Chapter

There are several important words and concepts throughout the upcoming chapter. The words appear several times in different places in order to help you remember the words and understand the chapter. The words are defined several times:

- Immediately below right before the chapter begins
- In text boxes throughout the chapter
- In red and boldfaced within the chapter
- In a glossary in expanded form at the end of the units

Some of the words also appear in other chapters. Talk about the words with other students, teachers, friends, and family members before you read, while reading the chapter, and after you have read the chapter.

Historiography

1. The writing of history; *especially*: the writing of history based on the critical examination of sources, the selection of particulars from the authentic materials, and the synthesis of particulars into a narrative that will stand the test of critical methods.
2. The principles, theory, and history of historical writing a course in *historiography*.

Contributed by Julie Lopez Figueroa and Macedino Figueroa. © Kendall Hunt Publishing Company.

Assimilation

Assimilation is the process by which a minority individual or group takes on the characteristics of the majority and attempts to be accepted as part of the majority group.

Bracero

A guest worker initiative that spanned the years 1942–1964. Millions of Mexican agricultural workers crossed the border under the program to work in more than half of the states in America.

Oral History

Oral history refers both to a method of recording and preserving oral testimony and to the product of that process. It begins with an audio or video recording of a first person account made by an interviewer with an interviewee (also referred to as narrator), both of whom have the conscious intention of creating a permanent record to contribute to an understanding of the past.

Family History

A record of incidents and occurrences important to our immediate families or ancestry.

Segregation

The separation or isolation of a race, class, or ethnic group by enforced or voluntary residence in a restricted area, by barriers to social intercourse, by separate educational facilities, or by other discriminatory means.

Research Question

The primary question guiding someone's research. The research question is usually large enough to have several subquestions within it.

Colonization

Political control of one nation over another that is institutionalized in direct political administration by the colonial power, control of all economic relationships, and a systematic attempt to transform the culture of the subject nation. It usually involves extensive immigration from the colonial power into the colony and the immigrants taking on roles as landowners, business people, and professionals. Colonialism is a form of imperialism.

Although I graduated from high school in 1987, I can easily remember taking high-school history courses. Memorizing history for the sole purpose of passing exams and in preparation to meet college requirements describes me as a learner in high school. Influencing this approach was the minimal representation of Mexican or Mexican American people in history textbooks that conveyed the silent, but firm message that anything of historical significance was already documented. Although my parents always taught me to be proud of my Mexican heritage, my history books in high school hardly recognized the presence or contribution of someone that looked like me. Parallel to this experience and outside of school, I loved listening to my family history for hours on end and enjoyed visiting local historical sites as well as museums. Needless to say, who I was as a learner inside and outside the classroom could not be more different.

This chapter explains how learning of my father's history in California impacted my outlook on history as well as opened my mind up to think about education so differently. To this point, learning of my father's history was one of the reasons I became a college professor in Ethnic Studies. In the end, this chapter urges you, the students, to become scholars and contributors to building a more inclusive and personal connection to history in collaboration with the teachers.

How Does One Learn History?

Traditionally, history seems to be taught as a series of indisputable facts. In this way, history seems inaccessible and at times inflexible to modern revisions or making personal connections. In truth, there is tremendous room to reinterpret history through what is called Historiography (Dray, 1971). Historiography is a method used to study how history is gathered and studied, written, and shared. Thinking back to my

> **Historiography:** beliefs, ideas, and events about history writing.

ninth grade, I remember looking at and memorizing continents, countries, and states that comprised the United States. Although I appreciated learning about these faraway places, these places were so far removed from my daily reality that I had no choice but to memorize versus learn. At the end of each year, I felt like a consumer of history rather than learner of history. I was a learner of history when I could relate to and respond to the history.

I understood history played an invaluable role in understanding my life, especially when I thought about my upbringing. To provide some context, I share some of my background.

Dr. Julie Figueroa.

Photo by Arya Allender West

I was raised in predominantly African American and Mexican American neighborhoods in San Jose, California. I attended an elementary school that was taught by teachers of color. My parents attended an American Indian Education Center to participate in different work-shops. While my father did the cooking at home, my mom attended workshops to learn nutritious recipes, given what local food was available. My father learned how to develop creative art lessons to facilitate learning for my sister, brothers, and myself. Needless to say, lessons on Slavery and American Indians marked moments of my being fully engaged with the readings and lectures because I wanted to understand my community members. To learn about myself in the ninth grade, the only lessons offered focused on the California Missions, the Mexican American War, and the Louisiana Purchase. These lessons seemed to underscore the theme of **assimilation**. Whether it was the Irish, Italians, or Mexicans discussed in Social Studies, history sent the strong mes-sage that finding a home and succeeding in the

> **Assimilation:** Where an ethnic group loses distinctiveness and becomes absorbed into a majority culture.

United States meant assimilating. One assimilates to blend in so that differences no longer exist. For me, blending in meant losing the ability to speak with my parents. As someone who grew up bilingual, I could not accept that losing Spanish would make my life better if I could no longer communicate with my family and friends who loved me. Living as a bilingual person in California where most of its cities are named in Spanish, completely agreeing with these messages on **assimilation** made little sense to me.

My Father's History: Developing a Sense of Place

As a young person in high school, I felt both alienated and villainized in the U.S. history lessons and textbooks. On the one hand, I could not personally connect to this history and on the other, it appeared to only represent folks that looked like me as the "Mexican Problem." Feeling demoralized and frustrated by these "facts," I remember going to my dad and asking him why he had decided to come to the United States. Like most other immigrants, he said: "Coming to the United States meant my children would have access to great educational opportunities." While my father's intention was both noble and admirable, this statement did very little to help me diffuse my feelings of frustration with the history I was learning in school.

I told him it was painful to learn history the way it was being taught in school. In response, my father told me he wanted to show me something. He returned to the kitchen and placed a small metal box on the table. Because I never saw that box before, my curi-osity was definitely high. He pulled out a paper card and handed it to me. I took the card and noticed the front cover of the card had English and Spanish words on the outside.

Once I finished carefully reading the words on the front of the card, I opened the card to discover my father's picture inside. Instantly, I knew it was some kind of identifi-cation card. Eagerly I explored the card again when my father's voice in the background came into focus. My father explained that card was his **Bracero** identification card. He explained that the U.S. Department of Labor contracted Mexican labors to address the labor shortage that resulted when a significant number of U.S. citizens were off fighting in World War II. After he spoke those words, I looked up at him with new eyes and new sense of understanding about myself in relation to history. I wanted to find out everything there was on the Bracero program, such as where were Braceros employed? how much were they paid? where did they live and work? I also wondered how my dad survived in the Southern states given that Jim Crow Laws were in full swing in the United States. Ultimately, I wanted to know why and how my father became a Bracero above all else. Unfortunately, my father's history exceeds the number of pages allotted for this discussion, but I will share the following brief history to offer some insight.

> **Bracero:** a guest worker initiative that spanned the years 1942–1964. Millions of Mexican agricultural workers crossed the border under the program to work in more than half of the states in America.

Macedonio Figueroa

My father was born in Jiquilpán, Michoacán in 1934. He worked in agriculture from the time he was 8 to 15 years old. In fact, when he was 11 years old he migrated to the United States to pick cotton in Texas. Years later, in 1954, at the age of 20, my father chose to become a Bracero as a way to move beyond the limited employment opportunities available for someone who grew up working in the farming and ranching industries and had no formal schooling. One year later, my father was relocated to Michigan where he picked beets and cucumbers. Then in 1959, my father came to California where he worked in Oxnard to harvest lemons, lettuce, and strawberries. In 1961, my father worked for an Italian farmer and owner named Mario

Backside of Macedonio Figueroa's Bracero identification card.

Inside of Macedonio Figueroa's Bracero identification card.

Photo courtesy of Julia Figueroa.

Lazzarini in Pescadero, California. Pescadero is a coastal town located off Highway 1 between Santa Cruz and Half Moon Bay, California. Although Michoacán was a coastal state, my father worked so hard from a young age that he had no free time to visit the ocean in Mexico. Needless to say, my father felt overwhelmed by seeing the ocean for the first time. The sounds, movement, and vastness of the ocean became my father's refuge at the end the day. One side note, he loved the ocean so much that growing up we spent every third weekend by the ocean.

Much later in 2004, while on one of those trips to the ocean, my father casually pointed to Mr. Lazzarini's farm. His former work site to this day continues to be located directly across the Pigeon Point Lighthouse on Highway 1. Interestingly enough, my father visited the Lazzarini farm with my older sister, Marina, in 2014 only to learn that Mr. Lazzarini grandson now owns the business and property. My father was welcomed like a long-lost family member. The grandson wanted to know everything he could about his grandfather and my father was kind enough to oblige. Working in Pescadero was an amazing experience for my father not just because of the ocean but also because Mr. Lazzarini sponsored my father's ability to apply to become a U.S. resident, which opened up the pathway for my father becoming a U.S. Citizen by 1964 just as the Bracero Program was terminated.

> **My father said he worked alongside African Americans, some poor Whites, Filipinos, and Chinese aside from other Braceros.**

Listening to this family history compelled me to jump up from the kitchen table, eagerly search for the U.S. map my parents kept and return to the table. I unfolded the map and began to circle all the places my father had worked as a Bracero. Knowing that my father along with other contracted Mexican laborers contributed towards stabilizing the economy during World War II gave me such immense pride. The geography lesson that was playing itself out as my father shared his labor history across the Southwest, Midwest, and some Southern states gave me a sense of belonging.

My father encountered different landscapes, but also confronted a variety of political views, unexpected warm welcomes, and learned about other people's histories that he would have not otherwise learned if he never left Mexico. He also learned about discrimination as he worked in many different states. One of the earliest forms of discrimination my father faced was in Texas. Although my father did not speak English, other Mexican Americans would interpret signs for my father indicating they were not welcomed into certain establishments because they were Mexican. My father said it was not unusual to find public signs that stated "No Mexican or Dogs Allowed" hanging in windows of stores, restaurants, barbershops, or bars. The more my father traveled across the United States the more he realized every single racial/ethnic group had its turn at being discriminated against.

My father said he worked alongside African Americans, some poor Whites, Filipinos, and Chinese aside from other Braceros. While these men were so different from him, it was when working alongside them that he could see how much they have in common.

Regardless of how they came into doing agricultural work, my father understood they were all working hard to improve their lives in spite of limited opportunities for advancement. Working in the Southern states, my father quickly grasped the public sentiment towards non-Whites, but in particular African Americans. Although my father witnessed how easily some of his non-African American coworkers would give in to public sentiment that African Americans were indeed more inferior, he consciously avoided the divide-and-conquer mentality. My father was not going to entertain the idea that he was somehow better than African Americans given his experiences facing racial discrimination.

The more I sat looking at the circled locations on the U.S. map, the more I began to see these circled locations as historical sites I would hope to visit someday. I considered these historical sites because my father contributed to the well-being of the United States. These historical sites served as anchor points and reminded me that in truth, history is much more multicultural than what is taught in a typical history course. I imagine it took a lot of courage for him to leave Mexico and come to an unfamiliar country without his family or knowing how to speak English. I cannot imagine what my father must have lived through, or the strength it took to survive the humiliation he most likely confronts as a Bracero in the United States. The circled places on the map gave me a sense of belonging and instantly made me confident and allowed me to let go of the imposed stigma I felt through the traditional teachings of history about Mexican and Mexican American people.

Transformed and Inspired by My Father's History

As an undergraduate, I declared Chicana/o Studies as a one of my two majors at the University of California, Davis. To fulfill major course requirements, I enrolled in a Mexican American history course and a course on Pre-Columbian History of Mexico taught by a well-known historian and scholar, Dr. Vicki Ruiz. Because Dr. Ruiz created assignments that brokered opportunities to locate our family history within U.S. history, I could take my father's labor history and relate it to what we were reading in my college textbooks. While I was emotionally pained to learn about how slavery, conquest, and colonization shaped the identity of Mexican and Mexican Americans, I also felt empowered by understanding how certain cultural foods and traditions have survived over 500 years. I was excited to formally learn a bit more about the positive contribution of Braceros during World War II, and thrilled to know we have color television today because of Mexican inventor Guillermo González Camarena. The oral history my father shared about being a Bracero ignited a passion for learning and a desire to expand my knowledge. Truthfully, I was surprised by my renewed enthusiasm for history. However, my response made sense according to Grebler, Moore,

Colonization: Political domination of one nation over another that is institutionalized in direct political administration by the colonial power, control of all economic relationships and a systematic attempt to transform the culture of the subject nation.

and Guzman (1970) who studied the impact of family oral history on Mexican American students. They found that when students learned about their **family histories** and how they strived for excellence, students used their family history as a source of inspiration to work though challenges with greater optimism. Understanding how one's family survived, lived through hardships, and succeeded opened the door to imagining what is possible in one's life regardless of the unknown.

My father's history inspired me to imagine how I could serve the world or at least provide another perspective on the world. The answer came to me while taking a Mexican American history course with Dr. Ruiz's class. I read an article by Gonzalez (1985) in which he discussed the segregation experience of Mexican American children. This article in part responded to my curiosity as to why so few Mexican Americans graduated from high school. In fact, I remained dissatisfied with much of the literature that blamed Mexican American culture or how the use of eugenics identified Mexican Americans as being genetically less intelligent to explain high dropout rates from school. At the same time, the literature offered no explanation as to why some Mexican Americans academically performed well without assimilating. My father's labor history along with the educational history of Mexican Americans influenced my decisions on how to use my education as a form of service but also helped me understand how to apply history in my work.

References

Dray, W. H. (1971). On the nature and role of narrative in historiography. *History and Theory*, *10*(2), 153–171.

Gonzalez, G. G. (1985). Segregation of Mexican children in a southern California city: The legacy of expansionism and the American southwest. *The Western Historical Quarterly*, *16*(1), 55–76.

Grebler, L., Moore, J. W., & Guzman, R. C. (1970). *The Mexican-American people*. New York, NY: Free Press.

Chapter 13

Self-Silhouette

Carolina Corona
Ms. Sims' Ethnic Studies Class

For my project, I chose to do a self-silhouette. The drawings in my silhouette represent the Mexican culture in the United States and how they transitioned here. It also represents how the Mexican people got here and what they did. My goal for this project is to give people a better understanding of the Mexican culture and the impact it had on the United States and its people. I hope to teach people the struggles Mexicans faced when coming into the United States and the importance of the culture. My project relates to Ethnic Studies because it gives examples of the Mexican culture and represents who they are.

Some of the main aspects of my silhouette are the wall and the desert behind it. That part of my silhouette shows what the Mexicans had to go through to get here. Another main part is the fruit. The fruit is an important part because the Mexican men and women that came into the United States worked for hours picking fruit. Another reason the fruit is important is

because some of these fruits shown come from Mexico and are sold here, for example, watermelon, papaya, and avocados. One more important part of my project is the flag in the background. The flag is a combination of the Mexico and U.S. flag. It's importance is that although these people aren't from the United States, they still play a big role here and have done a lot for this country.

Chapter 14

A Story of the People: The Hmong, in CIA's Secret War in Laos During the Vietnam Conflict

Chao Vang

Introduction

There is very little that is more important for any people to know than their history, culture, traditions and, language; for without such knowledge, one remains naked and defenseless before the world.

> Marcus Tillus Cicero (*King & American Educational Research Association, 2005, p. 159*).

Important Words and Concepts in This Chapter

There are several important words and concepts throughout the upcoming chapter. The words appear several times in different places in order to help you remember the words and understand the chapter. The words are defined several times:

- Immediately below right before the chapter begins
- In text boxes throughout the chapter
- In red and boldfaced within the chapter
- In a glossary in expanded form at the end of the units

Some of the words also appear in other chapters. Talk about the words with other students, teachers, friends, and family members before you read, while reading the chapter, and after you have read the chapter.

Contributed by Chao Vang. © Kendall Hunt Publishing Company.

Assimilate

Assimilation is the process by which a minority individual or group takes on the characteristics of the majority and attempts to be accepted as part of the majority group.

U.S. Census

A periodic counting of all people living in the United States. The census also records information about people's employment, ethnicity, race, gender, and so on.

Migrate

The act or an instance of moving from one place to another often on a regular basis.

Immigrants

An immigrant is a person who lives in a country other than the country of their birth. There are many different kinds of immigrants: economic immigrants, students, refugees, undocumented, and so on.

Communist Party

A system of government in which a single party controls state-owned means of production.

Trauma

A disordered psychic or behavioral state resulting from severe mental or emotional stress or physical injury; an emotional upset.

Ho Chi Minh

Founder of the Indochina Communist Party (1930) and its successor, the Viet-Minh (1941), and president from 1945 to 1969 of the Democratic Republic of Vietnam (North Vietnam). As the leader of the Vietnamese nationalist movement for nearly three decades, Ho was one of the prime movers of the post-World War II anticolonial movement in Asia and one of the most influential communist leaders of the 20th century.

U.S. Central Intelligent Agency (CIA)

A U.S. spy agency.

1962 Geneva protocol

Documents signed in Geneva declaring procedures and rules for the withdrawal of foreign military—such as France, the Soviet Union, and the United States—from Laos and the neutrality of Laos.

Vientiane Agreement in 1973

A cease-fire agreement between the two warring Lao factions—the monarchial government of Laos and the communists.

Sovereignty

The authority possessed by the governing individual or institution of a society. Sovereign authority is distinct in that it is unrestricted by legal regulation since the sovereign authority is itself the source of all law.

1954 Geneva Accords

Documents from the Geneva Conference in 1954, attended by representatives of Cambodia, China, France, Laos, the United Kingdom (England), the United States, the Soviet Union (Russia), the Viet Minh (i.e., the North Vietnamese), and the State of Vietnam (i.e., the South Vietnamese). Agreements were finally signed on July 21 between the French and Vietnamese, Laotian, and Cambodian representatives. Calling for a cease-fire line effectively dividing Vietnam in two; 300 days for each side to withdraw its troops to its side of the line; and communist troops and guerrillas to evacuate Laos and Cambodia.

Refugee Camps

Temporary shelters for people fleeing their home country. The United Nations High Commissioner of Refugees administers camps sheltering a vast population displaced people. World conflicts often result in scores of refugees around the world seeking shelter in camps. Contrary to popular belief, many of these settlements are far from temporary, and today most of the largest ones are in Africa and South Asia.

History of the Hmong

The Sacramento region includes the largest population of Hmong Americans in this country, all of whom trace their roots back to Southeast Asia in the not-too-distant past. Although these people have established a large community here in America, the Hmong are people without a homeland, and the country of their origin continues to be the subject of disagreement by scholars and historians. We do know that the history of the Hmong people dates back to at least 4,000 years in northern China

© Peter Herms Furian/Shutterstock.com

(Quincy 1995; Vang & Flores, 1999). Beginning in the late 1700s and early 1800s, the Hmong people's refusal to adopt and **assimilate** into the Chinese society forced many to **migrate** into the Indochina peninsula, regions that included the mountainous areas of southern China, Vietnam, Thailand, Laos, and Cambodia (Quincy 1995; Vang & Flores, 1999).

   Culas and Michaud (2004) noted that during the **migration** from China, the majority of the Hmong people congregated and formed villages in one particular geographic region: the highest mountain peaks in Laos.

> **Migrate:** to move from one country, place, or locality to another.

In 1972, an estimated 300,000–500,000 Hmong had resettled in the hilltops of Laos (Tapp, 2004, p. 81). Despite the difficult geographical features of Laos, a landlocked country with two major plateaus, the Hmong and other minorities such as the Iu Mien thrived by practicing slash and burn agriculture (Chan, 1994, p. 4). The Hmong and others who lived in the mountain tops of Laos cultivated rice and corn as food staples to maintain their villages and opium as cash crops sold primarily for profit (Hamilton-Merritt, 1993, p. 29). The Hmong unbothered by outsiders thrived in these conditions for many years until America's involvement in Southeast Asia changed the course of history for the Hmong.

The Secret War in Laos

The Hmong people lived peacefully in the mountains for over 300 years until their culture was disrupted by history. In the years following World War II in 1945, two political ideologies quickly developed between two world powers: a western democratic movement in the United States and a communist movement supported by the Soviet Union.

These opposing views set the stage for the Cold War with lasting global impact (Chan, 1994, p. 23). In Vietnam, the leader of the **communist party**, **Ho Chi Minh**, believed that it was time to liberate Vietnam from France, which had ruled Vietnam for 80 years, and unite the country under his communist leadership. After a surprised defeat of France by the Vietminh, nationalist soldiers led by **Ho Chi Minh**, French troops withdrew and ended the **French colonial rule** in the country. In the aftermath of the conflict in 1954, leaders from the United States, Soviet Union, United Kingdom, and China met at the Geneva Conference in Switzerland to settle political differences in Southeast Asia and find a way to unite Vietnam. However, leaders agreed that Vietnam would be divided into two nations with the communists in control over North Vietnam "while an **anticommunist** regime aligned with the United States and the Western allies ruled South Vietnam" (Chan, 1994, p. 22). The United States saw **Ho Chi Minh's** efforts of unifying Vietnam as a threat to democracy and thus began providing military advisors and American troops to defend South Vietnam from the communist North Vietnam encroachment and influence.

Laos, a country that was a neighbor to Vietnam, also experienced turmoil between the central government and pro-**communist** soldiers, the Pathet Lao. Thus, under the signed agreement of the **1962 Geneva protocol**, Laos was to remain neutral, and all nations were to respect the neutrality, **sovereignty**, unity, and independence of Laos (Hamilton-Merritt, 1993, p. 101). Despite this understanding, the North Vietnamese began violating this neutrality with the invasion and infiltration of troops into Laos. Hope faded quickly when Prince

© Peter Herms Furian/Shutterstock.com

…all nations were to respect the neutrality, sovereignty, unity, and independence of Laos.

Souvanna Phouma, prime minister of Laos, requested U.S. assistance, hoping that the accords would lead to real neutralization (Quincy, 2000, p. 222). Chan (1994) noted, "alarmed by the communists' military advances, the United States gave up any pretense at abiding by the 1954 Geneva Accords" (p. 29). According to Hamilton-Merritt (1993), some U.S. military advisors shared the conclusion to "not worry about the words in Geneva, they are only words. Worry about the Vietnamese soldiers in Laos, they are real" (p. 64).

At this point, it was very clear that Laos was a major geopolitical player as it was seen as the gateway to the countries of India, Burma, and Thailand (Hillmer, 2010, p. 63). Laos' significance would be echoed in 1961 by outgoing President Dwight Eisenhower who cautioned incoming President John Kennedy "Laos is the key to the entire area of Southeast Asia, if we permit Laos to fall, then we have to write off all the area" (Quincy, 2000, p. 3). According to Mahajani (1971), [President] Kennedy adhered to the domino theory coined by President Eisenhower that a "fall" of one country to communism would lead to "fall" of other countries (p. 90). Ultimately, the domino theory would be America's foreign policy that forced U.S. involvement into the affairs of Laos.

On April 28, 1963, during a National Security Council meeting President Kennedy once again reiterated the geopolitical importance of Laos: "If Laos fell to Vietnam the West would likely lose the rest of Southeast Asia and Indonesia" (Loewen, 1995, p. 45). Eisenhower's message of urgency would mark the beginning of the "Secret War" in Laos from 1961–1973. A U.S. Central Intelligent Agency (CIA) covert operation in Laos was termed the "Secret War" because little to no detail was made public. In fact, the United States had started bombing Laos to rid it of the communist soldiers. According to Loewen (1995), the United States government and its officials "kept our bombing of Laos secret for years, later citing national security as its excuse" (p. 222). To conceal the extent of America's involvement, most of U.S. operations in Laos were funneled through the CIA. Likewise, to keep the air war a secret, the U.S. Air force banned the news media's coverage from major air bases (Quincy, 2000).

By accident of geography, the Hmong who lived in the hilltops of Laos were recruited and trained by CIA secret agents as guerilla soldiers to fight Vietnamese communist forces that were penetrating into Laos (Morrison, 1999, p. 9). A CIA agent who identified himself as Colonel Billy approached General Vang Pao, a Hmong military leader, to command the Special Guerilla Unit (SGU) in efforts to push back the communists in Laos. Chan (1994) discovered that CIA agents had made verbal agreements to Hmong elders that if Americans should suffer defeat, then the Americans would "find a new place to relocate the Hmong" (p. 30). Vang Pao agreed to help and enlisted the support from Hmong villages and began recruiting Hmong men and boys to be trained by American CIA at base camps. Remember that all of this involvement of the Hmong was secret. Although the Hmong had been promised a new beginning, this promise was kept secret should the United States suffer defeat. The Hmong forces were trained to launch guerilla attacks, to destroy supply routes that the communists used, and to collect intelligence (Hillmer, 2010, p. 118). According to Hamilton-Merritt (1993), Vang Pao stated that "he needed his own men flying the air" because "only they knew the territory and the enemy and could talk to the troops on the ground" (p. 140). As a result, the Hmong soldiers performed search and rescue operations for downed American pilots.

...the Hmong soldiers performed search and rescue operations for downed American pilots.

During the decade long war in Vietnam, stories began to surface to the American public regarding U.S. involvement in Laos. The alarming activities in Laos reached the United States Congress, when the U.S. Senate held hearings that unraveled America's intervention in Laos (Hamilton-Merritt, 1993, p. 246).

Knowing that it was impossible to win the conflict in Vietnam and fully aware of the unpopularity of the war at home, on January 23, 1973 United States security advisor Henry Kissinger reached an agreement with North Vietnamese negotiator ending the war in Vietnam without the knowledge of Hmong military leaders. The United States retreated and deserted the Hmong people they promised to protect in the case of American defeat (Hamilton-Merritt, 1993; Quincy, 1995; Vang & Flores, 1999). Under the **Vientiane Agreement in 1973**, the United States government agreed to disband 18,000 Hmong troops while "all Americans military advisors in Laos left the country"

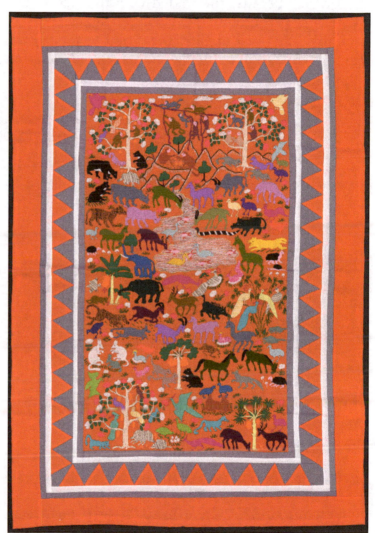

Anti-communist Hmong guerrilla troops in 1961. Air America Archives - Kenneth Conboy, War in Laos 1954–1975, Squadron/Signal Publications 1994

© Peter Herms Furian/Shutterstock.com

(Chan, 1994, p. 44). The following year in 1974, the Laotian government surrendered to the communist group, Pathet Laos, and as a result Laos became under communist rule.

Without U.S. protection that was promised "the Hmong, suspected of being U.S. spies, became unwanted people and had to flee from Laos to escape persecution" (Vang & Flores, 1999, p. 9). From 1976 to 1979 the Vietnamese and Laos government attacked the Hmong people, who had been promised American protection, using chemical weapons such as napalm to eliminate the pockets of Hmong resistance in the jungle of Laos (Chan, 1994). Subsequently, large numbers of Hmong fled to refugee camps in Thailand and eventually as political refugees to France, Australia, Canada, French Guyana, with the majority of Hmong immigrants settling in the United States (Chan, 1994, p. 48).

To this day, there are still a large number of Hmong trapped and hunted in the jungles of Laos because they sided with the U.S. to fight **communism** in Laos during the Vietnam War. Forgotten by the United States, which had spent about 20 billion dollars to wage the Secret War in Laos, the ordeal to the Hmong was devastating including 35,000 Hmong who fell in battle defending U.S. ideology (Quincy, 2000, p. 5).

Photo courtesy of Chao Vang.

My parents with two of my sisters in 1979 before they left Namyao Refugee Camp in Thailand to St. Paul, Minnesota.

Photo courtesy of Chao Vang.

My father with four of my sisters taken in 1982 3 years since their arrival to St. Paul, Minnesota.

Settlement of the Hmong in the United States

In December 1975, the United States Congress authorized the first wave of 3,466 Hmong refugees many of whom were from the camps in Thailand, to resettle in America under the Refugee Assistant Act (Faruque, 2002, p. 39). Since the first wave of

> The 2010 U.S. Census also reveals that the majority of Hmong concentrate in specific regions of the United States. California ranked number one with the largest Hmong population of about 91,224 followed by Minnesota with 66,181, and Wisconsin with 49,240.

Hmong immigrants, the Hmong population has grown significantly (Carroll & Udalova, 2006). In 1990, the **U.S. Census** estimated that the Hmong population was about 94,439, which nearly doubled to 106,310 in 2000 (Hmong National Development, 2004). Despite this increase, many Hmong American scholars argue that the Hmong like other minority in America are significantly undercounted. It is a matter of speculation but it was estimated that during the 2000 U.S. Census, over three million U.S. individuals may have not been counted. Given this margin of error, the Hmong population in 2000 could have totaled 204,948 (Carroll & Udalova, 2006). A decade later, the Hmong census continues to grow. The recent **2010 U.S. Census** reported that 260,076 people identified themselves as Hmong. The 2010 U.S. Census also reveals that the majority of Hmong concentrate in specific regions of the United States. California ranked number one

The author of this chapter, Vao Chang as a young child (sitting down) with his brother and sisters in Stockton, California.

Photo courtesy of Chao Vang.

with the largest Hmong population of about 91,224 followed by Minnesota with 66,181, and Wisconsin with 49,240. Specifically in California, the Hmong have moved to establish ethnic enclaves in Central Valley cities such as Fresno with 31,771, Sacramento with 26,996, and Stockton with 6,968 Hmong residents (Hmong National Development, 2011). Today, the largest group of Hmong outside of U.S. resides in China whose population is estimated to be around 2.8–5 million (Chan, 1994, p. 1).

Southeast Asia and Middle East: History Repeating?

Most Americans then and present day are not aware of the covert operation in Laos. Similarly, the decision to engage in Vietnam and current military policy decisions in the Middle East are controversial and much debated. As noted by Record and Terrill (2004), there are some parallels and analogies that historians will mark that are significantly similar between the war in Iraq, Afghanistan and the war in Vietnam. From **communism** in Vietnam to terrorism in the Middle East, the striking parallels were the basis for America's military encroachment in the region and influenced America's military tactics. These conflicts have led to widespread destruction and a wave of refugees flooding into Europe from Syria as it did in the 1970 in Southeast Asia for the Hmong, Mien, and many other groups. Although many students' parents were directly involved in this war and left Southeast Asia as refugees, many students like you are unaware of their own history. Essentially, students need information about the past to make sense of the present.

My Story—A Hmong Us

The story of the Secret War in Laos is important to me as a teacher of History. But it also holds tremendous personal importance for me. My parents left the refugee camps of Thailand on December 18, 1979 and came to "teb chaws Amelika" or "homeland America." Shared by hundreds of Hmong refugee families in America, their struggle shaped their children's identity. For me, to be Hmong, I relived their struggles and trauma, but simultaneously, I was their beacon of hope for the future. As an emerging young Hmong son, I am conscious of my place in the Hmong community and the role I play in the larger society. I hope to serve as a catalyst to begin a courageous conversation regarding the educational challenges that plague Hmong students, including the lack of academic interventions that benefit other similar at-risk groups. For this reason, as the children of refugees, we all should be reminded of the journey our parents undertook to be here, which wasn't easy; it never has been and maybe for their generation it will never be a full transition to life in America. But, it also reminds us that it is possible, possible that in the next 40 years we carve a place in America for our children as Hmong American.

Photo courtesy of Chao Vang.

A picture of my six sisters, three brothers, myself and my parents in 2016.

Photo courtesy of Chao Vang.

The author of this chapter, Chao Vang, seated with his parents after graduating with his Ed.D. in Educational Leadership, 2016.

Conclusion

Stories of a single event that altered the course of history for an entire people's life and culture have been part of my consciousness for as long as I can remember. This consciousness humanized me with the craving to search, reflect, and understand my parent's story, a journey and history of displacement and loss. We, the first generation of college students, known as the "rising suns" generation of Hmong will always be conflicted and challenged to explore what it means to be Hmong in America.

This search for my cultural identity reminds me that I am a Hmong male raised in South Stockton in a low-socioeconomic community, the son of refugee parents both of whom had no formal education, one of ten siblings, and a product of the public school system. These experiences capture the passion I have as an advocate for disadvantaged students and communities of color. My readers must understand that my position as a Hmong-American, engaged member of the higher education community in the Sacramento, California region have shaped this chapter from the ground up to promote a sense of cultural pride and appreciation for one's heritage.

References

Carroll, W., & Udalova, V. (2006). Who is Hmong? Questions and evidence from the U.S. census. *Hmong Studies Journal, 6*(1), 1–20.

Chan, S. (1994). *Hmong means free: Life in Laos and America*. Philadelphia, PA: Temple University Press.

Culas, C., & Michaud, J. (2004). A contribution to the study of Hmong (Miao) migration and history. In C. Culas, G. Y. Lee, J. Michaud, & M. Tapp (Eds.), *Hmong/Miao in Asia* (pp. 63–64). Chiang Mai: Silkworm Books.

Faruque, C. J. (2002). *Migration of Hmong to the Midwestern United States*. Lanham, MD: University Press of America.

Hamilton-Merritt, J. (1993). *Tragic mountains: The Hmong, the Americans, and the secret wars for Laos, 1942–1992*. Bloomington, IN: Indiana University Press.

Hillmer, P. (2010). *A people's history of the Hmong*. St. Paul, MN: Minnesota Historical Society Press.

Hmong National Development & Hmong Cultural Center (St. Paul, MN). (2004). *Hmong 2000 census publication: Data & analysis*. Washington, DC: Hmong National Development. Retrieved from http://www.hmongcc.org/ResearchDataandPublications.html

King, J. E., & American Educational Research Association. (2005). *Black education: A transformative research & action agenda for the new century*. Mahwah, NJ: L. Erlbaum Associates.

Loewen, J. W. (1995). *Lies my teacher told me: Everything your American history textbook got wrong*. New York, NY: New Press.

Mahajani, U. (1971). President Kennedy and United States Policy in Laos, 1961–63. *Journal of Southeast Asian Studies, 2*, 2.

Morrison, G. (1999). *Sky is falling: An oral history of the CIA's evacuation of the Hmong from Laos*. Jefferson, N.C: McFarland & Company.

Quincy, K. (1995) *Hmong history of people* (2nd ed.). Washington, DC: Eastern Washington University Press.

Quincy, K. (2000). *Harvesting Pa Chay's wheat: The Hmong and America's secret war in Laos*. Spokane, Washington, DC: Eastern Washington University Press.

Record, J., Terrill, A. (2004*) Iraq and Vietnam—Differences, Similarities, and Insights*. PA: Strategic Studies Institute. Retrieved from http://www.strategicstudiesinstitute.army.mil/pubs/display.cfm?pubID=377

Tapp, N. (2004). *Hmong/Miao in Asia*. Chiang Mai, Thailand: Silkworm Books.

Vang T., & Flores, J. (1999). The Hmong Americans: Identity, conflict, and opportunity. *Multicultural Perspectives, 1*(4), 9–14.

Mikala Her Ms. Sims Ethnic Studies

The history with the woman bringing her hands against her loved ones face is, in the Secret War many of the men that fought in this war had died, her loved one was just a shadow she was imagining. The girl with the Hmong clothing on is an outfit that girls would wear, it can be paired with a white skirt or black pants. The cross represents my religion of being a Christian. The Laos flags meaning, the white circle on the blue field is said to represent the moon shining over the Mekong river, the blue stripe represents wealth, and the red represents the blood shed during the internal struggle for freedom. The number 13 is the average age that the parents would marry their daughter off. The airplane is the transportation that the Hmong people took to fly away from the Secret War. The shoe prints are for those that didn't make it on the airplane, they went to Thailand on foot. The background is a pattern that woman's would create when they are sewing.

This relates to me because my family didn't get to go on the plane they had to go to Thailand by foot and my grandpa who served as the leading soldier who led many of the other people. My dad only has a sister because they had to leave behind their other siblings that were still little babies, they did this because the babies would cry and they didn't want to get caught, leaving their kids was something hard to do but it had to be done that way or they all could have got caught and shot. My parents were not forced to get married they wanted to get married but my grandpa and grandma thought that the time wasn't right for them to get married. My parents decided to disobey them and ran away to get married on their own, my mom at the age of 13 and my mad at the age of 19.

Chapter 16

Haitano

Molaundo Jones

© Peter Hermes Furian/Shutterstock.com

© Peter Hermes Furian/Shutterstock.com

The island of Hispañola, sometimes called La Española, La Isla Española, Haiti, or Santo Domingo is about 100 miles off the coast of Florida in the Atlantic Ocean between Cuba and Puerto Rico. The Taino Indians are the original inhabitants of Hispaniola; they called it Quisqueyo. Today, the island is divided into two countries: Haiti on the Western side of the Island, and the Dominican Republic on the East. During the 1920s and 1930s, the island—and both Haiti and the Dominican Republic—was occupied by the United States.

Although the two countries share the island, they are in conflict over land, citizenship, and labor. France colonized the West—Haiti, bringing enslaved Africans to cultivate the land; Spain took over the East—the Dominican Republic. After each country gained independence from France and Spain, Haiti's population was primarily made up of formerly enslaved Africans; the Dominican Republic mostly had Spanish descendants and citizens mixed with Spanish and Africans who had a lighter skin complexion than Haitians.

This difference in skin shade has caused many conflicts over the decades—from the massacre of Haitians and Dominicans of Haitian descent in the 1960s to forced deportation of Haitians and Dominicans of Haitian descent from the Dominican Republic. The following graphic is a true story of Molaundo Jones' visit to the Dominican Republic in 2002.

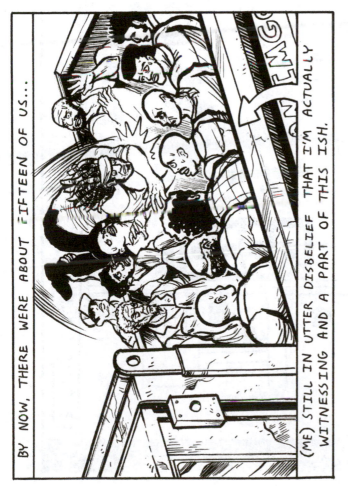

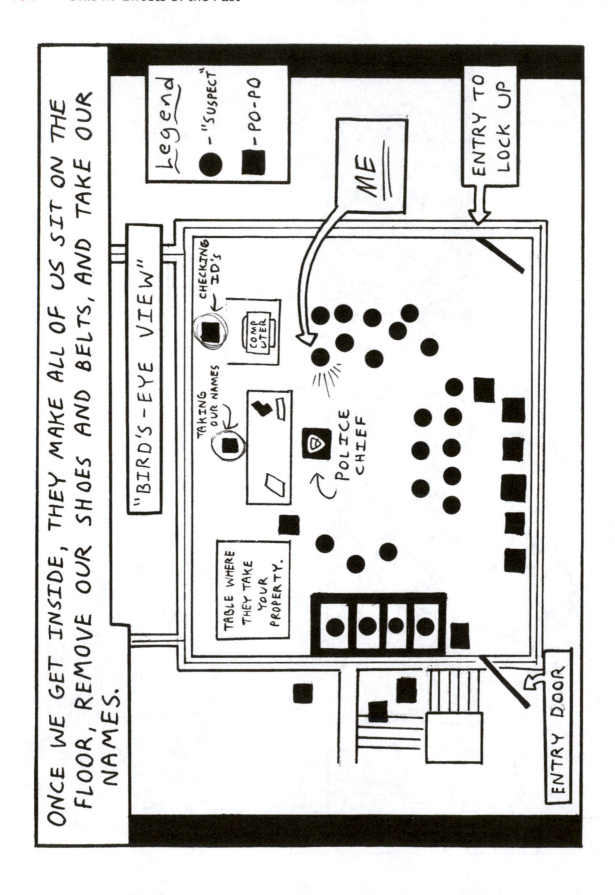

Chapter 17

Iu Mien—We the People

Fahm Khouan-Saelee Saetern

Important Words and Concepts in This Chapter

There are several important words and concepts throughout the upcoming chapter. The words appear several times in different places in order to help you remember the words and understand the chapter. The words are defined several times:

- Immediately below right before the chapter begins
- In text boxes throughout the chapter
- In red and boldfaced within the chapter
- In a glossary in expanded form at the end of the units

Some of the words also appear in other chapters. Talk about the words with other students, teachers, friends, and family members before you read, while reading the chapter, and after you have read the chapter.

Ethnicity

Membership or affiliation in a particular ethnic group.

Totemic Ancestor

An object (such as an animal or plant) serving as the emblem of a family or clan and often as a reminder of its ancestry.

Immigrate

The movement of peoples into a country or territory (movement of people within countries is referred to as migration). Some immigration is voluntary and some immigration is forced. Immigration can involve small number of people or masses of people in orderly or chaotic, dangerous conditions.

Migrate

The act or an instance of moving from one place to another often on a regular basis.

Southeast Asia

Southeast Asia consists of a vast territory encompassing 11 countries that reach from eastern India to China and is generally divided into mainland and island zones. Burma, Thailand, Laos, Cambodia, and Vietnam are in the mainland zones. Malaysia, Singapore, Indonesia, and the Philippines are part of the island zone.

Sinocentric

Any ethnocentric political ideology that regard China to be central or unique relative to other countries. A hierarchical Sinocentric model of international relations, dominated by China, prevailed in East Asia until the weakening of the Qing Dynasty and the encroachment of European and Japanese imperialists in the second half of the 19th century.

Refugee

A person who flees to a foreign country or power to escape danger or persecution.

Refugee Camps

Temporary shelters for people fleeing their home country. The United Nations High Commissioner of Refugees administers camps sheltering a vast population displaced people. World conflicts often result in scores of refugees around the world seeking shelter in camps. Contrary to popular belief, many of these settlements are far from temporary, and today most of the largest ones are in Africa and South Asia.

Linguistic Diversity

Different forms of verbal communication based on ethnicity, geography, culture, and age.

Myths

Sacred stories from communities around the world that help explain how things were created and how they came to be.

Theories

A belief, policy, or procedure that guides action.

Transliteration

To represent or spell the characters from an alphabet different from your own.

Fred Korematsu, Min Yasui, Gordon Hirabayashi

Korematsu from Oakland, California failed to report to an Assembly Center.
Yasui from Portland, Oregon violated a curfew order.
Hirabayashi from Seattle, Washington violated a curfew order and failed to report to an Assembly Center.
All three cases were appealed to the U.S. Supreme Court but all lost. The U.S. Army stated that evacuation and incarceration were carried out because of Military Necessity.
In the late 1960s, after the Federal Freedom of Information Act was passed, documents were discovered which showed the U.S. Army knew there was no Military Necessity. Government prosecutors had these documents, but did not disclose this information. All three cases were refiled under a rarely used legal procedure. They used Corum Nobis, which means to right a wrong. This time they won.

When people ask what ethnicity I am, I say, "I am Iu Mien." They then ask who are the Iu Mien and where are we from? My short response is "we do not have a country of our own but we originated from China." Often times, this response is enough to satisfy their curiosity. However, for many Iu Mien Americans, this answer does not suffice.

Although they immigrated to the United States over four decades ago, there are limited resources exist about the Iu Mien. As I explore my identity and feed my own curiosity about "who, what, when, where, and why" of the Iu Mien, I realize that I must do my part in ensuring that our rich traditions, customs, and culture survives the impact of past, current, and future social, political, and economic events. This article examines Iu Mien history, statistical data regarding the Iu Mien, and includes my personal experiences as an Iu Mien American.

Iu Mien History and Background

The Iu Mien are one of "the smallest major refugee groups in the U.S. and the least known in the refugee literature" (Macdonald, 1997, p. 3). Due to the Sino-centric biases of the mostly Chinese records, the early history of the Iu Mien is obscure and unclear. There is no reliable history of the Iu Mien before the tenth century A.D. (Macdonald, 1997, p. 70). Before the tenth century A.D., the Han did not distinguish among the different ethnic minorities. All southern China ethnic minorities were labeled "Man" (蛮). "Man" is derived from the ancient Chinese word for "barbarian" (Eberhard, 1982; Fortune, 1939; Wiens, 1967). In modern China, the Iu Mien are more commonly known as "Yao" (瑶). "Yao" is a government classification given to ethnic minority groups in China. In the United States as well as other parts of the Western world, the "Yao" identify themselves as Iu Mien or Mien.

Origin of Iu Mien Surnames

"The Iu Mien have various myths concerning the origin of the world, of the gods, of the Iu Mien, and other humans." Influences from the highland cultures and Han Chinese culture have contributed to the various versions that exist (Macdonald, 1997, p. 75).

A popular legend states that the Iu Mien's 12 surnames derived from the sons and daughters of Bienh Hungh, the Iu Mien totemic ancestor. The first six clans descend from the six sons of Bienh Hungh. The other six clans descend from the six daughters of Bienh Hungh.

Iu Mien surnames include Saephan (Bienh), Saelaw (Lorh), Saelee (Leiz), Saechou (Zuoqv), Saetern (Dangc), Saeyang (Yaangh), Saechao (Zeuz), Saelio (Liouh), Saefong (Bungz), Saechin (Zanh), Saetang (Dorngh), and Saehu (Huh). Although it is believed that there are 12 clans, there are other surnames that exist. This is not an inclusive list of Iu Mien surnames and variations in spelling do exist.

When Iu Mien migrated to Thailand, Thai authorities added "Sae" as the prefix to all Iu Mien last names. "Sae" in Thai means "last name." Today, it is more difficult to distinguish Iu Mien from other ethnicities solely based on their surnames since many Iu Mien Americans are reverting to their traditional names by dropping the prefix "Sae."

Iu Mien Migration to Southeast Asia

The Iu Mien migrated across national boundaries long ago. Records indicate that the first southward migration from China to Vietnam occurred during the seventeenth and eighteenth century. Throughout the late nineteenth and early twentieth century, the Iu Mien migrated into Laos, Burma (formerly Myanmar), and Thailand. Reasons for these migrations remain controversial varying from political to socio-economic ventures (Saeteurn, n.d.).

A large number of Iu Mien families settled in the mountains of northern and central Laos. Here, the Iu Mien practiced slash and burn agriculture, which involves cutting down trees and brush, burning the area to clear it, and then planting. They grew rice and other crops such as squash, beans, and poppies. Men crafted beautiful silver jewelry and women embroidered intricate designs on clothing and accessories (Gogol, 1996, p. 20).

© Popartic/Shutterstock.com

The Secret War

The simple and serene lives of the Iu Mien were abruptly interrupted by a civil war. "When the French struggled to retain control of Laos from 1945 to 1954, the Central Intelligence Agency (CIA) starting in 1958 began heavy recruitment among the hill tribes in order to counteract the Chinese and Vietnamese communists across the border and the Pathet Lao in Laos" (Gross, n.d.). By the early 1960s, a full-fledged civil war broke out in Laos. This war in Laos "quickly became part of a larger regional conflict known in the United States as the Vietnam War. Supported by the United States, the Royal Laotian government opposed Communist forces. An anti-Royalist group in Laos known as the Pathet Lao received military aid from North Vietnam, a neighboring Communist country" (Gogol, 1996, p. 20).

This civil war is known by many Iu Mien as the "Secret War." During this war, "Iu Mien men were recruited as anti-guerrilla forces by the CIA" (Macdonald, 1997, p. 88). In the documentary, *Voices from the Mountains*, Eric Crystal stated, "the United States dropped more conventional bombs in Laos than has ever been dropped in any country in the history of warfare, more than were dropped in Japan in World War II" (Saeliew, 2007). Many hill tribes including the Iu Mien fought a bloody secret war for the United States. Iu Mien men and teenage boys fought bravely and suffered many casualties.

In 1975, Pathet Lao forces won the war in Laos. Because the Iu Mien fought alongside the United States, they became targets for persecution. "Over 70% of the Iu Mien in Laos were forced to leave, abandoning their livelihood and walking two to three months to settle in large camps where they survived on the limited supplies provided by the American army" (Moore-Howard, 1989, p. 75). To escape danger, many families and even entire villages began to flee Laos. The majority of the Iu Mien population fled to Thailand resettling in **refugee camps**. "After several years, the United States returned to fulfill their contract made with the ethnic minorities. They offered a **refugee** rescue program, which gave the Iu Mien and other groups the choice to reset-tle in the United States" (Saeteurn, n.d.). U.S. residents aided by sponsoring Iu Mien families from the refugee camps. In 1976, the first Iu Mien families reached the United States to settle in Portland, Oregon.

> **Refugee:** Someone who flees their home to another country to avoid persecution.

Iu Mien Migration to the United States

The first significant group of Iu Mien arrived in the United States during the late 1970s. The number of arrivals increased in the 1980s. The majority of Iu Mien families settled on the West Coast in California, Oregon, and Washington. A smaller number of families settled in Alabama, North Carolina, Illinois, Minnesota, Kansas, Texas, and Oklahoma. Between 1980 and 1982, approximately seven families settled in Sacramento, California (Saechao, 1992).

Although the Iu Mien community grew significantly since their first arrival, the U.S. Census fails to recognize them as a separate ethnic group. The U.S. government includes the Iu Mien in the subgroups, "Laotian" and "Other Asian." One main reason why the Iu Mien are not recognized as an independent group is due to the fact that this community has yet to establish a consensus on one specific name. Some individuals from the community identify themselves as Iu Mien while others identify them-selves as Mien. Variations of the spelling of Iu Mien include Iu-Mien, Iu Mienh, Iu-Mienh, Yiu Mienh, and Mien. Since the Iu Mien remain aggregated under the "Laotian" and "Other Asian" categories, exact numbers for the Iu Mien popula-tion are unknown. Estimates vary from as little as 30,000 to as much as 150,000 Iu Mien residing in the United States.

Photo courtesy of Fahm Khouan-Saelee Saetern. © Kendall Hunt Publishing Company.

Author's Personal Experiences

I, Fahm Khouan-Saelee Saetern, was born in Ban Vinai refugee camp located in Loei, Thailand. On June 27, 1988, at the age of 2, my family and I migrated to the United States. My parents, Wern Khouan Saelee and Khae Luang Saelee raised their children with traditional

Iu Mien values and norms. They communicated with us in Mien. My parents expected my siblings and I to understand, participate, and respect Iu Mien traditions. We retain the ability to speak Mien today.

While studying abroad at Peking University (北京大学) in Beijing, China from August 2006 to July 2007, I encountered many people who asked what nationality I am. Very few thought I was Chinese—most assumed I was Korean or Japanese. When I told them I was American, some were immediately surprised and asked how could that be since I have the black hair, a petite stature, and the face of someone from the East, not the West. I couldn't claim I was Thai. Sure, I was born in Thailand, but I left the country at age 2 and never learned the language or culture. I couldn't tell them I was Chinese. I knew my ancestors descended from China, but how long ago and exactly from where, I wasn't sure. I realized then that my uncertainty about my identity was why I was in China.

Photo courtesy of Fahm Khouan-Saelee Saetern. © Kendall Hunt Publishing Company.

After a few months in China, I began to seek out Iu Mien living in China. I contacted an Iu Mien woman, Li Shaomei, a professor at the Central University for Nationalities (CUN) (中央民族大学). To my surprise, Mien literacy classes are offered at this university. I also discovered the Museum for Nationalities of CUN. This museum, created in 1951, is a professional museum that collects, displays, and researches the culture relics of 56 ethnic groups in China (Beijing, n.d.). I was both astonished and excited that I was surrounded by an abundance of resources that could potentially help me find answers I've been searching for.

After my studies in China ended in 2007, I continued on this journey of self-reflection and self-discovery. In 2014, I returned to China for a short visit. I traveled to Thailand in 2014 and 2017 to visit family members, continue my research about the Iu Mien, and collect artifacts and artwork created by the Iu Mien.

Fortunately, since I speak Mien, I am able to communicate with the Iu Mien of China and the Iu Mien of Thailand. I can connect with my parent's generation and can communicate in Mien with my cousins and distant relatives who live in Thailand. So many of the Iu Mien youth today struggle to speak and understand Mien. This is a reality in the United States, China, Vietnam, Laos, and Thailand. It is my goal as a parent to pass down my mother tongue to my children so that they too can describe the world in the one language their great-grandparents once spoke and understood.

Survey on Iu Mien Language

When the Iu Mien fled China, they brought with them "an Iu Mien spoken dialect, which had no written characters, and Mandarin, which was both spoken and written by a select, male, educated elite" (Egert, 2009, p. 5). Today, the Iu Mien language, Mien, has a form of romanized transliteration that was developed in the late twentieth century. Mandarin survives among the Iu Mien in the United States only as written characters of texts for ceremonies, which can be interpreted by shamans (Egert, 2009, p.5).

In November 2007, shortly after returning from China, I surveyed 135 Iu Mien currently living in California. The results indicate that the majority of Iu Mien Americans cannot speak Mien. Eighty-six percent of those surveyed have lived in the United States for less than 25 years. Fourteen percent have been in the United States for over 25 years. The data show half are fluent in Mien and 92% are fluent in English. Eighty-two percent feel most comfortable speaking English, while only 18% indicate that they feel most comfortable speaking in Mien. Within just a few decades, the Iu Mien language is on the brink of extinction in California. The relevance of learning Mien has been replaced by the need to learn English. Many Iu Mien, especially the 1.5, second and third generation Iu Mien Americans are losing their ancestral language despite the fact that 99% of first generation Iu Mien Americans are fluent in Mien.

As alarming as these survey results are, Iu Mien Americans show an interest in preserving their language. Many are not fluent in Mien, but are interested in learning the language. The survey asks, "If Mien language courses are offered at a community college, a university, or a place nearby you, will you consider taking a course?" Seventy-one percent responded yes. Twenty-two percent were unsure and only 7% responded no. Ninety-seven percent believe it is important for Iu Mien people to be able to speak their ethnic language. One particular individual stated, "Language is one of the most critical factors for ethnic association. Without our language, we essentially would lose part of our identity. Further, our future generations need to be able to speak Mien to prevent our own extinction. Once a language is extinct, it is impossible to revive it as we have seen with many other extinct languages." He also feels it is important for Iu Mien to read and write Mien. It is important for the Iu Mien to learn the romanized script "because of the nature of societal changes that necessitate us to have our language in a written form to make it useful. Furthermore, that would be one way of trying to increase usage and perhaps preserve what is left of our language." The overall consensus is it is important to take measures in preserving the Mien language. The Iu Mien have concerns about the availability of resources for them to maintain and learn the language. Ninety-one percent of the Iu Mien surveyed don't think there are enough learning materials available.

Conclusion

The Iu Mien struggle to maintain our community and culture in the United States. It is our responsibility as Iu Mien and Iu Mien Americans to preserve our identity. We need to contribute to the resources by doing academic research and oral history projects. We need

Photo courtesy of Fahm Khouan-Saelee Saetern. © Kendall Hunt Publishing Company.

to work together and advocate for our community. It is vital that we diligently record and document the different facets of Iu Mien life. Let's preserve linguistic diversity. Let's preserve our cultural heritage. Let's not allow scholars to draw conclusions about the Iu Mien based on assumptions and theories. We can take measures today to combat the loss of the Iu Mien language and culture. With our combined efforts, future Iu Mien Americans can more accurately define who we are and who they are. Until then, there are more questions to be explored and more research to be done.

References

Beijing Museum for Nationalities of Central University for Nationalities, Beijing Museums-Beijing China Travel Agency. (n.d.). *Beijing Tours, Beijing Tour, Beijing China Tours—Beijing Travel Agency and China Tour Operator*. Retrieved from http://www.tour-beijing.com/museums_guide/museum_for_Nationalities_of_central_university_for_nationalities.php

Eberhard, W. (1982). *China's minorities: Yesterday and today*. Belmont, CA: Wedsworth Publishing.

Fortune, R. (1939). *Yao society: A study of a group of primitives in China*. Canton, China: Department of Sociology, Lingnan University.

Gogol, S. (1996). *A Mien family*. Minneapolis, MN: Lerner Publications.

Gross, M. (n.d.). Wildflowers Institute—Iu Mien Community Portrait. *Wildflowers Institute—Home page*. Retrieved from http://www.wildflowers.org/community/IuMien/portrait2.shtml

MacDonald, J. L. (1997). *Transnational aspects of Iu-Mien refugee identity*. New York, NY: Garland Publishing.

Moore-Howard, P. (1989). *The Iu Mien: Tradition and change*. Sacramento, CA: Patricia Moore-Howard.

Saechao, S. (1992). *The Iu Mien community*. Sacramento, CA: Asian Community Center of Sacramento Valley.

Saeliew, J. (2007). Voices From The Mountain by Jai Saeliew | IMMIEN—Connecting Iu Mien with the world. IMMIEN.com—Connecting Iu Mien people with the world. Retrieved from http://www.immien.com/entertainment/arts-and-entertainment/videos/voices-from-the-mountain-by-jai-saeliew-2/

Saeteurn, F. F. (n.d.). United Iu-Mien Community, Inc.—Iu-Mien History. *United Iu-Mien Community, Inc.* Retrieved from http://www.unitediumien.org/MienHistory.php

Wiens, H. J. (1967). *Han Chinese expansion in South China*. Hamden, CT: Shoe String Press.

Chapter 18

Filipino Americans: From "Indians" to "Asians" in America

James Sobredo

Important Words and Concepts in This Chapter

There are several important words and concepts throughout the upcoming chapter. The words appear several times in different places in order to help you remember the words and understand the chapter. The words are defined several times:

- Immediately below right before the chapter begins
- In text boxes throughout the chapter
- In red and boldfaced within the chapter
- In a glossary in expanded form at the end of the units

Some of the words also appear in other chapters. Talk about the words with other students, teachers, friends, and family members before you read, while reading the chapter, and after you have read the chapter.

Colonists

A government official, employee, or citizen of a colonial or occupying country.

Unfree Labor

Indentured servants and enslaved persons.

Contributed by James Sobredo. © Kendall Hunt Publishing Company.

Social Darwinism

The theory that persons, groups, and races are subject to the same laws of natural selection as Charles Darwin had perceived in plants and animals in nature. According to the theory, which was popular in the late 19th and early 20th centuries, the weak were diminished and their cultures delimited, while the strong grew in power and in cultural influence over the weak.

Tydings–McDuffie Act of 1934

A law that (a) promised independence to the Philippines and (b) excluded Filipinos from entering the United States by setting a very low yearly quota of 50 immigrants a year. It was a compromise bill between Americans who wanted to exclude Filipino immigration and Filipinos who wanted independence for the Philippines.

National Identity

The depiction of a country as a whole, encompassing its culture, traditions, language, and politics.

Angel Island

Between the end of the 19th century and the beginning of the 20th century, millions of people—in numbers which have not been seen since—came to America in pursuit of a better, freer life. On the east coast, most of the huddled masses were met by the Statue of Liberty and Ellis Island. On the west coast, between 1910 and 1940, most were met by the wooden buildings of Angel Island. These immigrants were Australians and New Zealanders, Canadians, Mexicans, Central and South Americans, Russians, and in particular, Asians. Of these Asians, the majority were from China. They numbered 175,000.

Manilla Galleon Trade

Trade exchanging porcelain, silk, ivory, spices, and other items from China for silver from what was then considered New Spain, today Mexico. Some of the goods from China would be sent through Mexico and back to Spain.

Colonialism

Political control of one nation over another that is institutionalized in direct political administration by the colonial power, control of all economic relationships and a systematic attempt to transform the culture of the subject nation. It usually involves extensive immigration from the colonial power into the colony and the immigrants taking on roles as landowners, business people, and professionals. Colonialism is a form of imperialism.

The Katipunan

A Philippine revolutionary society founded by anti-Spanish Filipinos in Manila in 1892, whose main goal independence.

Mixed Race Heritage

Having two or more racial or ethnic heritages from parents who represent different race or ethnicity.

Philippine–American War

After its defeat in the Spanish–American War of 1898, Spain ceded its longstanding colony of the Philippines to the United States in the Treaty of Paris. On February 4, 1899, just 2 days before the U.S. Senate ratified the treaty, fighting broke out between American forces and Filipino nationalists led by Emilio Aguinaldo who sought independence rather than a change in colonial rulers. The ensuing Philippine–American War lasted 3 years and resulted in the death of over 4,200 American and over 20,000 Filipino combatants.

Spanish–American War

It is an important event in American history because it signaled the entry of American as a world superpower. The war started because the USS Maine sank in Havana Harbor, Cuba, and the Spanish government was blamed by newspapers and "Yellow journalism." These news reports argued that the USS Maine was sunk by a Spanish mine, but later reports and investigations case doubt this explanation. Still, the United States went to war with Spain based on these rumors. During this war, the United States invaded the Philippines, Guam, and Puerto Rico and made these islands American colonies.

Multilingual Family

A family whose members speak more than one language or dialect.

Multiracial

See "Mixed Racial Heritage."

Mestiza

It refers to racial and/or cultural mixing of Amerindians with Europeans, and the resulting tensions, contradictions, and ambiguities of this mixing.

Great Depression

Economic downturn across the world began in 1929 and lasted until about 1939. It was the longest and most severe depression ever experienced by the industrialized Western world.

Philippine Commonwealth and Independence Act

Also called the Tydings–McDufe Act, signed in1934, is the U.S. statute that provided for Philippine independence, to take effect on July 4, 1946, after a 10-year transitional period of Commonwealth government. The bill was signed by the U.S. President Franklin D. Roosevelt on March 24, 1934, and was sent to the Philippine Senate for approval.

Labor Union Organizer

A union representative who organizes nonunion workers to form union chapters at nonunion companies or worksites in order for all members to get the best possible salaries and working conditions.

Migration

The act or an instance of moving from one place to another often on a regular basis.

Manila

Capitol of the Philippines located on the island of Luzon. Manila was founded in 1571.

Bataan

After April 9, 1942, U.S. surrender of the Bataan Peninsula on the main Philippine island of Luzon to the Japanese during World War II (1939–1945), approximately

75,000 Filipino and American troops on Bataan were forced to make an arduous 65-mile march to prison camps.

Agricultural Workers Organizing Committee

Agricultural Workers Organizing Committee (AWOC), during its 7-year existence was made up primarily of Filipino Farm workers, called many strikes against growers and farm labor contractors and achieved some success in raising the wages of farm laborers. Additionally, AWOC sought job security, union recognition, and better working conditions for its members.

National Farm Workers Association

A labor union for farm workers established by Cesar Chavez in 1962.

Grape Strike

Also known as the Delano Grape Strike: a labor strike between the AWOC and the United Farm Workers against grape growers in California.

Nonviolent Protests

Nonviolent action refers to those methods of protest, resistance, and intervention without physical violence in which the members of the nonviolent group do, or refuse to do, certain things.

National Boycott

To engage in a national refusal to have dealings with a person, a store, an organization, and so on, usually to express disapproval or to force acceptance of certain conditions.

Filipinos Arrive on Spanish Galleons in California

Important Words and Concepts in this Section

Unfree Labor
Manilla Galleon Trade
Colonialism

In the sixteenth century, the Spanish ship *Nuestra Señora de Buena Esperanza* arrived at Morro Bay, a harbor close to San Luis Obispo in California's Central Coast. The ship's captain was Pedro de Unamuno and his ship's crew included "ocho Luzones Indios"—eight "Indians" from Luzon, a region in northern Philippines. These eight Filipinos would be the first documented Asians to arrive in America. They would land in California's shores in October 1587, 20 years before the 1607 Jamestown landing by English colonists. These Filipinos would arrive in America as "unfree" labor; they were captured from their native lands and forced to work on Spanish galleons. At that time, the Philippines and Mexico (*Nueva España* ["New Spain"] as it was called by the Spaniards) were both Spanish colonies, and the galleons were sailing back and forth across the Pacific Ocean between the Ports of Manila and Acapulco. As unfree labor, Filipinos had a similar experience with African; they were both forced to come to the New World as "unfree" labor on European ships, and they were forced to work in the New World.

Europeans first came into contact with Filipinos in 1521, when Magellan and his crew of Spanish explorers landed in the Visayan islands of the Philippines. Magellan was a Portuguese navigator who defected to Spain, became a naturalized Spanish citizen, and was in command of a small Spanish fleet searching for an alternative route to Asia (China and India). Magellan himself would not live to return to Spain. He was killed in battle by *Datu* (Chief) Lapu-lapu in Mactan Island in Cebu. Under the command of Juan Sebastián Elcano, a small crew of 18 were able to miraculously survive and to sail through southeast Asia, through the Indian Ocean and past the Cape of Good Hope in Africa, up the South Atlantic Ocean and return to Spain; thus, Spain became the first nation to circumnavigate the globe. When Elcano and his crew returned to Spain, his cargo included cinnamon and cloves—the precious spices that drove Europeans to risk their lives and "sail the ocean blue"—which they sold for a huge profit that paid for the price of the expedition.

For nearly 44 years, the Philippines would repel any attempts at European colonization and the Philippines and Filipinos would not be colonized until 1565 when Miguel Lopez de Legazpi, with a Spanish crew from Mexico, would successfully establish a Spanish colony in the Philippines. It was also under Legazpi that the *tornaviaje* ("return trip") to Mexico was discovered in 1565. A Spanish galleon sailed from the Philippines up to Guam and the Micronesian Islands, where it

> **Colonialism:** Complete and total control of one group of people or country by another group of people or country for economic gain of the controlling group.

resupplied with fresh water and food, and then it followed the currents across the Pacific Ocean and arrived near the California coast. From there, it sailed down the coast to the Port of Acapulco in Mexico. This was the route that the "Manila galleons" would eventually take for over 240 years.

In 1571, Legazpi switched his capital from Cebu to Manila when he saw the huge harbor that offered better protection for Spanish ships, which was important since the Philippines has frequent monsoons and typhoons. The actual "Manila galleon trade" would not start until 1571 when Chinese merchants were rescued during a storm by Legazpi in the Philippines. For hundreds of years, Chinese ships (junks) would sail from China and trade their goods of porcelains and silks with Filipinos in exchange for gold, spices, and food items. Following Asian tradition, these rescued Chinese merchants returned the following year bringing gifts—precious porcelains and silks—to show gratitude for their rescue. The Spaniards accepted those gifts, brought them back to Mexico and sold them for a huge profit. Recognizing a financial opportunity, the Spaniards returned to Manila the following year and offered to buy more silks and porcelains from the Chinese merchants and paid for those goods in Spanish silver pesos coins. Thus began the high successful "Manila galleon trade" across the Pacific Ocean; silks, porcelains, and other luxury goods from Asia (mainly China) were exchanged for precious metals (primarily silver, as well as gold) from the Americas (mainly Mexico). For over 240 years, this Manila galleon trade among Manila, Acapulco, and China comprised the largest and most lucrative economic system in the world. The Manila galleon trade was also the first global economic trading system; goods from Asia, the Americas, the Pacific Islands, Africa, and Europe were traded at a global level.

To complicate matters further, Filipinos were called "Indios" by the Spaniards, and the ships they arrived on were called *Nao de China* ("ship from China"), although the ships were really Filipino-built ships from the Philippines and were part of the highly profitable "Manila galleon trade." Thus, Filipinos on the Spanish galleons were often referred to, mistakenly, as "Chinos" (Chinese). While there were indeed Chinese merchants on the Spanish galleons, they were in fact a minority of the passengers. These Spanish galleons carried silks, porcelains, spices, and other Asian luxury goods to Mexico. The Asian goods the galleons carried mostly came from China (silks and porcelains) and also from Indonesia and Malaysia (spices),

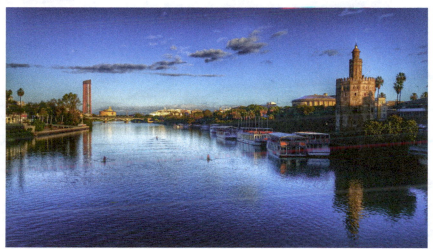

Tore del Oro in Seville where gold and silver from the New World arrived in Spain. This is the same river from which Columbus and Magellan sailed to America and the Philippines.

India (cotton, ivory, and furniture), Japan (silver, amber, swords, and bronze), as well as from Vietnam, Thailand, and Cambodia (ivory, musk, rubies, and sapphires).

When they arrived in Mexico at the Port of Acapulco, Spanish merchants bought the Asian goods and paid with Spanish silver mined and minted in South America (Potosí in Bolivia) and later Mexico. These Asian goods would be distributed throughout Latin and South America. Not surprisingly, upon arriving in Acapulco, many Filipinos jumped ship to escape from their forced labor and blended into the local Mexican population. In sum, these "Indios" from the Philippines became "Mexican," which was fairly easy given that they shared similar cultures and language as Spanish colonies. Some Filipinos would eventually travel all the way up to Northern California, including one Filipino named Felix Domingo, who, in 1830, married into the local Native American community at Point Reyes. Today, a large number of the Miwok and Pomo population in Sonoma and Santa Rosa are part-Filipino, including Greg Sarris, the chairman of the Federated Indians of Graton Rancheria.

The Manila galleon trade will continue until 1815 when the last galleon arrived in Mexico, and, by this time, Spain would lose their ports during the Mexican War of Independence (1818–1821). During the rest of the nineteenth century, the Philippines continued to be a Spanish colony, and Filipinos would begin their struggle to gain a national identity and eventually fight a war of independence against the Spaniard. One of the Filipino leaders of this fight against Spanish colonialism is a young doctor named Jose Rizal, a mixed race Filipino of Spanish and Chinese ancestry.

Rizal and Filipino National Identity

Important Words and Concepts in this Section

Mixed Race Heritage
Angel Island
Social Statement
The Katipunan

Dr. Jose Rizal was educated in Europe and spent a lot of time in Spain where he joined a group of Filipinos who were writing about the abuses of the Spanish government in the Philippines. Through his published writings, Rizal became one of the leading Filipino nationalists who were advocating for a Filipino national identity. Rizal would publish two novels (*Noli Me Tángere* ["Touch me Not"] and *El Filibusterismo* ["The Subversive"]) that told about the abuses done by the Spanish friars and colonial government in the Philippines. Rizal was a member of the newly formed *Ilustrado* ("Learned" or "Enlightened One") class. He was of mixed race heritage: Filipino, Chinese, and Spanish. Rizal was born to a privileged family, highly educated, and spoke several languages, including Filipino, Spanish, Portuguese, German, French, Dutch, Latin, and Japanese. He lives a significant part of his life in Europe, especially Germany and Spain, where he wrote and spoke of the abuses committed by the Spanish government against Filipinos.

In 1888, Rizal also spent time in California and traveled across the United States to New York on his way to Europe. However, his visit to California did not go well. Upon arriving in San Francisco, he was quarantined in Angel Island, which he found most objectionable and wrote about it bitterly in his journal. At this time, Asians were "quarantined" in Angel Island, presumably for health reasons, but Rizal saw it as simply racially motivated. He wrote in his diary: "Here [in San Francisco] we are in sight of America since yesterday without being able to disembark, placed in quarantine on account of the 642 Chinese that we have on board coming from Hong Kong where they say smallpox prevails. But the true reason is that, as America is against Chinese immigration, and now they are campaigning for the elections, the government, in order to get the vote of the people, must appear to be strict with the Chinese, and we suffer. On board there is not one sick person."

> **Rizal became one of the leading Filipino nationalists who were advocating for a Filipino national identity.**

After 7 days of quarantine, Rizal was allowed to enter and as a social statement, he booked a room at the Palace Hotel, which was one of the most prestigious and most expensive hotels in San Francisco. Today, there is a monument at the corner of Market and Montgomery commemorating Rizal's 1888 stay at the Palace Hotel. From San Francisco, Rizal boarded a ferry for Stockton, where he caught a train for Sacramento. He noted in his diary: "Dinner in Sacramento. 75 cents. We slept in the coach. Regular night. We woke up an hour from Reno, where we took our breakfast at 7:30." Rizal would continue on his train ride through the Midwest, stopping in Chicago, and continuing on to New York where he caught a trans-Atlantic ship to England and continued on to his European journey. The Filipino community in Sacramento honors and acknowledges Rizal's visit by naming a major community center on 7320 Florin Mall Drive, the "Jose P. Rizal Community Center." Every year for the last 20 years, the Filipino American community holds a "Filipino Fiesta" to celebrate its Filipino culture and heritage. Of his time in the United States in 1888, Rizal wrote: "I'll not advise anyone to make this trip to America, for here they are crazy about quarantine, they have severe customs inspection, imposing [duties] on anything."

Rizal noted that America was very ambitious and wanted to become an empire, and he feared that those ambitions about empire would reach all the way to the Philippines. Ten years later, Rizal's fear would become a reality when the United States would invade the Philippines during the Spanish-American War.

When he arrived in Spain, Rizal would belong to a powerful group of *Ilustrado* Filipinos who formed a newspaper, *La Solidaridad*, and would write propaganda that was heavily critical of the Spanish colonial government in the Philippines. Rizal and his fellow *Ilustrados* (most notably, Marcelo H. del Pilar and Mariano Ponce) were very well received by members of the educated population in Spain and the rest of Europe, but not by the Spanish colonial government in the Philippines.

Ultimately, however, Rizal was a reformist, and he did not advocate independence. Rizal wanted more equality between the "Indios" (what the Spaniards called Filipinos) and Spaniards. Still, the Spanish government in the Philippines accused Rizal of associating with the Katipunan, a secret and armed organization that was actively trying to overthrow the Spanish colonial government. When he returned to Manila, Rizal was arrested, held in prison, tried, and then executed in 1896 by the Spaniards for rebellion and sedition. The Katipunan, under the leadership of Andres Bonifacio and Emilio Aguinaldo, would eventually form an army and wage a war of independence against the Spanish government, which did not succeed. However, the Spanish government could also not defeat the Katipunan, so they paid the Filipinos to stop fighting and to leave the country. Under the leadership of Aguinaldo, the remaining Katipunan leaders left the Philippines and went into exile in Hong Kong in 1897, where they planned their return and goal to overthrow the Spanish colonial government.

> **The Katipunan:** A secret and armed organization that was actively trying to overthrow the Spanish colonial government.

America Invades and Colonizes the Philippines in 1898

Important Words and Concepts in this Section

Spanish-American War
Philippine-American War
Social Darwinism
Multiracial
Multilingual Family
Mestiza

By 1898, the Spanish-American War broke out between the United States and Spain. The war occurred because of an explosion that sank the USS Maine in Havana, Cuba. America declared war against Spain, but instead of attacking Cuba, the first act of war the United States did was to send a naval fleet to the Philippines and to attack an unprepared Spanish fleet. Under the command of Commodore George Dewey, the Americans were under secret orders to sail into Manila Bay from Hong Kong and to destroy the outdated and unprepared Spanish fleet. When news of the declaration of war reached Dewey, he sailed in to Manila on May 1st, 1898 and destroyed an unprepared Spanish fleet. These secret orders were sent to Dewey in Hong Kong *before the start of the Spanish-American War*, which meant to many historians that the United States had secretly planned the attack and had plans to take the Philippines prior to the outbreak of War. In the Battle of Manila Bay, Dewey was sailing onboard the *USS Olympia*, America's most modern warship that was built in San Francisco and completed at Mare Island Naval Shipyard (Vallejo). With the defeat of the Spanish fleet, this also signaled the arrival of the United States as a world superpower, a position that it maintains today.

After the naval battle, Dewey did not sail away. Instead, he and the American naval fleet waited in Manila Bay for the arrival of U.S. ground troops, who had been training in the San Francisco Presidio for a land invasion. The Spanish-American War was so popular that hundreds of thousands of young Americans across the country volunteered to fight in the War. When the U.S. troops arrived, they attacked and fought the Spanish army in Manila and took control of Manila. Filipino troops also participated in the battle, but the official "surrender" occurred between Spain and the United States. The Spanish colonial government made sure that they surrendered to the Americans and not to the Filipinos. Some scholars even refer to this batter and surrender as the "Mock Battle" of Manila. Meanwhile, Aguinaldo had returned to the Philippines and established an Philippine government. Thus, when the 1898 Treaty of Paris was signed to end the Spanish-American War, the United States only had control of Manila, while the rest of the Philippines was under the control of Filipinos. The 1898 Treaty did not involve Filipinos, and officially the Spain "ceded" the Philippines to the United States for a payment of $20 million. The 1898 Treaty essentially made the Philippines a U.S. colony.

A few weeks later, in February 1899, fighting and another full-blown war would occur between Filipinos and Americans. The Philippine-American War (1899–1902) was very one sided. The Philippines did not have the military resources and power that the United States had. The Philippines had no navy that could bombard its enemy; they had an inexperienced military; and the Philippine "army" was in very short supply of weapons and resources. In contrast, the United States had modern naval ships; a highly trained and experienced group of senior officers who spent their early years fighting against Native Americans; and they had a larger supply of guns and ammunitions.

The war was devastating to the Philippines and it led to the massacre of hundreds of thousands of Filipinos. E. San Juan, Jr., a leading Filipino American scholar of Philippine history, argued that approximately1.4 million Filipinos were killed at the end of the war and that the war amounted to genocide. What was also clear that the racism in the United States was also brought to the Philippines. At this period, the Unites States was at the height of social Darwinism, a racist belief that white people were the superior race and that they should be segregated from the "inferior" races. In its worse form, social Darwinists believed in the extermination of inferior races.

> **Social Darwinism:** A belief based on Darwin's theory of evolution arguing that social progress resulted from conflicts in which the fittest or best adapted individuals, or entire societies, would prevail.

Some U.S. soldiers were fighting the war by describing the Filipinos in racist terms and calling Filipinos "savages," "Injuns," and "niggers." Some African Americans fighting in the war were so disturbed by the racism directed against Filipinos that they defected from the U.S. Army and joined the Filipino army—although the majority of Black soldiers stayed and served their country honorably. The most famous African American to join the Filipinos was Corporal David Fagen. The *New York Times* described Fagen as a "captain in the Filipino National army" and noted that "Fagen's actions in the fall of 1899 mark the beginnings of an extraordinary expression of African-American solidarity with Filipino nationalist aspirations for independence." The connection between Filipinos and African Americans would continue at the end of the war. It was through African Americans that jazz was introduced to the Philippines. This early introduction to American jazz music and improvisation caught on with Filipinos. Today in Asia and in many parts of the world, Filipinos musicians are renowned for their talent and the origins of this can be traced to the aftermath of the Spanish-American War when jazz music was brought to the Philippines by African Americans.

> **The first documented Filipino American family to arrive in the United States was the family of Rufina Clemente Jenkins who arrived in San Francisco's Presidio in 1902.**
> **They were a multiracial and multilingual family: Rufina was a mestiza (Filipino and Spanish) and Frank was Black and Mexican, which is why he spoke Spanish.**

However, a much deeper connection would be through marriage and families formed between Filipinos and Blacks. The first documented Filipino American family to arrive in the United States was the family of Rufina Clemente Jenkins who arrived in San Francisco's Presidio in 1902. She was a "war bride" married to Sgt. Frank Jenkins, a "Buffalo Soldier," and a Spanish interpreter in the U.S. Army. The Jenkins family eventually settled in Fort Lawton in Seattle, Washington, and after Sgt. Jenkins's retirement from the Army, they lived in a home close to the main office of the Filipino American National Historical Society. They were a multiracial and multilingual family: Rufina was a mestiza (Filipino and Spanish) and Frank was Black and Mexican, which is why he spoke Spanish. At home in Seattle, the family spoke Filipino, Spanish, and English. This multiracial and multilingual theme would continue in many Filipino American families throughout California and the United States.

As a U.S. colony, Filipinos were not given U.S. citizenship rights. Instead, in 1904 the U.S. Supreme Court classified them as "nationals." This meant that Filipinos could come to America freely. They did not need a visa to immigrate, and Filipinos could not be excluded from immigration like other Asians before them. For example, racist immigration laws were passed against Chinese, Japanese, Koreans, and Indians that prevented them from entering the United States. However, it meant they could not have the full rights of U.S. citizenship; for example, they could not vote or hold public office.

Filipino Workers and Racism in California

Important Words and Concepts in this Section

Migration
Great Depression
The Tydings–McDuffie Act of 1934
Philippine Commonwealth and Independence Act

When Filipino immigrants finally came to the United States in large numbers in the 1920s and 1930s, they came first to Hawaii to work in the sugar cane plantations and later to California to work in the farms of the San Joaquin Valley. The town with the largest Filipino community was Stockton, located a 50 miles south of Sacramento, where Filipinos formed a community they called "Little Manila." Filipinos found work as migrant farm workers and followed the harvest season in California and the West Coast: picking asparagus in Stockton in spring, and then lettuce and strawberries in Salinas and Watsonville, and going up north to Seattle and Alaska to work in the fish canneries in the summer. After a summer of working in the canneries, they returned in early fall to pick grapes in the Central Valley. These were difficult jobs, and Filipinos were paid very little money, as little as a "dollar a day" and had very few workers benefits.

Unfortunately for Filipinos, their peak **migration** occurred when the United States was facing the **Great Depression**. Filipinos were blamed for stealing white workers' jobs and for dating white women. After two major "riots" against Filipinos, the U.S. Congress passed an immigration restriction law that essentially stopped this "Third Asiatic invasion." **The Tydings–McDuffie Act of 1934** was a compromise between (a) politicians who wanted to exclude Filipinos for economic and social reasons and (b) Filipinos who wanted independence for the Philippines. When the bill was finally signed into law, it was officially called the "**Philippine Commonwealth and Independence Act**," because it granted the Philippines Commonwealth status and a promise of independence in 1944. For immigration reasons, it also meant that Filipinos will now become "aliens" and can join the ranks of the other Asians who were excluded from the United States. Thus, as the "Third Asiatic invasion," Filipinos were finally excluded from America. In a word, these "Indios" from Luzon had become "Asians." And, as Asians, they could be and were in fact excluded from entering the United States. This period was a difficult time for Filipinos living in the United States. They had lost what little legal protection they had, and to make matters worse they were now in the midst of the **Great Depression**. There were very few jobs and millions of Americans were unemployed. Filipinos were facing discrimination and racism by white society because they dared to date and even marry white women. Carlos Bulosan, a Filipino American writer who wrote about the hardship and life of Filipinos in America, expressed it well when he wrote, "It is a crime to be a Filipino in America." And in many hotels in Stockton and the Central Valley, Filipinos looking for lodging were greeted with signs that said, "Positively No Filipinos Allowed."

> **Migration:** The act or an instance of moving from one place to another often on a regular basis.

Filipino Americans in World War II

Important Words and Concepts in this Section

Manila

Bataan

World War II will change the attitude of America toward Filipinos. A few hours after the December 7th, 1941, attack on Pearl Harbor, Japanese planes also attacked U.S. military bases in the Philippines. A few days later, on December 10th, Japanese troops were landing in Northern Luzon. To save Manila from the destruction of War, General Douglas MacArthur declared Manila an "open city." MacArthur decided to make his stand against the invading Japanese army in Bataan, at a military base across from Manila. By this time, the U.S. Armed Forces in the Philippines were united with the Philippine military into an umbrella united called the "United States Armed Forces in the Far East" (USAFFE), which meant that members of the Philippine military were not serving as part of the U.S. military. For practical purposes, this meant that Americans and Filipinos were now fighting together against a common enemy, which is ironic given that less than 42 years ago, they were fighting a war against each other in the Philippine-American War. Still, Filipinos saw themselves as defending their homeland and Americans saw themselves as serving their duty fighting for the U.S. military. Eventually, the USAFFE were defeated by battle experienced Japanese military troops who were armed by more advanced and faster war planes and a steady stream of supplies. To make matters worse, the USAFFE air bases were completely unprepared for the Japanese air attack even though they had radar and were following the incoming Japanese war planes. Filipinos took their last stand at an island fortress south of Bataan called Corregidor. MacArthur and the leadership of the Philippine Commonwealth Government (President Manuel Quezon and his cabinet) escaped from the Philippines. MacArthur went to Mindanao and then to Australia, and Quezon to American where he eventually established a government "in exile" in Washington, DC. When MacArthur arrived safely in Australia, he made his famous, "I came through and I shall return" speech to American troops and to the Filipino people in the Philippines.

Filipinos and Mexicans form the United Farm Workers Union

Important Words and Concepts in this Section

Labor Union Organizer
United Farm Workers Union
Agricultural Workers Organizing Committee
National Farm Workers Association
Grape Strike
Nonviolent Protest
National Boycott

By the 1950s and 1960s, the remaining Filipinos in the United States are now much older. They were also working side-by-side with other Mexican farm workers. Then in 1965, under the leadership of Larry Itliong, Filipinos went on strike for better salaries and working conditions in Delano. Itliong had been a long-time labor union organizer, but although they won strikes in the past, they had never been able to gain recognition as a union for farm workers. To make matters worse, when Filipinos went on strike, Mexican farm workers were brought in by the farmers to break the strike; in the same way, when Mexican farm workers went on strike, Filipinos were brought in to break their strike. Itliong recognized this problem, so he asked Cesar Chavez and Dolores Huerta, who had been organizing

> **Labor Union Organizer:** A union representative who organizes nonunion workers to form chapters at nonunion companies or worksites in order for all members to get the best possible salaries and working conditions.

Mexican farm workers, to meet with him. Itliong asked Chavez to join the Filipino grape strike, but Cesar refused because he did not feel that they were ready. It was Huerta, who had known Itliong when she lived and worked in Stockton, who convinced Chavez to join the Filipino strike. Thus, for the first time in history, Filipinos and Mexicans joined forces and had a unified strike for union recognition and workers' rights. This lead to the establishment of the United Farm Workers union (UFW), which brought together the Filipino workers of the Agricultural Workers Organizing Committee (AWOC) and the Mexican workers of the National Farm Workers Association (NFWA) in a joint strike.

One of the important labor actions the UFW did to gather support for the Grape Strike was a 300-mile march from the UFW headquarters in Delano in the Central Valley to the State Capitol in Sacramento. The march started on March 17th, 1966, when 75 Filipino and Mexican farm workers started their long trek down from Delano, taking country roads close to Highway 99, all the way up to Sacramento. They were stopping and spending the night at small towns along the way, giving speeches, theater performances, and singing songs. They were following in the tradition of nonviolent protests started by Mahatma Gandhi in India and Dr. Martin Luther King, Jr. in the South. The march to Sacramento was very successful. By the time, the Filipinos and Mexicans arrived in Sacramento, they were now 10,000 marchers strong, and the march brought more media coverage and national support to the UFW grape strike.

Among the Grape Strike marchers who started the walk from Delano with Chavez was Andy Imutan, a former Sacramento resident who lived in his retirement years near the Mack Road area of Sacramento. Imutan was an immigrant from the Philippines who arrived in Los Angeles with his wife in 1965. They then moved to Delano to be closer to family. After hearing Itliong speak of the plight of Filipino farm workers, he immediately became involved with AWOC as a volunteer. Imutan was one of the original union organizers to sign the charter to form the UFW union. Because of their closeness in age, Imutan and Chavez quickly became close friends. When the UFW started a national boycott of California grapes, Imutan was responsible for organizing the East Coast boycott. The national boycott was a strategy that eventually won the Grape Strike, and Imutan played an important role in the success of that boycott.

The connection to the Filipino and Mexican farmworkers remains a strong thread in the California Assembly. Rob Bonta (Democrat, 18 District) is the first Filipino American Assembly member to be elected to office. He is the son of Filipino labor union organizers and grew up in La Paz, in Kern County, in a "trailer just a few hundred yards from Cesar

Chavez's home." His parents were civil rights activists and labor union organizers who worked with the UFW to organize Filipino and Mexican farm workers. Cynthia Bonta, his mother, eventually settled and lived in Sacramento for several years and was a very active member of the Filipino American community. Rob Bonta attended Bella Vista High School in Fair Oaks and went to college at Yale University and at Oxford University and earned a law degree from Yale. He served as a lawyer in for the City and County of San Francisco and eventually became elected into the California Legislature in 2012, the first Filipino to be elected into the State Assembly.

Today, the first Filipino American Chief Justice of the California Supreme Court is a Sacramento-born resident whose Filipino-Portuguese father is from Hawaii and whose mother is Filipino. Tani Gorre Cantil-Sakauye is the 28th Chief Justice of the Supreme Court and the first Asian American to be appointed to the Court. She is a graduate of C.K. McClatchy High School and Sacramento City College. She went on to earn her undergraduate college and law degree from the University of California at Davis. After serving more than 20 years as a judge in Sacramento, she was nominated by Governor Arnold Schwarzenegger as Chief Justice of the California Supreme Court, and approved unanimously by California voters in November 2010. She was sworn into office on January 3rd, 2011.

木屋拘留幾十天，所因墨例致牽連。可惜英雄無用武，只聽杳來策程鞭。

從今遠別此樓中，各位鄉君家歡同。莫道其間囚西武，災感軍顏夾如籠。

No hea a hele mai wau? No hea a hele mai wau?
No hea a hele mai wau? No hea a hele mai wau?
No hea a hele mai wau? Where I come from?
No hea a hele mai wau? No hea a hele mai wau?
No hea a hele mai wau? No hea a hele mai wau?
No hea a hele mai wau? No hea a hele mai wau?
No hea a hele mai wau? No hea a hele mai wau?
No hea a hele mai wau? No hea a hele mai wau?
No hea a hele mai wau? No hea a hele mai wau?
No hea a hele mai wau? No hea a hele mai wau?
No hea a hele mai wau? No hea a hele mai wau?
¿De donde vengo? No hea a hele mai wau?
No hea a hele mai wau? No hea a hele mai wau?
No hea a hele mai wau? No hea a hele mai wau?
No hea a hele mai wau? No hea a hele mai wau?
No hea a hele mai wau? No hea a hele mai wau?
No hea a hele mai wau? No hea a hele mai wau?
No hea a hele mai wau? Where do I come from?
No hea a hele mai wau? No hea a hele mai wau?
No hea a hele mai wau? No hea a hele mai wau?
No hea a hele mai wau? No hea a hele mai wau?
No hea a hele mai wau? No hea a hele mai wau?
No hea a hele mai wau? No hea a hele mai wau?
No hea a hele mai wau? No hea a hele mai wau?
No hea a hele mai wau? No hea a hele mai wau?
No hea a hele mai wau? No hea a hele mai wau?
No hea a hele mai wau? No hea a hele mai wau?
Where I come from? No hea a hele mai wau?
No hea a hele mai wau? No hea a hele mai wau?

Unit III

A Glimpse of California

Chapter 19

No Utopia: The African American Struggle for Fair Housing in Postwar Sacramento From 1948 to 1967

Damany Fisher

Important Words and Concepts

There are several important words and concepts throughout the upcoming chapter. The words appear several times in different places in order to help you remember the words and understand the chapter. The words are defined several times:

- Immediately below right before the chapter begins
- In text boxes throughout the chapter
- In red and boldfaced within the chapter
- In a glossary in expanded form at the end of the units

Some of the words also appear in other chapters. Talk about the words with other students, teachers, friends, and family members before you read, while reading the chapter, and after you have read the chapter.

Utopia

(a) An imaginary and indefinitely remote place, (b) a place of ideal perfection especially in laws, government, and social conditions, and (c) an impractical scheme for social improvement.

Contributed by Damany Fisher. © Kendall Hunt Publishing Company.

Jim Crow System

As African Americans obtained political power and began the long march toward greater social and economic equality, Whites reacted with panic and outrage. Southern conservatives vowed to reverse Reconstruction . . . Their campaign to "redeem" the South was reinforced by a resurgent Ku Klux Klan, which fought a terrorist campaign against Reconstruction governments and local leaders, complete with segregation, bombings, lynchings, and mob violence.

Second Great Migration

Historians will argue that the effects of the second migration precipitated a more enduring transformation of American life, for both Blacks and Whites. However, many of the factors that spurred migration remained the same. The economy, jobs, and racial discrimination remained top factors for Black migration to the North. The advent of World War II contributed to an exodus out of the South, with 1.5 million African Americans leaving during the 1940s; a pattern of migration which would continue at that pace for the next 20 years. The result would be the increased urbanization of the African American population, with fewer Blacks working in agriculture or domestic labor.

Segregation

The separation or isolation of a race, class, or ethnic group by enforced or voluntary residence in a restricted area, by barriers to social intercourse, by separate educational facilities, or by other discriminatory means.

Double V Campaign

A symbol and a national campaign that urged Black people to give their all for the war effort, while at the same time calling on the government to do all it could to make the rhetoric of the Declaration of Independence and the equal rights amendments to the Constitution real for every citizen, regardless of race.

Nonviolent Direct Action

Nonviolent action refers to those methods of protest, resistance, and intervention without physical violence in which the members of the nonviolent group do, or refuse to do, certain things.

Racially Restrictive Covenants

An agreement between a person selling property and a person buying the property to restrict the future sale of the property to people of a particular race. Race-restrictive covenants are recorded on property deeds.

Federal Housing Administration

The The Freedom of Information Act (FOIA) generally provides that any person has the right to request access to federal agency records or information except to the extent the records are protected from disclosure by any exemptions contained in the law or by one of the three special law enforcement record exclusions.

Veterans Administration (VA)

The U.S. Department of Veterans Affairs is a government-run military veteran benefit system with Cabinet-level status. The VA provides health, home loan, and education benefits and other services to U.S. military veterans.

Congress of Racial Equality (CORE)

Founded in 1942 as the Committee of Racial Equality by an interracial group of students in Chicago. Many of these students were members of the Chicago branch of the Fellowship of Reconciliation (FOR), a pacifist organization seeking to change racist attitudes. The founders of the CORE were deeply influenced by Mahatma Gandhi's teachings of nonviolent resistance.

Home Owner's Loan Corporation (HOLC)

It is a former U.S. government agency established in 1933 to help stabilize real estate that had depreciated during the depression and to refinance the urban mortgage debt. It granted long-term mortgage loans to some one million homeowners facing loss of their property. The HOLC ceased its lending activities in June 1936, by the terms of the Home Owners' Loan Act.

Sacramento Committee for Fair Housing Colored (SCFH)

A civil rights organization advocating for fair housing in Sacramento alongside other organizations such as CORE and the National Council for the Advancement of Colored People (NAACP).

National Council for the Advancement of Colored People (NAACP)

The mission of the NAACP is to ensure the political, educational, social, and economic equality of rights of all persons and to eliminate race-based discrimination.

Introduction

In August 1948, the highly influential Black newspaper, the *Pittsburgh Courier*, described Sacramento, California, as "near utopia" and one of the most democratic and progressive cities for African Americans. "There is comparatively little concern with regard to where Negroes may own and occupy property here

> **Utopia:** A place of ideal perfection especially in laws, government, and social conditions.

[in Sacramento]," the article read, "consequently, one finds Negroes owning property and dwelling in all sections of this beautiful little city which justly has become recognized as the melting pot of the West. Here in this tranquil valley town one finds Caucasians, Japanese, Mexicans, Negroes, Filipinos and Indians, living, working and playing side by side together in peace and harmony."[1] In his weekly editorial for the *Sacramento Outlook*, attorney Nathaniel Colley, no doubt, spoke for many Blacks living in the city when he accused the *Courier* reporter of being "guilty of a little exaggeration of the virtues of Sacramento." He encouraged the reporter to return to the city and attempt to purchase a home in one of Sacramento's sprawling postwar suburbs. "For from nothing to about five hundred dollars down, any White ex-GI may move into one of these new homes today or tomorrow," said Colley, "But no Negro ex-GI, no matter how honorably he served his country, nor how much he can pay down, may buy one of these houses." Although he acknowledged that Sacramento was more "democratic" than other cities, it was no "Utopia" for Blacks. Colley insisted that if Black Sacramentans agreed with the *Courier's* conclusion regarding conditions in their city, "one of these days we are going to wake up and find Sacramento no different from Birmingham [Alabama]."[2]

Colley's warning that Sacramento might become another Birmingham, Alabama, must have frightened many African Americans living in the city. Like other cities across the South, Birmingham's neighborhoods, schools, and public places were racially segregated. Blacks were not permitted to live or attend school with Whites. Although the color line in Sacramento was not as rigidly drawn as it was in Birmingham, Black Sacramentans encountered enough obstacles to justify Colley's statement. Since many

---

1   Williams (1948).
2   Colley (1948), 2010/036, Center for Sacramento History, Nathaniel S. and Jerlean J. Colley Papers, c. 1940–1992.

of Sacramento's Black population had left the South to escape its Jim Crow system, they had no desire to see Jim Crow flourish in the city. Thus, over the next two decades, African Americans and their allies took part in a movement that challenged housing discrimination in Sacramento.

Jim Crow System: A system of extremely unfair and often violent legal and illegal acts committed against African Americans after Slavery ended and Reconstruction began.

This movement began after World War II as hundreds of African Americans moved to Sacramento. This wave of Black migration to Sacramento during the 1940s and 1950s reflected a larger migration pattern called the Second Great Migration. Between 1940 and 1970, over 5 million Blacks moved out from South of the America to northern and western cities like New York, Chicago, and Los Angeles. The main reason why so many Blacks left the South was due to the expectation that cities in the North and West offered higher paying jobs, a quality education for their children, and better race relations. This certainly motivated newcomers like Nathaniel Colley to move to Sacramento in the 1940s. African Americans, however, learned quickly that the reality of conditions in their newly adopted homes did not always match their expectations. Racial discrimination in jobs, housing, and recreation existed in cities like Sacramento too. Such conditions inspired a new generation of activists to try to make Sacramento a place of greater opportunity for everyone, regardless of race. They lent their talents and skills to civil rights groups like the National Association for the Advancement of Colored People (NAACP). Originally founded in 1909, the NAACP fought to end segregation and give Blacks the right to vote. Though it was a national organization, the NAACP had chapters in cities and towns across the nation. The Sacramento chapter, for example, led several campaigns to end segregation and discrimination in the city, including the removal of "Whites only" signs from businesses and pressuring firms like Campbell's Soup to hire more African Americans. The Sacramento NAACP did not operate alone; rather, it operated alongside other groups such as the Sacramento Committee for Fair Housing (SCFH), the Congress of Racial Equality (CORE), and concerned individuals committed to change. This movement to end racial discrimination in Sacramento's housing market took place in the courts, in publications, and in public demonstrations.

The Origins of Residential Segregation in Sacramento

Housing discrimination in Sacramento contradicted the myth of a "utopian" city for African Americans. Before World War II, the city's housing market relegated the majority of African Americans to the West End, an area of downtown Sacramento located between the Sacramento River and the state capitol building. Although Blacks had lived in the West End since the 1850s, they remained concentrated in the district well into the twentieth century. This pattern did not result from accident but rather through coercion. Convinced that African Americans and non-Whites lowered property values and quality of life, White real-estate agents and property owners tried to keep them out of certain neighborhoods. The most common and effective means of racial exclusion were informal agreements among real-estate agents and property owners not to rent or sell houses to Blacks in a specific area. Realtors, meanwhile, steered Blacks into areas that were either all-Black or areas with an increasing Black population. Another practice of homeowners and the real-estate industry that became particularly widespread in the 1920s was the application of racially restrictive covenants. A covenant is a promise written into a deed that tells a property owner what he or she can and cannot do to their property. In this case, a racially restrictive covenant barred homeowners from selling or leasing their property to African Americans and other non-Whites, usually for a period ranging from 20 to 30 years. As in other cities, the combination of day-to-day practices and racially restrictive covenants in Sacramento meant that many of its neighborhoods excluded Blacks, Mexicans, and Asians.

Lack of housing options for African Americans occurred at the same time many White residents enjoyed almost unlimited access to new suburbs—areas located directly outside the city—such as Oak Park, Curtis Park, East Sacramento, and Land Park. The Home Owner's Loan Corporation (HOLC) confirmed this pattern in its survey of Sacramento neighborhoods in 1937–1938. Established in 1933, the HOLC supplied emergency loans to some struggling homeowners at risk of having their property seized by a bank or lending association. In 1935, HOLC staff began conducting surveys to determine mortgage risks in 239 cities, including Sacramento. Although these surveys did not determine eligibility for HOLC loans, they did provide revealing neighborhood patterns and trends. Typically for a neighborhood to receive a high grade, it had to have new single-family homes, fewer people, no poverty, and *no* people of color, including African Americans, Asians, and Latinos. Surveyors desired to know whether an area had homes with race-restrictive covenants and whether these covenants had been in effect. Land Park and the majority of neighborhoods in Curtis Park and East Sacramento received the highest ratings largely due to their all-White population or, as the survey stated, "racial homogeneity"; whereas, the West End and other neighborhoods with either large or growing non-White populations received the lowest ratings. Surveyors stated that the West End suffered from congestion and "large numbers of subversive racial elements," an unsubtle ref-

> **Race-Restrictive Covenants:** An agreement between a person selling property and a person buying the property, to restrict the future sale of the property to people of a particular race. Race restrictive covenants are recorded on property deeds.

erence to Blacks, Japanese, and other non-White ethnic groups in the district. In contrast, the HOLC had much better evaluations for the various neighborhoods comprising Oak Park. In the late 1930s, Oak Park was a mostly White neighborhood. Although a few Black, Asian, and Latino families had moved into the area, the HOLC considered their numbers small enough so as to not raise concern. According to the area description, "[Oak Park] Realtors state that the few scattered Negro families [six known] are old residents and do not affect values beyond adjoining property." Even still, their evaluation mentioned the "danger of subversive racial infiltration" and the "age and obsolescence" of its buildings as warning signs of future deterioration and low desirability.[3] The significance of these surveys is that they confirm how real-estate agents and homeowners had successfully excluded African Americans from much of the city's suburbs. Moreover, they foreshadowed later housing patterns in neighborhoods like Oak Park whose Black population skyrocketed as real-estate agents steered more and more Black families into the district.

As the rate of Black migration to Sacramento increased in the 1940s, so too did the number of hurdles Blacks had to go through to find decent housing. Many Whites reacted with alarm and fear as the Black presence became more noticeable. For example, on January 21, 1944, homeowners in the Curtis Oaks subdivision of Curtis Park circulated a "Declaration of Restrictions" that excluded "any person of either Hindu, African, Japanese, Chinese, or Mongolian descent" from renting, leasing, or owning property in the neighborhood. Over 200 homeowners in the subdivision signed the declaration.[4] Such measures help to explain why some Black residents like Vincent "Ted" Thompson recalled feeling that it "began to get … harder and harder to rent property or to buy property and it came to the point where they [real-estate agents] did try to corral the Blacks into staying in the West End…"[5] Indeed, the West End remained the main point of entry for most Black migrants to Sacramento in the 1940s. Many migrants took up residence in boarding houses and homes that used to belong to Japanese Americans sent to concentration camps during World War II. Others moved into Del Paso Heights, an unincorporated, semirural district north of the city. The process of steering Blacks to the West End, Del Paso Heights, and Oak Park accelerated after the war. "Any lack who ventured from the confines of the lower end [West End] or Del Paso Heights, the black areas, and attempted to purchase property was faced with much opposition," said Dr. Kenneth Johnson, a prominent Black doctor in Sacramento who arrived in the 1940s.[6] Johnson blamed much of this opposition on Sacramento real-estate agents. Another Black migrant, Freddie Martin, agreed. In 1944, a real-estate agent told Martin that he was only going to show him houses in Oak Park and Del Paso Heights. Faced with little choice, he settled on a home in Oak Park. "The realtor would take you to Del Paso Heights," said Martin, "if that didn't suit you, he would take you to Oak Park, and if that didn't suit you, they had to see you later." One of Martin's friends had a similar experience. After showing a White real-estate agent a house he wished to buy, the agent advised him to "pick a block that had colored [people] living on it."[7]

3　Mariano, Goldberg, and Hou (2013). This website includes digital copies of original documents and maps from the Federal Home Loan Bank Board's "City Survey Program" for Sacramento, the Bay Area, Stockton, and Los Angeles.

4　Tract restrictions of Curtis Oaks to Joseph Korn (1945).

5　Thompson (1984).

6　McMahon (1972).

7　See Footnote 6, p. 82.

The housing dilemma for Blacks in Sacramento only worsened as a result of government policy. During the 1930s and 1940s, the Federal Housing Administration (FHA), created by the National Housing Act of 1934, and the Veterans Administration (VA), revolutionized home financing by providing mortgage insurance and other incentives that revived the nation's construction industry, providing millions of Americans the opportunity to purchase homes, typically in new suburbs. At the same time, these federal agencies contributed to the residential segregation of African Americans by encouraging real-estate developers and agents to apply race-restrictive covenants to their properties. Like elsewhere, FHA- and VA-insured subdivisions throughout Sacramento County usually contained such clauses in their deeds or contracts.

Post-World War II Migration and the Beginning of the Fair Housing Movement in Sacramento

During the 1940s and 1950s, California became one of the main arenas for organizing around fair housing and equal employment. The "Double V" campaign—victory over fascism abroad and racism at home—spearheaded by the *Pittsburgh Courier* during World War II inspired African Americans and their allies to redouble their efforts to end Jim Crow in the United States and force the nation to live up to its creed. This spirit fuelled a surge in membership in the Sacramento NAACP; by the late 1940s, the branch now had the energy, manpower, and resources to demand better housing and jobs in the city. Reflecting the diverse range Sacramento's expanding Black population, this movement included everyone from university-trained professionals to city sanitation

> The "Double V" campaign—victory over fascism abroad and racism at home—spearheaded by the *Pittsburgh Courier* during World War II inspired African Americans and their allies to redouble their efforts to end Jim Crow in the United States

employees. It also involved a growing number of Black military personnel stationed at McClellan and Mather Fields. Some had come from all-Black communities in the Midwest and South and were accustomed to seeing Blacks working in skilled trades and professions.

Virna Canson had come from such a community and embodied this new Double V spirit. She had spent her early years in the historically all-Black town of Lima, Oklahoma, where it was not unusual to see Black teachers, attorneys, physicians, insurance agents, and entrepreneurs. "We were constantly exposed to people who were contributing," said Canson, "and people who had a very high sense of values and assumed the responsibilities of leadership." Upon graduating from high school, Canson attended Tuskegee Institute where she met her future husband and Sacramento native, Clarence Bernard Canson. After they got married, the couple decided to move to Sacramento. Upon arriving, Mrs. Canson expressed shock and disappointment over the striking absence

Percentage of Black Residents by Census Tract, 1950
Sacramento, California

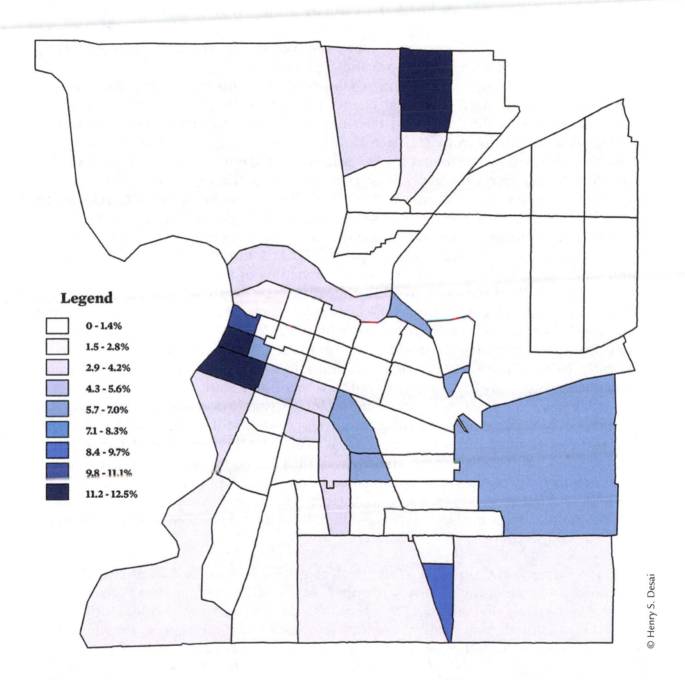

Legend

- 0 - 1.4%
- 1.5 - 2.8%
- 2.9 - 4.2%
- 4.3 - 5.6%
- 5.7 - 7.0%
- 7.1 - 8.3%
- 8.4 - 9.7%
- 9.8 - 11.1%
- 11.2 - 12.5%

© Henry S. Desai

of Black professionals and Black-owned businesses. "I didn't see any [positive] symbols for black people [in Sacramento]," remembered Canson, "Clarence's father was in business … But there were no [black] teachers … no [black] policemen." She recalled the difficulties her university-educated husband had trying to find work in Sacramento that matched his education. Faced with little choice, Clarence worked as a sanitation employee at McClellan Field in Sacramento under a White supervisor who, in her words, possessed only a "third-grade education."[8] Black conditions in Sacramento persuaded her to join the NAACP and fight. Canson represented the postwar generation of Blacks who had been lured to Sacramento by the prospect of finding their "utopia" only to be betrayed by the reality that such a place did not exist for them. Though disappointed and perhaps discouraged, many resolved to stay and transform the city to bring it more in line with Black hopes and expectations.

Still the absence of Black attorneys who could take up civil rights cases continued to be a frustrating reality. That changed, however, in 1948, with the arrival of Nathaniel Sextus Colley. Born and raised in Snow Hill, Alabama, Nathaniel Colley graduated with honors from Tuskegee University in 1941. Despite being turned away from the University of Alabama for law school after serving in World War II, Colley was admitted to Yale University. After graduating near the top of his class in 1948, several universities offered him teaching posts. Colley, though, decided to relocate to his wife's hometown, Sacramento. His entrance marked an important turning point in the civil rights struggle in Sacramento, which at the time had no practicing Black attorneys. Colley helped transform the Sacramento NAACP into a more effective organization, winning several suits on behalf of Black victims of police brutality and various forms of racial discrimination. In 1951, the West Coast Regional Office of the NAACP (NAACP-WC) designated Colley as the legislative representative of the NAACP for the state of California and the following year he helped form the NAACP-WC Regional Legal Redress Committee along with attorneys Loren B. Miller and Terry Francois. By the early 1950s, Colley had distinguished himself as a brilliant lawyer and champion of civil rights not only in Sacramento but throughout the state.

Colley was at the center of the most important legal battle over housing in Sacramento County. On May 10, 1954, the legal committee of Colley, Miller, and Franklin Williams filed suit on behalf of Oliver A. Ming, a Black World War II veteran and McClellan Field employee, and nine other African Americans against several of the largest real estate and construction firms operating in Sacramento county. Ming had attempted to purchase a home in McClellan Meadows, a section of North Highlands. Despite the fact that Ming met all qualifications, the NAACP charged that the real-estate broker, Milton G. Horgan,

In 1961, Leonard Cain Jr., a White professor of sociology at Sacramento State College and one of the founding members of the SCFH, published a report entitled *Housing Discrimination in Metropolitan Sacramento*. This particular study was the first detailed analysis of residential segregation in Sacramento, drawing on census reports and other documents to support his conclusions.

8 Regional Oral History Office, Oral Interview with Virna M. Canson, Waging the War on Poverty and Discrimination in California through the National Association for the Advancement of Colored People, 1953–1974, 1984, ROHO, The Bancroft Library, University of California, Berkeley, Government History Documentation Project, Ronald Reagan Gubernatorial Era.

Percentage of Black Residents by Census Tract, 1960
Sacramento, California

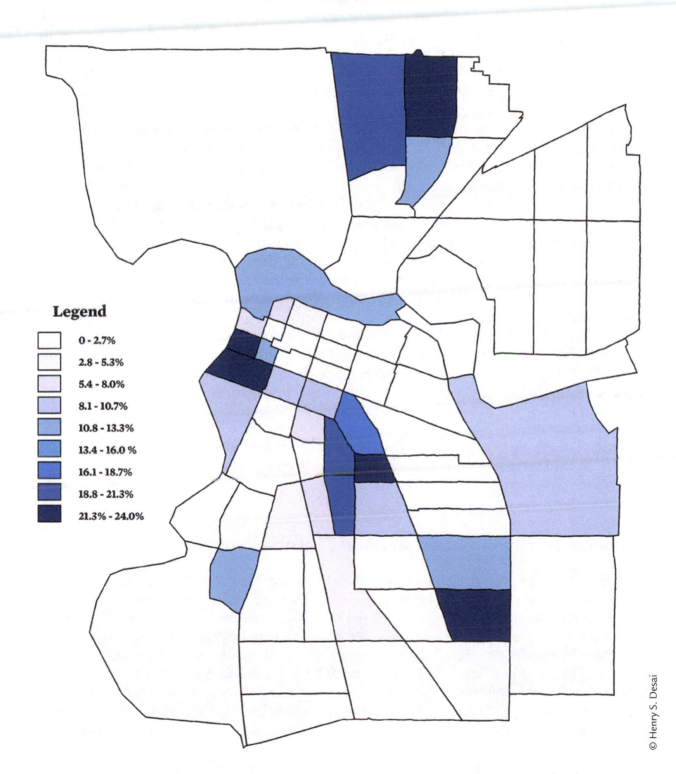

Legend

- 0 - 2.7%
- 2.8 - 5.3%
- 5.4 - 8.0%
- 8.1 - 10.7%
- 10.8 - 13.3%
- 13.4 - 16.0 %
- 16.1 - 18.7%
- 18.8 - 21.3%
- 21.3% - 24.0%

© Henry S. Desai

rejected his application because of his race. Other defendants named in the suit included the Sacramento Real Estate Board (SREB), McBride Realty Company, Hackes & Hurst Real Estate, and other homebuilders and real-estate brokers that had built and sold the majority of houses in Sacramento County since 1944 with the use of federal mortgage insurance. The suit accused the defendants of having conspired not to sell homes to African Americans in violation of federal and state law.

Coming in the wake of the 1954 Supreme Court decision, *Brown v. Board of Education*, which declared racial segregation in public schools unconstitutional, NAACP legal committee felt that the *Ming* case would give the court's decision real meaning. What good would it be to desegregate schools and not desegregate neighborhoods where those schools exist? On June 23, 1958, Sacramento Superior Court Judge James Oakley ruled in favor of Oliver Ming. He agreed with Ming's attorneys that the National Housing Act of 1934 sought to provide adequate housing for all Americans regardless of race; therefore, the FHA, he argued, could not "play favorites as to race, color, or creed." Because real-estate developers benefited from receiving mortgage loan guarantees from the federal government meant that they had to treat all applicants equally. Borrowing a quote from Colley, Judge Oakley stated that "when one dips one's hand into the Federal Treasury a little democracy clings to whatever is withdrawn."[9] Judge Oakley issued an injunction or court order that forbade racial discrimination in the purchase or sale of homes built with federal assistance in Sacramento County; it also ordered the defendants to accept and process the applications of Ming and other African Americans for whom the defendants had previously rejected. The Ming case marked the first successful legal challenge to racial discrimination in federally supported private housing and Colley's signal achievement in his long and illustrious legal career.

> Judge Oakley issued an injunction or court order that forbade racial discrimination in the purchase or sale of homes built with federal assistance in Sacramento County.

Nonviolent Direct Action and Civil Disobedience

Unfortunately, the *Ming* decision came too late to reverse decades of residential segregation in Sacramento. By 1960, restrictive covenants, redevelopment, and government policies had created a landscape where the vast majority of Blacks tended to be concentrated in Oak Park, Del Paso Heights, and Glen Elder. This residential pattern did not go unnoticed. In 1961, Leonard Cain Jr., a White professor of sociology at Sacramento State College and one of the founding members of the SCFH, published a report entitled *Housing Discrimination in Metropolitan Sacramento*. This particular study was the first detailed analysis of residential segregation in Sacramento, drawing on census reports and other documents to support his conclusions. "It is abundantly clear," he declared, "that Oak Park

---

9   Oliver A. Ming v. Milton G. Horgan, et al., 3 Race Rel. L. Rep. 695-97 (Calif. Super. Ct. 1958).

has replaced the redeveloped West End as Sacramento's new downtown Negro community, with a concentration of Negroes not previously experienced in the West End." Cain charged that local real-estate firms, lending agencies, and home sellers were primarily responsible "for keeping many Negroes from exercising a wider choice in the purchase or rental of homes."[10] Oak Park, Del Paso Heights, and Glen Elder, reported Cain, accounted for approximately half of African Americans living in the Sacramento Metropolitan Area; by contrast, northeast Sacramento County, which included the districts of Arden-Arcade, Carmichael, Fair Oaks, Citrus Heights, and Orangevale—not coincidentally, areas where the vast majority of FHA-insured housing had been built—had only 42 Blacks out of a population of 71,356, or less than 0.06%. Since the end of World War II, African Americans in Sacramento had charged the local real-estate industry of steering them into Oak Park, Del Paso Heights, and Glen Elder; Cain's research supported this trend. Fair housing activists in Sacramento understood that the fight against housing discrimination was just beginning.

At the dawn of the 1960s, new organizations like the SCFH joined existing organizations such as the CORE in drawing attention to challenges Blacks faced trying to secure decent housing. Established in 1961, the SCFH drew from a cross section of academics, civic, and religious leaders "to help insure equality of opportunity for housing for all persons of metropolitan Sacramento without regard to race, religion, or national origin."[11] The SCFH specifically singled out the local real-estate industry as the main obstacle to open housing in Sacramento. To prove this they organized into five different teams, each consisting of one Black and one White prospective buyer, and visited 13 new subdivisions throughout the county to inquire about purchasing a home. Each team member had roughly the same qualifications, including education, occupation, and income level. Not surprisingly, White participants received more tours of model homes than their Black counterparts. Generally, White participants received far more encouragement from agents of housing developments and offered more incentives to move into the unit. Deeply shaken by the results of this experiment, SCFH members determined to go on the offensive. Using **direct action** to draw public attention to racial bias in Sacramento's housing market, in June 1962, the SCFH began a 3-month campaign protesting housing discrimination in the new South Land Park Hills tract after Arthur Lyman, an African American physicist at Aerojet-General Corporation, had recently been denied a home in the development. Standing in solidarity with Lyman, the committee staged demonstrations outside new model homes in the South Land Park Hills. After weeks of protest and public scrutiny, the SCFH campaign began to produce its desired effect and scare away many potential customers. The campaign ended only after the SCFH received assurances from the developer, Shepard and Skover, that it would

> **Nonviolent Direct Action:** Methods of protest, resistance, and intervention without physical violence in which the members of the nonviolent group do, or refuse to do, certain things.

---

10 Cain (1961); "S.S.C. Prof says" (1961).
11 "Fair Housing Committee" (1961).

include a nondiscrimination policy regarding home sales. But 5 years after this incident, the same firm became the target of a civil suit after a Black dentist alleged discrimination after being denied a home in the same tract.

Although the SCFH staged its direct action on the streets of Sacramento, CORE's direct action campaign took place at the state capital. On February 14, 1963, California Assemblyman W. Byron Rumford from Berkeley introduced A.B. 1240, which prohibited discrimination in publicly assisted housing to private housing in addition to the selling, renting, or leasing of property. On May 28, 1963, a dozen Black and White CORE members invaded the rotunda of the state capitol and promised to remain until the legislature passed the Rumford Act. Over the next few days, dozens of CORE members from across the state came to Sacramento to take part in the demonstration. Rumford and several of his supporters, including the NAACP, expressed concern over CORE's action, fearing that such a move would alienate state legislators and undermine support for the bill. The NAACP preferred to work within the system and negotiate with state legislators. Many of the older NAACP members came to regard the actions of CORE and other civil rights organizations as potentially harmful to the civil rights cause. CORE, meanwhile, had grown increasingly impatient over the slowness of the legislature to enact fair housing laws.

> **The California state legislature finally passed the Rumford Act in June 1963. The final version prohibited racial discrimination in all publicly assisted single-family homes and apartments of five or more units.**

Despite determined opposition from the real-estate industry and many Republican legislators, the California state legislature finally passed the Rumford Act in June 1963. The final version prohibited racial discrimination in all publicly assisted single-family homes and apartments of five or more units. The Rumford Act was one of the most comprehensive fair housing laws passed in the postwar era and its passage precipitated a fierce counterattack by its opponents. One such opponent, the Committee for Home Protection, sponsored an initiative that was later designated as Proposition 14. The proposed constitutional amendment sought to overturn the Rumford Act. With help from mostly volunteer petitioners, the committee, along with other supporters, succeeded in collecting enough signatures to qualify for the next general election.

The battle over Proposition 14 became one of the most contentious initiatives in state history and many African Americans in California regarded it as a litmus test to determine the state's attitude toward civil rights. Therefore, when California voters overwhelmingly passed the proposition on November 3, 1964, by a two to one margin, many African Americans became disillusioned. Those who had migrated from other states felt particularly dejected because they had been led to believe that conditions in the state provided Blacks greater chances to lead fulfilling lives free of the blatant racism in the American South. Fair housing activists breathed a sigh of relief on May 10, 1966, when the California State Supreme Court ruled that Proposition 14 violated the U.S. Constitution. This decision was later upheld by the U.S. Supreme Court the following year.

Percentage of Black Residents by Census Tract, 1970
Sacramento, California

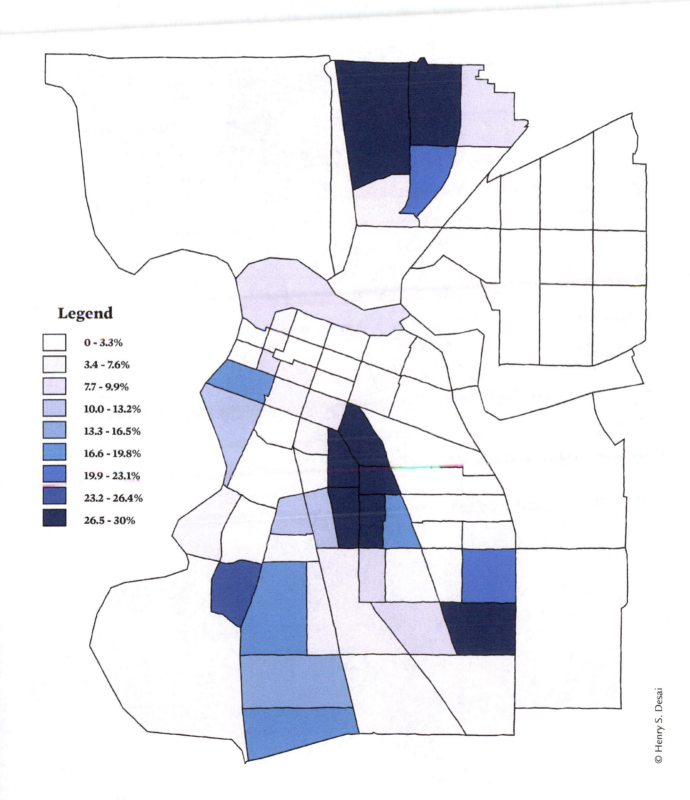

Legend

	0 - 3.3%
	3.4 - 7.6%
	7.7 - 9.9%
	10.0 - 13.2%
	13.3 - 16.5%
	16.6 - 19.8%
	19.9 - 23.1%
	23.2 - 26.4%
	26.5 - 30%

© Henry S. Desai

Percentage of Black Residents by Census Tract, 1980
Sacramento, California

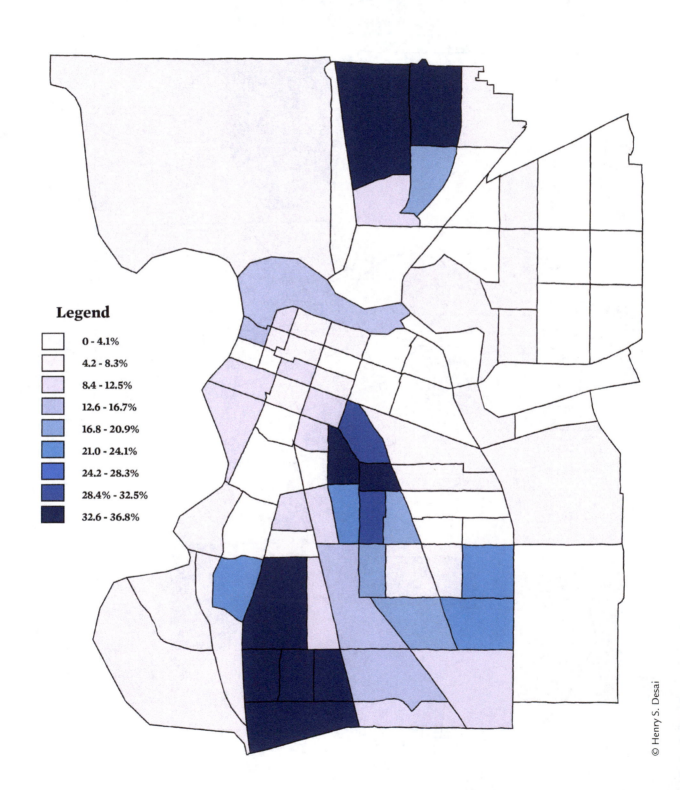

Legend

	0 - 4.1%
	4.2 - 8.3%
	8.4 - 12.5%
	12.6 - 16.7%
	16.8 - 20.9%
	21.0 - 24.1%
	24.2 - 28.3%
	28.4% - 32.5%
	32.6 - 36.8%

© Henry S. Desai

Conclusion

News of the Supreme Court's verdict vindicated the work of grass-roots organizations waging war against housing discrimination in Sacramento. Like the SCFH, these organizations represented a continuation of multiracial civil rights organizations operating in Sacramento dating back to the early 1950s. They demystified the notion held by many White Sacramentans that their city was free of the type of structural racism tearing apart other urban centers with large Black populations and, in the process, connected the struggle in Sacramento to the larger, national discussion on civil rights. But in the final analysis, such organizations failed to make significant progress in reversing housing discrimination trends in Sacramento. Older neighborhoods like Curtis Park and East Sacramento, along with suburban districts such as Fair Oaks and Carmichael remained overwhelmingly White through the 1970s and 1980s. Fair housing laws came way too late to prevent locking in the bulk of Sacramento's Black population into a few sections of the city. This pattern, of course, took place across much of America's urban landscape, leading historian Arnold Hirsch to the conclusion that the civil rights legislation that aimed to end housing discrimination in the 1960s "is not simply a matter of closing the barn door a little too slowly—the horse has not only escaped, but it has gotten into the trailer, moved down the interstate, and been put out to stud rural pastures."[12] In 1954, attorney Douglas Greer of the Sacramento NAACP had explained to the city council that unless the city guaranteed all of its residents equal access to housing, new slums would simply replace those located downtown. Unfortunately, his prophecy was fulfilled. The structural racism embedded in Sacramento's housing produced disastrous consequences for the city. By the late 1960s and early 1970s, Oak Park and Del Paso Heights had become Sacramento's symbol for the urban crisis. The flight of middle-class Whites and businesses from Oak Park in the postwar years, for example, left Oak Park in economic ruin. In 1973, the *Union* described Del Paso Heights as a "city apart," replete with substandard housing, inadequate services, and despair.[13] Bank redlining left Oak Park and Del Paso Heights mortgage deficient and starved of needed capital and resources. Indeed, the infrastructure of both districts had deteriorated to the point where each became the target of belated redevelopment efforts by the city in the 1970s that proved, ultimately, unable to reverse decades of neglect and decline. More than 20 years after the *Pittsburgh Courier*'s feature article on Sacramento, many African Americans found themselves still searching for that elusive "utopia."

---

12 Hirsch (1992).
13 Lee and Lee (1973).

Sacramento Neighborhoods

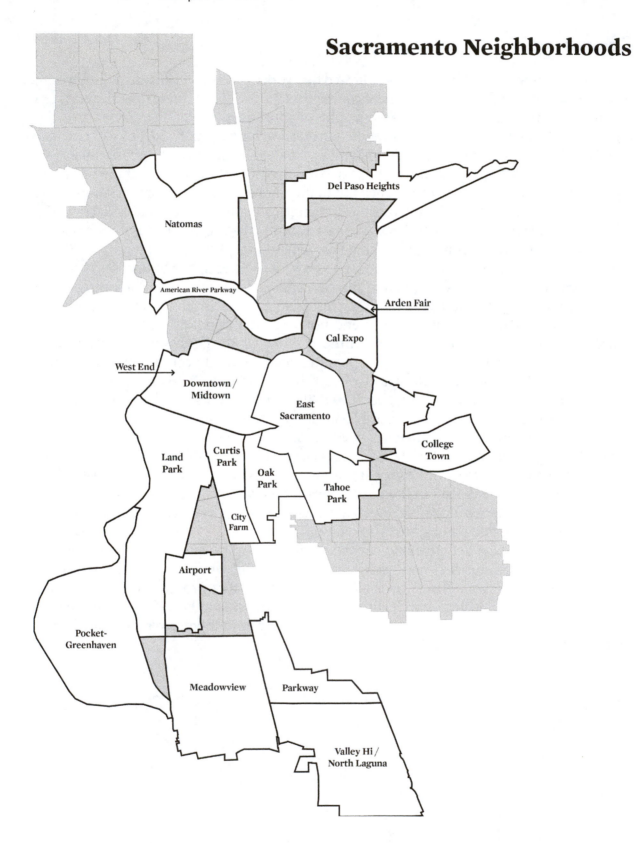

Natomas

Del Paso Heights

American River Parkway

Arden Fair

Cal Expo

West End

Downtown / Midtown

East Sacramento

Land Park

Curtis Park

Oak Park

Tahoe Park

College Town

City Farm

Airport

Pocket-Greenhaven

Meadowview

Parkway

Valley Hi / North Laguna

© Henry S. Desai

References

Cain, L. D. (1961). *Housing discrimination in Metropolitan Sacramento* (p. 3). Sacramento, CA: Sacramento Committee for Fair Housing.

Colley, N. S. (1948, August 31). One man's opinion. *Sacramento Outlook.*

Fair housing committee plans to elect officers. (1961, April 26). *Sacramento Bee.*

Hirsch, A. R. (1992). With or without Jim Crow: Black residential segregation in the United States. In A. R. Hirsch & R. A. Mohl (Eds.), *Urban policy in twentieth-century America* (p. 92). New Brunswick, NJ: Rutgers University Press.

Lee, K. W., & Lee, L. (1973). Del Paso Heights: A city apart. *Sacramento Union.*

Mariano, R., Goldberg, D., & Hou, C.-Y. (2013, May 11). *T-RACES: A testbed for the redlining archives of California's exclusionary spaces.* Retrieved from http://salt.unc.edu/T-RACES/references.html

McMahon, T. (Ed.) (1972). *A long look back: A special look at the history of Sacramento and the Black citizens who played a major role in that history* (p. 78). Sacramento, CA: William H. Lee.

S.S.C. Prof says segregation in city increases. (1961, May 22). *Sacramento Bee.*

Thompson, V. T. (1984, January 19). Interview by Clarence Caesar. Black Oral Histories 1983/146, Sacramento Ethnic Communities Survey, Sacramento, CA: Center for Sacramento History.

Tract restrictions of Curtis Oaks to Joseph Korn (p. 346). (1945, January 2). Sacramento, CA: Sacramento County Recorder's Office.

Williams, J. R. (1948, August 21). Color no handicap in Sacramento, California. *Pittsburgh Courier.*

Chapter 20

From Golden Empire to Valley High: A Mixed Girl's Education in Sacramento

Toni Tinker

Important Words and Concepts in This Chapter

There are several important words and concepts throughout the upcoming chapter. The words appear several times in different places in order to help you remember the words and understand the chapter. The words are defined several times:

- Immediately below right before the chapter begins
- In text boxes throughout the chapter
- In red and boldfaced within the chapter
- In a glossary in expanded form at the end of the units

Some of the words also appear in other chapters. Talk about the words with other students, teachers, friends, and family members before you read, while reading the chapter, and after you have read the chapter.

Black Political Thought

Originating from the institution of slavery, Black political thought has been framed by the historical and social experiences of the African American freedom struggle in the United States. The desire for liberty from enslavement provided initial parameters for the earliest political thinkers.

Assimilation

Assimilation is the process by which a minority individual or group takes on the characteristics of the majority and attempts to be accepted as part of the majority group.

Race

A classification of human beings into different categories on the basis of the way we look, for example, our skin color, head shape, eye color and shape, nose size and shape, and so forth.

Ethnicity

Membership or affiliation in a particular ethnic group.

Internalized Racism

Practices of inequality by racial ethnic minority group members against themselves or other members of their community.

Socioeconomic Status

Socioeconomic status is the social standing or class of an individual or group. It is often measured as a combination of education, income, and occupation. Examinations of socioeconomic status often reveal inequities in access to resources, plus issues related to privilege, power, and control.

Dominant Culture

Although *traditional societies* can be characterized by a high consistency of cultural traits and *customs*, modern societies are often a conglomeration of different, often competing, *cultures* and *subcultures*. In such a situation of diversity, a dominant culture is one that is able, through economic or political power, to impose its values, language, and ways of behaving on a subordinate culture or cultures.

Intersectionality

The interconnected nature of social categorizations such as race, class, and gender as they apply to a given individual or group, regarded as creating overlapping and interdependent systems of discrimination or disadvantage.

Spanglish

A hybrid language combining words and idioms from both Spanish and English.

Racial Restrictive Covenants

Restrictive covenants are agreements placed on people when they are selling their home. Racially restrictive covenants forbid the seller of a home to sell the house to people of different races, most often African American, Latinos, and Asian Americans. Racially restrictive covenants are illegal and homeowners can be Restrictive Covenant Modification to have the racially restrictive covenant removed from the property deed.

Ethnic Enclaves

Immigrant groups which concentrate in a distinct spatial location and organize a variety of enterprises serving their own ethnic market and/or the general population. Their basic characteristic is that a significant proportion of the immigrant workforce is employed in enterprises owned by other immigrants.

Social Construction

A theoretical approach which regard certain aspects of human experience and knowledge as originating within and cultivated by society or a particular social group, rather than existing inherently or naturally.

Cultural Values

Relatively general cultural prescriptions of what is right, moral, and desirable. Values provide the broad foundations for specific normative regulation of social interaction.

In late 2008, I found myself in quite a precarious position. I was a recently divorced mother of two small children and in my junior year of university, I was much older than most of the students. I was working an overnight stocking job at Target and living with my mother in order to make ends meet. My mother also helped me with child care so I had time to study. I was both excited and nervous, here I was taking political science and ethnic studies classes—two subjects I thoroughly enjoyed. I had transferred my credits from the community college to Sac State and I was determined to be the first person in my family to walk away with a 4-year degree.

So here I was sitting right in the front of my first black political thought class. I was ready. "Ready for what?" I was not sure. A few of my peers had warned me not to take this professor's course. "He's difficult and argumentative," they warned. "And his politics are so radical!" So, I was just ready for whatever this professor had to throw at me. Unfortunately, based solely on classmates descriptions I expected a very intense experience that would most likely result in my first official "F" at Sac State; but the professor that walked in and began talking—gave me reason to have a raised eyebrow.

He was a very tall, black man with an afro (of sorts). His posture could easily be described as open. He handed out the syllabus and immediately began to discuss the class. He cracked jokes and laughed at himself. We had a short conversation on the syllabus and class was over. Based on that day, I felt this was going to be easy. However, as the weeks moved on, I slowly began to get glimpses of the type of professor I had. Many times, I left the class angry. I felt sometimes at odds with my professor and many times at odds with my classmates; I was the lone opposing voice against most of the ideas and viewpoints that floated around my classroom. I felt left out of the conversations. At some point in the class, I even became very confused and angry. I was not sure that I wanted to continue with this course let alone, the major.

It was about the same time that I began to question my educational choices and my own position in the world. It is possibly not a coincidence that the politics of the country were doing much of the same thing. It is often that when things are happening in the world around you, you notice those same things happening in your personal life. Senator Barack Obama was running for President and up until that point, there had never been an African American candidate that had real potential to win. So, there was a lot of buzz that he was going to be the next great African American leader—a new age Martin Luther King.

However, this was not without much controversy. A good portion of the country was in as much turmoil as I was over race, ethnicity, and social status. The idea of an American President who was of African American decent had everyone on edge and trying to learn as much about this young mixed race senator from Chicago as they could—this included me and the members of my family. There was so much contradictory information about him circulating that it was difficult to tell what was true and what was not. I began to research who this man was on my own. The black political thought class was still always in the forefront of my thoughts. My involvement with the class along with my own self-interest in Barack Obama prompted me to read his autobiographical book entitled "Dreams from my Father."

I had a hard time putting the book down. I quickly discovered that Barack Obama and I had many things in common. The more I read and attended class, the more I began to reflect on my own life and upbringing. I began asking myself why I was taking this course of study. I wondered what a woman of my race and ethnicity, and socioeconomic status could contribute to the conversations. Why was I so seemingly different than other African Americans in my class?" One of the passages from Obama's book that stuck with me more than others and really echoed all of my questions: "I was too young to realize that I was supposed to have a live-in father, just as I was too young to realize I need a race." I was shocked that another person felt like this.

I felt that, because I was a woman of mixed heritage, I was often forced to choose a race. Race and socioeconomic standing play a huge part in how people live and work in Sacramento. The more I began to think about this, the more I kept going back to those original questions. I began to realize that everything about what made me feel so different in my black political thought class had everything to do with the **intersectionality** of race and class.

For much of my early childhood, I grew up in a very white, upper-middle class neighborhood in Mather and Rosemont. These areas at the time were predominantly white, with many of the military kids from the active base mixed in. I always thought life was good and simple coming from a mixed-race family. However, me being the mixed one, I occasionally got questioned when my very blonde, blue-eyed mother would pick me up from school. People were always asking "What are you?" or "Are you adopted?" to which I would reply, "No, that's my mom!" Race, to me, had no boundaries. I had white people who were part of my family and black people who were a part of my family. And although I did not know this at the time, I was being raised with a core ethnic studies understanding that race is a **social construction**.

Photo courtesy of Toni Tinker. © Kendall Hunt Publishing Company.

> . . . being the mixed one I occasionally got questioned when my very blonde, blue-eyed mother would pick me up from school. People were always asking "What are you?" or "Are you adopted?" to which I would reply, "No, that's my mom!"

I lived with my grandparents in a big house in a cul-de-sac that had a pool filled with frogs all the time. I had a pink and white frilly bedroom. My little brother and I were very lucky; our lives were simple. We had a room full of toys, new clothes that hung neatly in our closets, and we went on vacations—and not just in the summer.

I was lucky that my family had the ability to take vacations in the middle of the school year. During the time that I was in grade school, my grandparents could easily take my brother and I out of school for weeks at a time in the middle of instruction, and off we would go. We were sent with homework packets to keep up with our school work and told "I'm sure you will have a great time" or "what a lucky little girl you are." I never heard any negative discussions about my grandparents for taking us out of school during the school year. No threats of police or child welfare being called because my family wanted to spend time together and allow us to experience other opportunities that could not be found solely in school.

In the summer, my family and I made multiple trips to Disneyland, Universal Studios, San Diego, and camping trips in my grandparents RV. Summers passed way too quickly. I remember fishing with my grandfather from our boat, watching my brother water ski, and taking leisure rides on Lake Berryessa and Folsom Lake. In the winter, we enjoyed the holidays. We went on snow trips and skied, and decorated our Christmas tree with the big old fashion glass lights and glass icicles. My early childhood was brilliantly filled with the experience that I now reflect

back on; it was something that could be found in a Norman Rockwell painting.

As brilliant as I thought everything was, in 1985, my grandparents moved from our house in the cul-de-sac to a house closer to the public elementary school—Golden Empire Elementary. We moved because that year a plane that crashed at Mather AFB. It happened in the field behind our house. I remember that the force of the impact shook the entire house and the water in the pool sloshed out. After that my great-grandmother felt it wasn't safe for us to live there—plus she didn't drive. My great-grandmother refused to drive! She was also the caregiver to my younger brother and me while my grandparents worked as cross-country truck drivers. So, our access to a car was limited to only when my grandparents were home and as a result, my great-grandmother walked with my brother and me everywhere! Moving made it easier to get to places on foot.

My great-grandmother, Dorothy, was born in a tiny little town outside of Champaign, Illinois. She grew up during the depression and had a young family by World War II. The town she grew up in was a tiny town where everyone knew each other. All the residents there were white and because of the Racial Restrictive Covenants in the town, no one who was black was allowed to live in the town. My great-grandmother as she would explain, "never had any real reason to socialize with anyone black. It just wasn't needed."

My great-grandmother was divorced young and never remarried. She was a tough lady for her time. She worked at a dry cleaners, a bar, and in a shoe store that made custom shoes. When she came from Illinois to Sacramento by train with my 25-year-old divorced grandmother and my four-year-old mother, she worked as a waitress and bar manager at Mills Station in what is now Rancho Cordova. They moved around Sacramento quite a bit, but always stayed together. But the moves, from what I could tell, always revolved around the fact, according to my great-grandmother, that the neighborhood was bad. What I eventually learned is that this meant the neighborhood had too many people of color moving in.

My mother, however, did not live by my grandmothers' rules of who to live by or who to interact with. Despite several attempts to stop my mother from interacting with the "black side of town," I eventually was born and 2 years later, we welcomed my brother. My mother soon learned that as a young single parent, she did not have the time or resources to raise two small children. So, my brother and I eventually went to live permanently with my great-grandmother, my grandmother, and step-grandfather, in the big house with the pool.

I went to elementary school at Golden Empire Elementary. I played with my friends and interacted with my family. I had so few cares in the world. In my early years, my world and the outside world rarely touched each other. The color of my skin was not an issue for me and frankly, there was little reason for it. At this stage in life, the color of my skin was definitely not discussed in our house. In spite of the absence of talk about race from my close-knit family in a segregated community, race was everything and everywhere.

It was all the little things that every child learns while growing up; how to speak, how to sit at the dinner table, how to dress, how to wear your hair, and so forth. This, of course, all had its merits in how to interact with society, but for my great-grandmother it also had another purpose: how to not be too black. This message was front and center in every aspect of our education and upbringing. And, I was all too happy to accept this critique of my very make up. That's the funny thing about assimilation and internalized racism—they are quite effective tools in use in our culture that frame the mind to accept the dominant culture. As a young child learning how to lose these cultural aspects, you think nothing of it. However, later when you have matured, you realize quite quickly how you don't fit in with other people who look like you. You realize how much you've lost and how much is lost to you. You are angry and desperate to find ways to fit in and take in everything and anything you've lost.

> **Internalized Racism:** Accepting racist ideas or stereotypes from the dominant culture about one's own race or ethnicity.

I lived with my grandparents from birth to about age 13. I was happy until I reached the sixth grade. I enjoyed my life and loved my family. However, over the last year in sixth grade, my grandparents bought a trucking company in Woodland and we had to make the move there. For the first time, I was surrounded by kids who came from families that were very different than mine. Most of the families were Mexican; there were a couple of black kids, with the rest being white, poor, and working-class families. The kids I went to school with lived outside of the newly gated community in which I lived. They did not have a grandmother who took care of them. Most had keys to their houses and rode their bikes to school. Many spoke Spanish or Spanglish, had big extended families, and interacted like no families I had ever seen. Aunts, uncles, and cousins would get together on the weekends. Not all the families were like this but they all were very different in the way that they spoke to one another and interacted. As exciting as the new friends and their families were, I did not fit in. I lived in an area that many were not allowed to go to. Many of my friends were told that they should stay away from where I lived because they had no business there.

At 13, I was often hurt when I was told this. In hindsight, I now realize that it was a move by their parents to protect them from the people who lived in my community. Many of the parent's employers lived in the gated community. The mothers of a couple of the kids I went to school with cleaned house for some of our neighbors. My brother and I were the only African American kids who lived in the gated neighborhood. All of the African American kids lived in other parts of town. It became a lonely time for me. I began to make more and more contact with my mom who lived in Sacramento. I began to spend more and more of my weekends in Sacramento.

Sacramento in the late 1980s and early 1990s was a confusing time for people trying to understand the sociopolitical climate of the area; It was a time when there was a lack of diversity but the politicians wanted us to believe that we were in the forefront of progress in terms of racial diversity. However, Sacramento at times felt like a time warp, a bubble to the past.

Like most places, its ethnic populations were segregated into distinct **ethnic enclaves** throughout the city. North Highlands representing the poor white populations; the Central Sacramento area still housing many Chicano/Mexican populations; Oak Park and South Sac/Meadowview housing black populations; and of course, Folsom and Granite Bay remain the white enclaves that they are today. As a young girl, I knew nothing about any of them. But when I turned fourteen and my mother extended an invitation for me to come live with her in a 1950s bungalow in what is now lower Oak Park, behind the bar, The Touch of Class, I couldn't believe my luck because it all sounded exciting—I jumped at the chance. Unfortunately, I knew very little about where I was going to live. I did not know how different going to school at Kit Carson Middle School would be from Albert Einstein middle school, which I had previously attended. On my first day at Kit Carson, my whole world changed. I had never gone to school with so many other black kids in my life!

The interesting thing I realized is that the same feelings that I had as a kid living in Woodland with my grandmother are the same feelings I had living with my mother in Oak Park: I was surrounded by people and ideas that reflected their **Cultural Values**. My family did not raise me with a sense of being a mixed person. I was raised as an upper middle class white child. I had many privileges. However, as I grew and eventually came in contact with studies that both intrigued me and challenged me to look beyond my own comfort levels, I began to understand my own discomfort. Through this process, I began to understand that the discomfort that many of my classmates experienced was ongoing. I learned that many do not have the means or ability to fight back or even protect themselves from racism or prejudices of others. I also realized that the anger that I was experiencing had nothing to do with my classmates, and in some ways had everything to do with my own embarrassment and frustration with myself. I have always had the ability to walk away from any experience that made me feel threatened or uncomfortable.

Photo courtesy of Toni Tinker. © Kendall Hunt Publishing Company.

Chapter 21

Growing Up Mixed in Sacramento

Tiaura McQueen
Ms. Sims Ethnic Studies

This is a drawing of a mixed race girl titled "Growing Up Mixed In Sacramento." In the blue writing are quote about me and the things I went through, as a mixed race girl. She has black curly hair, as I do. She has a darker skin complexion and she also has freckles on her face.

Contributed by Tiaura McQueen. © Kendall Hunt Publishing Company.

This poster relates to me a lot because it's a drawing of a mixed race girl, and the quotes represent her experiences growing up in Sacramento, as I did. When I was growing up the things that would annoy me were the questions and the assumptions about my ethnicity. Most people would see me as a black person, but I always identified myself as being a mixed race person.

But people wouldn't see that, for example, people use to think my hair was fake because it was so curly and poofy. My message here is **don't be ashamed** about yourself no matter what your race or color. You shouldn't be afraid of being a mixed race person or wearing your natural hair out no matter what people have to say about it or what people think.

Chapter 22

Japanese Americans—Incarceration to Redress

Masayuki Hatano

Important Words and Concepts in This Chapter

There are several important words and concepts throughout the upcoming chapter. The words appear several times in different places in order to help you remember the words and understand the chapter. The words are defined several times:

- Immediately below right before the chapter begins
- In text boxes throughout the chapter
- In red and boldfaced within the chapter
- In a glossary in expanded form at the end of the units

Some of the words also appear in other chapters. Talk about the words with other students, teachers, friends, and family members before you read, while reading the chapter, and after you have read the chapter.

Japanese Aliens

In 1941, Japanese Americans were labelled as Enemy Aliens or Japanese Aliens.

Justice Department Internment Camps

After Japanese Americans were arrested during World War II they were taken to temporary Immigration and Naturalization Services (INS) detention centers. They were

Contributed by Masayuki Hatano. © Kendall Hunt Publishing Company then transferred to Department of Justice Internment camps where they awaited a hearing from the Alien Enemy Hearing Board to determine where they would stay for the remainder of the war.

Executive Order 9066

The Presidential Executive Order signed in 1942 by President Franklin D. Roosevelt requiring Japanese Americans to be imprisoned during World War II.

Federal Freedom of Information Act

The basic function of the Freedom of Information Act is to ensure informed citizens, vital to the functioning of a democratic society.

Relocation Camps

Another name for internment camps or concentration camps.

Immigrated

To have completed the immigration process and become established in some significant way in a new country.

Assembly Center

Another name given to the Internment Camps during World War II that imprisoned Japanese Americans.

Ancestry

1. Usually refers to an individual's family from many generations (e.g., an individual's grandparents' parents).
2. The origin of a phenomenon, object, idea, or style.

Concentration Camps

1. A camp where persons (such as prisoners of war, political prisoners, or refugees) are detained or confined.
2. A prison where people who are not soldiers are kept during a war and are usually forced to live in very bad conditions.

Public Law 96-317

To establish a Commission to gather facts to determine whether any wrong was committed against those American citizens and permanent resident aliens affected by Executive Order Numbered 9066, and for other purposes.

Start of World War II

On December 7, 1941, planes from the Empire of Japan attacked military installations at Pearl Harbor, Hawaii. Americans were totally surprised and extensive damage was done to Naval ships, aircrafts, military installations, and loss of lives.

The Federal Bureau of Investigation (FBI) had lists of primarily Japanese aliens. Within 48 hours, they had arrested over 1,000 men in Hawaii and the mainland. More would follow. These were ministers, schoolteachers, and presidents of various clubs such as local martial art clubs, prefecture clubs, owners of businesses, and others who were classified as leaders of their communities. They were placed in Justice Department Internment Camps in Santa Fe, New Mexico; Bismarck, North Dakota; Crystal City, Texas; and Missoula, Montana. Some of these men were incarcerated at these camps for the duration of the war while others were allowed to join their families in one of the ten permanent Relocation Camps.

On February 19, 1942, President Roosevelt issued Executive Order 9066 which authorized Military Commanders to establish Military zones and incarcerate anyone of Japanese ancestry, who lived in these zones. The commander, General DeWitt

Courtesy of Mas Hatano

Mas Hatano and family before World War II

of the Western Zone designated Alaska, part of Washington, part of Oregon, all of California, and part of Arizona as the Exclusion Zone. When the orders were issued. This included aliens and citizens (two-third were citizens), families, children, and anyone with 1/16th Japanese blood. Most were incarcerated in "Assembly Centers." These were temporary camps to hold the prisoners for 1–4 months until the 10 permanent camps could be built. These temporary camps were constructed or were County fairgrounds and the Santa Anita and Tanforan Race tracks where the people were housed in the horse stalls.

It is interesting to note that the Military Commander (General Emmons) in Hawaii chose not to incarcerate the Japanese relying on the FBI, Naval Intelligence, and State Department reports that indicated the Japanese were loyal and would not be a problem. Other considerations were that they were one-third of the population and their labor considerations would be acute if they incarcerated and had to replace them from the mainland.

Other actions were taken such as curfews, turning in guns, short-wave radios, cameras, and explosives. Travel was restricted to 5 miles away from home and no one could be out after dark.

Personal Narrative of Mas Hatano

In 1921, at Kumamoto, Japan, Yoshimasa Hatano and Yaeko were married. Shortly, after they immigrated to Isleton, California, and worked as farm laborers. A daughter Gerry was born in 1925 and a son Masayuki in 1928. I was 13 years old living in Loomis, California, attending the Loomis Union Grammar School and in the eighth grade. In May 1942, we were preparing to graduate when I went outside for recess and saw a poster from the U.S. Army that all persons of Japanese Ancestry will meet at a designated location and time with only what we could carry (one suitcase each) in 10 days. We were getting out from a depression and most families were poor and didn't have much. By law, my parents could not become citizens or own land so we didn't have a house.

We went to an Assembly Center near Marysville, California (Camp Arboga), where we stayed for about 6 weeks. It had a population of about 2,400. We didn't do much and life got to be rather boring. I remember the restroom was an outhouse with four holes and you could stretch your arm out and touch the person next to you. The holes were back to back. No partitions. I had used out houses before but they were one hole. We got on the train at Marysville one night and were forbidden to raise the curtains. We were guarded by American soldiers. When we got to Tule Lake, it was early morning the next day. I turned age 14. I lied and told them I was 16 and got a job as a carpenters apprentice and got paid $12.00/month. The camp was Tule Lake (Figure 3) which had a population over 18,500 at its peak. We were a family of six that lived in a barrack 20' × 24'. About the same as we had at Arboga. They had a separate building for men and women's restroom with flush toilets but no partitions. There was a separate building for doing your laundry. There was a separate building where 250 people ate their breakfast, lunch, and dinner.

There were lines all the time. We stayed at Tule for about 3 years when we were released. It was around June 1945. I turned 17.

In Tule, school started late and we went to school in an empty barrack with benches and tables made from scrap lumber. We always didn't have enough basic things such as paper, pencils, books, teachers, and microscopes (biology) chemicals (Chemistry class). Anyone with a Junior College education could teach in the elementary grades. They required a credential to teach in High School. There were not enough credentialed teachers so the teachers were hired from the outside. I could never understand why anyone with a degree would come to a concentration camp to teach the kids of our enemy during wartime when jobs were plentiful. But they came. The Japanese teachers were paid $19.00/month.

I recall my older sister came home from school and told me she was taking a typing class. She showed me a piece of paper with the keyboard drawn on it and told me she was supposed to practice her typing on that.

During summer vacation, some of the older students were able to get part time jobs on the camp farms for $12.00/month.

They tried to keep us busy and we had different activities. I played basketball, baseball, football, did sumo wrestling, and was in the Boy Scouts.

I don't think I was much affected being UPROOTED. I grew up during the depression and didn't have much. Didn't have much in camp. Every day was work before camp (chores after school). Didn't have this in camp. I lived in the country and my nearest neighbor was about half mile away. In camp, I had not seen so many Japanese kids my age and every day was play day. I think that the biggest thing that I began to miss was my freedom. My life was quite different from the young men who were working and of draft age and should be in college. My parents lost everything and were constantly thinking of the future of their children. This is something you don't know or understand until you become a parent.

10 INTERNMENT CAMPS

Amache, Colorado	7,318
Gila River, Arizona	13,348
Heart Mountain, Wyoming	10,767
Jerome, Arkansas	8,947
Manzanar, California	10,040*
Minedoka, Idaho	9,397
Poston, Arizona	17,813
Rohwer, Arkansas	8,475
Topaz, Utah	8,130
Tule Lake, California	18,789
Total	112,581

*Manzanar had about 100 children (known as the children's village) from orphanages in Los Angeles and San Francisco run by the Catholic Church (Figure 3). The church protested and stated these were children, already institutionalized and would not be spying or sabotaging anything. Besides, some of the children had half or less Japanese blood. The Army said that anyone with 1/16 Japanese blood must be incarcerated because of Military Necessity.

Life in the Camp

They had jobs for everyone who wanted to work. Cooks, waiters, and dishwashers in the mess hall; firemen in the camp fire department; orderlies, janitors, nurses, aides, doctors, optometrist, and dentists in the hospital. When they had serious medical problems, they would take the patient to a nearby city for treatment.

They also had farms outside the camps where the "inmates" raised vegetables. Some camps had pigs, chickens for eggs and eating, cows for milk and eating. We had adequate food but did not have choice of entrees. They fed us for $0.39/day. As a comparison, the American soldier was fed for $0.50/day. We were under the same rationing restrictions as the general public.

People worked as secretaries, clericals, and administrators. Train loads of food, mail, and other supplies were being delivered each day and had to be distributed to the mess halls and inmates. Garbage had to be picked up disposed of. The camps operated like a small city which required services for the residents.

We occasionally had movies and held talent shows where the "Inmates" performed. Baseball, football, and basketball games were well attended. Each block held about 250 residents and each had their own teams and they played against each other. Japanese and American card games and board games were played.

They held religious services, which were conducted by lay people because the ministers were incarcerated in another concentration camp.

The weather at Tule was much like Sacramento, California. The winter was colder and we had snow. However, it never got to be more than several inches.

Loyal and Disloyal

The government decided they had to determine which "inmates" were loyal or disloyal to the United States. They decided the easy way to do this was to ask them. They developed a questionnaire with a series of questions.

> **Two Controversial Questions From the Loyalty Questionnaire**
>
> **Question 27: Are you willing to serve in the armed forces of the United States on combat duty wherever ordered?**
>
> **Question 28: Will you swear unqualified allegiance to the United States from any or all attack by foreign or domestic forces and forswear any form of allegiance or obedience to the Japanese Emperor or any other foreign government, power or organization?**

Suspicion and mistrust of the Army who forced them into concentration camps with loss of property, their freedom, jobs, education, and rights without due process and no idea how the government was going to use the data resulted in failure of the loyal/disloyal issues. The Army realized the problems involved and changed the questionnaire but the damage had already been done. Nonetheless, the Army followed through with another questionnaire and anyone not answering or not marking yes—yes were designated Disloyal. Tule Lake had the largest number of Disloyal inmates and therefore was designated as the Disloyal Camp. All the Loyal inmates and their families from Tule were moved to one of the other nine camps. All the Disloyals from the other nine camps were moved to Tule. However, there were about 4,000 Loyals who didn't want to move and they were allowed to stay at Tule. Tule became a high security camp.

Tule started getting a bad reputation because of some dissidents who were very vocal about things like incarceration, food, demanding to give up their citizenship, and be sent to Japan.

Some Japanese Americans renounced their citizenship and were sent to Japan at their request in exchange for Americans who were caught in Japan or its territories in 1943.

Military Service

Japanese Americans in the U.S. Army Infantry in European Theater of Operations

In Hawaii, there was a National Guard unit of mostly Japanese Americans (100th Battalion). After Pearl Harbor was bombed, the unit was kept intact and sent to Camp Shelby in Mississippi. When some of the men went into town, they were told to use the white restrooms and ride in front of the bus. Ironically, some had family members in the Internment Camps. By June 5, 1942, **1,432** men landed in North Africa, then went to Italy. In the first month and a half, 78 were killed and 239 wounded. By the time they were pulled out of the line, they were down to an effective strength of **521** men. They had earned 900 purple hearts and earned the nick name "Purple Heart Battalion." On June 15, 1944, the 100th became part of the 442 Regimental Combat Team.

The draft was started about a year before Pearl Harbor was bombed. There were about 5,000 Japanese Americans in the Army who volunteered or were drafted. Some of these men were discharged and others had their guns taken away and they were assigned menial tasks after Pearl Harbor was bombed. After Pearl Harbor was bombed and World War II started, the Japanese Americans were not drafted into the military. In January 1943, they started accepting volunteers into the Army. Many of these men came right out of the Internment Camps. In January 1944, they started drafting eligible men into the Army. They were not accepted in the Air Force or the Navy. This created problems because some refused to go. Some were arrested, tried, and convicted for evading the draft and sentenced to a Federal penitentiary. Most went and were assigned to the special all Japanese 442 Regimental Combat Team. All Japanese Americans were transferred into this new unit. The officers were all White.

In Hawaii, when they started accepting volunteers in the Army, over 10,000 volunteered. Dan Inouye who was in Medical School and working in the Red Cross applied and was deferred because they needed doctors. He resigned from Medical School and the Red Cross. He reapplied and was accepted into the Army.

After basic training, he was sent to the 442 in Europe. Subsequently, he lost an arm in combat. He was awarded the Distinguished Service Cross which was later changed to the Medal of Honor, the nation's highest award. On his way home to Hawaii, he stopped at a barber shop to get a haircut and was told that they don't cut Jap hair. This in spite of being an officer in uniform having many decorations and the loss of one arm. After Hawaii became a State in 1959, he became Hawaii's and America's first Japanese American Representative elected to Congress. He later became the first elected Japanese American Senator to Congress. He never lost an election and served in Congress longer than anyone.

The 442 became the most highly decorated unit in the history of the U.S. Army for a unit this size and length of service. In seven campaigns,

they had 9,480 casualties, including 600 killed, 21 Congressional Medals of Honor, 47 Distinguished Service Crosses, 350 Silver Stars, 810 Bronze Stars, and over 8,800 Purple Hearts.

Japanese Americans in the Military Intelligence Service Language School

In the Spring of 1941, Lieutenant Colonel John Weckerling and Captain Kai Rasmussen were two Intelligence Officers in the U.S. Army who recognized there were no trained persons in the Army familiar with the Japanese language. Japan was looked at as a future enemy. They received approval to start a Japanese Language School in an airplane hangar at the Presidio in San Francisco. This was a **TOP SECRET OPERATION** that the newspapers were forbidden to write about. The students could not even tell their families what they were doing. They didn't want the Japanese military to know the U.S. Army had the capability to read, listen to, and understand their communications.

They started the school on November 1, 1941 with 58 Japanese Americans students, two White students and four Japanese American instructors. The best students and instructors were the Kibeis. They were born in the United States but educated in Japan.

Many went to Japanese Schools in Japan through high school. The school was designed to graduate the students in one year. However, that was cut to 6 months after the bombing of Pearl Harbor and start of World War II.

Evacuation of persons of Japanese ancestry on the West Coast started after President Roosevelt signed E.O. 9066 on February 19, 1942. This necessitated moving the school to Camp Savage, Minnesota. The first graduates were sent to the Aleutians and Guadalcanal. They were assigned in small numbers to various units. In some cases, the commanders didn't know what to do with them so they were given menial tasks. They soon found out they were very valuable. The linguists questioned prisoners (Figure 7), translated documents, listened to radio transmissions and could advise their commanders about the custom and culture of the Japanese soldier. The Japanese military did not know the U.S. military had this capability. The school graduated 6,000 linguists and they served in small groups with every allied unit in the Pacific.

People did not know what they contributed to winning the war in the Pacific because of the Top Secret nature of their work. When the Federal Freedom of Information Act was passed in 1967. People went into the archives and were able to discover their contributions. According to General Willoughby, Chief of Intelligence for General Mac Arthur, the linguists shortened the war and saved thousands of lives on both sides.

After World War II ended, the linguists were utilized in the occupation of Japan. They were used to make the Japanese people understand that MacArthur wanted to democratize Japan which led to a smooth transition from a defeated enemy to reconstruction of their country. They quickly changed from a devastated, destroyed, hungry country to an economic powerhouse and today is one of America's best ally in Asia.

Camps Closing

Mitsuye Endo

Endo was a California State employee with the Department of Motor Vehicles before the war started. She was a U.S. citizen, had never been to Japan, didn't know the language and had a brother in the U.S. Army. She was incarcerated at Tule Lake and Topaz, Utah. She had lawyers who challenged the government to prove she had committed any act against the United States or planned to do so. In the absence of any charges, they had to release her from camp. The Supreme Court ordered her release. This decision applied to all person of Japanese ancestry being held in the Internment Camps.

In January 1945, the government announced they were going to close all the camps. It didn't matter whether you were classified loyal or disloyal. Everyone was to leave as soon as possible. For many, it was like telling a homeless person to go home. We each received $25 and a train ticket to wherever we wanted to go. Most people lost everything and had no home to return to. It was difficult times for all of us. The GI's were now returning home and going to school, starting families, and needed housing and jobs.

It was difficult for Japanese Americans trying to get resettled because discrimination was worse than when they left. They faced things such as drive by shooting, arson, dynamiting of buildings, and signs on buildings of businesses stating "NO Japs Allowed." It was hard to understand because they compiled an outstanding military record proving their loyalty beyond any doubt. There was not one case where a person of Japanese ancestry was charged with a crime against the United States. They had been wrongly incarcerated while their sons were sacrificing their lives for their country.

My father found a place to live and a job working on a fruit orchard in Loomis. I completed my senior year at the Placer Union High School and went to the Placer Junior College in Auburn, California. We moved to Sacramento after about 2 years and I have lived here ever since. The first home they bought was in my name because it was against the law for them to buy land at that time.

On July 31, 1980, President Jimmy Carter signed **Public Law 96-317**, which created a Commission for determining what happened to result in the incarceration of over 110,000 people of Japanese ancestry. They interviewed over 750 people on both side of the fence and examined over 10,000 documents, many now available because of the Freedom of Information Act. The Commission was also to recommend remedies. They concluded that there were three primary reasons that led to the incarceration: wartime hysteria, racial prejudice, and failure of political leadership to uphold the constitution.

> **Public Law 96-317:**
> This law established a commission to investigate the effect of Executive Order 9066 and make recommendations for redress to the Japanese American community.

Concluding Thoughts

My younger brother Billy served in another war, the Korean War (1950–1953), despite serving in combat for a years and a prisoner of war for 2 years, he survived. He came home and lived a pretty good life. Here is his story.

Story of Billy Kazuyoshi Hatano

In 1930, the Hatano family took a vacation to Japan to visit their families. Billy, a son was born. He was a citizen of Japan but came back with the family to Loomis, California, as a foreign alien. All Japanese immigrants were aliens by Federal Law they could not become American citizens. Their children who were born in the United States were automatically citizens. Yoshimasa and Yaeko worked on a fruit orchard.

After my family was released from Tule Lake, we relocated to Loomis for about 2 years. Yoshimasa and Yaeko worked on a fruit orchard. The family then relocated to Sacramento, California.

Billy graduated High School and wanted to get his U.S. citizenship and get a government job. Immigration told him that if he renounced his Japanese citizenship and served for 3 years in the U.S. Army, he could get his U.S. citizenship. He renounced his citizenship and became a man without a country. He also enlisted in the U.S. Army in 1950.

Military Service

The Korean War started right after he finished his basic training and he was sent to Korea. He survived many harrowing situations but survived combat for about 1 year. One experience he related was when his platoon was dug in on a hill and Billy was sent out as point man about 50 yards in front of his platoon where he dug in. He sensed and heard the North Korean soldiers were crawling past his position about midnight. He threw a grenade and all hell broke loose. His platoon opened up with flares, machine guns, rifles, mortars, and grenades. After a short while, everything was quiet. The next morning he started crawling up the hill and yelled for the platoon officer, sergeant, and other members of his platoon. He made it back safely without getting shot by his own people.

Another situation was when they were getting close to the Yalu River, General Douglas MacArthur told his troops they would be home for Christmas. Then the Chinese entered the war and charged the American lines in human waves blowing their bugles. My brother and his fellow soldiers were holding their own but they finally ran out of ammunition, threw down their guns, and threw up their hands. Billy was reported Missing in Action on November 4, 1950. It was devastating news for the family and we assumed he had died.

Prisoners

They were marched North to a Prisoner of War Camp. No medical care, inadequate food, and supplies resulted in a number of deaths. They finally reached their camp and had about 30 men housed in a small hut. There was not enough space to lie down and they were a tangle of arms and legs when they woke up the next morning. After the first winter, about half of the men died and the remainder had adequate space in the hut. It was a case of inadequate food, clothing, harsh winters, and lack of medical services. Those that survived the first winter had acclimated to conditions and most of the others made it through the war as prisoners. Billy indicated he was emaciated and was skin and bones. After the Peace Talks began, both sides released a list of prisoners they had. Billy's name was on the list. The family was elated but worried about his physical condition. It was August 6, 1953 before the prisoner exchange and the Americans could come home.

Billy Kazuyoshi Hatano returns from the Korea War.

Courtesy of Mas Hatano

Civilian Life

He went to immigration and asked for his citizenship. They told him the law had been changed and he would have to apply and pass an exam before he could become a U.S. citizen. He did that and became a citizen. Now the Aliens of Japanese ancestry could become citizens if they applied and passed an exam like aliens from other countries.

He got a job at the U.S. Army Signal Depot in Sacramento doing computer-related work and retired in 1985. He got married in 1955 to Grace Yamamura and they had two sons, Brian and Kevin. Billy had a heart attack and passed away on March 6, 2017.

I was a Civil Engineer for Caltrans during my working years. I have three sons and seven grandchildren. I have been retired for 25 years and in reasonably good health. Overall, I had a good life and lucky to have lived in the United States. I think about the young men who went off to war and didn't return and didn't live one day of the good life that I had. Today, I continue to tell my story to many public school students, universities, and as a docent at the California History Museum. I tell my story as a Japanese American who like thousands of others was unjustly incarcerated in a dark part of U.S. history.

Courtesy of Mas Hatano

Billy Kazuyoshi Hatano greeted by his parents returning from the Korea War.

Redress

In 1988, Congress passed a law providing for redress of $20,000 for each person still living who had been incarcerated and a letter of apology from the President of the United States. About 60,000 (50%) were still living who had been incarcerated. My father was deceased. My mother was in a nursing home and flat on her back 24/7. They sure could have used that money when they left the camps. They also provided funds for educational purposes.

Chapter 23

Double Happiness: Chinese American History—Through the Lens of Family, Community, and Food

Gregory Yee Mark and Christina Fa Mark

Contributed by Gregory Yee Mark and Christina Fa Mark.

Some of the words also appear in other chapters. Talk about the words with other students, teachers, friends, and family members before you read, while reading the chapter, and after you have read the chapter.

Central Pacific Railroad (CPRR)

The western portion of the Transcontinental Railroad. Originating in Sacramento and ending in Promontory Summit, Utah. The most difficult part of the Transcontinental Railroad to create, given the huge blockade of the Sierra Nevada Mountains in the way.

Transcontinental Railroad

The first railroad uniting the western and eastern United States. Before the Transcontinental Railroad was completed on May 10, 1869, the two "halves" of the United States were "impossibly" far from each other.

Chinese American Council of Sacramento (CACS)

A Chinese American political and advocacy organization founded in 1987 by the late Frank Fat, Sacramento's renowned restaurateur and philanthropist.

Chinese American

A term originating with the term *Asian American*, coined in 1968 by Yuji Ichioka, then a graduate student at University of California, Berkeley and Emma Gee, a writer. Ichioka and Gee were founders of the Asian American Political Alliance. Any U.S.-born person of Chinese ancestry. Or, a person born in China (or any part of Asia, who identifies ethnically as Chinese), later emigrating to the United States, who identifies with being Chinese American.

Locke's Community Garden

Previous resident, Connie King grew a few Chinese vegetables along with an assortment of other vegetables and an array of flowers. Her plot showed the remnants of its previous gardener, her late husband Tom King. Tourists would often find her in the plot and she was delighted to give them a tour and the opportunity to teach them about the history of Locke. Since Connie passed away, volunteers for the Locke Foundation have turned her old plot across from her former home on Key Street into a Chinese vegetable demonstration garden. Each year, several residents have cultivated a variety of traditional Chinese vegetables.

Right of First Refusal (RFR)

The Right of First Refusal (RFR) requires that any Locke property for sale after the 2004 subdivision and sale of land by the County to then-current building owners would be subject to an RFR granting the Locke Management Association the first opportunity to purchase the property after notifying interested parties that the land was for sale.

Xenophobia

An individual's irrational and obsessive hatred of people perceived as different and foreign. Related to the concepts of racism and ethnocentrism. All of these can be overcome by the study of the social sciences and coming to appreciate the ideas of culture and social structure as tools for understanding ourselves and others.

Rock Springs Massacre

An especially brutal anti-Chinese riot in Wyoming, 1885. White coal miners, who scapegoated Chinese American coal miners for their poor working conditions, rioted and massacred 28 Chinese American coal miners, and drove hundreds more out of town.

Introduction

Double Happiness is the double combination of the Chinese character "Happiness" (喜). Combined, the word means "Double Happiness" (喜喜). Traditionally, "Double Happiness" refers to two fortuitous events, bringing happiness to a family—such as a wedding celebration and the return of a Gold Mountain sojourner after decades away from China.

This chapter is based on the 2016 Sacramento State University, Asian American Studies (AAS) Exhibit *Double Happiness: Chinese American History Through the Lens of Family and Restaurants*. Three Chinese American restaurants in different Northern California communities are examined.

Restaurants are important to Chinese and to Chinese American culture because they have been the cornerstones of celebrations of auspicious events. Traditionally, Chinese restaurants not only serve food, but they also function as family, clan, and even as community centers where people gather together.

Chinese families have always been the backbone of the Chinese American community. First, the community has undergone a progressive evolution of the changes from a single bachelor society to families made of women and children. Second, Chinese restaurants have served as important celebratory sites for Chinese American communities. Third, they have been external contact points with the local communities that they are a part of, such as Frank Fat's in Sacramento. In fact, Frank Fat's restaurant was extremely popular among California's lawmakers; it is said that many backroom deals were negotiated in the restaurant—these same deals eventually turned into state law and policy.

In the context of this chapter, "Double Happiness" examines three twentieth century Chinese American communities in Northern California: Sacramento (almost next door to California's capitol and near its Chinatown); El Cerrito (an unincorporated town in 1945, 30 minutes from Oakland Chinatown), and Locke (a rural town in the Sacramento Delta built by Chinese Americans).

Historical Background

Since the first arrival of Chinese to the United States in 1850, Chinese immigrants started their own businesses such as hand laundries, grocery shops, import/export businesses, and restaurants. These businesses provided the opportunity for these Chinese pioneers to create their own independent business establishments as opposed to working for non-Chinese such as the Big Four developers of the Central Pacific Railroad (1863–1868; part of the Transcontinental Railroad). The big four were: Leland Stanford, Collis P. Huntington, Mark Hopkins, and Charles Crocker.

In fact, Chinese began opening restaurants as early as the Gold Rush era. Their restaurants were known for their cleanliness, "excellent cookery," and good value. As of September 1849, there were at least three Chinese restaurants in San Francisco: Kong-Sung's by the bay, Whang-Tong's on Sacramento Street, and Tong-Ling's on Jackson Street.[1] Travelogue writer Bayard Taylor says of these restaurants: "The latter are much frequented by Americans, on account of their excellent cookery, and the fact that meals are $1 each, without regard to quantity." Newspaper publisher James Ayers says of Gold Rush era restaurants: " . . . the best restaurants . . . were kept by Chinese and the poorest . . . by Americans."[2] Little has changed in over 150 years.

Ironically, in this early Gold Mining era, White Americans would gladly eat at Chinese "chow chow houses," yet outside the restaurant arena, they would generally treat the Chinese with disdain and prejudice.

Chinese restaurants continued flourishing in the United States, even influencing American food culture. Standbys such as the fortune cookie were in fact American inventions. Renowned American chef Emeril Lagasse grew up eating Chow Mein Sandwiches in his hometown of Fall River, Massachusetts. Even our word *ketchup* comes from the Fukienese dialect *kôe-chiap* or *ké-tsiap*, meaning fish sauce.

---

1 Taylor (1850).
2 Liu (2016).

So, even though Chinese food is commonly thought of as a quick source of cheap food, Chinese cuisine is actually one of America's oldest cuisines. The persistence of Chinese restaurants in American culture is a testament to the entrepreneurship of Chinese Americans, from the 1800s until today.

Growth of Chinese Restaurants

By 1882, the United States government passed the first Chinese Exclusion Act that restricted Chinese laborers from immigrating to the United States. This Exclusion Act was the lowlight of anti-Chinese sentiments and discrimination. Besides contributing to an atmosphere of anger and hate, the Chinese American population declined, and since the beginning of immigration, in 1920, it reached a low point of 61,639[3] (Loo, 1991, p. 47).

Despite the population decline due to the anti-Chinese exclusion laws, Chinese cuisine in the United States steadily increased in popularity. One reason for this success was that many Chinese American restaurants were resourceful and creative in their appeal to the mainstream American palette. They did this by first adapting Chinese dishes to be Americanized such as in the case of chop suey and egg foo yung. In addition, restaurants such as Frank Fat's and the Wong family's Violet's Dining Room were among the pioneering restaurants which had separate menu sections for Chinese food and American food, a practice that became standard in Chinese restaurants' menus across the United states.

During this period of discriminatory practices, these restaurants were very important sources of employment for Chinese American community members. According to the 1920 U.S. census, out of 45,614 Chinese workers, 11,438 (25%) were restaurant workers and 12,559 (28%) were laundry workers (U.S. Census, 1920). Chinese restaurants emerged not only in urban Chinatowns, but also in mining and agricultural regions such as in California's Central Valley.

These Chinese American restaurants were able to build the foundation for future generations and communities to thrive. Even today, these specific restaurants tell different stories. First, Frank Fat and his family have continued to make a difference in serving the needs of the contemporary Sacramento Chinese American community. Second, Violet Wong's family has left a pioneering legacy in the culture and arts such as contributing to early American filmmaking. Third, the National Historic Landmark town of Locke, a rural Chinese American town, continues the fight to maintain its historical and cultural integrity.

Chinese American families fought in their own ways to bridge the gap between being Americans and Chinese Americans while taking pride in being both Chinese and American. These Chinese American restaurants reflected the historical status of

---

3 Loo (1991).

each period. A prime example of such a family is the well-known and politically influential Sacramento-based Fat family.

Frank Fat's

Frank Fat, also known as Dong Sai-Fat, was born on May 12, 1904 in WuLong village, in the Toi Shan Sub-District which was a part of the Sze District, in Guandong Province. In 1919, 16-year-old, Frank Fat migrated to the United States as a paper son. The paper name he purchased was Wong Bing-Yuen. He was detained on Angel Island for 2 months. After entering the United States, Frank worked many jobs such as fruit picker, laundryman, dishwasher, busboy, waiter, host, and restaurant manager.

Frank Fat and his family, circa 1946

At the age of 20, Frank went back to China and married Yee Lai-Ching. She took the English name "Mary" and they were life-long partners. While Frank was busy with his businesses, Mary became the backbone of their family. Other than her housework, she held jobs cooking, cleaning, growing Chinese vegetables, and raising chickens, all while raising six children: four sons and two daughters.

After years of hard work, Frank Fat was able to open his own business. During a gambling event in his uncle's restaurant, Frank helped a prestigious state official place a bet and the official ended up winning $900. The winner left before picking up his money, yet Frank gave him his winnings when he later returned to the restaurant. As a result, the official offered Frank a business loan. With this loan, in 1939, Frank was able to purchase property at 806 L Street. Today, the L Street restaurant

Frank Fat in front of his first L Street restaurant, Frank's 806, circa 1939.

continues to be the focal point of the Frank Fat Corporation which includes three Sacramento area restaurants.

Originally named Frank's 806, Frank renamed his Chinese restaurant, "Frank Fat's." He worked hard to build up his business, and after 8 months, he began to see the product of his labor. His was one of the first Chinese restaurants to expand its menu to include American food. Located just down the street from California's State Capitol, due to his high quality and reasonably priced food, the restaurant soon attracted government officials and business people. It became a popular place for politicians to discuss important matters. Frank soon earned the respect of these officials, who started to refer to him as "Senator Fat." Prior to World War II, one of Frank Fat's moves as a "self-appointed lobbyist" was to gain support from legislators for an embargo of U.S. war materials to Japan, which had already invaded China[4]

As a restaurateur, Frank Fat was a tremendous success. His Banana Cream Pie alone was—and still is—legendary. In 2013, Frank Fat's earned the distinction of being the only Sacramento restaurant to be the recipient of the James Beard Foundation America's Classics Award for "lifetime achievement."

Frank Fat and his restaurant catering truck, circa 1951.

Courtesy of the Fat Family.

A Community Advocate

Frank always believed himself to be both a Chinese and an American. Despite being a restaurateur, Frank Fat's heart was always in helping his community. He wanted to bridge the gap between Chinese and other Americans and to create a better Chinese American community. He believed community service was key to improving relations between the Chinese American community and the larger local community. Lonnie Wong, a Fox40 reporter and friend of Frank Fat, states, "Frank was always a big ideas guy. He was also the man behind Sacramento's Pacific Rim Street Festival which over 22 years drew tens of thousands of people to Old Sacramento. In the early 1990s, Frank urged community activists to create a venue where people could learn about Asian Pacific Islander cultures that exist within the city . . . (The Pacific Rim Street Festival) is another demonstration of Frank's belief that the world is a better place if people knew and understood each other more."

Far from an armchair philanthropist, Frank Fat truly advocated for the Chinese American community . . . and he urged other Chinese Americans to do the same. Legend

---

4   A Tribute to Frank Sai-Fat (1997).

has it that after Frank observed politicians and community leaders forging decisions while eating at his "L" restaurant, he realized how much strength there was in numbers. "That was the beginning of his dream, to form an organization that could speak out on behalf of the Chinese community" (CACS flyer).

In 1987, Frank Fat is credited with cofounding the advocacy group **Chinese American Council of Sacramento (CACS)**, an organization that is still active today. Besides the founding of Sacramento's Pacific Rim Street Fest, some of Frank Fat's greatest legacies were the advocacy and history projects of CACS. The Council's most notable achievements were: (a) spearheading a permanent exhibit at the Robert T. Matsui United States Courthouse of Sacramento Chinatown relics; (b) producing the book *CANTON FOOTPRINTS: Sacramento's Chinese Legacy*, a history of Chinese Americans written by the late Phil Choy; and (c) leading the Asian American community in advocating for Locke's revitalization, especially the creation of the Right of First Refusal (RFR)—an attempt to address the wrong of anti-Asian discrimination barring Asians from owning land.

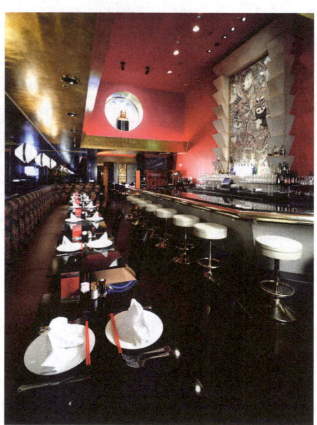

Courtesy of the Fat Family

At the 1996 national convention of the Organization of Chinese Americans in San Francisco, Frank Fat was the keynote speaker. His health appeared to be weakening, but he walked steadily to the center of the stage, resplendent in a tux. His speech consisted of just two words: "Get involved." He then walked off the stage, to a rousing standing ovation from a crowd surprised and energized by his words. Never was there a better message encouraging Chinese Americans to advocate for their own community.

Interior of Frank Fat's flagship restaurant, 806 L Street, Sacramento, California, circa 2004.

Violet's Dining Room, 1945–1968

In a similar Chinese American restaurant, an hour and a half drive to the south, Chinese American husband-and-wife team Violet and Albert Wong opened Violet's Dining Room in August 1945. In the town of El Cerrito, Violet's Dining Room was the first and only Chinese American Restaurant—and remained so for the next 20 years. Violet's served Chinese food, westernized Chinese food, and American food. It offered *war won ton*, *sub gum chow mien*, water chestnut *chow yoke*, New York cut steak, roast tom turkey with cranberry sauce, French sourdough bread, and homemade apple pie.

One of Violet's Chinese specialties was *Da Bin Lo* (*Huo Guo*; 喜喜喜) or Hot Pot (Fire Pot), according to the "Sang Wor Dinner" offering in the Dining Room's 1945 menu. Violet's Dining Room was one of the first—if not the first—in the United States to offer this specialty dish. (*Note*: *Sang Wor* was apparently how the Hot Pot was originally referred to in the 1940s in the United States.)

Sang Wor consisted of a charcoal heated soup stock from an original T'ang Dynasty recipe that was cooked on your table in a specially designed brass pot. Restaurant guests dipped abalone, oysters, fish, prawn, fish balls, chicken, lamb, black mushrooms, snow peas, and mustard greens in small metal nets into the bubbling broth. After retrieving their delicacy from the soup, they could use a variety of dipping sauces to enhance the *Da Bin Lo's* flavors.

Within the immediate and extended Wong Family, Violet's Dining Room was known as the gathering place for holiday dinners, especially Thanksgiving. All were invited—family, extended family, and family friends. Typically, there would be three generations of Wongs in attendance, including members of the aging Chinese American bachelor generation… all celebrating Thanksgiving at Violet's Dining Room. At the end of the evening, Kem Lee, the noted San Francisco Chinatown photographer who also was Violet's son-in-law, took family group pictures.

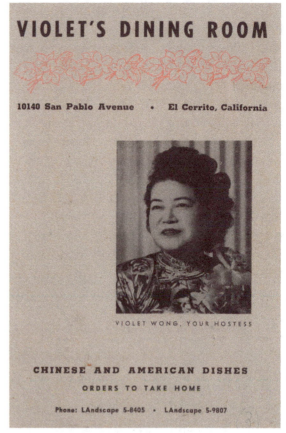

Front cover of "Violet's Dining Room" menu, 1946, featuring owner and movie star Violet Wong.

Three generations of the Wong Family, Thanksgiving circa 1954. Seated are Violet & Albert Wong, and Marion Wong, among others. Note the elaborate ceiling treatments made up of Cantonese Opera backdrops.

Besides the traditional turkey, cranberry, and mashed potatoes: there were bowls of rice and stuffing made out of Chinese ingredients such as sweet rice and *lop cheong* (Chinese sausage). The "American food" chef was Albert Wong (1891–1969), a third generation Chinese American born in San Francisco Chinatown, who was Violet's husband. In 1911, during the Dr. Sun Yat-Sen led Chinese Revolution, Albert sailed with his parents and younger sister Marion to Hong Kong. There, he was introduced to Violet Jung, whom he married a short time later.

Interior, Violet's Dining Room, circa 1955. Note the brass Hot Pots (Fire Pots) in the foreground.

Courtesy of the Contra Costa Historical Society

Violet's Dining Room By Mai-Lon Wong Gittelsohn (Violet's daughter)[5]

Late afternoon. A time of day like a double-edged sword,
    sun glare gone, shadows beginning to lengthen.
    Watch me enter the double doors, touch the dark wood of the teak table—

lacquered, black. See me brush by the silk tapestry embroidered
    with peonies, enter the dining room, marbled pink Formica tables
    lined up against the walls, wooden chairs pushed in.

On each table, a candle holder made from rice whiskey pots,
    sides caked with wax—green, yellow, red.
    It is the restaurant, of course, because I see her,

see my mother holding menus covered in plastic,
    trimmed in black, each menu typed up on the Royal typewriter.
    Today she is not wearing Chinese dress, but her favorite pants suit,

forest green, a gold buckle at the waist.
    Thirteen years old, today I will wait on tables for the first time.
    A young family comes in, two children under five in tow.

---

5 Gittelsohn (2014).

They order sweet and sour pork, a platter of fried rice.
    I write on a small tablet, announce the order to the cook
    in my best American style Cantonese.
    He answers with a smile and a flash of teeth,
    turns to the wok pouring in a dollop of peanut oil
    which begins to pop and crackle.

In the dining room, I sit against the wall, trying not to watch
    as a shower of fried rice scatters on the tale, the chairs,
    and ends up on the floor. The young father digs deep, leaving me

a fifteen cent tip. I'm left to mop up the rice, sticky like floury paste.
    The dining room empty, I sit at a table with my sisters, Ermah and Marcella,
    fill wonton wrappers. I struggle to copy them—the way they scoop up

the filling of ground pork and shrimp, the way their nimble fingers
    fill each square, sealing the edges with water. It looks so easy.
    I attempt the same switch movements dipping and filling

The last step is my undoing. My wraps unfurl as if possessed
    by an unruly spirit, spill their contents into the soup, a quagmire
    of pork, shrimp and wont ton skins, that float on sea of chicken broth.

Thirty years before starting her restaurant, Violet Jung Wong (1895–1981) starred in the very first known Asian American film, *The Curse of Quon Gwon*. Violet's sister-in-law, Marion Wong (1895–1969), directed this full-length feature film in Oakland, California. In addition to directing, Marion was the pioneering film's creator, producer, and even a key actor (she played the villainess). She received a great deal of support from her extended family and the local Chinese American community. Financial support came from each branch of Marion's family such as her eldest sister Alice Lim and husband, Lim Ben. Actors were family and friends; costumes were made by her sisters (Alice Lim of Oakland and Rose Ah Tye of Stockton).

Of major historical significance was that the film portrayed Chinese

Courtesy of the Violet Wong Family.

Photo taken on set of The Curse of Quon Gwon (1916–1917), the first known Asian American film. Actor Violet Wong on far left. Actor Harvey SooHoo on far right, and "Chin-See" Wong to his right.

and Chinese Americans as normal everyday people and did not negatively stereotype Chinese Americans, as happened too frequently after 1916 and continues to occur today. Ironically, *The Curse of Quon Gwon* was one of America's first feature length films—pre-dating Hollywood—yet it portrayed Asian Americans more accurately than Hollywood has ever portrayed Asian Americans since the ground breaking 1916 film.

Locke, California

Historical Background

In 1915, Chinatown burned down. That is, the Chinatown in the small Sacramento Delta town of Walnut Grove.

Chinatown residents, largely farmworkers, were now homeless. This was not only a physical catastrophe, but a major cultural hit as well. Walnut Grove's Chinatown—which started as early as 1875—was the heart of the regional Chinese American community. Hundreds of laborers would come to Chinatown on their days off to socialize, get haircuts, gamble, and have meals. Now, Chinatown was no more.

Some residents asked neighboring farmer George Locke, a White American, if they could rent land on his pear orchard. Three residents had already built buildings there: a saloon, gambling hall, and boarding house. George Locke agreed to lease an additional nine acres[6]

Main Street, Locke, California. (Undated photo). The National Historic Landmark of Locke, California looks very similar today to its formation 100 years ago.

Source: Library of Congress

of land and so the famous town of Locke was born. (Originally known as Lockeport, later as Locke or "Lockee" as some original residents called it.)

Not all the Chinese of Walnut Grove left. The group who departed were the Jungshan (*joong–sahn*) (Chungshan) Chinese, a minority Chinese group from the Guangdong Province. Most early Chinese immigrants in the United States were Toisanese, also from the Guangdong Province.

Chinese American and Japanese American laborers were vital to California's growing agricultural industry. The Sacramento-San Joaquin Delta was the "pear capital of the world" by the late nineteenth century—due largely to Chinese laborers transforming

---

6   https://www.nps.gov/nr/feature/asia/1999/locke.htm

500,000 acres of swampland into rich farmland. By 1910, the Delta produced almost 90% of the entire world's asparagus.[7]

These Asian American laborers made up the lion's share of the "unskilled" labor force California's agriculture required.[8]

Locke's mainly Chinese American residents were farmworkers or tenant farmers. Due to anti-Chinese laws, they earned at most $1 a day. The young town grew quickly. It had a church, boarding houses, a movie theatre, and even a post office. School kids had to attend either "Oriental School" (Walnut Grove) or "White School" (Courtland). In the mid-1920s, Locke had more than 600 Chinese Americans residents.[9]

Locke soon became a favorite for visitors of all races. Two main reasons were: (a) Alcohol was sold in Locke, even during Prohibition (1920–1933), when it was illegal to sell alcohol; (b) Locke was unincorporated (it had no police force). There were speak-easies, gambling parlors, and brothels. The "oldtimer" Chinese Americans were quick to point out that the prostitutes were White, not Chinese.

Not a Chinatown

Another difference in Locke's birth was that it was distinctly *not* a Chinatown. Chinatowns were enclaves within cities where Chinese and Chinese Americans were forced to live, driven there by racist intimidation or actual fear of being killed if one lived outside of Chinatowns, such as in the Rock Springs Massacre (Wyoming, 1885).

Instead, Locke became one of many rural Chinese American towns that dotted the west. Living in such freestanding towns, and not "ethnic" enclaves, the mainly Chinese American-residents had the freedom to live, work, and socialize on their own terms, not defined by the dominant racial and ethnic groups immediately surrounding them. These rural Chinese American towns existed in places like Nevada, California, Idaho, and Oregon, and were often based on agricultural industries.

Of all these towns, only Locke remains. This is Locke's true "claim to fame."

Alien Land Law

Though the mainstay of Locke was its Chinese American residents, they were never allowed to buy the land they lived on.

Despite the tremendous contributions Asian Americans made to literally enrich California, the White American majority became more nervous about the might of Asian Americans and their potential to be a leading force in California's agricultural industry.

---

7   https://alumni.berkeley.edu/california-magazine/march-april-2006-can-we-know-everything/year-4702-reunion-no-other

8   https://www.nps.gov/nr/travel/asian_american_and_pacific_islander_heritage/locke-historic-district.htm

9   http://www.locketown.com/more_history.htm

After all, the Delta heartland was a major source of California's agricultural economy, and agriculture was a significant part of California's economy.

As a result of this xenophobic anti-Asian sentiment, the Alien Land Act became law in California in 1913. This law forbade those ineligible for citizenship from owning land. The law obviously targeted Asian Americans, who were not allowed to become citizens. (Similar Alien Land Laws had existed since at least the 1850s, during the height of the anti-Chinese Yellow Peril era. California's 1913 law mainly targeted Japanese Americans, for two reasons: (a) Chinese immigration had slowed by then, because of the Chinese Exclusion acts and (b) Japanese American farmers were becoming such successful businessmen that they posed a real threat to White Americans.

So, because of the racist Alien Land law, ever since Locke was founded, in 1915, Chinese Americans were never allowed to own the land under their own houses.

Modern History of Locke; National Historic Landmark status

Locke's decline began slowly in the 1930s as the agricultural industry declined and Prohibition ended in 1933. Children of original Chinese American Locke families began moving out, attending college, and becoming professionals.[10]

In the 1940s and 1950s, Locke's Chinese American population declined further. In the 1960s and 1970s, non-Asian Americans began moving in in larger numbers, many of them intent on honoring Locke's past. All the while, Locke has remained popular with artists, motorcyclists, history buffs, and filmmakers.

In 1990, Locke was designated a National Historic Landmark for being the "largest and most intact surviving example of an historic rural Chinese-American [*sic*] community in the United States."[11]

Ironically, many groups and some press, including the National Park Service, still erroneously refer to Locke with the slur "Chinatown."[12]

In 1977, Hong Kong millionaire developer Ng Tor-tai bought the town. But, his attempts to turn Locke into a "Chinese Disneyland" failed, thanks largely to the resistance of residents and local Asian American community members who protested the gross commercialization of their home. They organized rent strikes, testified at government meetings, and resisted Locke being turned into a world fair-style "cultural village." Later, they also resisted California Sate Parks' turning it into a state park. They received support from the Sacramento County Board of Supervisors, the governor's office, Sacramento-area Asian American advocacy organizations, Sacramento Housing and Redevelopment Agency (SHRA), and preservationists.[13]

---

10 https://www.nps.gov/nr/travel/asian_american_and_pacific_islander_heritage/locke-historic-district.htm

11 http://www.locke-foundation.org/locke-history/

12 https://www.nps.gov/nr/twhp/wwwlps/lessons/locke/lofacts3.htm;   http://articles.latimes.com/2001/jun/06/local/me-7133

13 http://www.csmonitor.com/1980/0515/051561.html

Revitalization

Locke began to decline physically, and by 2000, its degree of disrepair, especially its archaic septic system, was so great that the whole town was close to being deemed uninhabitable. SHRA convinced the developer's representative, longtime town figure and property owner Clarence Chu, to sell them the town. They planned to subdivide the town and finally sell parcels of land back to residents.

This entire revitalization process took 5 years. It was an extremely difficult and complex process. SHRA enlisted help from groups interested in Locke's future: the Sacramento County Board of Supervisors, Sacramento-area Chinese American advocacy groups, California's Office of Historic Preservation, residents, building owners and others. Not only did SHRA have to precisely subdivide the town, but also the committee of stakeholder representatives had the painstaking challenge of creating every detail of rules by which the town would be managed and preserved, both physically and culturally. The process was, to say the least, arduously challenging.

In 2004, Locke's revitalization was formally completed when Sacramento County officially sold the land to Locke residents. This was the first time in almost a century that any Locke resident had owned their own land.

Today, the tiny town of Locke is 102 years old. Visitors can "walk back in time" exploring this "hidden" gem, since Locke's wooden buildings and sidewalks, its narrow alleyways, look very similar to how it did in the early 1900s. Locke's Main Street resembles an old-fashioned Western movie set (yet residents resent it being called a "ghost town").

In reality, thanks to the efforts of past and present stakeholders, Locke is still thriving with restaurants, stores, and museums. Locke continues to have a multicultural community of residents, most of whom are loyal to preserving its rich history.

Chinese American residents of Locke hanging bok choy, a Chinese vegetable, which they grew in Locke's Community Garden, Key Street, Locke, 1975.

James Motlow, coauthor, *Bitter Melon: Inside America's Last Rural Chinese Town*. Photo courtesy of James Motlow.

Locke's Food and Restaurants

One of Locke's key features is its community garden. Created in the 1930s, when the Depression forced residents to grow their own food, residents grew Chinese produce such as *bok choy*, winter melon, bitter melon, and loquats. Legend has it that pigs were roasted on Sundays in an oven near the garden.

Throughout its history, Locke had many restaurants and stores. During its heyday in the 1920s, there were six restaurants and nine grocery stores in Locke.

One of the first restaurants was a Chinese restaurant on Main Street co-owned by Lee Bing (who is credited with founding Locke). In 1934 (some say 1924), it was sold to Al

Adami, an Italian American. Adami was Locke's first non-Chinese business owner. Adami named it Al's Place (nicknamed "Al the Wop's," with Al's blessing). Al's remains a popular spot for locals and tourists—especially motorcyclists. It offers free liver and onions every Valentine's Day, and how dollar bills get stuck onto its ceiling is still a mystery. The families who have owned "Al the Wop's" have been supportive of Locke's Chinese American residents and history.

Happy Café was a Chinese restaurant near the end of Main Street with a restaurant on the bottom and a "taxi dance" hall on the second floor. Another Main Street restaurant was the Japanese Bakery and Lunch Parlor. It started as a gambling hall, and had a bakery downstairs. There was a fish market on Main Street as well.

One of Locke's first-ever buildings, built in 1915, became the Moon Café, flanking River Road and Main Street. Known as the Hing Lee Building, it was built by Lee Bing for his residence, general store, and headquarters. After Lee Bing sold the building to the Chee Family, it became a Chinese restaurant in 1937. Chee Fat's wife was named Moon, hence the restaurant's original name: the Fat Moon Company. After Chee's death, Joe Chow married Moon and together they ran the restaurant. It was renamed the Moon Café.

The Moon Café served Chinese food, authentic and Americanized. It still stands today, although now it is an artists' gallery and store. Remarkably, it still has its original neon "Chop Suey" sign hanging on the River Road side.

As of 2016, the only remaining Chinese restaurant in Locke is Locke Garden. It was Locke's first building, built in 1912 by Tin-Sin Chan and the Owyeung families. Originally, a beer parlor, then a pizza parlor (Tule's) in the 1960s and 1970s, Locke Garden became a Chinese restaurant in the 1980s. Since 2000, Locke Garden has been owned by Catherine and Ivan Zhang, from Jungshan, China. Fittingly, the Zhangs own the house next to that owned by Connie King, Locke's "Mayor" and "Mom" for many years (see the following). Their house's previous owner, Spanish American Laurence "Larry" Gimenez, was Connie King's adopted "paper son."

Locke's "Right of First Refusal"

Symbolically "Righting a Historic Wrong"
It is rare that living communities have the chance to help right historic wrongs. But, the Sacramento and Locke communities helped do just that with the passage of the historic RFR.

During the planning of Locke's revitalization, three representatives of Sacramento Chinese American advocacy groups wanted to address the racist Alien Land Act and its impact on Locke. They sat on SHRA's stakeholders' committee charged with drafting plans for how Locke would be managed in the future. One of them was the actual chair of the committee.

The three community representatives believed Locke's revitalization would be incomplete without addressing the appalling Alien Land Act barring original residents from owning land in Locke. Unfortunately, there was no way to actually legally right the historic wrong of the law.

But in the spirit of righting this historic wrong, the representatives conceived of an RFR, which they considered the next best thing. Both symbolically and in reality, this RFR would—at long last—allow prior Locke residents to finally own the homesteads of their ancestors. The idea—granting the town's governing body, the Locke Management Association (LMA), the RFR to purchase any future Locke property for sale—was intended for the LMA to act on behalf of original Locke residents and their families, eventually selling the property to these families.

The RFR was the brainchild of these three Chinese American representatives on the Locke CAC (the Sacramento County committee overseeing Locke's revitalization): CAC Committee Chair Christina Fa of the CACS; community-at-large member Derrick Lim; and Jon Barnato of the Organization of Chinese Americans-Sacramento. Their *pro bono* legal counsel was Remy Thomas Moose Manley, LLP. The California Insurance Commissioner (then Sacramento Vice Mayor), Dave Jones, was instrumental in securing this legal assistance. The late consultant Karen Tomine provided invaluable guidance and vision.

The Right of First Refusal Prevails

After 3 years of tireless support by its advocates, the RFR won the backing of Sacramento's Asian American community, the Locke CAC, and finally the Sacramento County Board of Supervisors (approved May 13, 2003).

The passage of this policy was historic. It was covered in a Sunday edition of *The New York Times* in their feature of Locke's revitalization (June 29, 2003), albeit inaccurately crediting the County for coming up with the RFR.

In 2016, there was a major legal triumph for the LMA: the RFR withstood a major legal challenge. Property owner Martha Esch bypassed the RFR and bought her property in a private transaction in 2011; she argued in part that the RFR should not apply because it discriminated against non-Chinese Americans. In February 2016, the Sacramento Superior Court of the County of Sacramento essentially ruled against this 5-year long challenge of the RFR, thus validating the RFR and its legality.

"Locke Mom" and "Locke Mayor" Connie King

One of the most well-known Locke figures in the twentieth century was Constance "Connie" Tom King or Connie King. Born in nearby Isleton, she moved to Locke in 1948 after marrying Locke resident Tommy King. Connie King was the unofficial "Locke Mom" and Locke "Mayor" for decades.

For years, Connie effectively lobbied for the rights for Locke residents to own their land. Every time she testified, Connie spoke without notes, from the heart, and powerfully. In one meeting, she said, "I'm here to represent the men who have gone . . . I promised those men we would own the land under our homes one day. We've been waiting a long time for this."[14]

14 https://alumni.berkeley.edu/california-magazine/march-april-2006-can-we-know-everything/year-4702-reunion-no-other

More than one Sacramento County supervisor attested to her compelling testimony in raising Locke's profile in their eyes.

Connie served as the first Vice Chairperson of the Locke CAC. She was so dedicated to Locke that at the first public event hosted by the LMA, Connie generously baked more than 2,000 of her signature almond cookies and gave them to friends and visitors.

On December 11, 2004, when Locke's land was officially transferred to Locke residents, Connie King raised her arms to Heaven. Later, she said she was saying to the former residents, "We finally got our land! We finally got our land!"

Connie King raises arms in elation when Locke's land was finally transferred to its residents after almost nine decades. December 11, 2004. (left to right: King's granddaughter Sabrina King; Connie King; Phyllis Sylvia, Placer Title Company)

© Christina Fa Mark

Connie continued to work tirelessly to keep things running smoothly in Locke, always willing to teach visitors about Locke's history and allowing them to view her private "toilet garden" (toilets of "old timers" who had passed away, now being used as planters). She used to garden by moonlight and walked 10,000 steps every day in her adopted hometown. When Connie passed away unexpectedly in 2009, it seemed the passing of an entire "oldtimer" generation of Locke. Thanks to her persistent work to "save" Locke, Connie King's spirit is felt, especially in the town's Memorial Park and a Chinese vegetable demonstration garden at the site of her Toilet Garden.

Closing Remarks

As discussed in the Introduction, this chapter was based upon the *Double Happiness: Chinese American History Through the Lens of Family, Community, and Food* exhibit. The Exhibit falls under the auspices of the AAS Program and the Wayne Maeda Asian American Studies Archive. Professor Maeda was one of the original Sac State AAS student founders, and he taught in the Program for 43 years. He passed away in February 2013, yet his legacy of educating our society about Asian Americans continues. On a personal level, Wayne always enjoyed a good meal and we had the chance to share quite a few. I remember the month before his passing—our last meal together was a *dim sum* lunch. At that time, he asked me to help preserve his artifacts and book collection, and to be sure that students and interested researchers had accessibility to his collection. Thus, the Wayne Maeda Asian American Studies Archives was created.

The Exhibit was in part, a product of my childhood thoughts and experiences. Our small group of Sac State students from the Wayne Maeda Asian American Studies Archive Student Club played a significant role researching and preparing for "Double Happiness." This exhibit truly provided me with food for thought.

The true inspiration for the Exhibit and this chapter was my family. My father, Yee Quon Wah (Byron Yee Mark to the larger American society), was detained at Angel Island for two months. He successfully passed his interrogation interviews, but in reality, Quon Wah was actually one of the many paper sons who immigrated to the United States.

Quon Wah lived and worked around both Oakland and San Francisco Chinatowns. He patronized Chinatown restaurants such as New Home, Sun Wah Kue, "Uncle H," and SF Chinatown's famous "Pork Chop House." All these restaurants served western dishes such as oxtail stew, pork chops, roast beef, raw vegetable salads, custard pie, and fruit cream pies. So, by eating at these restaurants, Dad was introduced to good "American food" with a Chinese twist.

On Sundays, I remember my father cooking roast beef, with either peas or cream corn and, of course, rice. There was plenty of gravy made from the roast drippings to be soaked up by the beef and rice. On special occasions, he made fried chicken, so that to this day—I still remember how good it tasted.

As a child, I didn't think Dad spent Sundays, his only day off, differently from any other American enjoying their weekend. But, to this man, an immigrant from China, who spoke little English and who worked his entire adult life in the United States as a Laundryman, he truly enjoyed his family's weekly outings to Chinatown, playing in a park, and ending with an "American dinner." As a child, I did not question how and why my father incorporated his taste for western food or how he learned to become an expert cook. It was ironic that this snapshot in time of one Chinese American family was simultaneously part of the uniqueness of Chinese America, and yet similar to how many American families enjoyed their weekends together.

Moon Café, Frank Fat's, and Violet's Dining Room were contact points in Chinese American community life where new immigrants were exposed to mainstream American society. The restaurant owners frequently made friends with customers from all walks of life that wanted good food at affordable prices. By the 1930s, urban Chinese restaurants such as Frank Fat's made "American food" just as good or even better than many mainstream "American" restaurants. As a result, Frank Fat's and Violet's Dining Room became gathering places for families and friends of all ethnic groups, and even for cross-cultural gatherings.

One of the most important people in my life was my grandmother, Violet Wong. In 1982, she passed away at the age of 87. She was the first Asian American actress and a pioneer in the Chinese American culinary world . . . but for me, she was Grandma. One night, I went to visit her as I was preparing to return to Hawai'i. I walked into her bedroom and she was semi-conscious. She asked me *"Nei yak jou?"* which literally means, "Have you eaten yet?" But what the phase really means is, "Are you well?" A few hours later, she passed away.

Whenever I think of my grandmother, family, community togetherness and sharing food comes to the forefront—and yes, Grandma, as you have taught me, I continue to eat well and be well.

—Gregory Yee Mark
The Great Grandson of a Gold Mountain Man

Note: Christina Fa Mark was the Chair of the Locke Community Advisory Committee, Sacramento County's committee charged with drafting plans for Locke's revitalization. For 5 years, she chaired its tempestuous meetings. She was the principal architect of Locke's Right of First Refusal.

References

A Tribute to Frank Sai-Fat (memorial booklet, November 1997). *Chinese American Council of Sacramento*.

Bailey, E. (2001, June 6). Hope for last rural Chinatown. *Los Angeles Times*. http://articles.latimes.com/2001/jun/06/local/me-7133

Gillenkirk, J. (2006, March April). Year 4702: A reunion like no other. *California Magazine*, Can We Know Everything issue.

Gittelsohn, M.–L., (2014). Choy Suey and Apple Pie Poems. *New Women's Voices Series*, 110.

Liu, H. (2016). *From Canton restaurant to Panda Express: A history of Chinese food in the United States.* New Brunswick, NJ: Rutgers University Press..

Loo, C. M. (1991). *Chinatown: Most time, hard time.* New York, NY: Praeger.

McBride, S. (1980, May 15). On this site: Chinese Disneyland? *The Christian Science Monitor*. http://www.csmonitor.com/1980/0515/051561.html

Murphy, D. E. (2003, June 29). This land is made, finally, for Chinese settlers. *The New York Times*. http://www.nytimes.com/2003/06/29/us/this-land-is-made-finally-for-chinese-settlers.html

Taylor, B. (1850). *El Dorado: Adventures in the path of empire* (p. 117). New York, NY: George P. Putnam.

Chapter 24

The Story of California, Ishi, and NAGPRA

Vanessa Esquivido-Meza

Important Words and Concepts in This Chapter

There are several important words and concepts throughout the upcoming chapter. The words appear several times in different places in order to help you remember the words and understand the chapter. The words are defined several times:

- Immediately below right before the chapter begins
- In text boxes throughout the chapter
- In red and boldfaced within the chapter
- In a glossary in expanded form at the end of the units

Some of the words also appear in other chapters. Talk about the words with other students, teachers, friends, and family members before you read, while reading the chapter, and after you have read the chapter.

Artifact

An object produced or shaped by human craft, especially a tool, weapon, or ornament of archaeological or historical interest.

Federally Recognized Tribes

Federally recognized Indian tribes or groups are eligible for funding and services from the Bureau of Indian Affairs (BIA). There are currently 566 federally recognized tribes throughout the United States. This is an important political and legal

Contributed by Vanessa Esquivido-Meza. © Kendall Hunt Publishing Company.

category, as there are also "state recognized tribes" and "unrecognized tribes," which are not officially recognized by the U.S. government.

Native Hawaiian Organizations

Native Hawaiian Organizations (NHOs) are nonprofit organizations authorized by the Small Business Administration (SBA) to participate in the 8(a) Business Development program. NHOs provide invaluable economic benefits to the State of Hawaii and the Native Hawaiian community by developing job opportunities, building the capacity of innovative industries, and supporting important social and economic programs.

Repatriation

To restore or return to the country of origin, allegiance, or citizenship *repatriate* prisoners of war.

Ishi

Ishi was labeled "the last wild Indian in North America" when he stumbled into an Oroville rancher's barn on August 28, 1911. T.T. Waterman and Alfred Kroeber determined him to be from a previously unknown Yana tribe in the Deer Creek region.

Anthropologist

Someone who undertakes the scientific study of the origin of a phenomenon, object, idea, or style. Anthropologists have been part of the destruction of culture and part of the preservation of culture.

Posttraumatic Stress Disorder

Recurring and ongoing experiences of trauma-related stress after a traumatic experience or set of experiences.

Postapocalyptic Stress Syndrome

Recurring and ongoing experiences of trauma-related stress from having direct experiences of a complete and total loss of culture, livelihood, and agency; or from having those experiences in one's family or ancestry.

Lets begin with a question; do you think it is ethical to dig up and study Native American remains and artifacts for scientific study?[1] This has been a topic of debate and controversy for over a century between the Native American and scientific communities. Until recently, native peoples have been powerless in protecting their deceased ancestors, and the Native American Graves Protection and Repatriation Act (NAGPRA), signed into law by George W. Bush in 1990, changed that.[2] NAGPRA was the response to Native American political activism, a legal mechanism by the U.S. government to address one aspect of injustice experienced by Native Americans. NAGPRA allows Federally Recognized Tribes and Native Hawaiian Organizations to file claims with museums, universities, and other repositories that receive federal funding.[3] Public museums and other collections that possess Native American skeletal remains, sacred objects, associated and unassociated funerary objects, and cultural patrimony (items held in communal ownership) are subject for repatriation

> **Repatriate:** To return someone or something to their or its homeland, country of origin or people.

Inside view of George Wharton James residence, showing a tremendous number of Native American artifacts, Pasadena, ca. 1908. The shelves, which were constructed close to the ceiling, house numerous vases and baskets. Two short totem poles sit on the shelf directly above a large tribal mask and a wooden cushioned bench. Over a dozen unique rugs (or blankets?) hang from their individual poles mounted on the wall. On the ceiling, several jugs hang at the upper left. In the left foreground is a wooden table covered with similar patterned rugs as those that are hanging. On top of the table are two vases, one with a plant, and a bowl. A thick rug and a leopard skin rug cover the wooden floor. Source: Digitally reproduced by the USC Digital Library; From the California Historical Society Collection at the University of Southern California.

Men with Native American artifacts in cases, in preparation for move to museum 1920. Public Domain image.

---

1   Throughout this chapter, I will use the terms Indian and Native American.
2   U.S. Congress, 1990. Native American Graves Protection and Repatriation Act (NAGPRRA). Public Law 101-601, 25 U.S.C 3001 et seq. 104 Stat. 3048. Federal law enacted 16 November 1990.
3   There is a difference between federally recognized tribes and nonrecognized tribes.

(transferring custody of ownership) to the culturally affiliated Indian tribe or Hawaiian organization (their closest living relative).[4]

So what does that all mean? In order for us to understand the significance of NAGPRA, we should explore this history, and by doing so, we focus on one of California's most known Indian: the story of Ishi, "the last of the Yahi" Indians and regarded as "the last wild Indian." In 2000, Ishi's brain was repatriated to the Redding Rancheria and Pit River Tribe in northern California.

California

California has always been immensely diverse, even before colonization. It is estimated that the population during the precontact period consisted well over 300,000 Native Americans. There were over 500 distinct tribes, and 90 different languages were spoken, not including the different dialects.[5] There are many Native stories that map California's landscape. Stories that explain why things are the way they are, why a mountain or river is important to certain peoples living near them, and stories to keep balance between the people and the land. In terms of the indigenous landscape, it is important to remember California Indians are a place-based people. This is significant, as California Indians believe that land is central to their worldviews because their homeland is where their religions, governments, languages, and judicial systems came into being. This is important to keep in mind that land and territory are vital to each California Indian tribe, it means a great deal to be laid to rest in the area where your people originated from, thus completing ones journey in a circular way.

NAGPRA requires the return of

1. **Native American Skeletal Remains**
2. **Sacred Objects**
3. **Funerary Objects**
4. **Cultural Patrimony**

In some ways, the history of California Indians is somewhat distinct from the history of Native Americans in general. California Indians lived through an intensive genocide that was waged against them by the state and the federal government. Although this is also true for Native Americans across the United States, the scale of genocide was comparatively larger and more extensive. Once California's Gold Rush started in 1849, millions of White settlers poured into every part of California looking to strike gold and settle the land. When miners made claims to the land in the search for gold, California Indians were forcibly displaced at the same time. In 1851, the governor of California, Peter H. Burnett, stated "[t]hat a war of extermination will continue to be waged between the races, until the Indian race becomes extinct, must be expected."[6] Given this policy of extermination, to be a California Indian during this time was very dangerous and frightening. By 1900, the California Indian population declined to a devastating 20,000, in five decades, nearly 280,000 Native lives had succumbed to colonization. This is the

---

4 Native American Graves Protection and Repatriation Act.
5 Starn (2004).
6 Heizer and Almquist (1971, p. 26).

time period when Ishi was a young person, and it was because of the dangerous policies instituted by settlers that Ishi's family went into hiding.

While the population decreased so rapidly in California, and throughout the United States, Americans began to view the indigenous peoples as *vanishing Americans*. For example, we see this *vanishing Indian complex* reinforced through James Fenimore Cooper's classic American novel, *The Last of the Mohicans*, published in 1826. Although Cooper's book is fiction, this happens to reflect Ishi's story as well; he quickly becomes a romanticized version of the last "wild" Indian, or the last Yahi. This creates a problem for Indians today, as little people know about 109 federally recognized tribes who still live in California.[7] The vanishing race complex is rooted in continuing the idea that California was void of Indians and settlers need to civilize the "wilderness."[8] Throughout the chapter, we see how the vanishing Indian complex is valued and continued through Ishi's story and experience.

Ishi's Story (Yahi)

Ishi's story is well known throughout California and beyond. He was born around 1860, a time when it was truly difficult for California Indians to survive. Not much is known about his early life, although it is very likely that he witnessed tremendous loss when it came to members of his family and village, as "[v]iolent clashes had broken out between the Yahi and the settlers, but the whites had the numbers and carried out attacks that culminated in 1871 with the massacre of as many as thirty Indians in place called Kingsley Cave."[9] The Yahi survivors of the massacre were small, and Ishi along with his relatives remained in hiding and in fear in the "*Wowunupo Mu Tetna*, or Grizzly Bear's Hiding Place" located in the foothills of Mount Lassen.[10] As an older man, Ishi eventually told people that he went into hiding with his sister, mother, and uncle. Yet, he did not reveal their names, abiding by his traditional Yahi culture, it was prohibited, as it would call their spirit back to earth. In actuality, many California tribes believed personal names should not be shared with strangers, *I'citi* or *Ishi*, which means "man" in the Yahi language, was given to him by Alfred Kroeber. Ishi never told the anthropologist or anyone else for that matter, his real name.[11]

> **Anthropologist:** Someone who studies human beings and their ancestors through time and space and in relation to physical character, environmental and social relations, and culture.

On August 9, 1911, Ishi walked into the local cattle slaughterhouse starving, desperate and alone in Oroville, California. Adolph Kessler, an employee, was wrapping up his

---

7   There are many more tribes that are not federally recognized in the state.
8   "Wilderness" is in quotations because many Native Americans tended to the land that the term wilderness was created to allow guilt free settlement.
9   See Footnote 5, p. 25.
10 See Footnote 5.
11 See Footnote 5, p. 40.

shift when a boy from up the road came running in a panic, when he saw the strange man approaching. Kessler was the first to interact with Ishi, although not sure what to make of him, as Ishi's traditional appearance seemed so out of place, wearing a tattered shirt, pierced septum, sinew strung through his earlobes, and short cut singed hair (a tribal indicator he was in mourning).[12] This was striking to Kessler, as tribes in the area, and for most of the state had already been removed to reservations some 30–40 years before, and the Indians who remained were known as "friendlies," they spoke English and dressed in Westernized attire.[13] Because of this ideology (way of thinking), Ishi was stereotyped as the last "wild" Indian and as such, gained considerable fame in the state even national attention. Kessler called the local sheriff, who came and arrested Ishi that day. Town's people started to gather to get a glimpse of the last "wild" Indian. Newspapers read outlandish headlines and created an interesting world for Ishi. Telegrams to the jail began to come in, offering to place him in carnivals or other attractions, offers that suggest that Americans, in general, did not view Ishi as human.[14] Through Ishi's story, we can see a snapshot of California Indian life. Imagine living during a time of high racial tensions, land encroachment, and fear of imprisonment just because of your racial background and ethnic identity.

Ishi and Anthropologists

When someone else is telling your stories, . . . in effect what they're doing is defining to the world who you are, what you are, and what they think you are and what they think you should be.

—*Lenore Keeshig-Tobias (Ojibwa)*[15]

It is important to talk about the relationships between native peoples and anthropologists before we move on with Ishi's story. Anthropology is the study of human beings, which include the past and present. Where ethnic studies focuses on race, ethnicity, gender, sexuality, class, and nation through structures of power.[16] Perspective is the key when we learn about different histories, and who is writing that history. Alfred Kroeber built the anthropology department at University of California, Berkeley, in 1900, and focused on salvage ethnography on California Indians. Salvage ethnography ideology centered on native peoples, mentioned above, as a vanishing race hence this information needed to be collected quickly before they went "extinct." Kroeber valued knowledge from (mostly male) Indians who did not assimilate into Westernized culture. This is where Kroeber was heavily critiqued; he failed to write about why

---

12 Thomas (2000, p. 84); see Footnote 5, p. 33.
13 See Footnote 5, p. 34.
14 See Footnote 12, p. 85.
15 Cooper (2008, p. 1).
16 This definition is from Gary Okihiro.

Indians were forced to assimilate, and purposely left out the impact of genocide on California Indians in his scholarship. Kroeber is known as the ". . . [Rescuer] and nemesis-the man who helped to 'salvage' the cultural experiences of 'savages' from likely oblivion; and the man who kept his 'silence about the costs of white conquest' [colonization]."[17] Now this is not to say, the information is not beneficial to tribes today, many of them seek out these salvage ethnographies to revitalize (bring back) parts of the culture that, as Dr. Cutcha Risling Baldy (Hupa, Yurok, Karuk) puts "went to sleep," and now we are reawakening them.[18]

> **Ishi also held a level of independence, not just as a victim but a true survivor. When the Bureau of Indian Affairs (BIA) sent an agent to check on Ishi's wellbeing and an offer to move him to an Indian reservation, Ishi declined. . .**

Once Alfred Kroeber heard of Ishi's capture, he sent Thomas Waterman, **anthropologist** and colleague, to visit Ishi in the Oroville jail. If Kroeber only valued traditional information from Indians, Ishi was his ultimate treasure, as the last "wild" Indian untainted by Westernization.[19] Waterman was able to connect with Ishi by speaking a couple words in the Yana language from a small vocabulary list he brought from the university. Ishi was excited to hear his language, even just a few words of it.[20] He was then moved to the **anthropology** museum in San Francisco, where "[i]t would be convenient to have the Indian there to study his language and culture."[21] Ishi was always the first and foremost scientific specimen to the people around him, the fact that he was also a human came in second.

Ishi also held a level of independence, not just as a victim but a true survivor. When the BIA sent an agent to check on Ishi's well-being and an offer to move him to an Indian reservation, Ishi declined by saying that "[h]e preferred to stay among the anthropologist, and wished to grow old and die in his new museum home."[22] The point here is Ishi was indeed traditional, but he also controlled how much he wanted to adapt to this new world outside of the foothills. He enjoyed luxury items of the museum, such as pillows and beds, coconut layer cake, and soda.[23] He wore suits and other Western clothing; Ishi was a person, not just an Indian.

---

17 Platt (2011).
18 Dr. Cutcha Risling Baldy is using Dr. Wesley Leonard's analysis of awakening languages for revitalizing culture.
19 This was inaccurate, as Ishi "to avoid starvation, he and the others stole canned beans, bags of barley, and tins of biscuit from nearby cabins . . . ." See Footnote 5, p. 25.
20 See Footnote 5, p. 38.
21 See Footnote 5, p. 40.
22 See Footnote 12, p. 47.
23 See Footnote 5, pp. 43–45.

Postapocalyptic Stress Syndrome

Ishi also suffered great loss in his life; he spoke little about his life prior to 1911 and if he did, the retelling of the events would leave him depressed, taking him time to recuperate.[24] Kroeber witnessed how Ishi "was occasionally 'bewildered,' broke into a 'high unnatural giggle,' and showed 'not the least initiative'. . . ." Today, these symptoms are connected to posttraumatic stress disorder (PTSD).[25] According to Dr. Lawrence Gross (Anishinaabe), native peoples live in a postapocalyptic world today, ". . . defined not as the end of time, but as the end of the world." That Ishi witnessed the end of his Yahi world but as Gross says this ". . . does not necessarily imply the end of the worldview (traditions) of those people (like the Yahi)."[26] Gross calls this, postapocalyptic stress syndrome (PASS). Removed from the foothills of Mount Lassen, Ishi lived in a very new world, far from what he knew and believed. At times, Ishi practiced aspects of his traditional life, such as volunteering to make arrowheads in the museum as a demonstration on Sundays.[27] He truly lived in two worlds. Maybe this was a form of self-healing, a way Ishi could control in his life, to not forget his Yahi roots.

> **Postapocalyptic Stress Syndrome:** On going and widespread stress within communities who have experienced their entire world and everything in it destroyed.

Many describe and remember Ishi as a kind soul. He was close to Alfred Kroeber, Thomas Waterman, and many others at the museum, going out for dinners or tours to different places. He even befriended Dr. Saxton Pope, a surgeon at the local hospital. They would practice their archery skills in the park. Ishi also helped out the nurses by cleaning their tools or singing Yahi songs to the sick patients.[28] But in 1915, Ishi became ill and was diagnosed with tuberculosis. Ishi was on his deathbed in California, while Alfred Kroeber was away in New York on business. Kroeber demanded he be kept up to date with Ishi's condition through daily telegrams. However, Kroeber received word that Ishi was dying. Kroeber instructed his colleagues to follow Yahi protocol, as Ishi would have wanted. There should be very little physical handling of his body, cremation, and a burial of his ashes in an urn (although, traditionally a basket would have been used). Unfortunately, on March 25, 1916, Ishi died in San Francisco, with Dr. Saxton by his side.[29]

Maybe it is here in death, Ishi found out who was friend and who was foe. Ishi made it clear that he did not approve of postmortem dissection. However, after he died, Dr. Saxton Pope chose science over Ishi's wishes and ordered an autopsy on his body. When Alfred Kroeber heard of the plan, he quickly sent a telegram to "shut it down" and "Say

---

24 See Footnote 5, p. 44.
25 See Footnote 5, p. 41.
26 Gross (2003).
27 See Footnote 5, p. 44.
28 See Footnote 5, p. 47.
29 See Footnote 12, p. 88.

for me that science can go to hell."[30] But the telegram came too late and the pathologist Jean Cook, another acquaintance of Ishi, performed the operation. After his head was decapitated, the doctors removed Ishi's brain and placed it in a large glass container filled with formaldehyde (a gas solution for preservation). As this is an interesting turn of events, much like a horror movie, the scientist, anthropologist, and physicians all held a fake funeral for Ishi, as if they were not a part of his demise and purposefully disregarded his death wishes. It was Kroeber who felt incredible guilt after the passing of Ishi. Shortly after Kroeber's first wife, Henrietta died of tuberculosis. Did Ishi contract tuberculosis from her or from his visits to hospital?[31] No one knows, but either way, there was considerable ethical reflection on everyone's part.

Ishi and Repatriation

Through this chapter, we see how native people have survived through genocide, forced and pressured to adapt to Western culture and if adapted were criticized for it. We see how Ishi was more valued as a scientific specimen than human, even when Kroeber said there would be no scientific value of dissecting Ishi because, ". . . We (UC Berkeley) have hundreds of Indian skeletons that nobody ever comes near to study."[32] How many is enough? How many tribes want their family members back to lay them to rest? Why continue to keep Native American remains when the communities have consistently asked for their return? James Riding In (Pawnee) compares the mass collection of Native American remains throughout the United States as a "spiritual holocaust."[33]

In 1997, 7 years after the passing of the Native American Graves Protection and Repatriation Act (NAGPRA), Arthur Angle (Maidu) stood up and declared to finally honor Ishi's burial wishes. People knew where Ishi's ashes were buried, in the Colma cemetery in California, but the big question remained. Where was Ishi's brain? Investigation perused, combing through Dr. Pope and Dr. Cook's notes did not provide any clues, had they removed his brain or did they put it back?

When the Phoebe Hearst Museum of Anthropology (where Ishi lived) was asked about the whereabouts of his brain, the reply specified that there was no evidence that Ishi's brain was located in the collection.[34] Soon after Arthur Angle sought help from anthropologist, Dr. Orin Starn, who located a file at Berkeley, which revealed that Kroeber had sent Ishi's brain to the National Museum collection on January 5, 1917 to Aleš Hrdlička, (Physical Anthropologist). Hrdlička's, ". . . replied that he would 'be very glad' to add Ishi's brain to his collection, which already contained more than two hundred human brains."[35] Later, in 1999, the National Museum Natural History (NMNH)

---

30 See Footnote 12.
31 See Footnote 5, pp. 47–48 and Footnote 12, p. 89.
32 See Footnote 12, p. 88.
33 Riding (2000).
34 Scheper-Hughes (2003), 120–122.
35 See Footnote 12, p. 221.

confirmed they held what everyone was looking for, "from 1917 until 1980 (Ishi's) remains were kept at the museum in an individual jar, wrapped in cloth and identified with two catalog number tags."[36] What if Ishi was able to fully enter the spirit world, as believed in his Yahi worldview, all that time ago in 1916?

On August 8, 2000, Ishi's brain was returned to the Redding Rancheria Pit River Tribes (neighbors to the Yahi) under the National Museum of the American Indian Act of 1989 (NMAI Act), heavily mirroring the NAGPRA process.[37] And in May of 2000, Ishi was laid to rest with a ceremony lasting several days, Maidu and Pit River Indians worked together in tending the fire, many other Native and nonnative peoples were invited which ended in a communal feast. I think it is also important to point out that during one of the many talking circles held during the ceremony, Alfred Kroeber was "forgiven" as this is a part of the healing process.[38]

NAGPRA Today

The NAGPRA is far from perfect as there are many loopholes that exists and make repatriation difficult. For example, the law can only be applied to institutions with federal funding, which means private collections and institutions are not included. NAGPRA cannot be applied outside of the United States, as other countries laws do not apply here, many of the colonizing countries such as France, Spain, Germany, and London collected Native American culture and remains, which now live in their museums overseas. And culturally unidentifiable remains (remains with no indicators from where they come from) are void to repatriation. Repatriation through NAGPRA is significant in the process of healing. As of 2014, according to the National NAGPRA website, 50,518 individuals have been repatriated.[39] This actively helps in dismantling the vanishing race complex, as native people are still here, and demanding their ancestor's return.

References

Cooper, K. C. (2008). *Spirited encounters*. Lanham, MD: Rowman and Little field Publishers.

"Frequently asked questions," National NAGPRA. Accessed May 20, 2016, https://www.nps.gov/nagpra/FAQ/INDEX.HTM

Gross, L. W. (2003). Cultural sovereignty and Native American hermeneutics in the interpretation of the sacred stories of the Anishinaabe. *Wicazo Sa Review, 18*(2), 127–134.

Heizer, R. F., & Almquist, A. J. (1971). *The other Californians: Prejudice and discrimination under Spain, Mexico, and the United States to 1920* (p. 26). Berkeley: CA: University of California.

Ishi: California State Indian Museum, Ishi Exhibit. Located: 2618 K St, Sacramento, CA 95816.

NAGPRA: Check out the NAGPRA. Retrieved from https://www.nps.gov/nagpra/INDEX.HTM

---

36 Speaker (2003).

37 See Footnote 12, p. 221 and Footnote 36, pp. 74–76.

38 See Footnote 34, p. 122.

39 Frequently asked questions.

Platt, T. (2011). *Grave matters: Excavating California's buried past* (p. 35). Berkeley, CA: Heyday.

Riding, R. (2000). Repatriation: A Pawnee's perspective. In D. A. Mihesuah (Ed.), *Repatriation reader* (p. 109). Lincoln/London: University of Nebraska Press.

Scheper-Hughes, N. (2003). Ishi's Brain, Ishi's ashes: Reflections on anthropology and genocide. In K. Kroeber & C. Kroeber (Eds.), *Ishi in three centuries* (pp. 120–122). Lincoln, NE: University of Nebraska Press.

Speaker, S. Repatriating the remains of Ishi: Smithsonian Institution report and recommendation. In K. Kroeber & C. Kroeber (Eds.), *Ishi in three centuries* (pp. 73–86). Lincoln, NE and London: University of Nebraska Press.

Starn, O. (2004). *Ishi's Brain: In search of America's last "wild" Indian* (pp. 24–25). New York, NY: W.W. Norton and Company.

Thomas, D. H. (2000). *Skull wars: Kennewick man, archaeology, and the battle for Native American identity*. New York, NY: Basic Books.

Chapter 25

The Angel Island Story: Asian Immigration, Paper Sons, and Poetry of Resistance

Gregory Yee Mark and Christina Fa Mark

Important Words and Concepts in This Chapter

There are several important words and concepts throughout the upcoming chapter. The words appear several times in different places in order to help you remember the words and understand the chapter. The words are defined several times:

- Immediately below right before the chapter begins
- In text boxes throughout the chapter
- In red and boldfaced within the chapter
- In a glossary in expanded form at the end of the units

Some of the words also appear in other chapters. Talk about the words with other students, teachers, friends, and family members before you read, while reading the chapter, and after you have read the chapter.

Angel Island

Between the end of the 19th century and the beginning of the 20th century, millions of people—numbers which have not been seen since—came to America in pursuit of a better, freer life. On the east coast, most of the huddled masses were met by the Statue of Liberty and Ellis Island. On the west coast, between 1910 and

---

Contributed by Gregory Yee Mark and Christina Fa Mark

1940, most were met by the wooden buildings of Angel Island. These immigrants were Australians and New Zealanders, Canadians, Mexicans, Central and South Americans, Russians, and in particular, Asians. Of these Asians, the majority were from China. They numbered 175,000.

Central Pacific Railroad

The western portion of the Transcontinental Railroad. Originating in Sacramento and ending in Promontory Summit, Utah. The most difficult part of the Transcontinental Railroad to create, given the huge blockade of the Sierra Nevada Mountains in the way.

Chinese Exclusion Act

The Chinese Exclusion Act of 1882 was the first significant law restricting immigration into the United States. Those on the west coast were especially prone to attribute declining wages and economic ills on the Chinese workers. Although the Chinese composed only 0.002% of the nation's population, Congress passed the exclusion act to placate worker demands and maintain White "racial purity."

Merchant Status Designation

Some Chinese Immigrants were able to adapt to Chinese Exclusion laws in the late 1800s by working within the U.S. Capitalist system and changing their status from laborers to business owners, or merchants. This allowed them to bring family members with them from China and into the United States.

Paper Name (Paper Sons and Daughters)

Due to the Chinese Exclusions Acts, many Chinese came into the United States by using the "Paper Name" system. They bought papers identifying them as children of American citizens and coaching books with detailed information on their "paper" families, which they studied in order to pass grueling interrogations.

Transcontinental Railroad

The first railroad uniting the western and eastern United States. Before the Transcontinental Railroad was completed on May 10, 1869, the two "halves" of the United States were "impossibly" far from each other.

Xenophobia

An individual's irrational and obsessive hatred of people perceived as different and foreign. Related to the concepts of racism and ethnocentrism. All of these can be overcome by the study of the social sciences and coming to appreciate the ideas of culture and social structure as tools for understanding ourselves and others.

Historical Background

In 1850, the first wave of Chinese immigrants began to arrive into the United States. They were predominately young men who faced language and cultural barriers, lack of capital, and little knowledge of American institutions. However, despite these challenges, many early Chinese sojourners set roots in the United States. Chinese Americans greatly contributed to the formation of the United States. They worked as laborers building the Transcontinental Railroad and river levees such as in the Sacramento Delta.

Along with others from around the world, Chinese men went to California to seek fortune in the Gold Rush of 1849. For many reasons, including the fact they were "late" for the Rush, Chinese miners rarely discovered large nuggets of gold. Instead, many eventually made a living by laundering clothes for White miners, establishing small restaurants, and doing shoe repair.

After the Gold Rush died down, the Chinese miners—and additional immigrants from Southern China—were hired to build the western part of the United States' cross-country railroad (Central Pacific Railroad [CPRR]). This railroad was historic because it was the first route connecting the west and east coasts of the U.S. Chinese railroad workers accomplished the "impossible" task of dynamiting and tunneling through the wall of the Sierra Nevada mountain range. Whole crews of men died in avalanches, dynamite explosions, and some even froze to death in the winters.

Four Chinese miners to right of sluice box, Auburn, California. Daguerreotype attributed to Joseph Blaney Starkweather. 1852. *Courtesy of the California History Room, California State Library, Sacramento, California.*

Largely because of these Chinese American workers' physical endurance and extremely backbreaking work, the entire Transcontinental Railroad finished ahead of schedule and under budget. Another reason the Railroad finished under budget was because of the exploitative labor practices of the railroad developers: In the beginning, Chinese workers were paid less than $1 a day.

Popular myth has it that Chinese workers were intentionally left out of the ceremonial photograph marking the completion of the Railroad on May 10, 1869 at Promontory Summit, Utah. In reality, some Chinese workers helped lay the last rails, at least a handful were probably at the ceremony, and speakers did acknowledge them in official remarks. It's actually believed that many Chinese American workers left Promontory Summit 1–2 days before the celebration (the celebration was originally set for May 8, 1869, but was delayed). The most formal recognition of Chinese laborers came after the ceremony, when the Superintendent of the CPRR, J. H. Strobridge, invited some Chinese workers to a private railway car celebration. There, he recognized the "Chinese foreman" before distinguished White guests. The truth was that Strobridge was well known for his anti-Chinese attitudes, so overall, the recognition of Chinese workers was token at best.

© Fotosearch/Stringer/Getty

Secret Town Trestle on Central Pacific Railroad, constructed by Chinese workers such as those seen in foreground. Sierra Nevada Mountains, Placer County, circa 1868. Mammoth Plate: Alfred A. Hart. Publisher: Carleton Watkins.

Chinese American agricultural worker harvesting stalks of celery in the fields. Circa 1932.
Source: Security Pacific National Bank Collection Agriculture-Labor/Los Angeles Public Library

After finishing their work on the Transcontinental Railroad, many Chinese American men found work in the agricultural industry, as farmworkers for the fruit bowl of the Central Valley. These early Chinese American and, later, Japanese American workers proved to be important to California's agricultural industry. Most were too poor to own their own farms; they either worked for farm owners, or became tenant farmers, renting small tracts of land from farm owners, on which they grew their own produce.

In fact, the creation of California's capitol, Sacramento, would not have been possible without the help of Chinese American laborers. Sacramento is flanked by rivers, which threaten to flood the town. As early as 1860, Chinese laborers were brought in from China to create levees to hold back potential floodwater from destroying Sacramento. Based on their knowledge of similar geography in southern China, these Delta laborers turned previously unfarmable swampland into fertile, farmable land.

Anti-Chinese Exclusion Laws

As early as the mid-1850s, anti-Chinese sentiments and actions—and outright racial discrimination—began to emerge.

Many White Americans falsely believed that Chinese workers were taking over their jobs. They considered the Chinese to be barbaric—and in particular, a threat to White men by taking "their" White women. Politicians stirred up racist-based fear of the Chinese, characterizing them as subhuman and denouncing them as rat-eating "heathen." This xenophobic attitude was called the Yellow Peril. These strong racist sentiments were due in part to pressure from various unions to eliminate the competition of the Asian American workforce in California.

In 1882, the United States passed the first of the Chinese Exclusion Laws, which severely decreased the Chinese American population by prohibiting entry of Chinese laborers to the United States. By 1920, the Chinese population in the United States was reduced to 61,639 (half of the number of Chinese in 1890), of which only 7,748 (12.6%) were women (Loo, 1991, p. 47).

Some Chinese Americans were able to resourcefully adapt to the discriminatory anti-Chinese legislation that restricted Chinese laborers from entering the United States. They changed their status from laborer to merchant, thus allowing them to bring their families over. These men became business owners by which they were given the status of businessmen (then called merchants by the government). For the fortunate ones, this exempt status meant they could attain Immigration and Naturalization Service (INS) merchant status designation, and thereby bypass these discriminating laws. As a result, they were able to sponsor family members including wives and children to migrate to the United States, and be reunited as a family. Other Chinese immigrants who did not attain merchant status used other methods to come to the United States.

The Angel Island Immigration Station (1910–1940)

Angel Island in San Francisco Bay played an important role in Chinese immigration to the United States. It has also served as a Native American hunting ground, an Army barrack, a prisoner of war (POW) camp, and, most notably, an Immigration Station. Active from 1910 to 1940, The Angel Island Immigration Station was founded after the destruction of the original Immigration Station in San Francisco in the 1906 San Francisco Great Earthquake.

The Immigration Station processed approximately 200,000 people primarily from Asia that included 100,000 Chinese, 85,000 Japanese, 8,000 South Asians, 1,000 Koreans, and 1,000 Filipinos (Lai, Lim & Yung, 2014). The remainder came from other parts of the globe. However, most came primarily from the Guangdong Province in southern China. Most of these immigrants were single young men from rural areas fleeing harsh economic climates and political instability in China.

Chinese immigrants entering Angel Island were treated more severely than immigrants from other ethnic groups. Often, they left their families in order to make enough money to return home as successful sojourners. Typical reasons for leaving China included catastrophes such as famines and floods, the inability to find work in China, and political and military instability. These young men intended to find jobs in the United States, but instead were detained, questioned, and treated like criminals.

Paper Names

In order to increase their chances of emigrating to the United States, thousands of Chinese immigrants tried to circumvent the Exclusion Laws. One way they did this was through the Paper Name system. How this worked was a Chinese young man (or woman) who wanted to emigrate to the United States would "purchase" the identity of someone who was legally able to emigrate to the United States and use this other person's identity as their Paper Name. An example of someone legally eligible to emigrate would be the son of

Chinese immigrant interrogated by three Angel Island Immigration Station inspectors. Circa 1932.
Source: National Park Services, U.S. Department of Interior.

a Gold Mountain Man (a Gold Mountain Man was a Chinese man who lived in the United States prior to the passage of the Chinese Exclusion Laws). Purchasing a Paper Name was very expensive. In 1928, Gregory Mark's father Byron Yee Mark paid over $3,000 for the cost of the Paper Name "Mark," including supporting documents plus ship passage to the United States. To pay for this cost, he had to borrow money from wealthier relatives but was required to pay back the "loan" soon after his arrival to the United States.

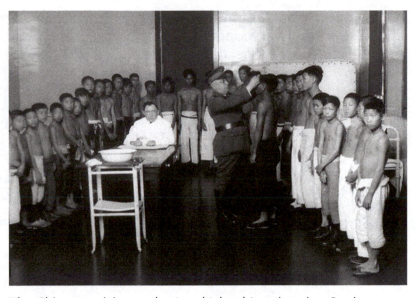

The Chinese arriving at the Angel Island Immigration Station were subjected to the humiliation of unusually scrutinizing medical exams in front of many other people, a practice many considered racist. Circa 1920s.
Source: National Archive.

After purchasing their Paper Name, the young person who wanted to go to the United States (now called a "Paper Son") would have to memorize hundreds of details about the person whose identity they were "assuming." These details were written in a coaching book, which the Paper Son needed to memorize during his long trip from China to the United States. The coaching book included names of all the person's relatives, often tracing back several generations, maps of their villages, and small details about their houses. The Paper Son frequently destroyed his coaching book and threw it overboard before docking in San Francisco. These books were destroyed so that immigration officials could not find evidence that he was a Paper Son when they searched him.

Typically, Chinese immigrants were detained for several months and in some cases, up to 2 years. They were subjected to intense interrogations by immigration officials to prove they were really the people they claimed to be. Questions were asked such as: "How many windows are in your home?"; "What are the marriage dates of your family members?"; "How many steps lead up to your house?"; "Who lived in the third house in the second row of houses in your village?"; and "How many guests were at your wedding?"

The paper name system required the potential immigrant to intimately learn the identity of someone else. If they passed the interrogations, they were allowed to stay in America. If they failed, they could be deported back to China.

Life on Angel Island

While being imprisoned, detainees lived in military-like barracks with no privacy. They were allowed only about 1 hour a day to go outside.

Subjected to such humiliating conditions over months and years, the Chinese detainees often carved poetry into the walls of their barracks as an outlet for their emotions. Even today, many of these poems are visible and the "Angel Island poems" are one of the lasting legacies of the detainees. Here are translations of two poems expressing the frustration and resistance of the detainees:

Coaching Book. A rare surviving example of a Chinese Exclusion Era coaching book, used by family and paper sons to prepare for rigorous immigration interviews at the Angel Island Immigration Station.
Source: From **YellowVisions**, the Asian Americana collection of Christina Fa Mark.

Instead of remaining a citizen of China, I
willingly became an ox.
I intended to come to America to earn a
living.
The Western styled buildings are lofty; but I
have not the luck to live in them.
How was anyone to know that my
dwelling place would be a prison?
~
I think back on the past when I had not experienced hardship.
I resolved to go and seek Taogong (wealth)
The months and years are wasted, and still it has not ended.
Up to now, I am still trapped on a lonely island.

(Lai, Lim, & Yung, 1980)

Food on Angel Island

Understandably, there was conflict between the imprisoned detainees and the immigration officials. One of the main conflicts was about food. Initially, the food served to the detainees was bland, stale, and low quality. As a result, there were food riots, in which some detainees aggressively threw food at the officials. Soldiers from nearby Fort McDowell had to come on to the island to quell the riots.

After several riots, immigration authorities reformed their policies in attempts to improve food quality. They also started employing Chinese cooks from San Francisco Chinatown at the mess hall. The new food was better. Examples of typical Chinese food that was served include pork with greens and salted fish; sweet tapioca soup; and codfish with dried lily flowers and olives. However, the food was still bland. This is likely because the Chinatown chefs were not allowed to stir-fry with traditional woks, but were forced to use steamers to cook the food. Supposedly, this was a safety precaution so that the all-wooden buildings would not catch fire. This steaming method imposed by the Immigration Station administrators resulted in unappetizing food that was tasteless and looked like mush (Lai, Lim, & Yung, 2014).

Poem carved on wall of detention barrack, Angel Island Immigration Station, 2013. Photo: Carol Highsmith. *Source:* Library of Congress.

Actually, the Chinese cooks who worked at the Immigration Station played critical roles for many of the detainees beyond just cooking for them. They helped smuggle information from Chinatown residents to the detainees, such as from concerned family members or Paper Name Family members. This was to assist the detainees with information that might be used in their interrogations. For example, messages were hidden in the bottoms of bowls, or even in bananas (between the bananas and the peels), and, Byron Yee Mark remembered, even under egg yolks. For many Chinese immigrants who came to the United States through Angel Island, their first experience in America was traumatic: the mess hall experience of unappetizing food, food riots, having to receive messages smuggled in food, intimidating interrogations by Federal agents, and being identified as foreign aliens. Today, they would be classified as "undocumented" immigrants.

In many ways, Angel Island was the unintended "birthplace" of thousands of Chinese American families. The racist nature of how Angel Island began and how it was run was unfortunately a precursor of decades more racism, which continues to cloak the Chinese American experience. In this day and age, it is even more vital for us to know and to remember our histories.

—*Christina Fa Mark & Gregory Yee Mark (The son of a Paper Son)*

References

Lai, H. M., Lim, G., & Yung, J. (1980) *Island: Poetry and history of Chinese immigrants on Angel island 1910-1940*. San Francisco: HOC. doi.

Lai, H. M., Lim, Genny, L., & Yung, J. (2014). *ISLAND: Poetry and history of Chinese immigrants on Angel island, 1910-1940* (2nd ed.). Seattle, WA: University of Washington Press.

Loo, C. (1994). *Most time, hard time*. Seattle, WA: University of Washington Press.

Chapter 26

Sacramento Teen On Stephon Clark's Death: "My Community Is Hurting"

Rachael Francois

When 22-year-old Stephon "Zoe" Clark was shot and killed by Sacramento police officers in his grandmother's backyard, he left behind two kids, a fiancé, and a broken, grieving community — my community.

I grew up in Sacramento. And even though I'm still in high school, I live in fear knowing that the next "unarmed black" male or female in the headlines could be my dad, uncle, cousin, or even myself.

Growing up in the black community here, we are trained to always be aware of our surroundings, more than other kids, because one blink too long could be fatal. We proclaim our love for one another before leaving the house or ending a phone call because that could be the last time we hear or see each other alive.

As black youth, we are angry — angry because our government officials do not take us seriously when we express our concerns after our sisters and brothers are slaughtered in the streets by the police.

As black youth, we are confused — confused because we are constantly raising the issue of gun control in America, but it seems like it only matters when white lives are in danger.

Unaware of their privilege, people tell us it's our fault the police kill us, or that we have no reason to fear the police. but many active community leaders such as my uncle, Les Simmons, or Berry Accius reassure us that what we feel is normal and justified, and the police should be learning how to interact with us, not the other way around.

My community is hurting. Stephon Clark's death opened old wounds here. I think back to last month's Sacramento city council meeting and I could see the tension in the room. The city council members stared emotionless at the lively crowd while we all

Sacramento Teen on Stephon Clark's Death: "My Community is Hurting", Youth Radio. Reprinted by permission.

poured our hearts out yearning for change. Just a few days later, at a youth forum, children as young as 8 expressed their pain through spoken word. Seeing and feeling the pain brought tears to my eyes.

It's time people outside the black community value that pain too.

If people valued our lives as much as white kids', gun control, #neveragain and #enough would apply to the cops too. We are being murdered — by the people who are trained to "serve and protect" us. We are seen as numbers rather than individuals. We plan protests, attend marches, but nothing we do is ever enough.

We have proven that we want change, but until the rest of America is ready for change, we will be forced to take the abuse.

Youth from all over Sacramento have come together to heal and change the culture of this community. Although we are all still grieving from this recent tragedy, we have unified as one to help lift each other up. Whether it's speaking at city council, youth town halls, or simply raising awareness, we have all been activated in our efforts to change Sacramento for the better.

THE BLACK PANTHER PARTY CALLS FOR A
RALLY AND NATIONAL PRESS CONFER[ENCE]
TO ANNOUNCE DATE AND PLAC[E]

REVOLUTIONAR[Y]
PEOPLE'S
CONSTITUTION[AL]
[CON]VENTION[AL]

[Mem]orial Washington
Panther Party Cha[irman]
[Direct]ive of Bobby S[eale]

Photo taken by Arya Allender West

Where am I going?   Where am I going?
Where am I going?   Where am I going?
Where am I going?   Where am I going?
Where am I going?   Where am I going?
Where am I going?   Where am I going?
Where am I going?   Where am I going?
Where am I going?   Where am I going?
Where am I going?   Where am I going?
Where am I going?   Where am I going?
Where am I going?   ¿Adonde voy?
Where am I going?   Where am I going?
Auhea wau e hele ai?   Where am I going?
Where am I going?   Where am I going?
Where am I going?   Where am I going?
Where am I going?   Where am I going?
Where am I going?   Where am I going?
Where am I going?   Where am I going?
Where am I going?   Where am I going?
Where I go stay?   Where am I going?
Where am I going?   Where am I going?
Where am I going?   Where am I going?
Kuv yuav mus qhov twg?

Unit IV

Solidarity

Chapter 27

Capitol City Civics and the Black Panther Party

Dale Allender

I would like to thank Billy "X" Jennings, Black Panther Party Archivist for his review of the chapter and for assistance with locating archival footage of the Black Panther Party Sacramento Chapter.

Important Words and Concepts in This Chapter

There are several important words and concepts throughout the upcoming chapter. The words appear several times in different places in order to help you remember the words and understand the chapter. The words are defined several times:

- Immediately below right before the chapter begins
- In text boxes throughout the chapter
- In red and boldfaced within the chapter
- In a glossary in expanded form at the end of the units

Some of the words also appear in other chapters. Talk about the words with other students, teachers, friends, and family members before you read, while reading the chapter, and after you have read the chapter.

Postcivil Rights Era

Often influenced by the Black nationalism of Elijah Muhammad and Malcolm X and by pan-African leaders, proponents of Black liberation saw civil rights reforms as insufficient because they did not address the problems faced by millions of poor Blacks and because African American citizenship was derived ultimately from the involuntary circumstances of enslavement.

Political Education (PE) Classes

A person wanting to join the Party had to attend Political Education PE classes as a Panther in training and read 2 hours a day to stay abreast of the changing situations in the community and world.

Coalition

A temporary alliance of distinct parties, persons, or states for joint action.

Oppression

Unjust or cruel exercise of authority or power. Also, a sense of being weighed down in body or mind: depression, an *oppression* of spirits.

Introduction

Decades into the Post–Civil Rights era, coalitions of youth and elders from many different racial and ethnic groups started coming together spontaneously and in organized advocacy efforts to demonstrate against and to disrupt police brutality. Groups such as the San Francisco 5 and Black Lives Matter started holding rallies in front of police stations, blocking freeways, conducting hunger strikes, and distributing videos of unlawful police activity all over social media. Where did it all begin? Some point to the demonstrations in Ferguson, Missouri after police shot Michael Brown while he held his hands in the air as the origins of this post–civil rights era activism; others point to the demonstrations in Oakland, California after a Bay Area Rapid Transit police officer shot and killed Oscar Grant in the back while he lay face down and handcuffed. The community's response to these two events demonstrates courage and outrage. However, the roots of contemporary antipolice brutality tactics, such as videotaping police officers while they are arresting citizens, direct confrontation about excessive force, and other kinds of activities to monitoring police misconduct can be found in the Black Panther Party for Self-Defense.

Considered a vanguard civil rights organization, the Black Panther Party stood up against police brutality with a combination legal knowledge, media savvy, and militant organizing.

This stylized group of activists wearing leather jackets, dark shades, and black berets tipped deep to one side and supported the community's health, education, nutrition, and safety. However, in spite of undertaking these broad efforts, the Black Panthers are most known and most maligned for their efforts to stop

1970 cover for Eldridge Clever Article about military industrial revolution; revolutionary peoples constitutional convention—coalitions with many groups to rewrite the constitution; Each copy of the paper had the ten-point program and a copy of Emory's art on the back . . . and the rules of the BPP party and who worked at the party headquarters.

Image courtesy of Bill Jennings

police abuse. This chapter will provide a broader understanding of the history, legacy, and personality of the Black Panther Party. The chapter concludes by highlighting the Black Panther Party's Sacramento Chapter.

Origins

In 1966, Part-time law student, Huey P. Newton organized the Black Panther Party for Self Defense, with his friend Bobby Seale in Oakland, California. Counter to many ideas, the Black Panther Party was started on a college campus—not a street corner. Indeed, many of the Panthers were scholars and writers who went on to publish books, such as Eldridge Clever's *Soul on Ice*, David Hilliard's *This Side of Glory*, Angela Davis's *Autobiography*, and Bobby Seale's *Seize the Time*. But, their intellectualism was not an "ivory tower" isolation. Frantz Fanon—one of the Panther's primary sources of inspiration taught them to work and build bridges between the African American intellectual class and common every day African Americans.

The Black Panthers wrote down their ideas in what was called a Ten-Point Platform. All ten points can be summed up in point number ten as a call for "land, bread, and

All Power
To All the People!

Selected Points from the Black Panther Party Ten-Point Platform and Program

1. WE WANT freedom. We want power to determine the destiny of our Black Community.
5. WE WANT education for our people that exposes the true nature of this decadent American society. We want education that teaches us our true history and our role in the present-day society.
7. We WANT an immediate end to POLICE BRUTALITY and MURDER of black people.
10. WE WANT land, bread, housing, education, clothing, justice, and peace. And as our major political objective, a United Nations supervised plebiscite to be held throughout the black colony in which only black colonial subjects will be allowed to participate, for the purpose of determining the will of black people as to their national destiny.

housing, education, clothing, justice, and peace." Other important points on the platform include a call for an immediate end to financial exploitation, police brutality, and murder of all Black and oppressed people. Ending police brutality is one of the last items on the platform. However, addressing this issue became an immediate need because it affected so many other areas of life, such as employment, income, health, relationships, education, and civic participation.

Huey Newton and Bobby Seal developed the idea for police patrols as a way to monitor and perhaps interrupt unlawful police action from the Community Action Patrol Association (CAPA) in Los Angeles. CAPA members used to follow and monitor police officers from a safe, nondisruptive distance to ensure fair and equal treatment of everyone in the community. CAPA members would carry tape recorders, polaroid cameras, and law books. CAPA members report that often the police would destroy their equipment if they were caught recording illegal police activity. As a law student, Huey P. Newton learned that, at that time the State of California law allowed citizens to carry weapons out in the open under certain conditions and contexts. For example, you could not point a gun at someone intentionally or unintentionally. During the Panther police patrols, members of the Panthers carried guns but they were always careful to act within the law. In fact, in addition to guns, they carried law books and often read the law to the police to defend their actions.

As a response, the California legislature created new laws restricting the Panthers right to carry guns in public. In an effort to prevent the new law from passing, the Black Panther Party protested by marching on the California State Capitol in Sacramento with their weapons. News footage of this march is widely available online. In addition to the change in state law, local law enforcement began an aggressive campaign to further disarm members of the Panthers. Further, the Federal Bureau of Investigation (FBI) initiated a program known as COUNTERINTELPRO, which stands for Counter Intelligence Program. Under this program, the FBI successfully used legal and illegal means to defame, disgrace, and shut down the Black Panther Party. Many members were arrested on a variety of charges, but most were ultimately found innocent of the crimes for which they were charged.

In order to become a member of the Black Panther Party, one had to first participate in political education classes. Political education classes lasted several weeks. The classes required prospective members to read a number of books by Frantz Fanon, Malcolm X, Jomo Kenyata, and W.E.B. DuBois among others. As a full-fledged member, one might or might not participate in Police Patrols. More likely a new member would participate in preparing and serving food for the free breakfast program; tutor adults in the night reading classes; work in a free clinic; or help transport elders to the bank or store on pay day. As Mumia Abu Jamal has said, being a Panther meant working long hours in the community.

Although members of the Black Panthers were often accused of feeling hatred toward other ethnicities, there is ample evidence to counter this claim. In fact, the Panthers

In this detail of an ad from the Black Panther Party Newspaper calls for representatives from all of the ethnic-based human rights organizations to come together and rewrite the U.S. Constitution. The ad shows a drawing of Bobby Seale bound and chained in court collaged on top of a photograph of Seale. This picture was taken by Arya AllenderWest.

The newspaper belongs to the Billy X Archives.

were very focused on coalition building—building bridges across communities and creating a unified front to end exploitation of all people. Japanese American, Richard Aoki is a third founding member of the Panthers along with Bobby Seale and Huey P. Newton. Aoki at first declined the invitation to join the Panthers because he was Japanese and not Black. Aoki quotes Huey P. Newton's response to his decision: "struggle against oppression for freedom and equality transforms racial boundaries." Aoki decided to join. Aoki was also part of the third world liberation strike at the University of California, Berkeley that led to the opening up of the curriculum for Ethnic Studies.

Black Panther Party Political Education Class Abbreviated Reading List

1. Malcolm X   The Autobiography of Malcolm X
2. Franz Fanon   The Wretched of the Earth
3. Kwame Nkrumah   I Speak of Freedom
4. C.L.R. James   A History of Negro Revolt
5. J.A. Rogers   Africa's Gift to America
6. W.E.B. DuBois   Black Reconstruction in America
7. John Hope Franklin   From Slavery to Freedom

Women of the Black Panther Party

1. Erica Huggins
2. Elaine Brown
3. Kathleen Clever
4. Angela Davis
5. Assata Shakur

Later, he became one of the first heads of the Asian American Studies program at University of California, Berkeley.

Another example of the Black Panther Party's **inclusiveness** can be found in the words of Fred Hampton, another law student and Chair of the Chicago Chapter. Hampton would often end his speeches by saying, "All power to all people. White power to white people; brown power to Brown people. Yellow power to yellow people; black power to black people; 'X' power to those people we left out; and panther power to the vanguard party." Later, the Party shortened this affirmation to "All power to all the people!

Artist Molaundo Jones' portraits of Erika Huggins, Assata Shakur and Angela Davis.

Black Panther Party Chapters

In addition to the chapters in Oakland and Chicago mentioned above, the Black Panther Party had chapters all over the United States and in several countries around the globe, including India, Australia, New Zealand, and Israel. They also had chapters in several African countries, such as Algeria and Tanzania. The Los Angeles chapter, started by Bunchy Carter included Elaine Brown and Angela Davis. The New York chapter included Assata Sakur, a member of the New York 21 who later escaped from prosecution and fled to Cuba where she is living under asylum to this day. Not all Panthers were able to escape false prosecution. Many members, such as Fred Hampton mentioned above, were killed in ambushes. And some, like Philadelphia Panther, Mumia Abul Jamal are currently still on a death row after serving decades in prison.

This photograph courtesy of the Billy X Archives.

Most Black Panther Party offices had a place where people could view, read, or listen to political material. Many people in the community couldn't afford to buy books or the Black Panther Party newspaper. The people in the community could at least go to the Panther office and read the paper. This is one way that the Panthers raised people's political consciousness. As the sign behind the young man reading explains, refreshments were served every hour. The Panther offices had an open door policy to the community. They saw it as the people's office.

Sacramento Branch of the Black Panther Party

In 1968, Charles Brunson opened the Sacramento Chapter of the Black Panther Party at 2941, 35th street in the Oak Park neighborhood. The Sacramento Chapter operated a number of Survival Programs similar to other chapters, including

- Teaching Ppolitical Eeducation classes that included a liberation school for youth to learn Black History.
- Serving free breakfast to over 150 school children every morning.
- Providing literacy tutoring to help people in the community learn to read.
- Offering legal aid for prisoners, and helping a number get out of jail.

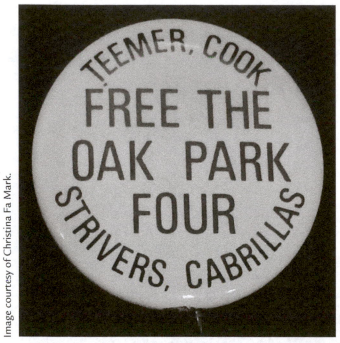

Image courtesy of Christina Fa Mark.

In addition to these efforts to support Black and poor residents of Sacramento, they also participated in rallies in Oakland, such as the free Huey campaigns. These campaigns helped raise political support and legal aid for Huey P. Newton during his incarceration.

Similar to other Chapters, the Sacramento Chapter of the Black Panther Party came under persecution from the federal government. State and local police raided the party office in 1969, destroying property, shooting, and firing tear gas into the building. Panthers and community members inside the building barely escaped out the back door with their

Photo courtesy of Bill Jennings.

Photographer Arya Allender West and Billy X Jennings. Bill X served as a personal aid to David Hilliard, Chief of Staff for the Black Panther Party. Later, Billy X became the personal aid of Huey P. Newton, the Black Panther Party's Minister of Defense.

lives. News footage archived by Billy Jennings and posted on YouTube shows the mayor of Sacramento and members of the Board of Supervisors walking with local Panthers viewing the damage and refuting various accusations of wrong doing with evidence and counter claims.

Again, like other Party Chapters in different parts of California and the country, the FBI and local police continued to pursue them. On one occasion, Panthers were investigated for allegedly creating a coloring book for children depicting people shooting police. Although the book was attributed to Mark Teemer, Lieutenant of Culture for the Sacramento Chapter, some believe that the book was false propaganda created by others. The pursuit turned violent again when Teemer and fellow Panther Jack Strivers were accused of killing a police officer. Teemer, Strivers, and two others were given the name the Oak Park 4 while they sat in jail and moved through the court proceedings. Although local newspapers sometimes cast a negative perception of these men, all four were eventually found innocent.

Although the Black Panther Party existed for a short and tumultuous time, they have had a lasting legacy in community clinics, free breakfast programs, and critical education. But, they are unfortunately still mostly known for their willingness to question abuses of authority and defend the community. This legacy of antipolicy brutality activism can be seen in Black Lives Matter, Say Her Name, the San Francisco Five, and similar movements to emerge early in the twenty-first century.

Chapter 28

Ifa in Oshogbo

Charles Vincent Burwell and Molaundo Jones

Important Words and Concepts in This Chapter

There are several important words and concepts throughout the upcoming chapter. The words appear several times in different places in order to help you remember the words and understand the chapter. The words are defined several times:

- Immediately below right before the chapter begins
- In text boxes throughout the chapter
- In red and boldfaced within the chapter
- In a glossary in expanded form at the end of the units

Some of the words also appear in other chapters. Talk about the words with other students, teachers, friends and family members before you read; while reading the chapter; and after you have read the chapter.

Awo

A person or people being introduced to or initiated into the West African Ifa tradition.

Divine (Verb)

Cultural rituals to provide information about a person's personality or future.

Contributed by Charles Vincent Burwell. © Kendall Hunt Publishing Company.

Ifa

Ifa is a common belief system originating among the Yoruba—a group of cultures who occupied an area bounded by the Niger River, and including what is now known as the Benin Republic, southwestern Nigeria, and part of Togo.

Initiate

One who has been introduced to or has attained some knowledge in a particular field.

Orisha

A divine force of nature within the Yoruba spiritual system of West Africa.

UNESCO

An agency of the United Nations established in 1945 to promote the exchange of information, ideas, and culture.

Babalawo

A Babalawo is a sage or high priest, who is well-versed in the rituals, lore, and history of the Yoruba tradition/religion called Ifa.

Embodiment

The act of giving a tangible, bodily, or concrete form to (an abstract concept).

Odu

A sacred story from the Yoruba people of West Africa, sometimes involving spiritual or supernatural beings that provide guidance on how to live in the world.

Introduction

In 2014, Charles Vincent Burwell and Molaundo Jones journeyed from their home in Brooklyn, New York to Osogbo, Nigeria in Yorubaland, West Africa. Charles Vincent Burwell traveled to Nigeria to become a priest of Ifa. Ifa is a traditional religion that began in nearby Ile Ife, Nigeria and can be found in many parts of West Africa. Charles asked Molaundo to accompany him to Africa to document the initiation. The photo essay illustrates various aspects of the largely secretive ceremony.

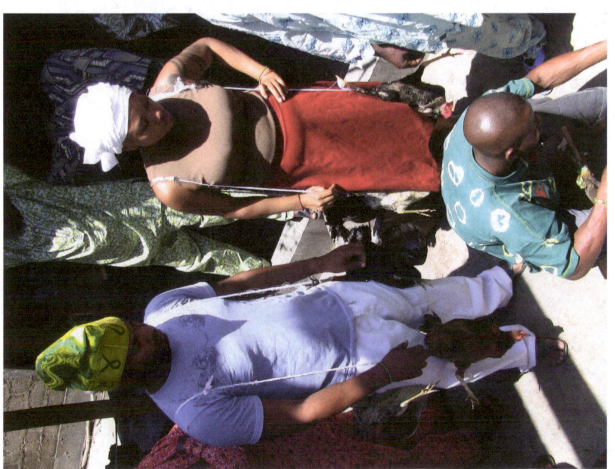

Awos (Ifa initiates) prepare to begin the process of initiating into Ifa. The priest (kneeling) divines to allow the initiation process.

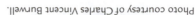

Photo courtesy of Charles Vincent Burwell.

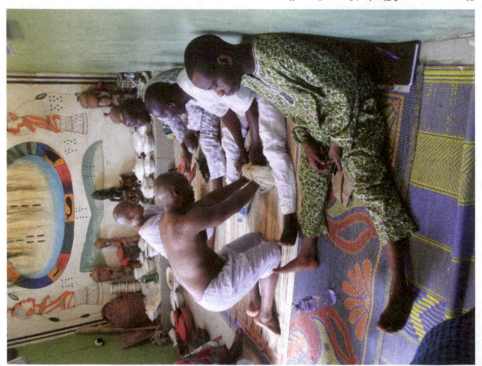

Senior **Babalawos** (priest of Ifa) **divine** and recite **odu** (sacred text) on day one of the initiation process. The conclusion of these divinations will determine whether the **initiates** will be permitted to receive **Ifa**.

Awos pictured being prepared and dressed for **initiation**. This includes bathing, receiving garments, and removing hair from the crown of the head.

Photo courtesy of Charles Vincent Burwell.

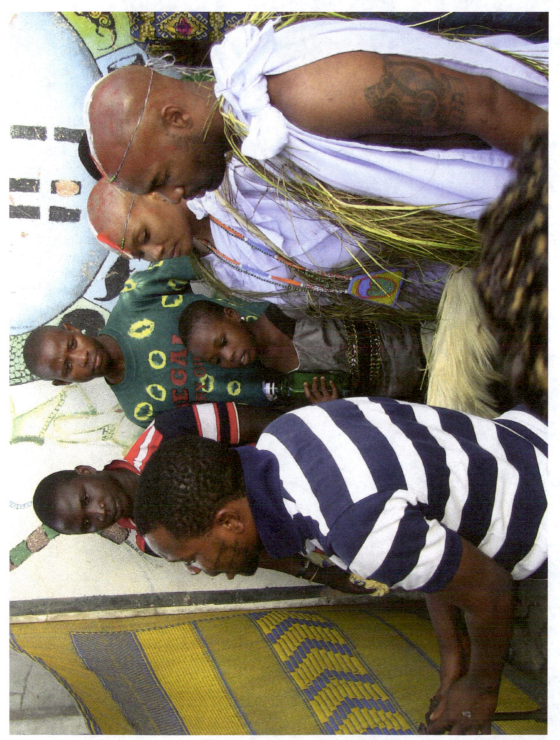

Photo courtesy of Charles Vincent Burwell.

Having been divined and acceptance as initiates of Ifa, the Awos prepare to enter the sacred shrine for initiation. As full initiates they are said to, now, carry Ifa with them. In this state, they are by proxy considered the **sacred embodiment** of the **orisha** Orunmilla. They will remain in this state until the conclusion of the initiation process.

CHIEF AWÓSANMÍ ÓSUNTÓGÙN SÉKOU ALÁJÉ stands on the banks of the Osun River in the Osun **Sacred** Grove.

Photo courtesy of Charles Vincent Burwell.

The initiates pray to the offerings for acceptance into Ifa by the creator (Oludumare/God). Each article offered will be divined upon by the senior Babalawos..

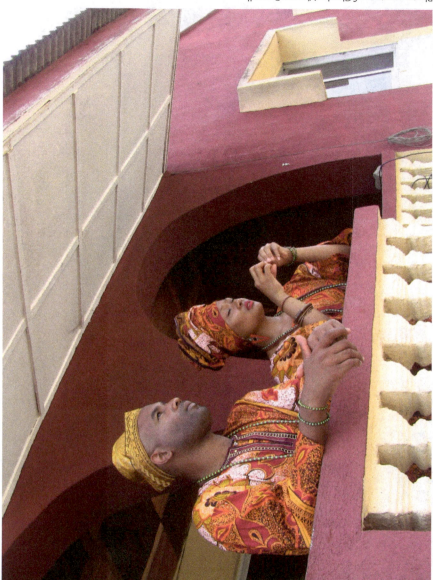

Photo courtesy of Charles Vincent Burwell.

At the conclusion of the initiation, the Awos are presented to the community as Babalawo and Iyanifa. Rather than the end of a process, initiating into Ifa is the beginning of a journey that will continue for many years. To become a Babalawo or Iyanifa with full rights and privileges, the Awos have committed to years of study and ritual. In Osogbo, Nigeria, a Babalawo must commit to no less than 12 years of concentrated study as the sacred text is vast. The Babalawo and Iyanifa, as high priests and priestesses of Ifa, must have a commanding understanding of botany, geology, the divinity of Odu and Orisha, and philosophy.

Photo courtesy of Charles Vincent Burwell.

An initiation into Ifa requires the efforts of a community of individuals. Many have initiated into Ifa at a very young age. Regardless of age, the young Awos retain a striking knowledge and understanding of the principles of Ifa and the Odu (sacred text).

Photo courtesy of Charles Vincent Burwell.

The Awos visit the Sacred Grove. The Osun Sacred Grove, on the outskirts of the city of Osogbo, is one of the last remnants of primary high forest in southern Nigeria. Regarded as the home of the Orisha of fertility Osun, one of the pantheon of Yoruba gods, the landscape of the grove and the Osun River is dotted with shrines, sculptures, and art works that honor Osun and other Orisha. The sacred grove, which is now seen as a symbol of identity for all Yoruba people, is probably the last in Yoruba culture. The Sacred Grove is listed as an UNESCO World Heritage Site.

Back in New York.

Photo courtesy of Charles Vincent Burwell.

I wanted to be sure that it is understood that one cannot "decide" to become a priest of Ifa, rather, they must be allowed to do so by the presiding Babalawos of the particular house. It must, then, be divined upon.

It is very uncommon for photographs to be allowed during an initiation—to many, it is frowned upon. This is more so the case in the west as African Americans are particularly sensitive to who has access to information based on the manner in which information has been used against them in the west. There is an omnipresent concern that once the White majority has access to the customs, rituals, and principles, African Americans will find themselves pushed toward the margins. This is less so of an issue in Africa as they are more enamored with the exposure that social media has provided them. This same access is, incidentally, the reason for the resurgence of African spirituality in the New World. Its emerging popularity in the west has created a renaissance in Yorubaland where Orisha and Ifa currently rank behind Christianity and Islam in terms of popularity despite being the birthplace of the sects.

—*Charles Vincent Burwell*

Chapter 29

Fiji and Fijians in Sacramento

Mitieli Rokolacadamu Gonemaituba,
Neha Chand, Darsha Naidu, Jenisha Lal,
Jonathan Singh, Shayal Sharma,
and Gregory Yee Mark

Introduction and Background

Mitieli Rokolacadamu Gonemaituba

Ethnic 14 Introduction to Asian American Studies is a course taught at Sacramento State University that focuses on topics concerning various Asian Pacific American (APA) groups through a historical perspective. The instructor for the course is Dr. Gregory Yee Mark.

In the Fall of 2016, Dr. Mark met and work closely with two Fijian students, Jonathan and Mitieli, from his Ethnic 14 class. They bonded over the topic of food. One day in lecture, Jonathan had asked Dr. Mark where in Sacramento was the best place for fried chicken. Dr. Mark responded by saying it was better to show him where, rather than just telling. From there, the three would often meet up at restaurants recommended by Dr. Mark, and a bond was formed. After the semester has ended, the three kept in touch. Jonathan and Mitieli would visit Dr. Mark during his Ethnic 14 lecture or met him for lunch. It was during these times that the conversation of having something written on the understudied community of Fijians in California arose. And Dr. Mark approached Mitieli and Jonathan on the idea of having them write something on their experiences of being a Fijian in California, and possibly publishing it in the Ethnic Studies textbook for ninth graders. When approaching the two about this idea, Dr. Mark explained that he understood that Fijians, like many other Pacific Islander groups, were understudied and that there are barely any academic/scholarly literature concerning the group. Dr. Mark was motivated to do this because he felt that all students, including Fijians, needed to be empowered and needed materials of their own in schools or classrooms. And he believed that through Ethnic Studies, this can be achieved.

After discussing this idea with Jonathan and Mitieli, Dr. Mark came to notice a good number of Fijian students in his current Ethnic Studies 14 class in the Fall of 2017. And so, he also approached them about the project he was conducting the Mitieli and Jonathan. Then around the fall of 2017, the group of six of his Fijian students came together and wrote this chapter on the Fijian American perspective on different aspects of the Fijian community in the United States today. Part of the

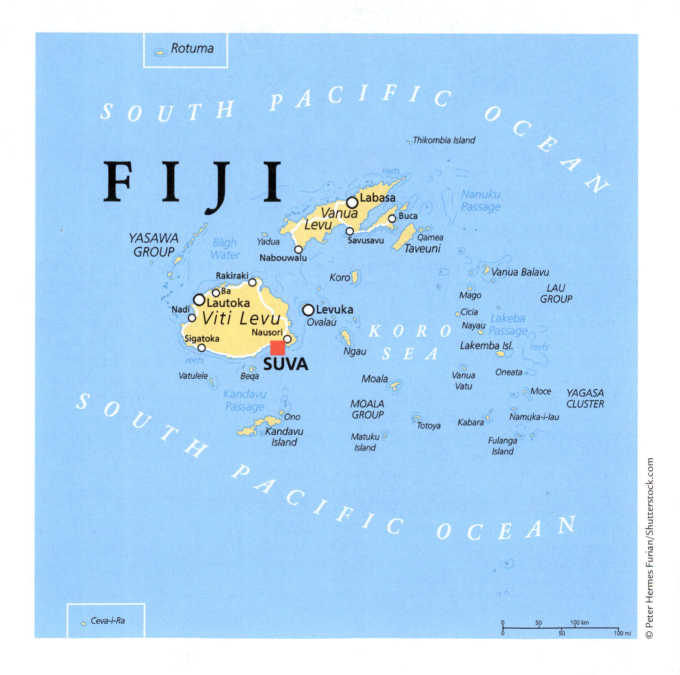

course, Dr. Mark assigns students to do research on one of the Asian American and Pacific Islander groups. The Fijian students were challenged by the general lack of research and information on Fiji and/or Fijians. One of the primary reasons to this chapter is to create more published materials on this small ethnic group in the United States. This starts with the Fijian American students telling their own stories in their own voices.

The islands of Fiji are one of the well-known pacific nations in the South Pacific region. Located in a more accessible location, Fiji owns one of the most strategic locations in the area in terms of commerce and trade. Falling in the line of one of the more important and advantageous trade routes of the world. The nation consists of over 300 islands, some of which are uninhabited. Two main islands are called *Viti Levu* and *Vanua Levu*. *Suva*, the capital of Fiji, is located on the eastern side of the *Viti Levu* island. The two main islands are home to a large number of the entire population of Fiji, which today can be estimated to be close to one million people. *Suva*, the capital, is one of the heavily populated cities in the entire country. It is the center of government and commercial activity. The major airport, Nadi International Airport, is located on the western side of Viti Levu, which serves to connect Fiji to the world and also bring large numbers of tourists who are attracted to Fiji's beautiful tropical climate and golden sandy beaches.

Naming Terms Used in Fiji

There are many terms of self-identification. Some of them are; Fijian, Native Fijian, Indian Fijian, Indo-Fijian, and *iTaukei*. Recently, the Fijian government has made the move to use the term "Fijian" to include those of who are Fiji nationals or citizens. This has made it rather useless to use the term Indian Fijian and/or Indo-Fijian to identify Indians living in Fiji, who were descendants of the indentured laborers from India. However, with this move by the Fijian government, there is still a need to have an identifying term for the native Fijians. The word used for this group is *iTaukei*, which loosely means "indigenous" in the native Fijian language. This chapter will mostly be using the terms "Native Fijians" to refer to the indigenous Fijians and will use the term "Indo-Fijians" to refer to Fijians of Indian ancestry, particularly descendants of the indentured laborers from India. The history of both these groups will be discussed in this chapter.

The First Fijians

The Native Fijians are considered to be descendants from one man, *Lutunasobasoba*. *Lutunasobasoba* and his family sailed the seas in search for new land to establish a new home. They came upon the shores of Fiji and made a home out of it. Their arrival on their new land was along the coastline of *Viti Levu*, known as *Vuda Point*. A timeline estimation of the first settler dates back to the 12th century.

After establishing a new home on the islands, Lutunasobasoba and his family (particularly his sons and family) had spread out and made homes in other parts of the islands. This is how they populated the land and other islands in the region. Those early settlers broke off into different places and formed different villages and tribes and are still around today. The story of Lutunasobasoba is one that was passed down through the generations and through time and is still told today in families and perhaps in school too.

Religion

Today, the majority of native Fijians are of Christians. The early exposure to Western Europeans was with Christian missionaries. Before the arrival of Christian Missionaries, native Fijians practiced a rather dark custom and religion. One of these practices was cannibalism. Fijians in those times ate other Fijians. Eating the flesh of their enemies was done under the belief that it was the ultimate method to totally defeat their enemies. With the introduction of Christianity, the Native Fijian society saw the end of this dark era, and the end of cannibalism. Native Fijians today have made Christianity the center of what they do as individuals and as a group. Sundays are considered to be sacred days and is observed in most places across the nation. With Indo-Fijians being the second largest population, there is a large number who practice Hinduism. So, the two most primary religions in Fiji are Christianity and Hinduism.

The Colonization of Fiji

Fiji was first introduced to Western Europeans through trade. With Fiji's vast natural resources and strategic location, channels of trade opened up from the late 1700s to the early 1800s. They were in business with many countries like Australia, New Zealand, the United States, China, and Great Britain. Around 1849, an American trading store that was stationed on one of the islands was looted, destroyed, and burned down by some of the natives. In reaction to this, the United States demanded reparations for these damages from Ratu Seru Cakobau, who had self-proclaimed himself to as *Tui Viti*, which translates to Chief of Fiji. This however, stirred some conflict with other chiefs of other villages because Cakobau held no authority over them. Foreign powers also showed doubt in his proclamation, but that did not stop the United States from demanding payments for damages to the store. This, in turn, placed Fiji, and especially Cakobau, in financial debt to the Americans.

To avoid further confrontation with the United States, Cakobau wrote to Queen Victoria offering to cede the islands of Fiji to Great Britain, and in return, for Great Britain to assume the burden of repaying debts to the United States. After a second invitation to do so, Great Britain finally accepted, and on October 10, 1874, Fiji became a colony of Great Britain. With this, Great Britain sent a government representative to govern the new colony. The representative was Sir Hercules Robinson, who became Fiji's Governor-General. He was later succeeded by Sir Arthur Gordon who gave some limited authority to local Fiji chiefs to handle local affairs.

With Fiji being a colony of Great Britain, it opened more economical, educational, and political opportunities for the islands. Now, Fiji's vast land and favorable climate gave way to the cultivation of several crops that were used to trade with other nations. Even though the islands were under the control and rule of Great Britain, land ownership was still controlled by the Fijian natives. This made it difficult for the colony to expand economically because the natives were not welcoming to the idea of working hard labor on their own land. With labor needed to work the plantations, Great Britain recruited indentured laborers from India to become plantation workers.

Indians in Fiji

Between 1879 and 1920, Indians immigrated to Fiji as indentured laborers. Approximately 60,000 Indians worked on the crop plantations, particularly sugar cane plantations, which became Fiji's largest exported good. Upon arrival, their first contact with the native Fijians was not a pleasant one. There was a mutual attitude of disdain. Native Fijians saw the Indians as people who would potentially take their land away from them, and Indians were frightened at the sight of native Fijians who were tall men with fine physique which reminded the Indians of savage people according to Indian mythology.

Indentured laborers were required to work for a certain period of time, depending on their contract agreement. When their contracts were up, some decided to go back to India and some stayed in Fiji. Most of these indentured laborers were recruited from a lower caste system in Indian society. The caste system was a class structure determined by birth and family. A simple way to understand this, if your parents are poor, then you are going to be poor too. Since most indentured laborers were from the poorer level of their caste system, going back to India meant going back to still be part of that same system, and that was not appealing. Also, most of them barely had enough money to go back. Although most of them stayed behind, some still decided to go back to India. One of the motives to do so was because Indians did not want to die in a foreign land.

Indians have been in Fiji for more than a 100 years. Although being in a foreign land, they ensured that some of their cultural practices were not completely lost. Today, Indians in Fiji still practice their religions such as Hinduism and Islam. With a long-standing presence in Fiji, Indians become the second largest group in the entire Fijian population.

This chapter focuses on some specific aspects of Fijian culture, community, family, practices, and identity. The case studies are from first and second year Sacramento State students forming a diverse group of six individuals from within the Fijian community. Some are individuals who were born in Fiji and moved to the United States, some were born in the United States and have not been to Fiji. The group consists of both a Native Fijian and Indo-Fijian perspective, each discussing briefly a small aspect of their experiences as a Fijian.

This map pinpoints locations on the map of Fiji where the families of the students are either from, or were born in.

© Peter Hermes Furian/Shutterstock.com

Most people have not actually heard a lot about Fiji, unless they are referring to its most famous product, Fiji Water. According to the 2010 U.S. Census, the population of Fijians living in the United States is around 32,000 and half of them are living in the state of California. The population of Fijians in the United States will continue to increase, and so will the demand for the conversation of Fijians to be discussed not only within the communities they are in, but also in most academic institutions.

Education and Discipline

Mitieli Rokolacadamu Gonemaituba

In Fiji's capital city of *Suva* was where I was born and raised. Moving to the United States at age 15 in 2013 was a major change for me, especially change in my experiences in education. Moving from a grade to the next is one all students go through. Most people would remember a time when they were both excited and scared to move from the eighth grade to the ninth. I felt the same way when I left high school to go to college. After graduating from Luther Burbank High School (LBHS) in Sacramento, California, I later enrolled into Sacramento State (California State University, Sacramento [CSUS]). Now, I am a second-year student and pursuing a degree in construction management. It was in my first ever college semester in 2016 that I had sat in my first Ethnic Studies class, Ethnic Studies 14 Introduction to Asian American Studies, where students would learn about basic aspects of the Asian American groups that are present in the United States today. Sitting in that class, students get to listen to Dr. Gregory Mark talk about Asian American history and being mindful of the presence of some Pacific Islanders like myself in his class, he also included some information on Pacific

Mitieli Gonemaituba (right) and Veronica Bourke (left) after Mitieli's high school graduation from Luther Burbank High School, 2016, Sacramento, California. Source: Kong Vang

Islanders in his curriculum. In this class, students get to learn about the many changes Asian and Pacific Islanders go through in American society. This played a part in my self-reflection on some changes I went through in the same society.

One of the most significant changes that I was exciting for was when I moved to the United States and entered high school. Everything was new, from the people, to the class structure, to attitude and behavior, to fashion, and so on. Back in Fiji, the school system was structured differently and was closely similar to the British school systems. In colonial times, Fiji was colonized by the British. First to eighth grade was compiled together into one school, usually called "Primary School." Then from the ninth grade to the 12th, it was called "Secondary School."

I can still recall the time I spent in school back in the islands, from kindergarten to ninth grade, and school uniforms were a major part of it. It was the school's identity. Anyone could name the school a student attended simply by looking at the uniforms they wore. The strict rules on school uniforms instilled a strong sense of discipline in students. I remember wearing my white and gray Stella Maris Primary School uniform. There were always strict rules to follow on uniforms. For example, our white shirt had to be tucked into our pants at all times, hair and nails had to be kept short and clean (girls had to braid their hair a certain style and were not allowed nail polish of any kind), only black sandals were allowed, most importantly without exception, you could only come school wearing your uniform. Without it could result in us being sent back home for the day. But that was not the same experience I had here in the United States. On my first day at Luther Burbank, I realized that I

Mitieli Gonemaituba (center) and his friends, Martin Taylor (left) and Alfred Yaya (right). Stella Maris Primary School, Suva, Fiji, 2012. Source: Mitieli Gonemaituba

had never had to pick an outfit for school because with school uniforms, there were no choices. In addition to that, it was quite interesting to see some new styles that I have never seen in person before, styles like "sagging" where a person's pants hung lower than their waistline. It was odd for me, but it was still interesting to see something new. Also, students had an extreme level of passion for their shoes. I never knew brands like Nike was so adored and liked by my fellow peers.

One of the changes that I experienced in coming to school here in the United States that I embraced was the fact that teachers were not allowed to physically hit the students as a form of punishment. In Fiji, there was little use for "detention," because when students did something wrong, they were just physically punished, like being hit on the hands with the teacher's yard stick. I remember a time in my second grade at Stella Maris where I was sent to the principal's office by my teacher, Ms. Williams, for quietly asking for my friend's eraser during quiet writing time. When entering the principal's office, the first thing I saw was a belt hanging in the room, which he used to punish students who were called to his office, which is also what he used on me that unfortunate day. That type of punishment in schools kept students on their best behavior, which is something I brought to the United States with me. During my time at Luther Burbank, I was never once written up for detention because I behaved well. I'd say it's because my time in Fiji really shaped me into a well-behaved student. I did what I was asked to do, turned in assignments on time, showed up early for school and class, and I always tried to respect my teachers. It was really shocking to see how different that was during my time in high school. I saw students talk back to teachers, show up late for class, and I saw students using their phone in class. Basically, I saw a lot of things that students did on a daily basis that would be highly prohibited in schools in Fiji. One of the things my friends do not understand is that, the forms of discipline that was used in school was pretty much the same as the kind Fijian parents used at home. It is the norm for Fijian parents to be highly strict, and using physical discipline is no stranger to nearly all Fijian children. Fijian parental skills may be harsh to some, but, it is a way that Fijian parents ensure that their children are well behaved when they are not around, especially in school. A high priority for Fijian parents is their children's education, and, molding them to be well behaved in school is a way to ensure their child's academic success. It sure has worked well for me. Being disciplined at home to behave well has made me into something of a good student, and that has pushed me to do good in school.

My stories of experiences in Fijian schools is something I have in common with many parents of Fijian American students. In other words, if you have parents who were born and raised in Fiji, my story about school in the islands may be the similar to their own. Now, as I tell my friends stories of what it was like to go to school in Fiji, I enjoy seeing their faces express how much they disliked the experience that they would have gone through if they were me. Some of my Fijian American peers even changed how they felt about their parents' attitude toward their education. Some of them have come to understand that their parents are so strict on them with school, because the school system they went through back in Fiji was strict and challenging. Going through firm and strict discipline in school, parents of Fijian American students have implemented some of that discipline into their child's education. Even though they are from two different systems, I know some Fijian American students who say that their Fijian parents are strict about their education to the point where they should focus on nothing else but school. Perhaps, if they have gone through the same experience of school as their parents, they would understand why they feel that way. Looking back and remembering a day sitting in that Ethnic Studies 14 class, I learned that this experience of change that I went through is definitely not something that only I have gone through. Any person who moves somewhere new will experience some form of change.

Our Indo-Fijian Roots

Neha Chand

I am a graduate of LBHS, class of 2017 (one out of 14 high schools in the Sacramento City Unified School District). Currently, I am a first-year student at CSUS, as for my major I am undecided. College is a time for self-exploration; therefore, at the beginning of the Fall semester, I got the opportunity to take Ethnic Studies 14: *Introduction to Asian American Studies*. This Ethnic Studies course enabled me to explore college, because it strengthened skills such as critical thinking. Therefore, the course aided in going beyond course content, and it enabled the students to reflect on our personal connections to Asian Pacific Islander American history. We learned about the narratives of the APA ethnic groups, and their experiences in America such as the creation of organizations, the labor-intensive occupations, and the strength to attain social and political rights in the United States. Relatively, in our Ethnic Studies course we were assigned to write a research paper on an APA ethnic group. We conducted research upon a factor we believed was important to an ethnic group we had selected. Some of the factors were in education, culture, and businesses, which reflected the sacrifices Asian Pacific Americans experienced to build a life in the United States. Through this assignment, it was brought to my attention that there is little to no research on Indo-Fijians. Therefore, the significance of this paper is to shed light upon the identity of the Indo-Fijians and their historical narrative in U.S. history.

During the late 1800s, the British colonizers wanted laborers that could work on the sugar cane plantations in Fiji. Therefore, the British recruited thousands of Indians that went on board the first ship that sailed to Fiji. The ship was called the Leonidas, which was a British-owned ship (V. Chand; D. Chand oral interview, January 4, 2018).

They were all told by the British that they would be paid a lot of money in Fiji. My great grandparents were among those on this ship. After the Leonidas departed India, the Indian passengers were told by the British sailors that they are under their control. In Fiji, the Indian workers worked in the hot sun as they cultivated the land and planted sugar cane with little pay. They were known as *"Girmityas,"* indentured laborers, and they had an agreement known as the *"Girmit"* (Pande, 2010, p. 58). The original 5-year agreement was extended for five more years. They were told they could return to India after the agreement ended (Pande, 2010, p. 58). However, the workers normally were unable to save enough money, and there was no means of transportation (D. Chand, oral interview, January 4, 2018).

The Indian workers were employed by the Colonial Sugar Refining Company (CSR) where they would plant and harvest sugar cane (V. Chand, oral interview, January 4, 2018). The profits were made at the company and part of the share was given to the Indian workers (Pande, 2010, p. 58). For many, like my great-great-grandparents, it was difficult to rebuild their lives in a new country.

Indo-Fijians are of Indian ancestry but they were born in Fiji. The second and third generations (my great-grandparents and grandparents) were Indo-Fijians. My great-grandparents and grandparents adapted to the Fijian culture, while maintaining their Indian heritage. Moreover, they helped their parents in sugar farming for the continuation of the business (V. Chand & D. Chand, oral interview, January 4, 2018).

I was born in Suva, Fiji. In 2000, there was a military coup in Fiji. The condition of the country was unstable due to racial tensions. Furthermore, for the safety and better opportunities such as in education and employment, my parents decided to move to the United States. It was difficult for my parents because they had to leave our family and begin a new life in the United States. They told me they were homesick for about a year until they realized that this is it, "We are here for a brighter future and for me to have a better life" (V. Chand; D. Chand, oral interview, January 4, 2018).

Furthermore, I was 2 years old when I moved to the United States. Therefore, I adjusted to the American culture. Yet, I grew up in a traditional home where we had a specific room that had statues of our deities. This room was a mini temple in our home where we could pray to our deities.

Photo provided by Neha Chand

My parents and I going to a cultural gathering. My mom and I are wearing cultural clothes, October 2001, 24th Street Florin Road.

Moreover, my parents told me when they immigrated to California it was important that they found a Hindu temple, because in Fiji they went to temples. In order to continue our Indian culture in the United States, the Hindu temples provided religious services for the Asian Indians, specifically the Indo-Fijian community. The services are organized by the Hindu temple founders and organizations. The religious programs, such as festivals, are held in the temples. For example, a main autumn celebration in the community is the 9-day festival to *Goddess Durga* known as *Navratri*. The

Sri Siva Sumbramaniya Temple, Queens Road, Nadi, Fiji, 2001. Source: Venay Chand

statues of deities are there to pray for prosperity. There are Indian priests (*Pandits*) or Indian teachers (*Swami*) who taught us the stories of our deities (V. Chand; D. Chand, oral interview, January 4, 2018). As a community, we came together to celebrate this important religious holiday. Also, the temples helped my family develop networks in the Indo-Fijian community, because we did not have many close relatives living in Sacramento. This is how our community strengthened and sustained our culture for future and younger generations in the United States.

To reflect on what it means to be a fifth generation Indo-Fijian, who resides in the United States, brings a deeper meaning to my life. By going to temples, it allows me to understand rituals that our ancestors have passed down. An example of a ritual will be religious ceremonies where we offer fruits, sweets, flowers, and incense to the deities. Along with our ceremonies, we sing devotional songs as a way to show our gratitude to our deities. These religious practices create a strong bond with my culture. As I learn more about my origins it helps

me connect to my family's history. When I have my own family in the future, I would like to go to the temples with them to learn more and embrace my beautiful culture.

In your Ethnic Studies course, I believe you will connect more to your ethnic identity through learning about historical narratives. The most important part is to see you being represented. Your representation can be seen by learning your ethnic group's history. As well as, to hear other ethnic group's histories, and see how they relate to your family's experiences in the United States. Ultimately, all of our personal narratives showcase how we are all apart of American history.

Laxmi Narayan Mandir Temple, Elder Creek Road, Sacramento, California, 2018. Source: Neha Chand

Arranged Marriages in the Indo-Fijian Community

Darsha Naidu

As a freshman at CSUS, I was granted with the opportunity to take an Ethnic Studies course titled, *Introduction to Asian American Studies*. I attended Monterey Trail High School in Elk Grove, which did not have an Ethnic Studies course and I saw the opportunity to take it in college. Even though this was a course requirement through the Full Circle Project, an organization that focuses on Asian American and Pacific Islanders achieving higher education, I found it to be a great class with a lot of fascinating topics. In this course, I learned about the history of different Asian American groups and the sacrifices made by them to make a living in the United States such as discrimination based on ethnicity. Being Asian American, my family can relate to other Asian Americans struggles. During this course, I found it interesting that there is little to no information published regarding Indo-Fijian. This gave me the motivation to write about my family's history and background.

According to my parents, my great-grandfather from my mom's side of the family, Mr. Dhalbal Prakash, was born in one of the ships used to transport laborers from India to Fiji. Indian arranged marriages originated from the period where Vedas, or large texts which contained sacred knowledge about the Indian teachings, rituals, and beliefs, were being chanted. During that time, there was no question about arranged marriages. Since cultural rituals are still practiced, most arranged marriages happen based on how much money your family has or if your family is respectable in the eyes of the society, which is why the main purpose of arranged marriages was to keep the traditional and cultural beliefs alive while creating a family.

My great grandfather's family stayed in Nasouri, Fiji, and had a huge influence on the village named Vuci since he was a prominent leader there. When migrating from India to Fiji, arranged marriages were one of the traditions still held by the Indians. Because of this, an arranged marriage was set up with a daughter, whose name was Chand Kaur, of another leader of a village in Nasouri. The tradition of arranged marriages was adopted by old religious scriptures and has continued ever since in the Indo-Fijian community. My great grandfather got an arranged marriage with my great grandmother, who was the daughter of another leader of the village. This arranged marriage took place when she was only 5 years old since getting married at an early age was appropriate. When she turned 13, her in-laws came and took her away since they believed she was mature enough to start having kids now. So, when my great-grandparents had an arranged marriage, all the rituals that were followed in India were followed in Fiji.

As time changed, some rituals were slowly being taken out of Indo-Fijian practice because the new generation of Indo-Fijians wanted more control of their lived and wanted to branch out of the traditional Indian practice. For example, one ritual practiced before getting an arranged marriage in Fiji is that before anything happens, the bride and groom exchange photos. If they approve each other, the groom side of the family is supposed to come visit the bride's family and tell her that she is reserved for that guy.

However, in the United States, this ritual that is part of arranged marriages have died out. Most potential bride and grooms know a little about each other before getting married. Since the United States is a diverse place, most immigrant Indo-Fijian families encourage kids to socialize with other Indo-Fijians kids. Parents, in other words, start looking for suitable mates for their children at an early age. Indo-Fijian families want their children to befriend other Indo-Fijian children at Indian weddings and religious events. In arranged marriages, divorce tends to be rare. That's because both partners have respect for each other's traditions and families.

Looking at the Indo-Fijian community in the United States, my parents have taught me a lot about my culture and the traditions we follow. Even in the United States, I wear my traditional Indian clothes and jewelry to represent my Indo-Fijian roots. Both of my parents, were born in Fiji, and in 1999, they immigrated to the United States. I was in my mother's womb at the time and they wanted a better life for me, which is why they came to the United States. Growing up in a diverse area, my parents made sure that the Western culture didn't influence our family customs by teaching us about holy texts and religious songs where the concept of arranged marriages appeared from. Even though certain rituals of arranged marriages have changed over time, I hope to continue this tradition in the United States. Now, it is up to the future generation of Indo-Fijians to keep the tradition going. Having this community helps the younger and future generation learn about our family traditions. I hope that through the ethnic's course, you can connect with your ethnic identity and learn about the struggles faced by many Asian American groups.

The Dance and Music of Fiji

Jenisha Lal

All throughout my life, I have always been asked, "How are you Indian but from Fiji? I thought that you were Indian from India? How did you end up in Fiji?" My repetitious answers to a multitude of people throughout my childhood frustrated me. As a student from Florin High, one of the nine high schools in Elk Grove, I was exposed to many different cultures. However, it was not until I was in college in my first semester at CSUS when I realized that I shared my frustrations with other students with similar backgrounds to me. I took the Ethnic Studies course: Introduction to Asian American (ETHN14) when I realized that there was a lot of things untold about Indo-Fijians and Native Fijians. For most people, Fiji is a tropical getaway. A vacation from work and stress. While many indulge in the tropical energy that Fiji has to offer, many do not know of the country's history or traditions.

Some traditions that are important in the Indo-Fijian culture are music and dance. Music and dance is said to be a universal language that one does not need to understand other's language or customs to interact. It can be a very powerful unifying force. Through music and dance, Indians and Native Fijians were able to cross culture forming a new culture of its own known as Indo-Fijians.

Coming From India

When the "Grimit" or "Girmityas" (indentured Indian laborers) came from Lucknow, Uttar Pradesh, India, to the country of Fiji, they brought their music and dance along with them. The type of music that Indians brought were described as folk tale since these songs told stories of myths. In addition, Indians brought along some of their traditional dances styles to Fiji as well. Although people may believe that Bollywood is a new phenomenon, it in fact known as the Indian Film Industry before being dubbed as Bollywood in present times. Most of which these dances at the time were inspired by Bollywood and these types of dances were known to most as the classical Indian dances.

While in Fiji

Ever since Bollywood were introduced to the Native Fijians, it has influenced the society in terms of music and dance, making Bollywood a crucial aspect of Indo-Fijian culture. Over time, Indo-Fijians and Native Fijians cross cultured for generations by sharing their traditions or style with each other. For example, Native Fijian influences such as reggae style music and traditional dances have added to how Indians celebrate music and dance. This fusion, Indo-Fijians, was different compared to Indians who were from India.

Examples of the "Fusion"

Bhajans, according to *The Garland Encyclopedia of World Music: South Asia: The India Continent* (2000) by Alison Arnold and Bruno Nettl is, "an informal, loosely organized devotional music . . . probably one of the ubiquitous genres of Indian religious music." Indo-Fijians have carried Bhajans with them to Fiji, it was the best way from most to remember god through music. However, in order to play this music there were certain instruments that are needed. One in particular instrument was the dholak, otherwise known as a "cylindrical drum," one of the major instruments used in the Indian culture played hitting the sides of the drum while in a sitting position. In addition to making music, the dholak is also used as a metronome as it helped dancers time their choreography. As the person created the beats, the dancer would have to listen and find a pattern in order to dance according to the beats.

Although the Indians introduced bhajians and dholaks, the Native Fijians introduced their music and traditional dances to the Indians as well. One Fijian dance in particular that is well known is the *Meke*, which "is the traditional style of dance, which is a combination of dance and storytelling through song. Both men and women perform in the *Meke*, and the dance is viewed as a group collaboration in which men are expected to demonstrate strong, virile movements, whereas women are expected to be graceful and feminine" (Meke, the Traditional Fijian Dance). In addition to the music and dance, many Indo-Fijians adopted the afro hairstyle that was common among Native Fijians when they performance their traditional dances (M. Lal, oral interview, January 17, 2018).

Closer to Home

Sadly, there is not much known about Indo-Fijians or Fijians music and dances in the United States. However, Brigham Young University (BYU, Hawaii) has a Polynesian Cultural Center where many cultural dances and traditions of Fiji along with many other islands are displayed. In fact, my father, who was offered admission to BYU and took a job as a part time dancer and performed many Fijian dancers with other students of Indo-Fijian or Fijian descendent. But closer to home in California, there are annual Fiji Festivals that take place at Cosumnes River College in Sacramento. Due to the lack of Indo-Fijian representation, most people will never know about the rich and unique culture in Fiji. From a quick sample taken from my Indo-Fijian friends and family have expressed their displeasure of having to constantly tell others about their background. In textbooks, we grew up learning little about Fiji's history. The most that we got was a footnote when there was a whole population of Indo-Fijian that lived in America not knowing whether to identify ourselves as Indians or Pacific Islanders.

Ethnic Studies are an important course because not everyone knows how important their culture or heritage is until you learn about your ancestors struggles and their journey. There is a lack of literature on the topic of Indo-Fijians, and being born in Hayward, United States of America, with parents who were born and raised in Suva, Fiji, I have been lucky to have the opportunity to learn more about my Indo-Fijian culture through Ethnic Studies.

Fiji Food

Jonathan Singh

Fijian food is a cultivation of two subjects, Fijian and migrant Indian, with involvement from many communities combined in order to produce the term "Fijian food." It involves the food types in each community that are beautiful and flavorful combinations that is the best of both worlds of distinct flavors. The restaurants in the Sacramento area did not meet requirements and therefore did not excite me. My mother's cooking could always cheer you up even when you were feeling down which why it was unique and delicious. She would always cook anytime she had free time, usually on the weekends. My favorite dish that she made was Lamb curry with Cassava and Dalo and this was an interesting dish because it combined aspects from more than one culture to create. Growing into a family that not only uses food as a way to communicate but is a method to bring people together. I never truly understood how grateful the life I was given is when food can be a catalyst for family emotions.

Being the first in your family to attend college meant that not only did you cross that high school stage senior year, but so did all of your loved ones who supported you. I graduated from Monterey Trail High School which is in the Elk Grove Unified School District in 2016 and then attended Sacramento State. I am currently a sophomore and up to this point, my *Ethnic Studies 14: Intro to Asian American Studies* class really made me more intrigued about my heritage. Professor Mark created a space where you actually felt proud of knowing who you were, the class was designed to appreciate Asian Americans and Pacific Islanders and seeing my ethnicity discussed really made me feel special.

Class discussions become like a family discussion in a community of people who valued who they were and were curious to finding out more about themselves. My Fijian heritage was something that honestly never rose interest in my mind prior to the class, to me it seemed like the past was exactly that and I already knew who I was and what I was all about. Regardless of what I thought, I never thought more information and discovery about my family would make me appreciate my life more.

I was born in 1997 in the island of Fiji, in the capital city known as Suva where I lived with my mom, and my uncle and my auntie down the street. We lived in a house down the street from my fellow relatives, this close community created a strong bond that was built upon family. Fiji is a small nation especially when my mom or uncle knew people that I had not even known existed, even when they had just met the person, they would somehow end up being family. My family moved to the United States as a result of chain migration which in turn started out as my first-generation relatives already living in the United States with my parents, uncles, and aunts moving over second. I realized that food was the magic key to bring people together (Figure 1).

The celebrations that brought all of us together would not change even with my move to the United States when I was 5 years old. For a kid, it is quite a journey to travel to another country. I have to thank all my family members because it was a team effort of love to make sure everyone is together again. With my mom and step dad, my palate for food increased not only culturally but I was able to see another point of view when visiting my dad's side of the family which was Scottish and Irish. The way that food was celebrated there was amazing and more on a grander scale and set out traditional American food such as Thanksgiving turkey and macaroni casserole. The spices used are drawn from oregano to cayenne pepper, indeed multi ethnicity spices infused together. To be completely honest, there were never really any Fijian restaurants in the city that could match up to the way my mother cooked food in my opinion.

Photographer Jonathan Singh

Figure 1: The removal of the banana leaves and tin foil (a substitute for coconut leaves) finalizing that the lovo is in its final stage. Sacramento California (2014).

Another thing that comes out of food in the Fijian community is the traditional lovo (Low-vo), an underground oven setup where meat is cooked. In other communities, the underground oven is also used for cooking, for example, in Hawaii the term is called imu (E-moo), in Samoa it is called the umu (Ooh- moo), and the Maori call in the Hangi (Han- gee), the Rotuman call it a koua (k-O-wa) yet no matter how it is said, it all comes down to an amazing way of cooking. In the islands of Fiji, meat was higher priced than in the United States, many Fijians in Sacramento like lamb, chicken, and pork all from your local Fijian supermarket, mine would be Fiji-mart down Del Paso road was easier to access for purchase. Fiji's meat industry can be traced back upon the discovery of early Europeans colonizing Fiji around the 1860s. The settlement soon evolved into a society composed of New Zealand and Australia. New Zealand brought in a number of imports other than meat items, these ranged from tea to chocolates as well. There are many choices to buying meat, one option is to purchase fresh lamb that was raised locally, usually from a farm that somebody who works at the store owns. The second option that is available at your local Fijian store would be to purchase lamb that comes from another country such as New Zealand. My mother would love to use spice in her cooking, back on the island there was spices imported from India such as curry powder considering it was not grown in Fiji. Spice is a flavor of life and I have tried my fare share thanks to my mother's amazing cooking. The lovo is meant to make the meat more flavorful. This preparation from the way to prepare and marinate the meat to covering it with tin foil then banana leaves makes it so the cultural appreciation is there and as a result makes the food taste twice as good. It is not only a unique taste, but it requires more than one person to help prepare thus bringing in more family through working together. Banana leaves are used to cover up the food as a final layer of protection against dirt, it creates an inner heating vent and unique smokehouse sensation. Digging the pit and setting it up takes the same amount of time as cooking the food and as such, a lovo is reserved for important events.

Food is the very idea that can bring people together who each has individual lives and dilemmas and for a brief moment have all their worries gone. It is the starting fire as an iconic symbol that cooks the meals and the burning embers that creates an everlasting bond.

Our Time is Now

Shayal Sharma

I am a freshman at CSUS and I am majoring in health sciences. I graduated from LBHS in 2017. I am currently in the Full Circle Project, which is a program at Sacramento State that increases the graduation rate for students from the Asian American and Pacific Islander community. It comes with several leadership opportunities, academic support, and all that good stuff. We are like our own little community within the school and we had to take two classes in the Fall semester of 2017 for that program which fulfilled our General Education requirement. I was placed in a course about the history of Asian Pacific Americans taught by Professor Mark, where I have noticed that I finally fit into the category of something I am learning, which indeed sparked my interest.

Since I was fascinated with the material, it made me feel like I was finally included in a class curriculum considering my family was alive during those old times as well. I instantly think of my parents when I hear the word "migration" because they migrated to America in 1991. My parents were one of those people searching for better opportunities and came to the land of freedom. They always emphasize on how they wanted a better future for us as their kids. The class was under the Department of Ethnic Studies and my professor was explaining the significance of the Ethnic Studies movement, especially how it played a major role for social justice within the community thus far. In the 1980s and 1990s, Fijian families left Fiji due to the British military taking over the government and built lives here in America. In fact, my parents and my whole family fits into that category and they always reminisce about when they first came to the United States. The Ethnic Studies class taught by Professor Mark also expanded my knowledge of the past of what Asian Pacific Americans had to go through to get to where they are now. As a result, Fijians and people from all origin are here today in America and our voices need to be heard. Meaning that broadening the curriculum is relevant to a high extent because after everything that happened in the past, it led up to the point where we are today including why we are here this very moment.

For my Ethnic Studies class, the assignment was to write a research paper about the significance of something that was a key contributor to a specific ethnic group, so I chose to write about my own people, Indo-Fijians. As I was writing my research paper about Indo-Fijians, I had questions about my own family roots and began to reflect. What is an Indo-Fijian? It is a person who is from the Indian descent but born in Fiji. They can be referred to as Fijians or even Indo-Fijians as well. Why were there so many Indians in Fiji? There were thousands of Indians who left India to work in Fiji as indentured laborers. In fact, my great grandparents, Rav Rattan and Chandmati Rattan were some of the indentured laborers who came on one of the boats to Fiji. They went to Fiji to work on the sugar cane plantation. Then my grandparents, Shanti Prasad and Dhayan Prasasd were born in 1929 and then later my parents Shashi and Hirendra Sharma were born in 1966.

Furthermore, my Ethnic Studies research paper concentrated on how the dominant group of the taxi industry in the early 2000s in Sacramento were mostly Fijians meaning that it greatly contributed to the success of those families. I was a part of one of those families because my dad became a taxi driver in 2004, so I understand how it plays a key contributor to the household. My dad, Rakesh Sharma, claims that 80% of the drivers in his company were Fijians. Based off my experiences, I made an inference that the taxi industry was the primary source of income for Fijian immigrants because it was not that easy getting a job being a minority and new to the country. My research paper was written from my dad's perspective because of his reasons of becoming an independent taxi driver, so he was my key informant. I learned how he survived in this country financially while being part of a minority group, which was by driving his taxi cab. He was an independent driver and told me that there were several of immigrants driving taxi to make a living during that period especially people from Fiji.

Although, I had another key informant who is a current taxi driver, Ajit Chandra. In fact, my dad and he know each other through the taxi company. Ajit has been driving taxi for 12 years and is still going. I had an interview with him regarding how the taxi company served as a stable source of income and how it helped provide his family with food and shelter. He is an independent taxi driver like how my dad was meaning that he decides his own hours, so that his income is up to him. The taxi industry was indeed a contributor to his household considering that he drives daily and as much as he possibly can. He continuously talked about the fact that the flexibility was a key factor as to why he chose that job. He has time to take care of his kids such as dropping them off to school and cooking or doing things around the house. He has some good days and some bad depending how the business is going. He picks his own hours, although the high demand is what really controls his income. The industry helped him and his family maintains financial stability.

He literally said that if it wasn't for his job then he wouldn't know what to do. Like that is where the money comes and goes, which is needed to live a decent life in America. There were and are many immigrants on the same boat as him, such as my dad, who were employed by the taxi company to make a living to support their families. There were and are people of all colors who relied on the taxi industry for steady source of income. A large number of families have been supported financially by the taxi company, in which AJ and I fall under that category.

He also confirmed that there are six taxi associations and as of now he claims that the taxi industry is culturally diverse. He also added that there are all types of people such as Indians, Fijians, Muslims, Arabs, Pakistanis, Polynesians, Asians, African Americans, and so on. For instance, the company he is working for is called, "The Island Star Cab" and the dominant group is Fijians. In fact, his uncle had come up with that name 20 years ago. He is from Fiji as well and he wanted to represent his pride, so that seemed like the perfect fit. There are plenty of families that have been sustained with the help of the taxi company and even I am a part of that. It is important to realize that there is not too many of us, Fijians, but we still contribute to the community and want to be acknowledged.

Along with that, I was conducting my research for my Ethnic Studies paper by trying to find scholarly journals, it has caught my attention that there was not really anything written about Fiji Indians. There was nothing about Fijians or Indians driving cabs, which is ironic because a majority of my dad's side of the family and friends drove taxi to get a good enough income to provide for the household. Even in the textbook that we had to read in class, there was just a section that mentioned something about Indians, but not much. After learning that we Fijians are understudied, I felt that as if it needs to change. We must broaden the curriculum in order for it to be inclusive for the APA community. When young students learn about themselves, it has the ability to empower them to be the change they wish to see in the world.

Conclusion

To have Ethnic Studies a part of the curriculum is significant to a high extent because young students can learn things they never knew before and feel included in American history. For instance, some students can finally relate to what is being taught it is their own people are getting some type of recognition. When you shed light upon some facts about being a minority, then it has the ability to affect social justice for all. Also, people should know their roots in general and be prideful. Ethnic studies can empower students to be the change and be inspired, which is definitely a positive impact. Then, people will start to question things like the continuity of race and racism. In addition, they realize things they never knew before, which lead to them learning their own cultural identities.

Before I took the Ethnic Studies class, I have not really taken being understudied personal, but it is 2018 and now it is time for a change. We still are a part of this community and should be acknowledged. This chapter has the potential to have our voices heard. We should be included in history textbooks because we existed at that same period. We always get the short end of the stick and even in the schooling system, which is unfair. There are more than just five races in the world and now is the time to broaden the curriculum to create change. We always have to come together to fight for what we believe in, which in other words, form coalitions to push for change and if that is what it takes then that is what we will do.

Minorities have voices that need to be heard because we are the people who build up this community too. Being inspired by the past can also influence them to become political activists, which can legally push to create change. We were all taught that everything that is written in black and white is the most important. We have the power to push for change because we were meant to evolve. So, let's start here and begin having a section in these history books regarding our people, which will have an impact on us as a whole. Ethnic studies represent an opportunity to show the significance of social justice and people of color, which builds the community stronger because it is more inclusive. Now there should be information regarding Fijians by conducting researches on them in other aspects such as health, education, employment, and so on (Figure 2).

Photo by Ann Thomas.

Figure 2:   The group that wrote this chapter. From left to right (behind the flag). Mitieli Gonemaituba, Jenisha Lal, Jonathan Singh, Darsha Naidu, and Dr. Gregory Yee Mark. From left to right (in front of flag). Neha Chand and Shayal Sharma.

Chapter 30

Move on the 45

Dale Allender and Molaundo Jones

© Molaundo Jones

Taekwondo is an international martial arts form that began in Korea. Taekwondo is practiced in over 140 countries by more than 40 million people, and it is an official event in the Olympic games. Taekwondo aims to cultivate a person into a righteous and true human being.

I study at Robinson's Tae Kwon Do in Sacramento on Florin Road. My teacher, Master Robinson, pictured above teaches the very young to the very old. He teaches boys and girls, men and women of all races and ethnicities. He teaches all of us the importance of courtesy, truthfulness, self-control, positive thoughts, and a winning spirit. He also teaches us how to have a healthy body and healthy mind.

The following comic strip is an adaptation of an experience I had one day while I was training. On that day I became aware of how our thoughts and actions are connected. I also learned how geometry and other areas of mathematics are related to how we move our bodies while exercising, training, or moving around in the world.

© Molaundo Jones

Chapter 31

Danos un Corazon Fuerte para Luchar (Give Us a Heart Strong Enough to Struggle): Living Undocumented[1]

Rhonda Ríos Kravitz, Marisela Hernandez, Ernesto Gutiérrez Topete, Violeta Urizar, and Oscar Sarabia

In this chapter, we examine the barriers and challenges DREAMers face living in the United States as unauthorized immigrants. We look at the difficulties they have accessing and completing a college degree, including efforts to make colleges pay attention to their unique needs as students. We also discuss the attitudes and unfair treatment DREAMers encounter prior to enrolling in college, along with their experiences living in high poverty and needing to help their families. We highlight critical California legislation that has improved DREAMers' ability to obtain college degrees and discuss a framework for immigration reform that creates a welcoming roadmap to citizenship. Finally, we address the impact of the presidential election on DREAMers.

ALIANZA is a collective of active college students, educators, and community activists working for comprehensive immigration reform.

Illustrators:

Antonio Sarabia, Chief Information Officer of Alianza.

Lorenzo Valdovinos, undergraduate student, Butte Community College, Alianza Board Member

Special Thanks to Chico State, Leaders Educating for the Advancement of Dreamers (LEAD)

DANOS UN CORAZON FUERTE PARA LUCHAR (GIVE US A HEART STRONG ENOUGH TO STRUGGLE): LIVING UNDOCUMENTED

Authors:

---

1 Lyric from a hymn by the singer–songwriter and priest Juan Antonio Espinosa

Rhonda Ríos Kravitz, MSLS, DPA, Retired Dean, Sacramento City College and Chief Executive Officer of Alianza; Marisela Hernandez, undergraduate student, Chico State, DREAMER and President of Operations of Alianza; Ernesto Gutiérrez Topete, undergraduate student, Pomona College, DREAMER and President of Education Outreach of Alianza; Violeta Urizar, Certificate in Medical Assisting, President of Health Outreach of Alianza; Oscar Sarabia, undergraduate student, Stanford University, Alianza Board Member

Illustrator: Sarabia, Antonio, Chief Information Officer of Alianza; **Photographer:** Valdovinos, Lorenzo, undergraduate student, Butte Community College, Alianza Board Member

Special Thanks to Chico State, Leaders Educating for the Advancement of Dreamers (LEAD)

DREAMers

Estella was 10 years old when she and her mother crossed the U.S. border from Mexico with six other immigrants. They walked in the desert for over 10 hours and rarely took breaks. There was little food and water. As risky as this journey was, her mother believed it was worth it for Estella to have a better life. As a college student today, that experience will be forever etched in Estella's memory. Each day she reminds herself that she will never give up. Her dream is to complete her education and become an immigration lawyer. She tells her friends, "I will work hard to succeed and make my parents proud.

I am part of the solution, not the problem."

The United States has long been a key destination for immigrants like Estella and her mother, along with many others from all over the world. According to the U.S. Department of Homeland Security (DHS), of the total 11.4 million undocumented immigrants living in the United States in 2012, nearly 8 out of 10 (78% or 8.9 million people) are from North America, including Mexico, Canada, the Caribbean, and Central America. The largest share is from Mexico (59%). The next largest populations are from Asia (15% or 1.3 million) and South America (8% or 0.7 million). This chapter focuses on one segment of the immigrant population, young undocumented youth, or DREAMers, who were brought to this country as children.

Photo contributed by Lorenzo Valdovinos.
© Kendall Hunt Publishing Company.

The term DREAMers originated from a bill in Congress, introduced in 2001, called the DREAM ACT (see Appendix B). DREAM was short for Development, Relief and Education for Alien Minors. This Act never passed, even though many versions have been reintroduced since 2001, the last in 2013. Had it passed, as many as 2.5 million undocumented youth, or DREAMers, would have been provided an affordable public college education and military service opportunities, providing them with a pathway to citizenship.

Most DREAMers have lived in this country for most their lives, usually arriving in the United States. between the ages of 5 and 12 years of age. They have been called "Generation 1.5". Born in another country but arriving in the United States as young children, they are distinct from both the first and second generations. The name DREAMer, although it had its origins in the DREAM ACT, is appropriate for another reason, as immigrant youth have high hopes and dreams for a better future. They came with their parents who wanted a better life for their children; some came to escape political or economic conflicts in their native countries; a great many put their lives in danger crossing the border; and some came legally with visas, but their visas expired.

Life in the United States is often difficult for DREAMers for several reasons. First, debates over U.S. immigration policy are often divisive and anti-immigrant rhetoric has become prominent. Second, immigrants have witnessed over the last several years an increase in the number of deportations, workplace raids, and restrictive local and state laws, heightening feelings of exclusion, discrimination, fear, uncertainty, and perpetual stress. Third, negative characterizations and stereotypes of undocumented immigrants take a hard toll on many immigrant families. Mayra, a DREAMer who came to this country when she was 5 years old, has been called *illegal*, *alien*, *foreigner*, and *not American*. These terms serve to criminalize and dehumanize Mayra and millions of others like her. They are used to justifying abuse by unethical employers who take advantage of many immigrants' fears of speaking up, making them work long hours, for example, in agricultural fields with few breaks and difficult working conditions. Min-Jun and others have been told that they have no right to fight back and no right to live and work in this country, despite having lived most of their lives in this country and knowing no other country but the United States. Violeta watched helplessly as her mother died prematurely as she did not have access to adequate medical care.

DREAMers cannot work unless they have a valid social security card reserved for those with legal status, and they can't travel out of the country to visit family and friends because they may be denied reentry to the United States. Without legal status, they can

face deportation at any time to countries they barely remember or do not know at all. DREAMers are often forced to live in the shadows, sometimes having to move every 6 months to remain hidden from U.S. Immigration and Customs Enforcement (ICE). They often watch with fear and hopelessness as family members and friends are deported, not knowing when they will be able to reunite with their families. Many times, parents of DREAMers did not tell them about their undocumented status to protect them from verbal and physical discrimination. However, they often learned firsthand of their status when they were asked for a social security card, when applying for a job, or applying to college.

Photo contributed by Lorenzo Valdovinos.
© Kendall Hunt Publishing Company.

Education

Despite their high aspirations, undocumented youth have low educational attainment rates.

According to the Pew Research Center, 47% of undocumented adults aged 25–64 have less than a high school education, compared with 8% of U.S. residents.[2] They also have low college attendance rates even though DREAMers are well aware that a college degree is often a critical step toward fulfilling their desire for a stable career.

There are approximately 80,000 undocumented immigrants that turn 18 each year and sadly, 16–20% of them do not graduate from high school. Of the approximately 65,000 that graduate each year, only about 5–10% go on to college and only about 1–3% obtain a degree. Undocumented immigrants have a right to obtain a K-12 education, but not a college education. In 1982, the Supreme Court issued Plyer v. Doe, a landmark decision that stated all children, regardless of immigration status, were entitled to a free public education in public primary and secondary schools. Supreme Court Justice Blackmun effectively argued that "when a state provides an education to some and denies it to others, it immediately and inevitably creates class distinctions of a type fundamentally inconsistent with the purposes of the Equal Protection Clause because 'an uneducated child is denied even the opportunity to achieve.'" Unfortunately however, this law did not include college enrollment.

There are many barriers preventing undocumented students from entering college. In the past decade, debates over immigration reform have been heated, especially as they relate to whether DREAMers should be provided financial aid and/or in-state tuition, which is the ability to pay the same tuition rate as what the state residents pay. Some opponents of immigration reform have even argued that undocumented immigrants should not have the right to enroll in post-secondary education and enacted state policies to that effect. In 2008, for example, South Carolina prohibited undocumented students from enrolling in public post-secondary institutions. Alabama also passed a similar draconian law in 2011. Supporters of this view argue that undocumented students live illegally in the United States and, therefore, are not deserving of any services; it is unfair to legal residents to "reward" this type of "illegal behavior," they say.

In the absence of the DREAM Act or any federal direction on the issue of a right to a college education for DREAMers, states can determine their own policies. Currently, only 16 states provide in-state tuition provisions, passed through their state legislative processes. In addition, five states offer in-state tuition through their state boards of higher education or by the advisement of the state attorney general. Even the Federal DREAM Act, as currently written, does not require states to provide in-state tuition. The DREAM Act lets states decide whether they will or will not offer in-state tuition, making access to college across the United States very unequal. Thus, DREAMers

Photo contributed by Lorenzo Valdovinos. © Kendall Hunt Publishing Company.

---

2 Passel and Cohn, A Portrait of Unauthorized Immigrants in the United States, iv. http://www.pewhispanic.org/2009/04/14/a

have advocated strongly on behalf of future federal immigrant legislation that would be inclusive of in-state tuition in all states and enable federal access for eligible students to federal programs such as Pell grants, federal work-study, and federal student loans. Without nationwide in-state tuition, states like North Dakota, Georgia, Arkansas, and Nevada, all of which have large undocumented populations and do not have in-state tuition policies, have made it very difficult and oftentimes impossible for DREAMers to attend college.

Why is there so much opposition to DREAMers obtaining an education? Regrettably, anti-immigrant rhetoric has shaped the way immigrants are viewed and the opportunities they are afforded. This negative picture, however, is generally overshadowed by the successes of immigrants. When enrolled in college, DREAMers are often high-achieving students, or "undocuscholars." The image of the high-achieving student is in clear contrast to the image of the DREAMer as unqualified and unworthy of an education. Compared to their documented counterparts, DREAMers consistently hold higher GPA averages, according to the University of California, Los Angeles

Center for Labor Research and Education's hearing and conference in 2007. It is not unusual to find DREAMers as honor students, exceptional students in search of a better life. They consistently debunk the negative stereotypes often attributed to undocumented individuals.

Contesting the Negative Construction of Immigrants: Standing up for Change

Over the last 15 plus years, DREAMers have emerged as a powerful force with effective and compelling messaging. They have become the important and vital face of immigration reform. Part of their messaging was storytelling that helped the public, legislators, other college students, faculty, administrators, and other policy makers understand who they were as people and as advocates. In California, as in other states, DREAMers organized campus clubs and worked with well-established networks (see Appendix C).

DREAMers are a powerful, dedicated group of student political activists. They proudly stand for social justice and publicly state: "Unafraid, Unapologetic, and Undocumented." As activists, they refuse to live in a state of invisibility and fear. They call for greater access to higher education and for a pathway to citizenship. They have changed the language around their status and proudly call themselves undocuscholars and predocumented, not undocumented. Living with strong hearts, they are resilient and imaginative. They live their lives with meaning and determination to make the world a better place and believe they have a right to be heard, to be safe, and to be treated fairly. As leaders, they stand up for their beliefs and values and purposefully choose not to keep their status private.

Photo contributed by Lorenzo Valdovinos. © Kendall Hunt Publishing Company.

DREAMers know they have a great responsibility to be accountable not only to themselves and other predocumented individuals, but also to their families, allies, organizations, and citizens working for comprehensive immigration reform and justice for immigrants. Their accountability and conscious decisions are often guided by the Iroquois proverb, "In every deliberation, we must consider the impact of our decisions on the next seven generations."

As DREAMers, they have transformed the immigrants' rights debate and have talked about the civil rights of immigrants, the right of immigrants to live their lives full of hope and dignity. Immigrant rights are human rights, the basic rights and freedoms to which all humans are entitled, whether or not they are documented. They have transformed the dialogue from only asserting legal rights and the right to a pathway to citizenship to one that also includes and recognizes locally, statewide, and nationally that they are a politically autonomous group with the right to rights. Their vision is inclusive and their fight is for social and policy change. Given the chance to gain an education and the ability to maximize their skills and talents, they can contribute substantially to the long-term growth and prosperity of the nation embodied in a vision for empowerment, integrity, equality, and justice for all.

Dreamers/DACA and the Trump Effect

The 2016 presidential election has dramatically shaken but *not* eliminated DREAMers ideals and vision for empowerment. While running for office, Presidential candidate Donald Trump put forth tough immigration stances including promising to fully fund the building of a wall along the United States–Mexico border, arguing that Mexico was sending "criminals" and rapists to the United States, advocating for the creation of a deportation force to deport millions of undocumented individuals, as well as endorsing the extreme vetting of Muslim noncitizens seeking entry into the United States. He also promised to end President Obama's executive decision program, Deferred Action for Childhood Arrivals (DACA). Obama created this program because the U.S. Congress could not pass comprehensive immigration reform. This program enabled undocumented immigrants who came to the United States before age 16 to have temporary protection from deportation, work authorization, the ability to apply for a social security card, and in California, the ability to apply for medical care (Medi-Cal). However, it fell short of providing a pathway to citizenship. Because President Obama issued this program as an executive action and it is overseen by the DHS, the next secretary of the Department, who will be appointed by President-elect Trump, will have the authority to end it immediately.

Given Trump's victory on November 8, 2016 and his anti-immigrant rhetoric during the presidential campaign, DREAMers and DACA recipients have expressed worry and despair, as well as fear they could be forced back into the shadows and/or deported. They worry about their families being separated and what the future will hold for them. Their fears are not unique or unfounded. A survey by Southern Poverty Law Center's Teaching Tolerance project in November 2016 found that "the results of the election are having a profoundly negative impact on schools and students in K-12. About 90% of educators' report that school climate has been negatively affected, and most of them believe it will have a long-lasting impact. A full 80% describe heightened anxiety and concern on the part of students worried about the impact of the election on themselves and their families."[3] This survey was administered to over 10,000 teachers, counselors, administrators, and other school personnel. As reported in the press, these same results are being seen on college campuses as well.

Teachers in the survey reported that the election has unleashed a spirit of hatred they have not seen before. Some of the survey's major findings were: nine out of ten educators reported a negative impact on their students' moods; eight out of ten educators saw heightened anxiety on the part of marginalized students, including immigrants, Muslims, African-Americans, and LGBT students; four out of ten educators heard derogatory language directed at marginalized students; and sadly, four out of ten educators didn't feel their schools had action plans to respond to incidents of hate and bias, although two-thirds felt that individual administrators had been responsive. Finally, "over 2,500 educators described specific incidents of bigotry and harassment that can be directly traced to election rhetoric. These incidents include graffiti (including swastikas), assaults on students and teachers, property damage, and fights.

Activist DREAMers in California and the nation have vowed to fight against the anti-immigrant policies and practices and the bigotry and racism expressed in their schools and other institutions. They have stated that they will not let fear and despair mute their voices. DREAMers' rallying cry across the nation, "Unafraid, Undocumented, and Unapologetic," remains as vital today as it was in 2011.

In California, activists have urged the state as well as cities, counties, school districts, and colleges to adopt sanctuary/safe-haven policies. In response to their actions and calls from state policy makers, Sacramento City Unified School District's (SCUSD) Board of Education voted unanimously on December 8, 2016 to safeguard students and families by protecting student data and requiring ICE officials to obtain written permission before entering any campus. Shortly after this vote, California State

Superintendent of Education, Tom Torlakson, called on other K-12 organizations throughout the state to adopt "safe-haven" resolutions like SCUSD's. He stated: "Our schools are not and will not become an arm of the U.S. Customs and Immigration Enforcement (ICE)."

California policy makers are also at the forefront of developing legislation to support undocumented immigrants on the local and state levels. California Senate President pro Tempore Kevin de León (D-Los Angeles) introduced SB 54, the California Values Act, in December 2016 to prevent the use of state and local public resources to aid federal ICE agents in deportation actions. Democratic mayors in major cities have vowed to fight Trump's policies and continue their efforts to not ask residents their immigration status when providing services. In Sacramento, California, Mayor Darrell Steinberg stated in

---

3 *After election day, the Trump effect: The impact of the 2016 Presidential election on our Nation's* A report by the Southern Poverty Law Center © 2016. http://www.tolerance.org/sites/default/files/general/After%20 the%20Election%20Trump%20Effect%20Report.pdf

the Sacramento Bee in December 2016 that: "I can't say it strongly enough: We are going to assure families and kids and anybody who is worried about their status in our community that we are going to stand with them"

(http://www.sacbee.com/news/local/article115282793.html

On the college and university levels, University of California President Janet Napolitano, California State University Chancellor Timothy White, and State Chancellor-Designate of the California Community Colleges, Eloy Ortiz Oakley sent a letter on November 29, 2016 to President-Elect Trump urging him to continue the DACA program and to allow DREAMers to pursue their educations in the United States. Petitions supportive of undocumented immigrants are also being signed by students and faculty members and alumni in colleges and universities across the nation. These petitions are calling on postsecondary institutions to limit their cooperation with federal immigration enforcement authorities and to declare their educational institutions as sanctuaries/safe-havens.

All the actions listed above are cause for hope and send a unified message to undocumented communities that K-12 schools, colleges, and government institutions will stand up against hate and racism. These efforts also confirm that California agencies that have adopted safe-haven policies will protect the civil rights of the undocumented and that they will direct police departments not to undertake joint efforts to enforce federal immigration laws, allaying deportation fears for many.

Leading With the Values of Human Rights, Inclusion, and Dignity: Creating Hope for All

Now more than ever, considering Trump's election and the positions on immigration which he reiterated as a candidate, it is important that policies and power structures on the local, state, and national levels reflect the values of inclusion, respect, and dignity and that they also reflect the fundamental observance of human rights and freedoms. When the government uses its powers to deny legal rights and due process to vulnerable groups, such as the undocumented, Muslims, LGBT, and African-Americans, then everyone's rights are at risk. Alianza, a Sacramento area immigration rights group, along with other civil rights groups is committed to seeing that the civil liberties and civil rights of all vulnerable groups are upheld and that we lead with the values of inclusion and dignity. When our nation leads with these values, we embrace immigrant and refugee communities. When we lead with these values, we "Keep the Dream Alive." When we lead with these values, as individuals and as a nation, we have a responsibility to stand up against injustice and give each other hope. Together, as students, educators, academicians, policy makers, public officials, and activists, we can challenge nativism, xenophobia, and the widespread conception of immigrants as undeserving criminals whenever, and wherever we see it.

As Martin Luther King Jr. stated in his remarkable *"I Have a Dream"* speech, "we refuse to believe that the bank of justice is bankrupt. We refuse to believe that there are insufficient funds in the great vaults of opportunity of this nation. And so, we've come to cash this check, a check that will give us upon demand the freedom and the security of 'justice.'"

Together, both documented and undocumented immigrants, we can harness and transform immigrant fears, sadness, and rage into building a strong human rights movement and a culture that protects the most vulnerable from the threats of deportation and hate. Together we can dare to dream of a world we want to live in and back those dreams up with strategies bold enough to make substantive change, policies that will honor the security of justice, as Dr. Martin Luther King, Jr. has stated; poli-

Photo contributed by Lorenzo Valdovinos.
© Kendall Hunt Publishing Company.

cies that will encourage people to speak up and address bias, policies that will correct misinformation and help others to stand courageously; policies that will affirm that hate and intimidation have no place on our campuses, in our institutions, in the state, and in the world; and policies that will enable all individuals to be welcome regardless of immigration status.

Questions:

1. What words have positive connotations when describing DREAMers? What words have negative connotations when describing DREAMers? (Connotation is an idea or feeling that a word invokes in addition to its literal or primary meaning.)
2. How important are words or terms used to describe immigrants in framing a supportive or negative argument about immigration reform?
3. For example, notice how the sentence meaning shifts when the underlined word is changed:
   Positive: Enrique is a *proud* DREAMer
   Neutral: Enrique is a *young* DREAMer
   Negative: Enrique is an *illegal alien*
4. Why do some young undocumented DREAMers choose to keep their status private?
5. Should a college education be a right for all, regardless of immigration status? Why or why not?
6. What advice would you give to President Trump as he begins his presidency in January 2017?

Activity:

Watch the ALIANZA documentary: http://alianza-dream.org/documentary

How did you feel about the hopes and aspirations identified by the DREAMers in this documentary?

ALIANZA is a collective of active college students, educators and community activists working for Comprehensive Immigration Reform.

Artwork contributed by Antonio Sarabia.© Kendall Hunt Publishing Company.

APPENDIX A CALIFORNIA LEGISLATION AB 540

Assembly Bill 540 allows qualifying students, including undocumented immigrant students, to pay in-state tuition fees at public colleges or universities. This means AB 540 students will be allowed to pay the same amount for college tuition as a resident or U.S. citizen.

Requirements:

1. Attended a California high school for 3 or more years.
2. Graduated from a California high school or attained a GED.
3. Registered or is currently attending a public college or university in California.
4. Filed an affidavit with his or her college or university stating that the person will apply for legal residency.

AB 2000

This is an expansion of AB540. It increases the scope of student eligibility for students who graduated early from a California High School with the equivalent of 3 or more years of credits. If a student graduates early, they must have attended California elementary or secondary schools for a cumulative total of 3 or more years; a student may qualify for exemption from nonresident tuition pursuant to the abovereferenced provision either by high school attendance in California for 3 or more years or by either elementary or secondary school attendance, or both, in California for a total of 3 or more years and attainment of credits earned in California from a California high school equivalent to 3 or more years of full-time high school coursework, in addition to the other conditions referenced above.

California Dream Act

The California DREAM Act is composed of two parts: *AB 130 and AB131*.

AB130 allows eligible AB 540 students to apply for privately funded scholarships and grants given out by public colleges and universities in California.

AB 131 allows eligible AB 540 students to receive limited state financial aid, which includes: the Board of Governor's Fee Waiver, Competitive Cal Grants, and grants and scholarships awarded by public college and universities in California.

Requirements:

Must be eligible to apply for AB 540 (must meet the four requirements for AB 540 previously mentioned). For AB 130: must meet scholarship's requirements. For AB 131: must meet GPA and income requirements.

Available Aid from the California Dream Act: Cal Grant, Chafee Grant, Middle Class Scholarship, UC Grants, State University Grants, California Community College (CCC) BOG Fee Waiver, EOP/EOPS, some University scholarships, some private scholarships administered by campuses

SB 1159 Professions and Vocations: License Applicants: Individual Tax Identification Number

Authorizes agencies to accept tax identification numbers (TIN) in lieu of social security numbers (SSN) from individuals applying for professional licensure, and **prohibits the denial of licensure applications based on citizenship status or immigration status.**

AB60 Driver's Licenses

Requires the California Department of Motor Vehicles to issue an original driver license to an applicant who is unable to submit satisfactory proof of legal presence in the United States. Driver license applicants under AB 60 must meet all other qualifications for licensure and must provide satisfactory proof of identity and California residency.

AB 4 Trust Act

Limits local jails from holding people for extra time just so they can be deported. County jails can no longer respond to requests to hold individuals solely based on their immigration status, unless certain conditions are met. Even then, local law enforcement always has the discretion not to use local resources to detain immigrants for extra time. The TRUST Act ensures that people with most low-level, non-violent offenses (misdemeanors) are not wastefully held for deportation purposes. At the same time, the law allows detention of people with felony convictions and of those charged with felonies under certain circumstances. It also allows detention of people with several higher level misdemeanors (https://www.aclunc.org/our-work/legislation/trust-act-ab-4)

SB75—Medi-Cal for all Children

Children under 19 years of age are eligible for full-scope Medi-Cal benefits regardless of immigration status, if they meet the income standards. DHCS is working with CWDA, county human services agencies, Covered California, advocates, and other interested parties to identify and provide Medi-Cal coverage to all children under 19 with qualifying income. (http://www.dhcs.ca.gov/services/medical/eligibility/Pages/SB75Children.aspx

SB 54—California Values Act—Introduced 12-5-16

The California Values Act will keep California law enforcement out of painful deportations which separate families and communities, damage public safety, and undercut due process. The bill would ensure that public officials such as police, sheriffs, and school security officers are not involved in reporting, arresting, detaining, or turning community members over to Immigration and Customs Enforcement (ICE) for deportation. It would also keep schools, hospitals, and courts safe and accessible, with each developing a clear policy to limit deportation activities on their premises to the fullest extent possible.

Other key provisions of the California Values Act would guarantee that California plays no part in creating any kind of national registry to profile Muslims or other groups at risk of discrimination, barring state and local officials from providing information on religion, national origin, or other protected characteristics. The bill would also bolster confidentiality practices at state agencies so immigrants can continue to successfully participate in California's public life. http://www.caimmigrant.org/cipc-praises-ca-valuesact/

APPENDIX B FEDERAL LEGISLATION

Deferred Action for Childhood Arrivals (DACA)

On June 15, 2012, the Secretary of Homeland Security announced that certain people who came to the United States as children and meet several key guidelines may request consideration of deferred action for a period of 2 years, subject to renewal, and would then be eligible for work authorization. Determinations will be made on a case-by-case basis under the DACA guidelines.

Requirements:

1. Was under the age of 31 as of June 15, 2012.
2. Came to the United States before reaching the 16th birthday.
3. Has continuously resided in the United States since June 15, 2007.
4. Was physically present in the United States on June 15, 2012.
5. Is currently in school, graduated from high school, or received a GED or is an honorably discharged veteran.
6. Has not been convicted of a felony, significant misdemeanor, or does not pose a threat to national security or public safety.

Deferred Action for Parents of Americans and Expanded DACA Programs (nilc.org)

On November 20, 2014, President Barack Obama announced that the U.S. DHS would not deport certain undocumented parents of U.S. citizens and parents of lawful permanent residents (LPRs). The president also announced an expansion of the DACA program for youth who came to the United States as children. Under a directive from the secretary of DHS, these parents and youth may be granted a type of temporary permission to stay in the U.S. called "deferred action." These programs are expected to help up to 4.4 million people, per the DHS.

Requirements for Deferred Action for Parents of Americans (DAPA)

1. Be the parent of a U.S. citizen or LPR.
2. Have continuously lived in the United States since January 1, 2010.
3. Have been present in the United States on November 20, 2014. It's also likely that you will need to be present in the United States every day from Nov. 20, 2014, until you apply for DAPA.
4. Not have a lawful immigration status on November 20, 2014. To meet this requirement, (a) you must have entered the United States without papers, or, if you entered lawfully, your lawful immigration status must have expired before November 20, 2014 and (b) you must not have a lawful immigration status at the time you apply for DAPA.
5. Have not been convicted of certain criminal offenses, including any felonies and some misdemeanors.

Status of Extended DACA and DAPA—Court Summary from National Immigration Law Center (NILC) https://www.nilc.org/issues/immigration-reform-and-executive-actions/united-states-v-state-oftexas/supreme-courts-tie-vote-means-dapa-daca/

In December 2014, Texas and 25 other states filed a lawsuit in the Federal District Court for the Southern District of Texas to stop DAPA and the *expansion* of DACA (DACA+) from being implemented. In February 2015, just 2 days before the federal government was set to begin accepting applications for DACA+, Judge Andrew Hanen of the Texas district court issued an order—a *preliminary injunction*—that temporarily blocked DAPA and DACA+ from being implemented. When the Obama administration appealed this order, the Fifth Circuit Court of Appeals affirmed Judge Hanen's decision. This kept DAPA and DACA+ blocked. The Obama administration then appealed the Fifth Circuit's decision to the U.S. Supreme Court, arguing that DAPA and DACA+ should be allowed to go forward. Having voted 4-4 in *United States v. Texas*, the Supreme Court issued its ruling in the case on June 23, 2016. *U.S. v. Texas* is about whether two of President Obama's immigration relief initiatives— DAPA and LPRs and an *expansion* of Deferred Action for Childhood Arrivals (DACA+)—may be implemented. The tie vote means that decisions by lower courts that temporarily blocked DAPA and DACA+ from being implemented remain in effect.

(*Note*: Usually there are nine Supreme Court justices, but currently there are only eight. Since Justice Antonin Scalia died earlier this year, Senate Republicans have refused to hold confirmation proceedings for Merrick Garland, the man President Obama nominated to fill the vacant position.)

The Supreme Court case does not directly involve the DACA program that has been in place since 2012. People who qualify under the original terms of the DACA program can still apply for that program. However, the Supreme Court case does affect the expansion of DACA that the President proposed. That expansion remains on hold.

Dream Act (as it appeared in Senate Bill 744—has not passed)

An expedited road to citizenship would be available to those who entered the United States before the age of 16, graduated from high school (or received a GED) in the United States, and attended at least 2 years of college or served 4 years in the uniformed services. DREAMers would apply for Registered Provisional immigrants (RPI) status, and, after 5 years, would be eligible to apply for adjustment to LPR status. They then would be able to apply immediately for U.S. citizenship.

- **No age cap.** There would be no upper-age limit for those who apply under this provision. This makes sense, since the relevant issue is the person's age at the time of entry into the U.S., not his or her current age.
- **DACA streamlining.** The DHS secretary would have the discretion to establish streamlined procedures for people already granted DACA.
- **No penalty for offering in-state tuition.** The bill would repeal a provision of the Illegal Immigration Reform and Immigrant Responsibility Act of 1996 that prohibited public universities from offering in-state tuition rates to undocumented students on the basis of residence in the state, unless they offered the same rates to nonresidents of the state.
- **Educational loans.** RPIs who entered the United States prior to age 16 (and agricultural workers with blue card status) may qualify for federal work-study and federal student loans. They remain ineligible for federal Pell grants until they adjust to LPR status.

Bridge Act—"Bar Removal of Individuals Who Dream of Growing Our Economy"—S. 3542

The following information is from https://www.nilc.org/issues/daca/faq-bridge-act/

Senators Lindsey Graham (R-SC) and Dick Durbin (D-IL) have introduced the BRIDGE Act, bipartisan legislation whose intent is to allow people who are eligible for or who have received work authorization and temporary relief from deportation through DACA to continue living in the United States with permission from the federal government

The BRIDGE Act would make it possible for people who meet certain requirements to apply for and receive "provisional protected presence" and work authorization for a 3-year period. The 3-year period would end 3 years after the bill becomes law. The requirements people would have to meet are essentially the same as the <u>requirements for DACA</u> under the program that was created in 2012.

People who already have DACA would be deemed to have provisional protected presence until their DACA's expiration date, then they would be eligible to apply affirmatively for provisional protected presence.

The BRIDGE bill also would impose restrictions on the sharing of information in DACA and provisional protected presence applications with U.S. ICE and U.S. Customs and Border Protection for purposes of immigration enforcement.

Is the BRIDGE Act the same as the Dream Act?

No. The Dream Act did not pass when Congress voted on it in 2011, and it has not been reintroduced since then. The Dream Act would have permitted certain immigrants who grew up in the United States to obtain temporary legal status and eventually apply for and obtain permanent legal status, then U.S. citizenship. To be eligible, they would have had to meet certain education-related requirements or have served in the U.S. military.

The BRIDGE Act would not provide a pathway to U.S. citizenship. It would only allow people who are eligible for—or who already have—DACA to receive work authorization and provisional protected presence.

Why is the BRIDGE bill being introduced?

Members of Congress from both parties recognize the positive impact providing work authorization and protection from deportation has had on the lives of people with DACA, as well as on the broader society and economy. (These benefits are detailed in a recent report, <u>New Study of DACA Beneficiaries Shows Positive Economic and Educational Outcomes</u>.) The BRIDGE bill would allow DACA recipients the opportunity to continue contributing to our society and economy. In addition, policymakers recognize the need to protect DACA recipients. Since the November 2016 election, many DACA recipients and their allies have expressed concerns over whether President-elect Trump will follow through on his campaign threat to end the DACA program. If it were enacted, this bill's provisions would provide assurance to DACA recipients that they could continue being both authorized to work in the United States and protected from deportation.

APPENDIX C: RESOURCES

ALIANZA—http://alianzadream.org

Alianza is a collective of active college students, educators, and community activists from the Sacramento area personally committed to issues related to immigration reform, especially those regarding DREAMer students. Its activism takes shape in creating awareness, delivering meaningful outreach, and building systems of support for DREAMer students.

California Dream Network/CHIRLA—http://chirla.org/CADREAMNetwork

The California Dream Network is a project of CHIRLA, a statewide network of existing and emerging college campus organizations who actively address undocumented student issues and who work to create broader social change around immigration reform and access to higher education. The California Dream Network's work is carried out through: college campus organizing; statewide conference calls; regional summits; and annual statewide conferences.

California Immigrant Policy Center (CIPC)—http://caimmigrant.org

CIPC advances inclusive policies that build a prosperous future for all Californians, using policy analysis, advocacy, and capacity building to unlock the power of immigrants in California.

California Rural Legal Assistance Foundation (CRLAF)—https://www.crlaf.org/

CRLAF provides community outreach and education, public policy advocacy, litigation support, and technical and legal assistance for California's rural poor. We target our work in the areas of agricultural workers' health, civil rights, education, labor and employment, immigration and citizenship, pesticides and worker safety, rural housing, and sustainable communities.

Educators for Fair Consideration (E4FC)—http://www.e4fc.org/

Their mission is to empower undocumented young people to achieve their academic and career goals and actively contribute to society.

Immigrant Legal Resource Center (ILRCI)—https://www.ilrc.org

The Immigrant Legal Resource Center (ILRC) is a national nonprofit resource center that provides immigration legal trainings, technical assistance, and educational materials, and engages in advocacy and immigrant civic engagement to advance immigrant rights

National Immigrant Law Center—http://nilc.org

The National Immigration Law Center (NILC) is one of the leading organizations in the United States exclusively dedicated to defending and advancing the rights of low-income immigrants.

Own the Dream—http://www.weownthedream.org/

Own the DREAM is a national campaign to help aspiring Americans brought to this country as children take advantage of the opportunity to apply for DACA and work permits. The campaign will join the resources of United We Dream and its partners to offer assistance to a significant number of the hundreds of thousands of DREAMers eligible for this opportunity to stay in America to complete their education and contribute to the economy.

United We Dream—http://unitedwedream.org

United We Dream is the largest immigrant youth-led organization in the nation. Its non-partisan network is made up of over 100,000 immigrant youth and allies and 55 affiliate organizations in 26 states. They organize and advocate for the dignity and fair treatment of immigrant youth and families, regardless of immigration status.

DREAM Educational Empowerment Program (DEEP)—http://unitedwedream.org/about/projects/education

DEEP is a catalyst for educational justice and empowerment for immigrant students. DEEP educates, connects, and empowers immigrant students, parents, and educators to close the opportunity gap and engage in local efforts to improve educational equity. DEEP seeks to lay the groundwork that advances the educational justice movement in the United States by focusing resources and research on the needs and realities of immigrant students in order to increase educational attainment rates.

For more resources go to Alianza's website: http://alianzadream.org/resources

Chapter 32

Danza Azteca: Movement, Music, and Memories

Sohnya Castorena

Important Words and Concepts in This Chapter

There are several important words and concepts throughout the upcoming chapter. The words appear several times in different places in order to help you remember the words and understand the chapter. The words are defined several times:

- Immediately below right before the chapter begins
- In text boxes throughout the chapter
- In red and boldfaced within the chapter
- In a glossary in expanded form at the end of the units

Some of the words also appear in other chapters. Talk about the words with other students, teachers, friends, and family members before you read, while reading the chapter, and after you have read the chapter.

Transnational Social Movements

A group of people organized, outside of institutions and across more than two countries established for this purpose, so as to bring about political and social change which will satisfy their shared interest or goal.

Contributed by Sohnya Castorena. © Kendall Hunt Publishing Company.

Maestro

A master usually in an art; *especially* an eminent composer, conductor, or teacher of music.

Decolonized, Pan-Indigenous Consciousness

An awareness of the connection and freedom to think and live according to their own collective desires among different indigenous communities across many different regions.

Cosmology

Cosmology explores how and why the universe works. Cosmology involves the philosophy and the scientific study of the large-scale properties of the universe as a whole.

Nahua

The **Nahuas** are a group of indigenous peoples of Mexico.

Colonialism (Colonization)

Political control of one nation over another that is institutionalized in direct political administration by the colonial power, control of all economic relationships, and a systematic attempt to transform the culture of the subject nation.

Pan-Indigenous Ideology

The term Pan-Indigenous or "Pan-Indianism" has been applied to social movements among both Asian Indians and North American First Nations peoples.

Kinesthetic (Kinesthesia)

Of or relating to Kinesthesia (The sense that detects bodily position, weight, or movement of the muscles, tendons, and joints.)

Multiplex Identity

Multiplex identity refers to people who hold multiple cultural identities or who hold identities that locate them in the intersections of oppression.

Colonist

A government of cial, employee, or citizen of a colonial or occupying country.

Symbol

Something that represents something else by association, resemblance—a material object used to represent something invisible.

Indigenous Spiritual Belief Systems

Ideas from people whose family and ethnic group lived in a particular land first about how the world was created, where people came from, and where we will go when we die; also how we should treat our families and other people living or dead.

Chicano Movement

The Mexican American Civil Rights Movement, one of the least studied social movements of the 1960s, encompassed a broad cross section of issues—from restoration of land grants, to farm workers' rights, to enhanced education, voting, and political rights.

Elders

An influential member of a tribe, community, or family—often considered wise.

Anthropologist

Someone who undertakes the scientific study of the origin of a phenomenon, object, idea, or style. Anthropologists have been part of the destruction of culture and part of the preservation of culture.

This chapter explores the transformative power of Danza Azteca. Danza Azteca, also commonly referred to as Danza Mexica, involves more than just the physical act of dancing. Danzantes are engaged in the movement, music, as well as multiple visual representations of danza. It is a modern **transnational social movement** that has now spread across California and the United States. Jesus Ortiz, the **Maestro** of Grupo Quetzalcoatl-Citlalli described Danza as "a spiritual movement, life movement …. Danza's not just one thing, Danza's life, Danza's everything …. A danza is a form

© Gerasimov/Shutterstock.com

Nahua art depicting Chicomecoatl, Goddess of food and produce. This image is in the public domain.

of prayer. Each danza has its own meaning, story, power and direction." (J. Ortiz, personal communication, 2011). Danza is seen not solely as a dance form, it is viewed among danzantes as a way of life, as prayer, tradition, heritage, history, an art form as well as something that grants danzantes the ability to express their different identities through dance. A danzante within the dance circle is surrounded by family, prayers, and one's history, and through the act of dancing, danzantes are able to access, reconstruct, and express sociohistorical memories, feelings, and their sense of space and place, effectively creating a *Mexica*[1] identity and way of life based in a decolonized pan-indigenous consciousness.

Danza has the ability to act as a vehicle of self-representation for individual danzantes as well as the larger Chicana/o and Native communities in which it exists. The danzantes described remembering and "prayer through movement" aids in transforming their identities, as well as focus on the remembering and rewriting of history, traditions, and identity through the recovery of historical and cultural memories through Danza's expressive cultural practices. A danzante may utilize one or more of danza's expressive cultural practices to produce and express different aspects of their identities. Upon speaking with a danzante who has danced for over 30 years, he stated that he continues to dance because of "everything that it's done for us as a people, and as a community. It gives us identity. It gives us something actual physical that is us, and I think we need that …. The danza is not a religion, it's a view and understanding of the universe. It's a tool to help us understand our place on this earth in the universe. It's a perspective, it's a way of seeing life …. it strengthens the individual." (Danzante1 personal communication, 2012). The practice of danza, the dancing connects danzantes with their history, community, both past and present, and connects the danzantes to their individual innermost feelings, sense of self.

> Jesus Ortiz, the Maestro of Grupo Quetzalcoatl-Citlalli described Danza as "a spiritual movement, life movement … Danza's not just one thing, Danza's life, Danza's everything … A danza is a form of prayer. Each danza has its own meaning, story, power, and direction … "

---

1   Term used by the Aztecs to describe themselves. Mexica are the people who resided in Mexico-Tenochtitlan.

Dance and its accompanying expressive cultural practices can communicate as much information and knowledge as oral or written communication systems. Each danzante is introduced to the movements, sounds, and symbolism of Danza Azteca. They first learn the shared danza language and knowledge of the movement system.

During this initial period, danzantes learn not only the movement system but also the cosmology and intellectual traditions of the Nahua, which grants them a new world-view and way of life based on the Nahua belief system.

Numerous danzantes stated that they had no knowledge of their history nor did they have a connection to their ancestry. Danzante 2 asserts that the danza has given her a connection to her ancestry, "I feel blessed, I feel tied to our people. Danza is part of our culture, part of our people and I'm just so appreciative of it … for me it fulfilled a void and I think that's just not really knowing myself, it's helped me to understand … about where I come from" (Danzante 2 personal communication, February 2011). Danza has provided the avenue to remember their sociohistorical memories and an indigenous belief system. With the history and knowledge of their past, danzantes are able to produce and express this shared notion of a Mexica identity based within a Nahua belief system.

Danzantes connect with sociohistorical memories via movement, as well as in Danza art through the images and symbols on their *trajes*[2] and *armas*[3]. Expressions of cultural and social identity are created and shared through the dance. Danzantes employ indigenous North, South, and Central American art and symbolism within danza art and *trajes* as representations of their gendered, social, and cultural identity.

> **Nahua:** a group of indigenous peoples of Mexico originating in the southwestern part of what is now the United States and northwestern Mexico. They migrated into central Mexico around 500 CE settling around the Basin of Mexico and spread out to become the dominant people in central Mexico. Nahua ethnic groups include the Toltecs, Aztecs, Tepanecas, Acolhuas, Tlaxcaltecs, Xochimilcas, and many others.

> **Symbolism:** an act, sound, or object having cultural significance and the capacity to excite or objectify a response.

The body is a powerful site for the dissemination of information, and has been used in both sacred and secular contexts throughout time to write one's memory and identity into history. The performance and reception of danza are a particularly powerful site for the representation, performance, and reception of sociohistorical memories and identity. Danza Azteca dance events encompass more than just the performance of the dance. These events are fluid and include the place and space surrounding it, the interplay between the dancers and observers, as well as the music. All aspects of a dance event influence the meaning garnered by the danzantes and the audience because, in the words of Maxine Sheets-Johnstone, "Movement is unique among the media of expression …. We produce sound kinesthetically, via muscular movement, but we hear it aurally, we paint kinesthetically but review it visually.

---

2 *Trajes* are the regaliaand attire the danzantes wear for presentations and ceremonies.
3 *Armas* are the tools and instruments a danzante carries with them at all danza events, that is, *ayacachtli*.

While the results of movement can be seen and heard, they are primarily received by the person doing it as felt experience, as kinesthesia. As a participant and observer at danza events, the multisensory nature of movement at Danza events that Sheets-Johnstone speaks about is clearly evident. Danza Azteca presentations and ceremonies require that we utilize each of our senses. As soon as you enter the location of any ceremonial site, as a danzante or observer your senses are overtaken by the sounds of the *armas*, huehuetls (drums), *xayayotes*, and conversations, all taking place simultaneously. You are at once immersed in the sight of danzantes performing their readying rituals, dressing, lacing up their *xayayotes*, placing their feathers in their *kopillis*. One also can hear the *xayayotes* ringing as danzantes are walking around, and you smell the *copal* or sage burning in the *sahumador*, and see the smoke in the air as the *sahumadoras* bless the altars and danzantes. Then the caracoles are called and the drums begin to beat. The heartbeat is set and the *ayacachtlis* and *xayayotes* carry that beat. Everyone begins to move in unison and the movement has begun. Songs and blessings are said in English, Nahuatl, Spanish, and sometimes the regional Native American languages. Every sense is overtaken by a multitude of happenings.

The danzantes are acting as agents of change constructing, expressing, and producing a *Mexica* identity, through the use of ancient *Nahua* material culture; by displaying *Nahua* symbolism, they publicly declare their *Mexica* identity in practices, presentations, and ceremonies. Danzantes use *Nahua* art and symbolism within danza art and *armas*, as representations of their gendered, social, and cultural identity.

The dances and each movement within the dance, are seen as words to a prayer. Through the movements and the utilization of the kinesthetic sense, the danzantes are able to experience in unison, the remembering of sociohistorical memories and the creation and expression of a new **pan-indigenous** representation. This shared pan-indigenous ideology and identity acquired through danza events and expressive cultural practices aids the danzantes in creating and expressing various aspects of their multiplex identity. Many scholars have shown that memories and access to one's identity are embodied and expressed through the senses in bodily practices such as dance, ritual, song, smells, and taste. These expressive productions and narratives of self and one's sense of history and place in the cosmos are just as powerful as written constructions of memory and identity.

> **Pan-Indigenous:** the coming together of many different indigenous people to advance political, economic, and social equity. Pan indigenous also explores the complimentary and common identities, experiences, and ideas among indigenous people.

Remembering

Why is memory, and more importantly, why is the erasure and remembering of one's cultural and historical memory so important? Many scholars have asserted that, "Memory is the foundation of self and society … and without it there can be no self, no identity.

Without memory, the world would cease to exist in any meaningful way ... memory, whether individual or collective, is constructed and reconstructed" (Climo & Cattel, 2002, p. 1). The danzantes are remembering and rewriting their cultural and historical memories based in a Nahua belief system and accessed through the performance of danza and its expressive cultural practices, such as art, songs, and music. Much care was taken by each **Nahua** generation to preserve and pass down the songs and dances. The elders taught and lectured the youth of each generation to memorize, recite, and perform the songs and dances because one's history and memories were contained within the poems, songs, and movements. These songs and dances of the Nahua, carried within them individual, familial, and communal histories and memories. The Maestro of the group spoke frequently about the importance of remembering "your history because if you do not know your history, if you don't know where you come from you can't move forward, your lost without it" (J. Ortiz, personal communication, 2011). I have observed the Danza group in the process of reclaiming their indigenous past. The group is invested in remembering and reconstructing key sociohistorical memories.

The act of colonization has produced conflict and destruction on multiple levels: physically, economically, intellectually, spiritually, and with respect to the loss of sociohistorical memories. The destruction and loss of memory affects identity formation which then results in an ongoing contentious relationship between the colonizers and colonized that has had lasting devastating effects on the colonized population (Aldama & Quinonez, 2002; Connerton, 1989; Fuentes, 1992).

I argue that during the performance and/or reception of these expressive cultural practices, danzantes are remembering and recreating historical memories based in an indigenous past rather than in an era of colonization. Danzantes are actively engaged in remembering and rewriting sociohistorical memories and are constructing new identities and a sense of space and place based in a **pan-indigeneous ideology**. These collective memories are not a given; rather, they are socially and culturally constructed through the performance and reception of cultural practices. Numerous danzantes stated that they had no knowledge of their history nor did they have a connection to their ancestry. Danza has provided the avenue to remember their cultural and historical memories, indigenous belief system, and created a sense of belonging. Many danzantes also expressed a feeling and sense of home; of being lost and finding their space and place; their indigenous history; a new perspective and world-view; and they found these through danza. The act of dancing, of performing in collective ritual or performance, grants danzantes the ability to express their indigenous identities, and create a sense of community, family, and belonging.

During the Chicano Movement, one of the primary modes of communication utilized to disseminate sociohistorical and cultural knowledge and information to both rural and urban Chicano/Latino communities was through cultural practices such as dance, poetry, and visual art. Stuart Hall argues that identity is a "production, which is never complete, always in process" (Hall cited in Velez-Ibanez & Sampaio, p. 85). The experience and reception of dance is a particularly powerful site for the embodiment, expression, and reception of identity and memory because, as argued by Williams, "When people dance, they are organizing, attaining, experiencing, communicating, or representing knowledge and belief" (Williams, 2004, p. 35). I have participated and observed the Danza group in the process of reclaiming their indigenous past. The Danza group is invested in remembering sociohistorical memories, and through the act of dance they are rewriting their gendered political, social, and cultural identities. The group has redefined and reshaped the Danza's ideology and traditions to speak to the specific concerns and interests of their community and the corresponding ideology of the Maestro.

The danzantes, I interviewed, all expressed feelings of unity and family when speaking about the Quetzalcoatl-Citlalli danza group. Turino argues that, "Through moving and sounding together in synchrony people can experience a feeling of oneness with others. Signs of social intimacy are experienced directly—body to body—and thus in the moment reflect to be true." (Turino, 2008, p. 2) The collective act of dancing together, in unison in such a supportive environment created a sense of home and family, a Mexica identity and sense of space and place based within a Nahua belief system. Additionally, the danzantes all spoke of instances when they were transported to another realm, they transcended through the dance, or felt transformed, but a stronger theme that came up time and again in the interviews and within the group palabras after practice was the creation of a danza family, a sense of belonging, and of being home.

Music

Throughout history across continents and cultural divides, one of the primary modes of communication utilized to disseminate sociohistorical and cultural knowledge, influence national identity, and inform rural and urban communities was, and still is, through cultural practices such as songs, poetry, dance, and drumming. Current research conducted on music, songs, and drumming has focused on drumming and music's ability to incite as well as record social change in the given sociohistorical time period. Music may operate simultaneously as a unifying force as well as a force of resistance. Within the lyrics of these songs, history was being recorded as well as genealogies, and cultural knowledge systems.

The music of *danza*; the singing, drumming, and sounds of the *armas* (*danza* term for regalia, vestments and musical instruments) are important and powerful forces utilized in both sacred and secular events. The sounds of *danza*, the songs, *alabanzas* and *cantos*, drums, flutes, mandolins, and other *armas* have agency, the means to send and receive encoded meaning, and produce socially and culturally constructed knowledge.

When interviewing both Native American and Danza elders, they all expressed the vital importance of song and music in dance. A Miwok elder shared her belief that song is of the utmost importance because, in her words, "if you don't have your song, your drum, your words, you don't have a people, you don't have something to carry on, something that gives you that pride, something that gives you that uniqueness, and if you don't have that then I think you get kind of lost" (Danzante 3 personal communication, August 2011). This idea is readily expressed and shared in danza circles. Songs index and incite many feelings, experiences, and histories. Songs have the power to make you feel: whether sad or happy, they may bring back memories of a time in your life, or speak of an individual or group history. Turino states that the power of song resides in the collective power of voice, in his words, "The very fact of many voices sounding together creates the experience of unity, directly and concretely felt …. The constant repetition of a few simple ideas in the texts cement them in people's minds as truth, and thus help generate courage to act on that truth in the face of opposition" (Turino, 2008, p. 217). I agree with this wholeheartedly, and I would add that, when you add in the sound of the drum and armas, with the visuality of the movements of the danzantes moving and sounding in unison, and the visuality and smell of the copal, with the smoke drifting up from the sacred fire at the altar; this visual, auditory, and kinesthetic event creates a multisensory overload, and creates a hyper-sense of awareness and experience.

Music production is a complex powerful site and experience. In particular, the drum has special significance and has often been called the heartbeat of a community, as it carries the heart and energy of a community or a movement. The drum is a key component within danza events and danza movement systems. The movement, the dancing, and the drumming are linked, they coexist, each influences the other in turn, the dance is dependent on the drum and the drum is dependent on the dancers.

Singing and drumming are nearly always spoken of with reverence and awe.

> **…the music, the songs and drumming brought about feelings ranging from a sense of home and safeness, to sadness.**

Informants would often fall short in words, and move to describe their feelings or use sensory words and phrases. My informants, both the danzantes and Native American informants, echoed these sentiments often stating that the music, songs, and drumming brought about feelings ranging from a sense of home and safeness, to sadness. More often than not, they stated that the drums produced something that was hard to put into spoken words; feelings were more often deployed when addressing and describing the drum, it's sounds, and the emotions and meaning it produces for each *individual*.

Music and dance are key sites for the production, maintenance, and reception of social, political, and cultural identities, history, rites, traditions, and spiritual communication/invocation. Numerous anthropologists, ethnomusicologists, and Native American scholars testify to the fact that music in Native American communities has multiple meanings and functions, and that music may operate in a social, political, and sacred (religious/spiritual) capacity on different occasions depending on the situated event and audience.

When interviewing danzantes and audience members about the danza and their first experience or their first remembrance of seeing danza at any type of event, nearly all (90%) of the informants spoke of their memory of and reaction to the drum. They did speak of the regalia, the feathers, the colors, and movement of the dancers and feathers together but when they spoke of what drew them into danza, what pulled them to the dancing was the sound of the drumbeat. The danzantes as well as the California traditional dancers spoke about the drum with reverence and awe. They see the drum as key component in what brings us together as a community, as a danza community and in the larger sense as a pan-indigenous community.

A traditional California dancer who has never danced Danza Azteca spoke of the danza and the drum's first impression on her at a Native event as a youth, 20 years ago, "It was around the time when I started dancing, which was around age twelve, thirteen. It just became like a part of me …. It was at a Gathering and I said ok, because it was different from our style, and I was like that's different oh they're different. Then the music and the drums start and I said *OH* that's just like us, you know it was kind of like I felt it here (points to her heart), you guys are just like us." (Danzante 4 personal communication, July 2011) She and each of the other traditional dancers that I spoke to emphasized how they were at first cognizant of the difference between the styles, primarily because of the difference in regalia. But as soon as the drums started, they each felt a connection and feeling of sameness and a sense that although the movement styles were quite different, the essence of the song and the dances was the same, the role and function of the song and dance in each of their traditional dances were connected, and the integral component in making this connection was the sound of the drum.

In particular, the drum is seen as a universal heartbeat that creates a powerful sense of home and safeness. This idea is prevalent among all of the danzantes and traditional California dancers. The music, songs, dances, and other traditional expressive cultural practices are extremely important aspects of their indigenous identities.

When one participates in danza, in addition to learning the movements, the danzantes acquire intellectual, spiritual, and cultural traditions and memories. This process involves the acquisition of a new movement system based in movement as well as Nahuatl symbolism, in order to interpret and comprehend the meaning of the movement, trajes, structure of the dance, and other tools associated with the Danza. I argue that through the performance and reception of danza at Danza Azteca dance events, the shared indigenous knowledge systems are learned, and the expressive cultural practices shared by the danzantes, granting them the power to create, produce, and express a highly politicized pan-indigenous identity.

References

Aldama, A., & Quinonez, N. (Eds.) (2002). *Decolonial voices: Chicana and chicano cultural studies in the 21st century*. Bloomington, Indiana: Indiana University Press.

Climo, J., & Cattel, M. (Eds.). (2002). *Social memory and history*. Lanham, MD: Altamira Press.

Connerton, P. (1989). *How societies remember*. Cambridge University Press.

Fuentes, C. (1992). *The campaign*. HarperCollins.

Turino, T. (2008). *Music as social life*. Chicago, IL: University of Chicago Press.

Velez-Ibanez, C.G., & Sampaio, A. (Eds.). (2002). *Transitional Latina/o communities*. Lanham, MD: Rowman and Littlefield Publishers.

Williams. W. (2004). *The anthropology of dance*. Chicago, IL: University of Illinois Press.

Chapter **33**

Unmasking the Spirit: Danza at Sol Collective
A Photo Essay

Arya Dawn Allender-West

Contributed by Arya Dawn Allender-West. © Kendall Hunt Publishing Company.

Chapter 34

The Legacy of MLK Is Alive Today In These Young Activists

Youth Radio Editors

Fifty years ago, on April 4, 1968, civil rights leader Martin Luther King, Jr. was assassinated. Half a century later, some of the same battles he fought — for racial equality and justice, voting rights, and fair wages, and against poverty, war, and segregation — are still being waged, and new struggles have begun.

Meet some of the young activists who are, in various ways, carrying on in Dr. King's footsteps today. Here they explain in their own words what they're fighting for.

Celeste Aguilar, 16, Washington, D.C.

As a young Latina student, I'm fighting for justice in my society, like equality and safety for all individuals — no matter their immigration status, sex or race. I stand and I speak up for others and I attend marches and protests for rights and participate in any kind of protest that will benefit us, young and old, because it will make a change but we have to work together for change. I do this because I strongly believe that the more people who seek change, the quicker the change will come.

I'm only one, but when it comes to numbers, we can all work to make a difference. I matter, and my voice matters. MLK voiced his concerns, and we should join him in this effort.

Celeste Aguilar

It's pivotal for all living in the U.S. to stand for social justice issues because without it there wouldn't be any order. We need a change for future generations to have good morals, positive mindset and to live at peace.

Hamdia Ahmed, 20, Portland, Maine, University of Southern Maine | @hamdia_ahmed

I am fighting for a world where everyone is treated with respect and dignity. We must never watch people get oppressed on our own watch. We cannot be silent in the face of injustice because it is our duty to stand up for our brothers and sisters. Dr. Martin Luther King, Jr. inspired us to not stay silent, and we must continue his legacy.

I have been, in particular, fighting for Muslims, immigrants and black people in this country because I fit into these groups. We live in a country where people are told to go back to their country, the spread of hatred towards Muslims, and black people getting murdered by the police for no reason. We

Hamdia Ahmed.

Photo: Jason

have a leader who promoted hatred and division. What makes people a true patriot is when they fight for the rights of their fellow Americans.

Ziad Ahmed, 19, Princeton, NJ, Yale University | @ziadtheactivist

As an American-Muslim teenager, I am fighting for (in whatever capacity I can be helpful/useful) a tomorrow where every child can be loved, accepted, and confident/safe in their own skin.

More than that, I'm fighting for a world where every child has the space to dream unapologetically — and has the agency/ability to achieve their dreams, whatever they might be. I fundamentally believe that this world is better when every voice is empowered, when we are not limited by societal expectations, and when we disrupt the status quo to shift paradigms forward.

I am inspired by those before me — many of whom are people of color, women, queer, and representative of the diversity that exists in our world.

Ziad Ahmed.

Courtesy of Ziad Ahmed

I find hope in the strides that leaders like Dr. Martin Luther King Jr. were able to make — by speaking truth to power, by working tirelessly for better, and by resisting systems of inequality. I hope to be a part of that same fight, as I hope to follow the lead of those who have been doing this work far longer/better than me.

As I look around this world, I see institutionalized racism, patriarchal power, imperialist foreign policy, ignorant leaders, children being left behind, and broken justice systems. I see a world that needs radical change. I am fighting for that world because I believe in the power of humanity to create a more just world, because I believe it's my responsibility to love this world enough to want to make it better.

I fight for better, because InshAllah (God willing), we will be better.

Santos Amaya Guevara, 20, Washington, D.C., co-founder, Latin American Youth Center's Latino Youth Leadership Council

Martin Luther King was a great leader who fought for civil and human rights to protect and defend the dignity and value of his people, and all people for that matter. I believe that his spirit is still alive today because he is still a role model which has inspired and motivated other leaders across the world, including myself.

Santos Amaya Guevara.

As a Latina activist, I have been participating in different advocacy roles to combat discrimination and racism, while also celebrating and uplifting diversity.

I, alongside my friends, founded and developed the Latino Youth Leadership Council (LYLC), a group bringing together students from various high schools in D.C., with the mission to organize and mobilize to assess, develop, and implement opportunities and alternatives for recent immigrant Latino students in D.C. public schools and other educational systems in the District of Columbia.

The Latin American Youth Center supports us by providing community organizing support and mobilizing knowledge and skills, and together we are organizing powerful community conferences, youth summits, and we have even created a powerful book called "Voices Without Borders: Our Stories, Our Truth," hoping to counter the deceiving national anti-immigrant rhetoric that taints and dehumanizes immigrant youth.

What I have learned from Martin Luther King is that when we are quiet about the things that matter, darkness gets stronger, injustice rules, and people suffer. This is why I believe that there is power in fighting for what we believe in, especially us, the youth. If we fight, something will change. We must be committed to work hard to make changes and not give up until we get what we need and deserve.

I fight for justice, for equity, for a better future, for an education, and to make youth voices be heard because youth voices matter. Youth voices are powerful. Youth have more knowledge than people think, and they need to speak their truth.

Too many undocumented youth are scared to speak because they don't know English and because the real threat of police forces trying to separate them from their families, but we must not stay quiet, just like Martin Luther King did not stay quiet in the face of oppression.

I fight and represent undocumented youth because I believe one person can let them know that they are not alone, and — more important — that together we are going to win this fight against injustice.

Anya Andrews, 18, Policy Committee Leader, Million Hoodies Bard Chapter, Bard College, from Los Angeles, CA

I am fighting for Black and Brown people to reach the mountaintop King spoke about that many years ago. I am fighting for Black excellence. I am fighting for Black Liberation. I am fighting for Black education. I am fighting for the success of Black America.

However, this fight has many scales, and we must remember that there are levels to every fight, just as there are battles in every war. There are some of us who struggle just to get out of bed in the morning. We're battling ourselves just as we are battling systematic oppression, overt and covert racism, and the invisible White Only signs that exist across America.

Anya Andrews.

Photo courtesy of Anya Andrews

We are fighting a two-front battle, which makes it hard to see where we're going and where we can succeed as Black people. Our self-hate is reinforced by their hate, and thus reiterates the vicious cycle of loathing.

What I am fighting for is the belief in a future that we have yet to see. I am fighting for children to understand their rights and see their barriers so they can knock them down. As long as difference is used to define us, we will always be segregated.

And to answer your question as to why I fight: How can I not? I have been given the access to education and the privilege to study and participate in organizations that fight for our power, our rights, and our excellence. Not everyone has the privilege that I have had to learn about our oppression and articulate it to the world.

I see it as my responsibility to fight for those who cannot, to fight for those who are lost to the system, to fight for those who are hidden behind numbers and demographics, and to fight for those whose voice have been muted year after year, generation after generation, time and time again.

Young people like Giavonni and I are the Freedom Fighters of today, and we will always stand for our people.

Seun Babalola, 20, Bronx, N.Y., Penn State | @seuntheactivist

Fifty years after MLK's assassination, I am still fighting for social justice among my peers, which are Black youth and, specifically, college students. As a Black college student currently attending a predominantly white institution, I'm not blind to the injustices that people still face today in 2018, and especially on college campuses where there is a mix of ideas being put together in the same space.

There are many of my peers who are Black that have experienced various acts of hatred, and it only shows that more work needs to be done. One of the key driving forces to my activist work is the fact that I know we aren't where we need to be yet in terms of equity or equality, and Dr. King's vision for the future in terms of equality still needs to be reached.

Through my lens, until my fellow Black college students, especially those at PWI's, can

Seun Babalola.

Photo by Joe Green

have a college experience without being targeted, harassed, or physically hurt based off of the color of their skin, there is still work that needs to be done.

Emely Batista, 17, Power U Center for Social Change, Miami, FL

I am fighting for my freedom and the rights of LGBT students because love is love. Students deserve the right to feel however they feel and love whoever they love. We should be able to dress however we want without feeling judged.

Mari Copeny, AKA Little Miss Flint, 10, Flint, MI | @LittleMissFlint

I am fighting for Flint kids and for kids all around the country to be able to grow up in a world that sees their potential and not just where they are from or the color of their skin.

Mari Copeny, AKA Little Miss Flint.

Photo provided by Mari Copeny

Grace Dolan-Sandrino, 17, Washington DC | @graceadvocates

I fight for equality and dignity for trans individuals who are too often not awarded their human rights. I fight for trans students to who face legislated danger in their schools. I fight for the trans women of color who are killed every year.

We fight to be seen as humans. We fight for our dignity. We fight for our lives. We fight for justice.

Grace Dolan-Sandrino.

Photo courtesy of Grace Dolan-Sandrino

Katie Eder, 18, Shorewood, WI, founder, 50 Miles More | @katie_eder

I am fighting so every single child, no matter who they are or where they come from, can feel safe walking down the street, playing on the playground, and going to school.

I am fighting because 96 people die every day from gun violence in this country and that number is 96 too many. I am fighting because it's the only way change is going to be made.

Katie Eder.

Photo courtesy of Katie Eder

Nikhil Goyal, 22, Long Island, N.Y., University of Cambridge | @nikhilgoya_l

The legacy of Martin Luther King, Jr. has been sanitized over the past half century. He unapologetically campaigned for full employment: jobs for all, abolition of poverty, universal health care, affordable, desegregated housing, and integrated education, but unfortunately, little of this has been fulfilled. Too many Americans are still suffering from economic exploitation, systemic racism, and state violence.

Referred to as "ghetto schools" in the 1960s, our urban public schools remain deeply segregated, hamstrung by starvation funding, and thus, ultimately fail to educate the whole child and equip our

Nikhil Goyal.

Photo: Alberto Vargas

young people with the ability to think "intensively" and "critically," a core purpose of education according to King.

I have sought to carry on King's dreams by fighting for a child-centered, equitable public education system for all, not just the offspring of affluent, white families, fair housing measures to integrate our lily-white communities, and a federal job guarantee so that anyone able and willing to work will have a living wage job. We must revive the radical imaginations of our ancestors and struggle for a world free of oppression, violence, and injustice.

Shawn Goyal, 16, Birmingham, AL, member, Youth Action Council at YouthServe Birmingham

Insults, anger, and violence leads to us feeling further apart, with everyone becoming stuck in their right opinion and political discussions becoming increasingly polarized.

Over 50 years ago, Martin Luther King Jr. fought the polarizing issue of racism through nonviolent social change. Today, I fight for effective civil discourse. When people show up to their classrooms, workplaces, and political stages willing to listen to opposing viewpoints and participate in thoughtful discussions, only then can real change be achieved and effective solutions be implemented.

Photo courtesy of Shawn Goyal

Shawn Goyal.

Merrit Jones, 20, Columbia, SC, UNC-Chapel Hill, Executive Director, Student Voice | @merritjones

I'm fighting for education equity. Every student has a right to a quality education that allows them to find both their voice and passion. I continue to fight because I know we have a long way to go, but I know that students, now more than ever, are ready to see change enacted in schools. A youthquake is shaking America, and together we'll fight for equity.

Photo courtesy of Merrit Jones

Merrit Jones.

Brittany King, 28, organizer, Black Lives Matter of Columbus, IN

I fight for our chained ancestors. I fight for what the civil rights activists died for. I fight for what we continue to march for: liberation, equity, and freedom.

Brittany King.

MLK sacrificed his life and was murdered at 39 years old for the fight, and as a black person, I feel it's my duty to participate in mobilizing for the betterment of every aspect of our black lives.

The fight is long from over. We still have a lot to do. We still have a ways to go. But I won't let all the Black lives who fought for mine be in vain. The ones who escaped underground, the ones who continued to pick cotton, the ones who marched on Edmund Pettus Bridge, the ones who hung because of their existence. . .

White supremacy is no match to our defiance to matter. Our persistence is a threat, our existence is a reminder. We were never supposed to be free, we were never supposed to fight back. So no wonder the three scariest words in the English language is Black Lives Matter. I fight for all that.

Clifton Kinnie, 21, St. Louis, Missouri, Howard University, Founder, Our Destiny STL | @ CliftonKinnie

I'm fighting for black liberation. In August 2014 – shortly after my mother died from breast cancer – the killing of Michael Brown Jr. thrust my community of St. Louis and Ferguson into utter chaos. I stood side by side with several other high school students, while we were tear gassed and hit with rubber bullets.

Clifton Kinnie.

I founded Our Destiny STL, a network of over 300 students in 30 schools conducting voter registration and walkouts. I met with President Obama to discuss police reform during protests in the summer of 2016.

I'm organizing with other student activists now to make sure that police violence is included in the gun reform conversation during #MarchForOurLives.

Tiffany Dena Loftin, 28, Washington, DC, Director, NAACP Youth and College Division | @TiffanyDLoftin

I am still motivated and focused on fighting for my people who are victims of state violence. State violence shows up in different but real ways. When my people don't have access to clean water or healthy food, that is violence. When my people are denied health care because it is unaffordable, I see that as strategic violence. When kids can't learn in the classroom because the schools are underfunded or aren't taught real history of this country, that is mental violence. It shows up in more ways, in addition to police brutality and discrimination in the courtroom and I am fighting to end all of it. Why? Because I believe real freedom is possible.

Tiffany Dena Loftin.

Photo courtesy of Tiffany Dena Loftin

Sara Mora, 21, Hillside, N.J. | @misssaramora

I fight for the justice and for the rights of the lives of undocumented people. Not only in the Garden State, but also all across the United States. The USA is a melting pot, and we all have a generation in our family tree that migrated, if not ourselves.

Time and time again we are handed the leftover crumbs to work with. Our parents pay taxes and work many times up to three jobs but are still considered second-class citizens. I fight because I am an immigrant and DACA recipient. My parents are immigrants, but we are working day to day. Our parents work every single day.

Sara Mora.

Photo courtesy of Sara Mora

We as youth are rising up as leaders in education, science, business. When I fight, I fight for my family, for my community and for the rights of people who are not asking for anything more than the chance at living and creating a better future. There is power in fighting back because when we fight back, we say no to oppression and hate.

I believe it is important to fight back as a directly impacted person because I am telling the younger people behind me to not fear and to be brave. Fighting is a means of survival, and to not do so would be to give in to the fear.

RaeVen Ridgell, 25, Indianapolis, IN, National Action Chair, DONT SLEEP | @Dangerouslyrae

Photo courtesy of RaeVen Ridgell

RaeVen Ridgell.

I fight to dismantle oppression and the systems that accompany it. Unfortunately people don't recognize that today's civil rights movement doesn't look like that of our parents and grandparents; because of this, so many individuals have been dismissed, particularly Black and Brown women.

This is why I fight the hardest: so that no little Black or Brown girl after me may feel as if her voice doesn't matter because she doesn't speak the language individuals think she should speak, she doesn't practice the religion people say she should practice, she doesn't love who people say she should love, or she doesn't identity as people say she should identify. I want those little girls to always feel empowered.

I want the systems of oppression that govern their discomfort and the discomfort of so many others to be completely dismantled, and I'll do this until my last breath.

Courtney Roberts, 14, Nacogdoches, TX | @everydayblackgirl

Photo courtesy of Courtney Roberts

Courtney Roberts.

Not only do I fight for those that look like me, I fight for those within my generation, Gen Z. Many times we're told that we're just ruthless teenagers and we need to sit down and be quiet, when in reality, we are the change makers within our society. We are the current leaders and innovators.

Our voices, especially those of the marginalized, are needed more than ever under the current administration and political climate. Our opinions and our actions are needed to move this country forward. Our drive and our determination to make a change is what this country needs.

We give our country hope. No backing down now.

Sojourner Rouco-Crenshaw, 16, incoming president, YouthServe Youth Philanthropy Council, Birmingham, AL

Sojourner Rouco-Crenshaw.

For me, it is incredibly important to fight for gun control. As a youth in school right now, enough is enough. Schools should be a safe place that fosters a positive environment. That is why it is necessary to fight for a solution to the problem that will have a meaningful impact, like keeping dangerous weapons out of our communities. As youth, it is important for us to be involved in decisions that will impact our future because we must fight for change to better our world and save lives.

Giavonni Williams, Direct Action Committee Leader, Million Hoodies Bard Chapter | @MillionHoodies

I fight to survive, for the right to have accessible healthcare and security.

Giavonni Williams.

In April 2018, I am still fighting to prove that the Black experience is NOT singular. I fight because on a college campus where I am supposed to feel loved and supported, I experience hostility and scrutiny, all for being Black. I cannot move, I cannot resist, I cannot speak without being inspected and generalized. So, as sad as it may be, I am fighting and will always fight for these civil liberties.

I fight — *we* fight — to destroy the invisible wall that stands between Black and Brown bodies that hinders us from achieving greatness. My struggle for equality, security and equity is a beautiful nightmare, but I will never destroy barriers alone.

So my fight is also one for unity, a coalition of the underrepresented; if we do not protect and love each other, then no one else will. The fight goes on.

Glossary of Ethnic Studies Terms

Learn More, Read More, Change the Globe

—Nasir (Nas) Jones

This glossary was compiled by Dr. Dale Allender primarily from the terms that appear in the essays throughout the book. Definitions were gathered and paraphrased from a wide variety of sources. The online sources are listed at the end of the glossary. The terms and definitions were then reviewed by faculty from the Sacramento State University Ethnic Studies Department (Dr. Gregory Yee Mark, Dr. Christina Fa Mark, Dr. James Sobredo, and Dr. Brian Baker).

Acculturation

A process of cultural transformation initiated by contacts between different cultures. Individuals experience acculturation when their social roles and socialization are shaped by norms and values that are largely foreign to their native culture. Educational and occupational experiences are the primary agents of an individual's acculturation process. Some sociologists use the term to refer simply to the process of learning and absorbing a culture, making it synonymous with socialization.

Affirmation

A positive statement about someone or something; a compliment.

Agricultural Workers Organizing Committee (AWOC)

Agricultural Workers Organizing Committee (AWOC), during its 7-year existence was made up primarily of Filipino farm workers, called many strikes against growers and farm labor contractors and achieved some success in raising the wages of farm laborers.

Additionally, AWOC sought job security, union recognition, and better working conditions for its members.

American-Ness

1. The quality of or relating to the United States of America or its people, language, or culture. Historically American-ness most often referred to White Americans of European Ancestry. However, the term can also mean the following:
2. The quality of or relating to North or South America, the West Indies, or the Western Hemisphere.
3. The quality of or relating to any of the Native American peoples.
4. Indigenous to North or South America.

Ancestry

1. Usually refers to an individual's family from many generations (e.g., an individual's grandparents' parents).
2. The origin of a phenomenon, object, idea, or style.

Angel Island

Between the end of the 19th century and the beginning of the 20th century, millions of people—in numbers which have not been seen since—came to America in pursuit of a better, freer life. On the east coast, most of the huddled masses were met by the Statue of Liberty and Ellis Island. On the west coast, between 1910 and 1940, most were met by the wooden buildings of Angel Island. These immigrants were Australians and New Zealanders, Canadians, Mexicans, Central and South Americans, Russians, and in particular, Asians. Of these Asians, the majority were from China. They numbered 175,000

Anthropologist

Someone who undertakes the scientific study of the origin of a phenomenon, object, idea, or style. Anthropologists have been part of the destruction of culture and part of the preservation of culture.

Artifact

An object produced or shaped by human craft, especially a tool, weapon, or ornament of archaeological or historical interest.

Asian American Political Alliance (AAPA)

The goal of AAPA is political education and advancement of the movement among Asian people, so that they may determine their own destiny. AAPA was the primary political Asian American organization for those student strikers at San Francisco State College and the University of California, Berkeley. AAPA was founded by Yuji Ichioka and Emma Gee.

Asian American Movement

By watching African Americans expose institutional racism and government hypocrisy, Asian Americans began to identify the ways in which they, too, had faced discrimination in the United States. During the Asian American civil rights movement of the 1960s and 1970s, activists fought for the development of ethnic studies programs in universities, an end to the Vietnam War, and reparations for Japanese Americans forced into internment camps during World War II.

Asian Indian

Immigrants to the United States from India, Pakistan, and Bangladesh are referred to as Asian Indians. The first Asian Indians or Indian Americans, as they are also known, arrived in America as early as the middle of the nineteenth century. By the end of the nineteenth century, about 2,000 Indians, most of them Sikhs (a religious minority from India's Punjab region), settled on the West Coast of the United States, having come in search of economic opportunity. The majority of Sikhs worked in agriculture and construction. Other Asian Indians came as merchants and traders; many worked in lumber mills and logging camps in the western states of Oregon, Washington, and California, where they rented bunkhouses, acquired knowledge of English, and assumed the Western dress. Most of the Sikhs, however, refused to cut their hair or beards or forsake the wearing of the turbans that their religion required. In 1907 about 2,000 Indians, alongside other immigrants from China, Japan, Korea, Norway, and Italy worked on the building of the Western Pacific Railway in California. Other Indians helped build bridges and tunnels for California's other railroad projects.

Asian Laborers

They began with the building of the Transcontinental Railroad (1863–1869). Over 10,000 Chinese miners were recruited for the construction of the railroad through a 5-year contract. Their working conditions were exhausting and life-threatening. Many have died during their work on the railroad due to the weather and terrain of the route but no records of these deaths have been officially documented.

Assembly Center

Another name given to the Internment Camps during World War II that imprisoned Japanese Americans.

Assimilation

Assimilation is the process by which a minority individual or group takes on the characteristics of the majority and attempts to be accepted as part of the majority group.

Association

1. An organization of persons having a common interest.
2. Something linked in memory with another person, place, thing, or activity.
3. The process of forming mental connections or bonds between sensations, ideas, or memories.

Awo

A person or people being introduced to or initiated into the West African Ifa tradition.

Babalawo

A Babalawo is a sage or high priest, who is well-versed in the rituals, lore, and history of the Yoruba tradition/religion called IFA. He has become a master in the Cabalistic and ritualistic aspects of IFA. Babalawo (Baba-ni-Awo) means "Father in the knowledge of things material and spiritual."

The Cabalistic mastery makes the Babalawo a craftsman who has acquired the fine skills of the preparation of medications (curative, calming, preventive), some of which can be explained in western scientific terms. He also utilizes the power of invocation and evocation of spiritual forces to effect the expression of phenomena. He is therefore a redeemer from the Ajogun (evil forces of the material and spiritual systems).

In many IFA verses, the client is full of praise for his and her Babalawo after the feat has been performed. The Babalawo in turn then praises IFA who then in turn sings the praises of Olodumare (the Almighty).

In order to become a Babalawo, one needs to get initiated in to IFA and one needs to study with elders in order to get well-versed in IFA.

Baghdad

Capital city of Iraq on the Tigris River *population* 3,841,268.

Bataan

After April 9, 1942, U.S. surrender of the Bataan Peninsula on the main Philippine island of Luzon to the Japanese during World War II (1939–1945), approximately 75,000 Filipino and American troops on Bataan were forced to make an arduous 65-mile march to prison camps.

Bias

An inclination of temperament or outlook; *especially*, a personal and sometimes unreasoned judgment.

An inclination or outlook; especially a personal and sometimes unreasonable judgment; prejudice or an instance of an instance of such prejudice.

Binary Racial Hierarchy

A belief in the superiority of one racial group over one other racial group. The binary usually refers to Black people and White people, or White People and other people of color.

Black Political Thought

Originating from the institution of slavery, Black political thought has been framed by the historical and social experiences of the African American freedom struggle in the United States. The desire for liberty from enslavement provided initial parameters for the earliest political thinkers. In the years after the Constitution was amended and slavery abolished, Black theorists wrestled to define the meanings of liberty and equality for newly freed peoples. Political philosophers and activists struggled against White supremacy and its tools of slavery, state-sanctioned kidnappings, lynchings, peonage, and segregation all designed to deny the Black community property rights, full citizenship, and personal liberty. These attempts to control Black bodies and Black identities provide the backdrop for the queries and values that drive Afro-American political thought. The necessity of challenging social and governmental oppression founded on racial characteristics ensures that this intellectual tradition bridges both political theory and activism through a proclivity for social change.

Border

In Ethnic Studies, this refers specifically to the border between Mexico and the United States. It can also refer to the psychological state of being torn between two places. It's a particularly important concept in Chicano/a (Mexican-American) Studies.

Bracero

A guest worker initiative that spanned the years 1942–1964. Millions of Mexican agricultural workers crossed the border under the program to work in more than half of the states in America.

British Colonies

Comprised about one quarter of the world's land area and population and encompassed territories on every continent, including the British Isles, British North America, British West Indies, British Guiana, British West Africa, British East Africa, India, Australia, and New Zealand.

British Empire

A worldwide system of dependencies—colonies, protectorates, and other territories—that over a span of some three centuries was brought under the sovereignty of the crown of Great Britain and the administration of the British government. The policy of granting or recognizing significant degrees of self-government by dependencies, which was favored by the far-flung nature of the empire, led to the development by the twentieth century of the notion of a "British Commonwealth," comprising largely self-governing dependencies that acknowledged an increasingly symbolic British sovereignty. The term was embodied in a statute in 1931. Today, the Commonwealth includes former elements of the British Empire in a free association of sovereign states.

Bureau of Indian Affairs

Interior Department agency that serves as the principal link between federally recognized Native American populations (officially *American Indian tribes*) and the U.S. government.

California Racial Mascot Act AB30

In recent years, the use of Native American names and images within sports has been called into question and is see as a form of institutional racism.
    In Section 221.2, the California State Legislature declares

  a. The use of racially derogatory or discriminatory school or athletic team names, mascots, or nicknames in California public schools is antithetical to the California school mission of providing an equal education to all.
  b. Certain athletic team names, mascots, and nicknames that have been used and remain in use by other teams, including school teams, in other parts of the nation

are discriminatory in singling out the Native American community for the derision to which mascots or nicknames are often subjected.

c. Many individuals and organizations interested and experienced in human relations, including the United States Commission on Civil Rights, have concluded that the use of Native American images and names in school sports is a barrier to equality and understanding, and that all residents of the United States would benefit from the discontinuance of their use.

d. No individual or school has a cognizable interest in retaining a racially derogatory or discriminatory school or athletic team name, mascot, or nickname.

Following these acknowledgments, Section 221.3 stipulates
(a) Beginning January 1, 2017, all public schools are prohibited from using the term Redskins for school or athletic team names, mascots, or nicknames.

Through this enactment of this law, California became the first state in the United States to ban the use of "Redskins" in public schools.

Californio Era

In the California history, this is the time when the descendants of missionaries, soldiers and workers from New Spain (what is today Mexico) occupied California.

The **Californio era** spans approximately 80 years (1769–1848), during which the Californios navigated life under three different political systems, Spanish (1769–1821), Mexican (1821–1848), and American (1848 to present).

Castas System

During the Californio era of California history, this system spelled out 16 different categories of people produced through various intermarriages between Spanish, Indian and African men and women. The castas used race and place of birth to rank people; with the highest status being reserved for "pure blood" Spanish and the lowest status being assigned to Africans. In between were the various combinations that could be produced through intermarriage.

Census

An official counting of the population with details about race, ethnicity, employment, number of members in the household, and so forth.

Central Pacific Railroad (CPRR)

The western portion of the Transcontinental Railroad. Originating in Sacramento and ending in Promontory Summit, Utah. The most difficult part of the Transcontinental

Railroad to create, given the huge blockade of the Sierra Nevada Mountains in the way. The "Big Four," including Leland Stanford and Charles Crocker, are credited with building the CPRR. Actually built by Chinese and Chinese American laborers, who worked tirelessly and with both skill and brute force to dynamite/tunnel through mountains and lay down ties and rail. In creating 690 miles of track, hundreds of Chinese lost their lives in avalanches and dynamite accidents along the way. The might of the Chinese laborers, along with the ruthlessly exploitative labor practices of paying them purportedly less than $1 a day, was the central reason in the Transcontinental Railroad being completed ahead of schedule and under budget.

Contrary to myth, the Chinese workers were recognized at and after the May 10, 1869 ceremony marking the Transcontinental Railroad's completion. However, the recognition was token and scant, with only future generations of Americans recognizing what a massive feat these Chinese men accomplished in creating one of the most significant chapters in the building of America.

Cesar Chavez

Mexican-American Cesar Chavez (1927–1993) was a prominent union leader and labor organizer. Hardened by his early experience as a migrant worker, Chavez founded the National Farm Workers Association in 1962. His union joined with the Agricultural Workers Organizing Committee in its first strike against grape growers in California, and the two organizations later merged to become the United Farm Workers. Stressing nonviolent methods, Chavez drew attention for his causes via boycotts, marches, and hunger strikes. Despite conflicts with the Teamsters union and legal barriers, he was able to secure raises and improve conditions for farm workers in California, Texas, Arizona, and Florida.

Chicana

An American woman or girl of Mexican descent.

Chicano Gente

People of family of chicano/a/x descent.

Chicano Movement

The Mexican American Civil Rights Movement, one of the least studied social movements of the 1960s, encompassed a broad cross section of issues—from restoration of land grants, to farm workers' rights, to enhanced education, voting, and political rights.

Chicanx

See Latinx.

Chinese American

A term originating with the term *Asian American*, coined in 1968 by Yuji Ichioka, then a graduate student at University of California, Berkeley and Emma Gee, a writer. Ichioka and Gee were founders of the Asian American Political Alliance. Any U.S.-born person of Chinese ancestry. Or, a person born in China (or any part of Asia, who identifies ethnically as Chinese), later emigrating to the United States, who identifies with being Chinese American.

Note:

1. Any "*Asian American*" term should never be hyphenated.
   Example: Correct: "*Hmong American*"
                Incorrect: "*Hmong-American*"
   Hyphenation implies "half Asian, half American," negating the existence of the Asian American community in what's now the United States since the 1500s. Hyphenating "Asian American" is considered derogatory by the Asian American community.
   Hyphenation originally implied sojourner status, for example, "Italian American," with expectation that Italians would go back to Italy.
2. The term *African American* was purportedly adopted from the term *Asian American*, proposed by Reverend Jesse Jackson at a Black conference. (Ironic, since many major press style guides have agreed to not hyphenate *African American*, but persist in practicing subtle racism by regularly hyphenating the original term, *Asian American*.)

Chinese American Council Of Sacramento (CACS)

A Chinese American political and advocacy organization founded in 1987 by the late Frank Fat, Sacramento's renowned restaurateur and philanthropist. Founded on the principals of giving back to the community and fighting for what's right for the community. Issues of focus include social justice, discrimination, civil and human rights, voter education, legislation "not in the best interest of the API community."

Chinese Exclusion Act

The Chinese Exclusion Act of 1882 was the first significant law restricting immigration into the United States. Those on the West Coast were especially prone to attribute declining wages and economic ills on the Chinese workers. Although the Chinese composed only 0.002% of the nation's population, Congress passed the exclusion act to placate worker demands and maintain White "racial purity."

U.S. Central Intelligent Agency (CIA)

A U.S. spy agency.

Coalition

A temporary alliance of distinct parties, persons, or states for joint action.

Code-Switching

The switching from the linguistic system of one language or dialect to that of another

Colonialism (Colonization)

Political control of one nation over another that is institutionalized in direct political administration by the colonial power, control of all economic relationships, and a systematic attempt to transform the culture of the subject nation. It usually involves extensive immigration from the colonial power into the colony and the immigrants taking on roles as landowners, business people, and professionals. Colonialism is a form of imperialism.

Colonists

A government official, employee, or citizen of a colonial or occupying country.

Commonwealth

A political unit having local autonomy but voluntarily united with the United States used officially of Puerto Rico and of the Northern Mariana Islands.

Communist/Communism/Communist Party

A system of government in which a single party controls state-owned means of production.

Compatibility

Capable of existing together in harmony.

Concentration Camps

1. A camp where persons (such as prisoners of war, political prisoners, or refugees) are detained or confined.
2. A prison where people who are not soldiers are kept during a war and are usually forced to live in very bad conditions.

Congress of Racial Equality (CORE)

Founded in 1942 as the Committee of Racial Equality by an interracial group of students in Chicago. Many of these students were members of the Chicago branch of the Fellowship of Reconciliation (FOR), a pacifist organization seeking to change racist attitudes. The founders of the CORE were deeply influenced by Mahatma Gandhi's teachings of nonviolent resistance.

CORE started as a nonhierarchical, decentralized organization funded entirely by the voluntary contributions of its members. The organization was initially co-led by University of Chicago White student George Houser and Black student *James Farmer*. In 1942, CORE began protests against segregation in public accommodations by organizing *sit-ins*. It was also in 1942 that CORE expanded nationally. James Farmer traveled the country with *Bayard Rustin*, a field secretary with FOR, and recruited activists at FOR meetings. CORE's early growth consisted almost entirely of White middle-class college students from the Midwest. CORE pioneered the strategy of nonviolent direct action, especially the tactics of sit-ins, jail-ins, and freedom rides.

Conquistadors

One of the Spanish conquerors of Mexico and Peru in the sixteenth century.

Conscientious Objector

A person who refuses to serve in the armed forces or bear arms on moral or religious grounds.

Consonants

a speech sound produced by occluding with or without releasing (p, b; t, d; k, g), diverting (m, n, ng), obstructing (f, v; s, z, etc.) the flow of air from the lungs (opposed to a vowel).

Contact

1. Contact usually refers to a period when European colonizers, explorers or missionaries first had interaction with Native Americans or other indigenous peoples throughout the world, including the continents that became known as Africa, Latin America, and Australia.
2. Contact can also refer to anytime two different communities meet for the first time.
3. Contact can refer to human contact life in outer space for the first time.

Of or relating to the period of contact between an indigenous people and an outside, often industrialized culture.

Cosmology

Cosmology explores how and why the universe works. Cosmology involves the philosophy and the scientific study of the large-scale properties of the universe as a whole. It endeavors to use the scientific method to understand the origin, evolution, and ultimate fate of the entire Universe. Like any field of science, cosmology involves the formation of theories or hypotheses about the universe which make specific predictions for phenomena that can be tested with observations.

Cultural Genocide (Culturcide)

Comes from the word "gens," meaning a clan or community of people related by common descent. The idea of cultural genocide implies the process of undermining, suppressing, and ultimately eliminating, native cultures.

Cultural Imperialism

The practice of systematically spreading the influence of one culture over others by means of physical and economic domination. Usually involves an assumption of cultural superiority (ethnocentrism).

Cultural Pluralism

[A] mixture of different cultures where each culture retains its own identity and yet adds to the "flavor" of the whole.

Cultural Proscriptions

A restraint or restriction from doing or saying some things based on cultural heritage.

Culture

The generally shared knowledge, beliefs, and values of members of society. Culture is conveyed from generation to generation through the process of socialization. While culture is made up of ideas, some sociologists also argue that it is not exclusively ideational but can be found in human-made material objects. They define a separate "material culture."

Culture Shock

Where an individual encounters a new and different culture and experiences a major disruption of their normal assumptions about social values and behavior. Their old values seem unable to provide guidance in the new situation, yet the new culture seems strange and unacceptable.

Cultural Values

Relatively general cultural prescriptions of what is right, moral, and desirable. Values provide the broad foundations for specific normative regulation of social interaction.

Dawes General Allotment Act

This law was named after Senator Henry Dawes of Massachusetts who was main person who authored and introduced this act to Congress in 1887. The law allowed for the president to break up reservation land, which was held in common by the members of a tribe, into smaller allotments that were parceled out and assigned to individual tribal members as heads of households, generally in 160-acre allotments. After reservation land was allotted to tribal members, remaining land was deemed to be excess land and then sold to non-Indians. While in effect, the overall land based for Native Americans decreased from 138,000,000 in 1887 to 48,000,000 in 1934. The legacy and negative effects of the allotment policy continue to play out on many Indian reservations today.

Decolonized, Pan-Indigenous Consciouness

An awareness of the connection and freedom to think and live according to their own collective desires among different indigenous communities across many different regions.

Demographic

Information about the size and growth of groups in society.

Diaspora

Diaspora is the voluntary or forcible movement of peoples from their homelands into new regions.

Discrimination

The unequal treatment of individuals on the basis of their personal characteristics, which may include age, sex, sexual orientation, ethnic, or physical identity. Discrimination usually refers to negative treatment, but discrimination in favor of particular groups can also occur.

Disproportionate

Too large or too small in comparison with something else.

Divine (Verb)

Cultural rituals to provide information about a person's personality or future.

Defense Language Institute Foreign Language Center

The DLIFLC is regarded as one of the finest schools for foreign language instruction in the nation. As part of the Army Training and Doctrine Command, the institute provides resident instruction at the Presidio of Monterey in two dozen languages, 5 days a week, 7 hours per day, with 2–3 hours of homework each night. Courses last from 26 to 64 weeks, depending on the difficulty of the language.

The DLIFLC is a multiservice school for active and reserve components, foreign military students, and civilian personnel working in the federal government and various law enforcement agencies.

Dominant Culture

Although *traditional societies* can be characterized by a high consistency of cultural traits and *customs*, modern societies are often a conglomeration of different, often competing, *cultures* and *subcultures*. In such a situation of diversity, a dominant culture is one that is able, through economic or political power, to impose its values, language, and ways of behaving on a subordinate culture or cultures. This may be achieved through legal or political suppression of other sets of values and patterns of behavior, or by monopolizing the media of communication.

DNA

Various *nucleic acids* that are usually the molecular basis of heredity.

Double "V" Campaign

While A. Philip Randolph's threat of a massive March on Washington convinced Franklin D. Roosevelt (FDR) to ban discrimination against Blacks in the defense industry in 1941, segregation in the armed forces persisted. Covering the conflict posed a problem for Black newspapers: Either give in to the government's propaganda about racial harmony at home for the sake of the war effort and national unity or speak the truth and be smeared as coconspirators with the enemy. American history was replete with cautionary tales of disappointment and betrayal, starting with experiences by Frederick Douglass in the post-Reconstruction period and continuing through one involving W.E.B. Du Bois during World War I. What should Black journalists and spokespersons do?

Two months to the day after Pearl Harbor (February 7, 1942), the most widely read Black newspaper in America, the Pittsburgh Courier, found a way to split the difference—actually, the newspaper cleverly intertwined them into a symbol and a national campaign that urged Black people to give their all for the war effort, while at the same time calling on the government to do all it could to make the rhetoric of the Declaration of Independence and the equal rights amendments to the Constitution real for every citizen, regardless of race. And, in honor of the battle against enemies from without and within, they called it "the Double V Campaign."

Dravidians

Dravidian people are believed to have originated in Africa, and later migrated to Southern India. After migrating further North, they were later forced South again by invading Aryans. Dravidians were originally a peace-loving culture that worshipped all forms of life.

Dream Act

DREAM was short for Development, Relief and Education for Alien Minors. This Act was never passed, even though many versions have been reintroduced since 2001, the last in 2013. Had it passed, as many as 2.5 million undocumented youth, or DREAMers, would have been provided an affordable public college education and military service opportunities, providing them with a pathway to citizenship.

DREAMers

Most DREAMers have lived in this country for most their lives, usually arriving in the United States between the ages of 5 and 12 years of age. They have been called "Generation 1.5." Born in another country but arriving in the United States as young children, they are distinct from both the first and second generations. The name DREAMer, although it had its origins in the DREAM ACT, is appropriate for another reason, as immigrant youth have high hopes and dreams for a better future. They came with their parents who wanted a better life for their children; some came to escape political or economic conflicts in their native countries; a great many put their lives in danger crossing the border; and some came legally with visas, but their visas expired.

Economic Exploitation

Taking advantage of the labor or resources of someone else for personal financial gain.

Elders

An influential member of a tribe, community, or family—often considered wise.

Emancipation

The feeling or act of being free from a condition, experience, or system.

Embodiment

1. The act of giving a tangible, bodily, or concrete form to (an abstract concept).
2. Acting as an example of or express (an idea, principle, etc.), especially in action.
3. The act of collecting or uniting in a comprehensive whole, system, and so forth
4. Comprise giving, creating, or being a body or bodily form to a spirit; render incarnate.

Emigration

Refers to migration out of a nation. Emigrants are those who leave their home country.

Empathy

Identification with and understanding of another's situation, feelings, and motives.

Encomienda System

A system that was created by the Spanish to control and regulate American Indian labor and behavior during the colonization of the Americas.

Enslaved Africans (African Slaves)

While many use the term "slaves" or "African slaves" to refer to Africans and later African Americans who were captured in Africa and subjected to slavery, a more accurate term is enslaved Africans.

Ethnic Enclaves

Immigrant groups which concentrate in a distinct spatial location and organize a variety of enterprises serving their own ethnic market and/or the general population. Their basic characteristic is that a significant proportion of the immigrant workforce is employed in enterprises owned by other immigrants.

Ethnic Group

A group of individuals having a distinct culture—a subculture—in common. The idea of an "ethnic group" differs from that of "race" because it implies that values, norms, behavior, and language, not necessarily physical appearance, are the important distinguishing characteristic. Usually, ethnic groups are thought of as minority groups within another culture.

Ethnic Identity

An individual's awareness of membership in a distinct group and of commitment to the group's cultural values. This is the subjective aspect of ethnicity, but for many people their ethnic heritage has little subjective meaning although it can be objectively determined.

Ethnicity

Membership or affiliation in a particular ethnic group.

Ethnic Stereotyping

A fixed or generalized belief about an ethnic group and people from that ethnic group. Ethnic stereotypes are almost always negative and can lead to hurtful feelings, stress, sickness or destructive behavior.

To stereotype is to apply a gross generalization, to people from a specific ethnic group rather than seeing the individual variation.

Ethnic Studies

Ethnic studies includes units of study, courses, or programs that are centered on the knowledge and perspectives of an ethnic or racial group, reflecting narratives and points of view rooted in that group's lived experiences and intellectual scholarship. Ethnic studies arose as a counter to the traditional mainstream curriculum which included limited or inaccurate information about non-European ethnic groups.

Ethnobotanist

Someone who studies the stories, beliefs, and agricultural practices of an ethnic community.

Ethnocentrism

The tendency to view your own society or culture as superior and the standard by which other societies and cultures are judged.

Ethnohistory

Ethnohistory is the study of cultures that combines cross-disciplinary methods of historical document research and ethnographic studies such as anthropology, linguistics, archaeology, and ecology to give as complete a picture as possible of a whole culture. It employs maps, folklore, myth, oral traditions, music, and painting. Ethnohistory usually deals with small groups that do not have written histories instead of with large societies.

First used in Vienna in the 1930s by ethnologist Fritz Röck and the Viennese Study Group for African Cultural History, ethnohistory was not utilized in the United States until the 1950s as a result of the Indian Claims Act of 1946. Evidence used in Native American claims against the U.S. government employed both anthropological and historical reports and was presented at the Ohio Valley Historic Indian Conference. An outgrowth of the conference was the formation of the American Society for Ethno-history, which was established in 1954 and published the first issue of its journal, *Ethnohistory*, that same year.

Ethno Religious Minority Group

A group of people characterized by ethnicity and religion with limited political power due to domination or colonization.

European American

Americans with ancestry from Europe, such as Germany, Italy, England, Austria, and so on.

Evacuation Orders

In the Western United States evacuation was ordered by General John Dewitt for all Japanese Americans to leave their homes, jobs, friends, pets, and schools to go to Assembly Centers (May 1942) and then to one of the 10 permanent camps such as Tule Lake where Mas Hatano's family was incarcerated.

Executive Order 9066

The Presidential Executive Order signed in 1942 by President Franklin D. Roosevelt requiring Japanese Americans to be imprisoned during World War II.

Family History

A record of incidents and occurrences important to our immediate families or ancestry.

Federal Freedom of Information Act (FOIA)

The FOIA generally provides that any person has the right to request access to federal agency records or information except to the extent the records are protected from disclosure by any exemptions contained in the law or by one of the three special law enforcement record exclusions.

The basic function of the Freedom of Information Act is to ensure informed citizens, vital to the functioning of a democratic society.

Federal Housing Administration (FHA)

The Federal Housing Administration, generally known as "FHA,", provides mortgage insurance on loans made by FHA-approved lenders throughout the United States and its territories. FHA insures mortgages on single family and multifamily homes including manufactured homes and hospitals. It is the largest insurer of mortgages in the world, insuring over 34 million properties since its inception in 1934.

The Freedom of Information Act (FOIA) generally provides that any person has the right to request access to federal agency records or information except to the extent the records are protected from disclosure by any exemptions contained in the law or by one of the three special law enforcement record exclusions.

Federally Recognized Tribes

Federally recognized Indian tribes or groups are eligible for funding and services from the Bureau of Indian Affairs (BIA). There are currently 566 federally recognized tribes throughout the United States. This is an important political and legal category, as there are also "state recognized tribes" and "unrecognized tribes" which are not officially recognized by the U.S. Government.

Filipino Farm Workers Activism

During the 1920s, the Filipinos in Hawaii learned organizing strategies and tactics, such as strikes and work slow-downs. After the violent 1924 labor strikes, many Filipinos migrated to the continental United States. They applied the same strategies to oppressive labor conditions in their new homes. Filipino labor activists worked with Cesar Chavez, Dolore Huerta, and many others.

Foraker Act

The Foraker Act was signed on April 2, 1900, by U.S. President William McKinley to establish a civilian government in Puerto Rico. The purpose of the Foraker Act was to establish a limited government in the recently acquired territory of Puerto Rico.

Funerary Objects (Associated Funerary Objects)

U.S. Code ›Title 25 › chapter 32 ›§ 3001 **(A)** "associated funerary objects" which shall mean objects that, as a part of the death rite or ceremony of a culture, are reasonably believed to have been placed with individual human remains either at the time of death or later, and both the human remains and associated funerary objects are presently in the possession or control of a Federal agency or museum, except that other items exclusively made for burial purposes or to contain human remains shall be considered as associated funerary objects.

Geneva Accords (1954)

Documents from the Geneva Conference in 1954, attended by representatives of Cambodia, China, France, Laos, the United Kingdom (England), the United States, the Soviet Union (Russia), the Viet Minh (i.e., the North Vietnamese), and the State of Vietnam (i.e., the South Vietnamese). Agreements were finally signed on July 21 between the French and Vietnamese, Laotian, and Cambodian representatives. Calling for a cease-fire line effectively dividing Vietnam in two; 300 days for each side to withdraw its troops to its side of the line; and communist troops and guerrillas to evacuate Laos and Cambodia.

Geneva Protocol (1962)

Documents signed in Geneva declaring procedures and rules for the withdrawal of foreign military—such as France, the Soviet Union, and the United States—from Laos, and the neutrality of Laos.

Gender Roles/Expectations

Social roles ascribed to individuals on the basis of their sex. The term gender differs from sex because it refers specifically to the cultural definition of the roles and behavior appropriate to members of each sex rather than to those aspects of human behavior that are determined by biology.

Genocide

The systematic killing of an entire ethnic community.

Genotype

1. (genetics) The entire set of genes in an organism.
2. (genetics) A set of alleles that determines the expression of a particular characteristic or trait (phenotype).

Gentrification

A process of change in the social and economic condition of urban neighborhoods where poorer original residents are replaced by newcomers from middle-class and professional groups.

Geopolitical Importance

Geographic influences on power relationships in international relations.

Government-To-Government Relations

November 6, 2000, with Executive Order 13175, the United states in consultation with Native American tribes codified their government-to-government consultation policy. The government-to-government relationship is not new, but has strong roots that took hold with the very earliest contact between the American Indians and the first

European settlers. The settlers and the tribal leaders dealt with each other as separate sovereigns and that relationship is the foundation of all dealings that have taken place between the United States and Indian tribes throughout the history of the Nation. This Indian policy has found its way into federal statutes and case law and into Executive Orders. As nations separate from the United States, the internal affairs of tribes are the responsibility of the tribal entity and are not to be tampered or interfered with by the United States.

Grape Strike

Also known as the Delano Grape Strike: a labor strike between the AWOC and the United Farm Workers against grape growers in California.

Great Depression

Economic downturn across the world began in 1929 and lasted until about 1939. It was the longest and most severe depression ever experienced by the industrialized Western world.

Great Law Of Peace

The Great Law of Peace is the name given to the constitution of the Iroquois Confederacy, a union of Native American tribes centered south of Lake Ontario that thrived for 600 years up to the formation of the United States. The U.S. Constitution is based on the Great Law of Peace.

Heathen

Technically meaning one who doesn't practice the dominant culture's religion, that is, in the United States, a non-Christian. In the commonly used term "heathen Chinee," (heathen Chinese) used in the nineteenth and twentieth centuries, "heathen" is meant to indicate Chinese as "the other," strange and uncivilized.

Hijab

The traditional covering for the hair and neck that is worn by Muslim women.

Historicize

To use historical information in order to help understand or explain something or someone.

Historiography

1. The writing of history; *especially*: the writing of history based on the critical examination of sources, the selection of particulars from the authentic materials, and the synthesis of particulars into a narrative that will stand the test of critical methods.
2. The principles, theory, and history of historical writing a course in *historiography*.

Ho Chi Minh

Founder of the Indochina Communist Party (1930) and its successor, the Viet-Minh (1941), and president from 1945 to 1969 of the Democratic Republic of Vietnam (North Vietnam). As the leader of the Vietnamese nationalist movement for nearly three decades, Ho was one of the prime movers of the post-World War II anticolonial movement in Asia and one of the most influential communist leaders of the 20th century.

Home Owner's Loan Corporation (HOLC)

It is a former U.S. government agency established in 1933 to help stabilize real estate that had depreciated during the depression and to refinance the urban mortgage debt. It granted long-term mortgage loans to some one million homeowners facing loss of their property. The HOLC ceased its lending activities in June 1936, by the terms of the Home Owners' Loan Act.

Horticulture Techniques

The scientific and artistic practices of growing fruits, vegetables, flowers, or ornamental plants. These practices are influenced by culture.

Ideology (Or Political Ideology)

A set of opinions, beliefs, or attitudes (e.g., the "world view" of a social group or class).

IFA

Ifa is a common belief system originating among the Yoruba—a group of cultures who occupied an area bounded by the Niger River, and including what is now known as the Benin Republic, southwestern Nigeria, and part of Togo. Starting in the sixteenth century, large numbers of Yoruba natives were enslaved and transported to the Caribbean and the Americas. They combined beliefs and practices from their Ifa religion with beliefs from other newly enslaved Africans from different parts of West Africa with whom they were forced together. They also combined of Ifa with elements of Roman Catholicism, sometimes to hide their religion from plantation owners and missionaries. Over the years, this combination has become known as Candomblê, Palo Mayombe, Santeria, Vodun, and so forth. These religions are now flourishing in New York, Atlanta, Oakland, the Caribbean, Brazil, Colombia, Cuba, Grenada, the Guyanas, Jamaica, Puerto Rico, St. Kitts, St. Vincent, Tobago, and Trinidad.

Imaginary Indians

A concept used to emphasize the stereotypes and images related to and associated with Native Americans that appear in popular culture, especially through the mass media or typified by team names and mascots used in sports.

Immigrants

An immigrant is a person who lives in a country other than the country of their birth. There are many different kinds of immigrants: economic immigrants, students, refugees, undocumented, and so on.

Immigrate

The movement of peoples into a country or territory (movement of people within countries is referred to as migration). Some immigration is voluntary and some immigration is forced. Immigration can involve small number of people or masses of people in orderly or chaotic, dangerous conditions.

Immigrated

To have completed the immigration process and become established in some significant way in a new country.

Immigration

The movement of peoples into a country or territory (movement of people within countries is referred to as migration.) Some immigration is voluntary and some immigration is forced. Immigration can involve small numbers of people or masses of people in orderly or chaotic, dangerous conditions.

Immigration Act of 1924

A law that completely excluded immigrants from Asia (except the Philippines). The law was designed to protect and preserve immigration from Britain and Western Europe. Immigration from Southern and Eastern Europe were also restricted.

Imperialism

Domination by one or more countries over others for political and economic objectives. It can be effected by force of arms or through the economic and political power exercised by state and corporate agencies. Imperialism is sometimes organized in a formal empire, with a ruling nation and colonized territories, but it can also exist where one nation or region exercises dominant influence over international trade and investment, patterns of economic development, and mass communication.

Independence Act

See the Philippine commonwealth and independence Act.

Initiate

One who has been introduced to or has attained some knowledge in a particular field.

Initiation

The often secret ceremony initiating new members into an organization.

Inclusive

Covering or intended to cover all people, items, costs, or services.

Indentured Labor

Forced work performed for another for a specified period of time, especially such a person who came to America during the colonial period.

Indian Removal Act

Spearheaded during the administration of President Andrew Jackson, this law was passed in 1830. The intent of this law was to remove Native Americans from their ancestral homelands and to relocate them to "Indian Territory." This law initiated a series of removal treaties and one of the most known cases of removal had to do with the Cherokee Nation. The problems of Cherokee Removal have been well-documented, especially as they relate to problems associated with the Treaty of New Echota in 1835 followed by the Trail of Tears 4 years later.

Indian Subcontinent

Historically forming the whole territory of Greater India; now it generally comprises the countries of India, Pakistan, and Bangladesh; prior to 1947, the three nations were historically combined and constituted British India. It almost always also includes Nepal, Bhutan, and the island country of Sri Lanka, and may also include Afghanistan and the island country of Maldives. The region may also include the disputed territory of Aksai Chin, which was part of the British Indian princely state of Jammu and Kashmir, but is now administered as part of the Chinese autonomous region of Xinjiang.

Indigenous

Those people whose family and ethnic group inhabiting a land before it was taken over (colonized) by another nation. Indigenous can also mean not only the first people on a land, but also still alive and (possibly) still inhabiting some part of that land to which that person's ancestors inhabited.

Indigenous Cultures

The practices and beliefs of people whose family and ethnic group lived in a particular land first. Some of these practices and beliefs change over time and some of them stay the same for many years.

Indigenous Spiritual Belief Systems

Ideas from people whose family and ethnic group lived in a particular land first about how the world was created, where people came from, and where we will go when we die; also how we should treat our families and other people living or dead.

Individualism

An over-emphasis on the effort, interest, achievement, and wealth of the individual rather than the group.

Institutional Discrimination

Policies, rules, and practices created and followed by companies, agencies, and other government or nongovernment organizations favorable to a dominant group and unfavorable to another group that have existed for a long time, and that get repeated over and over.

Insular Cases

Following its victory in the Spanish–American War (1898), the United States acquired Hawaii, Puerto Rico, Guam, and the Philippines. In the Insular Cases (1901–1922), the U.S. Supreme Court determined the constitutional and political status of the new territories. In *De Lima v. Bidwell* (1901), a customs dispute, a 5-to-4 majority ruled that Puerto Rico was not a "foreign country" for tariff purposes. In subsequent cases, the court addressed the territories' relationship to the United States and whether "the Constitution follows the flag"; that is, whether and how constitutional provisions applied to these acquisitions.

Interdisciplinary

Involving two or more academic disciplines (such as English and Science), two or more artistic disciplines (such as music and painting), or two or more scientific disciplines (chemistry and biology) to understand or appreciate life.

Internalized Racism

Practices of inequality by racial ethnic minority group members against themselves or other members of their community.

Internment (Camps)

A place of confinement or imprisonment, especially for political or military reasons. During World War II, the United States President Franklyn D. Roosevelt signed Executive Order 9066, forcing all Japanese Americans onto prison camps. Another word for "internment camp" is "concentration camp".

Intersectionality

The interconnected nature of social categorizations such as race, class, and gender as they apply to a given individual or group, regarded as creating overlapping and interdependent systems of discrimination or disadvantage.

Intonation

The manner of utterance; specifically, the rise and fall in pitch of the voice in speech.

ISHI

Ishi was labeled "the last wild Indian in North America" when he stumbled into an Oroville rancher's barn on August 28, 1911. T.T. Waterman and Alfred Kroeber determined him to be from a previously unknown Yana tribe in the Deer Creek region. An overnight media sensation, newspapers across the United States were quick to emphasize Ishi's primitiveness and hastily conclude his lack of tribe members was the singular result of his Native people's extinction. Under authorization from the Bureau of Indian Affairs in Washington DC, Waterman and Kroeber brought Ishi to the University of California's Associated Colleges Museum in San Francisco, where he worked as a living diorama until his death in 1916, teaching the world much about his Native customs and culture in his 5 years at the museum.

Japanese Aliens

In 1941, Japanese Americans were labelled as Enemy Aliens or Japanese Aliens.

Jim Crow Systems

The backlash against the gains of African Americans in the Reconstruction Era was swift and severe. As African Americans obtained political power and began the long march toward greater social and economic equality, Whites reacted with panic and outrage. Southern conservatives vowed to reverse Reconstruction . . . .Their campaign to "redeem" the South was reinforced by a resurgent Ku Klux Klan, which fought a terrorist campaign against Reconstruction governments and local leaders, complete with segregation, bombings, lynchings, and mob violence.

The terrorist campaign proved highly successful. "Redemption" resulted in the withdrawal of federal troops from the South and the effective abandonment of African Americans and all those who had fought for or supported an egalitarian racial order. The federal government no longer made any e ort to enforce federal civil rights legislation.

Once again, vagrancy laws and other laws defining activities such as "mischief" and "insulting gestures" as crimes were enforced vigorously against Blacks. The aggressive enforcement of these criminal offenses opened up an enormous market for convict leasing, in which prisoners were contracted out as laborers to the highest private bidder.

Convicts had no meaningful legal rights at this time and no effective redress. They were understood, quite literally, to be slaves of the state. The Thirteenth Amendment to the U.S. Constitution had abolished slavery but allowed one major exception: slavery remained appropriate as punishment for a crime.

Jones Act

On March 2, 1917, President Woodrow Wilson signed the Jones–Shafroth Act. This law gave Puerto Ricans U.S. citizenship. The Jones Act also established three branches of the Puerto Rican Government: Executive, Judicial, and Legislative.

Justice Department Internment Camps

After Japanese Americans were arrested during World War II they were taken to temporary Immigration and Naturalization Services (INS) detention centers. They were then transferred to Department of Justice Internment camps where they awaited a hearing from the Alien Enemy Hearing Board to determine where they would stay for the remainder of the war.

Kinesthetic (Kinesthesia)

Of or relating to Kinesthesia (The sense that detects bodily position, weight, or movement of the muscles, tendons, and joints.).

Labor Union Organizer

A union representative who organizes nonunion workers to form union chapters at nonunion companies or worksites in order for all members to get the best possible salaries and working conditions.

LAPU-LAPU

He was a *Datu* (Chieftan) and leader of Filipinos in Mactan Island in Cebu, Philippines. He and over 1,000 heavily armed Filipino warriors killed Ferdinand Magellan and his Spanish landing party in 1521. As a result, the first attempt of Spanish colonization of the Philippines failed. Lapu-Lapu is considered a hero in the Philippines.

Latinx

Spanish nouns are gendered (o for masculine and a for feminine). By dismantling some of the gendering within Spanish, Latinx helped modernize the idea of a pan-Latin American experience—or *Latinidad*—one that reflects what it means to be of Latin American descent in today's world. The term also better reflects Latin America's diversity, which is more in line with intersectionality, the study of the ways that different forms of oppression (e.g., sexism, racism, classism, and heterosexism) intersect. Similarly, the terms Chicano and Chicana are becoming Chicanx in some activist and academic communities.

Linguistics

The study of human speech including the units, nature, structure, and modification of language.

Linguistic Diversity

Different forms of verbal communication based on ethnicity, geography, culture, and age.

Locke's Community Garden

Previous resident, Connie King grew a few Chinese vegetables along with an assortment of other vegetables and an array of flowers. Her plot showed the remnants of its previous gardener, her late husband Tom King. Tourists would often find her in the plot and she was delighted to give them a tour and the opportunity to teach them about the history of Locke. Since Connie passed away, volunteers for the Locke Foundation have turned her old plot across from her former home on Key Street into a Chinese vegetable demonstration garden. Each year, several residents have cultivated a variety of traditional Chinese vegetables. We have grown, long beans or dow gok, bok choy, see gwa, dong gwa, foo gwa, poo gwa, and gow choy along with a couple of strawberry plants for the children.

Loyalty Questionnaire

In 1943, the War Department and the War Relocation Authority (WRA) joined forces to create a bureaucratic means of assessing the loyalty of Nikkei in the WRA concentration camps. All adults were asked to answer questions on a form that become known informally as the "loyalty questionnaire." Responses to this questionnaire were meant to aid the War Department in recruiting Nisei into an all-Nisei combat unit and to assist the WRA in authorizing others for relocation outside of the camps. The registration program provoked a wide range of resistance due to its provocative "loyalty" questions and built resentment among Issei and Nisei over their unconstitutional wartime treatment.

Luzones Indios

The name that Spaniards gave to Filipinos who served on the Manila galleons that sailed between Manila and Acapulco, Mexico. The first documented "Luzones Indios" landed in California in 1587, which would make Filipinos the first Asians to be documented as arriving in America.

Maestro

A master usually in an art; *especially* an eminent composer, conductor, or teacher of music.

Maidu

An indigenous people to northeastern California. Collectively known as the Maiduan, separate yet interrelated groups are the Mountain Maidu of Plumas and Lassen counties, the Mechoopda of Butte county, the Konkow of Butte and Yuba counties, and the Nisenan of Yuba, Nevada, Placer, Sacramento, and El Dorado counties.

Manifest Destiny

A common belief in the eighteenth and nineteenth centuries that it was the destiny of the United States to expand its territory and extend its political, social, and economic influence over all of North America.

Manila

Capitol of the Philippines located on the island of Luzon. Manila was founded in 1571.

Manilla Galleon Trade

Trade exchanging porcelain, silk, ivory, spices, and other items from China for silver from what was then considered New Spain, today Mexico. Some of the goods from China would be sent through Mexico and back to Spain.

Mass Culture

A set of cultural values and ideas that arise from common exposure of a population to the same cultural activities, communications media, music and art, and so forth. Mass culture becomes possible only with modern communications and electronic media. A mass culture is transmitted to individuals, rather than arising from people's daily interactions, and therefore lacks the distinctive content of cultures rooted in community and region. Mass culture tends to reproduce the liberal value of individualism and to foster a view of the citizen as consumer.

Mecha

Movimiento Estudiantil Chicanx de Aztlán (MEChA) is a student organization that promotes higher education, cultura, and historia. Each word in MEChA symbolizes a great concept in terms of la causa. Movimiento means that the organization is dedicated to the movement to gain self-determination for Chicanx people. Estudiantil, identifies the organization as a student group. At the heart of the name is the use of the identity: Chicanx. At first seen as a negative word, now taken for a badge of honor. In adopting their new identity, the students committed themselves to return to the barrios, colonias, or campos and together, struggle against the forces that oppress. Lastly, the affirmation that they are Indigenous people to this land by placing our movement in Aztlán, the homeland of all peoples from Anahuak. At the time of this writing, Mecha is considering changing its name.

Merchant Status Designation

Some Chinese Immigrants were able to adapt to Chinese Exclusion laws in the late 1800s by working within the U.S. Capitalist system and changing their status from laborers to business owners, or merchants. This allowed them to bring family members with them from China and into the United States.

Mestiza

It refers to racial and/or cultural mixing of Amerindians with Europeans, and the resulting tensions, contradictions, and ambiguities of this mixing.

Microaggression

A comment or action that subtly and often unconsciously or unintentionally expresses a prejudiced attitude toward a member of a marginalized group (such as a racial minority).

Migrate

To move from one country, place or locality to another.

Migration

The act or an instance of moving from one place to another often on a regular basis.

Minority Group

A group distinguished by being on the margins of power, status, or the allocation of resources within the society. "Visible minority" refer to those racial or ethnic groups in a society which are marginal from the power and economic structure of society, not to those which are few in number.

Misogyny

Individual and institutional policies and practices that express a hatred of women.

Missions

A ministry commissioned by a religious organization to propagate its faith. Religious missions, such as Spain's Missions in California, are often one factor in the colonization of an indigenous community's land and resources.

Mixed Racial Heritage

Having two or more racial or ethnic heritages from parents who a represent different race or ethnicity.

Mosul

A city on the Tigris River in northern Iraq; *population* 1,637,000. During the second Gulf War, the prison in this city was used as a U.S. Army interrogation and detention center. After the Gulf War the city was taken by the Islamic State of Iraq and Syria (ISIS). At the time of this writing, the Iraqi Army is advancing on Mosul and has nearly retaken this Iraqi city.

Multiplex Identity

Multiplex identity refers to people who hold multiple cultural identities or who hold identities that locate them in the intersections of oppression.

Multilingual

Having the ability to speak two or more languages. Many countries in the world have citizens who speak two or more languages.

Multilingual Family

A family whose members speak more than one language or dialect.

Multiracial

See "Mixed Racial Heritage."

Muslim

A follower of the religion known as Islam.

Myths

Sacred stories from communities around the world that help explain how things were created and how they came to be.

National Association For The Advancement Of Colored People (NAACP)

The mission of the NAACP is to ensure the political, educational, social, and economic equality of rights of all persons and to eliminate race-based discrimination.

National Boycott

To engage in a national refusal to have dealings with a person, a store, an organization, and so on, usually to express disapproval or to force acceptance of certain conditions.

National Identity

The depiction of a country as a whole, encompassing its culture, traditions, language, and politics.

National Farm Workers Association (NFWA)

A labor union for farm workers established by Cesar Chavez in 1962.

Nationalism

Devotion, especially excessive or undiscriminating devotion, to the interests or culture of a particular nation-state.

Native Hawaiian Organizations (NHOs)

Native Hawaiian Organizations (NHOs) are nonprofit organizations authorized by the Small Business Administration (SBA) to participate in the 8(a) Business

Development program. NHOs provide invaluable economic benefits to the State of Hawaii and the Native Hawaiian community by developing job opportunities, building the capacity of innovative industries, and supporting important social and economic programs.

Naturalization Law Of 1870

After the Civil War, this law enabled formerly enslaved Africans to become natural citizens. However, in spite of this law newly freed African Americans were subject to all manor of racial terror to prevent them from acting on their citizenship.

Nahua

The **Nahuas** are a group of indigenous peoples of Mexico. Their language of Uto-Aztecan affiliation is called Nahuatl and consists of many more dialects and variants, a number of which are mutually unintelligible. About 1,500,000 Nahua speak Nahuatl and another 1,000,000 speak only Spanish.

Evidence suggests the Nahua peoples originated in the southwestern part of what is now the United States and northwestern Mexico. They split off from the other Uto-Aztecan speaking peoples and migrated into central Mexico around 500 CE. They settled in and around the Basin of Mexico and spread out to become the dominant people in central Mexico. Some of the most important Mesoamerican civilizations were of Nahua ethnicity, including the Toltec and Aztec cultures, as well as the Tepaneca, Acolhua, Tlaxcaltec, Xochimilca, and many others.

The name Nahua is derived from the Nahuatl word nāhuatl, which means "clear," "intelligible" or "speaking the Nahuatl language."

Neocolonization

Economic and political policies by which one country maintains or extends control or influence over another country, after formally withdrawing from occupying that country.

Nonviolent Direct Action (Nonviolent Protests)

Gene Sharp writes: "Nonviolent action refers to those methods of protest, resistance, and intervention without physical violence in which the members of the nonviolent group do, or refuse to do, certain things. They may commit acts of omission—refuse to perform acts which they usually perform, are expected by custom to perform, or are required by law or regulation to perform; or acts of commission—perform acts which they usually do not perform, are not expected by custom to perform, or are forbidden by law or regulation from performing; or a combination of both." (1980) *Social power and political freedom*, Boston: Porter Sargent Publishers, p. 218.

Nonviolent action refers to those methods of protest, resistance, and intervention without physical violence in which the members of the nonviolent group do, or refuse to do, certain things.

Norm

A culturally established rule prescribing appropriate social behavior. Norms are relatively specific and precise and elaborate, the detailed behavioral requirements that flow from more general and overarching social values. For example, it is a value in Western society that one should respect the dead, it is a norm that one should dress in dark colors for a funeral.

ODU

A sacred story from the Yoruba people of West Africa, sometimes involving spiritual or supernatural beings that provide guidance on how to live in the world.

Oppression

Unjust or cruel exercise of authority or power. Also, a sense of being weighed down in body or mind: depression, an *oppression* of spirits.

Oral History

Oral history refers both to a method of recording and preserving oral testimony and to the product of that process. It begins with an audio or video recording of a first person account made by an interviewer with an interviewee (also referred to as narrator), both of whom have the conscious intention of creating a permanent record to contribute to an understanding of the past. A verbal document, the oral history, results from this process and is preserved and made available in different forms to other users, researchers, and the public. A critical approach to the oral testimony and interpretations are necessary in the use of oral history.

Original Nation

A name for indigenous people, sometimes referred to as First Nation, Native American, or American Indian. These terms refer to many different ethnic groups (e.g., Cheyenne, Lakota, Maidu, Miwok, Mohawk, and Cherokee) all at once so they are not specific and may not be the way they refer to themselves.

Orisha

A divine force of nature within the Yoruba spiritual system of West Africa.

Other

A term that refers to an individual or group who is perceived to be different from the ruling colonial group. Someone perceived as Other is often treated like an outsider.

Pan-Indigenous Ideology

The term Pan Indigenous or "Pan-Indianism" has been applied to social movements among both Asian Indians and North American First Nations peoples. In both contexts, Pan-Indianism refers to a social movement and a political philosophy that asserts a peoples' common identity and unity across political or state boundaries and tribal divisions.

Paper Name (Paper Sons And Daughters)

Due to the Chinese Exclusions Acts, many Chinese came into the United States by using the "Paper Name" system. They bought papers identifying them as children of American citizens and coaching books with detailed information on their "paper" families, which they studied in order to pass grueling interrogations. Because official records were often nonexistent, an interrogation process was created to determine if the immigrants were related as they claimed. Questions could include details of the immigrant's home and village as well as specific knowledge of his or her ancestors. Interrogations could take a long time to complete, especially if witnesses for the immigrants lived in the eastern United States. The average detention was 2–3 months, but many stayed longer.

Paradox

A person, group, or situation that appears to have contradictory qualities or experiences.

Patrimony (Cultural Patrimony)

A right, a status or tangible asset inherited from a father or other ancestor. In principle, a patrimony may be inherited by either sex, although the term is generally associated with patrilineal transmission of status, property, and wealth.

Personifies

To represent something as having human qualities or powers.

Phenotype

1. The physical appearance or biochemical characteristic of an organism as a result of the interaction of its genotype and the environment.
2. The expression of a particular trait, for example, skin color, height, behavior, and so forth, according to the individual's genetic makeup and environment.

Philippine–American War

After its defeat in the Spanish–American War of 1898, Spain ceded its longstanding colony of the Philippines to the United States in the Treaty of Paris. On February 4, 1899, just 2 days before the U.S. Senate ratified the treaty, fighting broke out between American forces and Filipino nationalists led by Emilio Aguinaldo who sought independence rather than a change in colonial rulers. The ensuing Philippine–American War lasted 3 years and resulted in the death of over 4,200 American and over 20,000 Filipino combatants.

Philippine Commonwealth And Independence Act

Also called the Tydings–McDufe Act, signed in1934, is the U.S. statute that provided for Philippine independence, to take effect on July 4, 1946, after a 10-year transitional period of Commonwealth government. The bill was signed by the U.S. President Franklin D. Roosevelt on March 24, 1934, and was sent to the Philippine Senate for approval.

Phonetics

1. the system of speech sounds of a language or group of languages.
2. the study and systematic classification of the sounds made in spoken utterance.
3. the practical application of this science to language study.

Place Names

The name given to geographical location, such as a town or street. Often place names originate from Indigenous names.

Plebiscites

A vote by which the people of an entire country or district express an opinion for or against a proposal especially on a choice of government or ruler.

The following entry is an excerpt from the web site http://www.itsabouttimebpp .com/home/home.html.

Political Education (PE) Classes

The root of the growth and development of the Black Panther Party (BPP) has to be the political education that the BPP members taught and learned. I have mention before in articles that reading and studying was heavily stressed in the BPP. A person wanting to join the Party had to attend PE classes as a Panther-in training and read 2 hours a day to stay abreast of the changing situations in the community and world. Each one Teach one. Some of the basic reading to start you out was the 10-point program and platform, *the Red Book* by Chairman Mao and the centerfold of the Black Panther Party newspaper.

My section leader when I joined the BPP was Anthony Woods. We lived close to each other and would get together with other members in our section and study extra material, like selected works of Mao and books by Che and Fidel. We studied military writing by many revolutionaries. I was fortunate to have classes also taught by leading members of the BPP from the very beginning: George Murray who was Minister of Education, Wendell Wade, Landon Williams who was a wealth of knowledge and led by example. Bobby Seale taught classes as well, and when Huey got out of prison I attended some PE classes he taught, but the most dynamic teacher of all was Ray Masai Hewitt who replaced George Murray in 1969.

Before Huey got out of prison in 1970, the BPP started to focus more on the concept of Dialectical Materialism and study a more scientific approach to analyzing the world and our situation in America. We held PE classes on Sunday mornings and all had to attend; a must even for apolitical types. The Party's view was that information is the raw material for new ideas, the more information one received, the better adapted one was to solve problems in the community and bring the peoples' consciousness to a higher level.

Postcivil Rights Era

By the late 1960s, organizations such as the *NAACP, SCLC,* and *SNCC* faced increasingly strong challenges from new militant organizations, such as the Black Panther party. A series of major "riots" (as the authorities called them), or "rebellions" (the sympathizers' term), erupted during the last half of the 1960s. Often influenced by the Black nationalism of Elijah Muhammad and Malcolm X and by pan-African leaders, proponents of Black liberation saw civil rights reforms as insufficient because they did not address the problems faced by millions of poor Blacks and because African-American citizenship was derived ultimately from the involuntary circumstances of enslavement.

In addition, proponents of racial liberation often saw the African-American freedom struggle in international terms, as a movement for human rights and national self-determination for all peoples.

Postapocalyptic Stress Syndrome

Recurring and ongoing experiences of trauma-related stress from having direct experiences of a complete and total loss of culture, livelihood, and agency; or from having those experiences in one's family or ancestry.

Posttraumatic Stress Disorder

Recurring and ongoing experiences of trauma-related stress after a traumatic experience or set of experiences.

Precontact

1. Precontact usually refers to a period before European colonizers, explorers or missionaries first had interaction with Native Americans or other indigenous peoples throughout the world, including the continents that became known as Africa, Latin America, and Australia.
2. Of or relating to the period before contact of an indigenous people with an outside, often industrialized culture.

Prejudice

To make a judgment about an individual or group of individuals on the basis of their social, physical, or cultural characteristics. Such judgments are usually negative, but prejudice can also be exercised to give undue favor and advantage to members of particular groups. Prejudice is often seen as the attitudinal component of discrimination.

Primary Source Data

In research activities, *primary source* refers to information collected firsthand from such sources as historical documents, literary texts, artistic works, experiments, surveys, and interviews. Also called *primary data*.

Public Law 96-317

This law was passed to establish a Commission to gather facts to determine whether any wrong was committed against those American citizens and permanent resident aliens affected by Executive Order Numbered 9066, and for other purposes.

Puritanical Work Ethic

A belief in and devotion to hard work, duty, thrift, self-discipline, and responsibility; also called Protestant ethic, Protestant work ethic, or work ethic. Sometimes, this ethic is associated with rigid or overly strict ideas and attitudes.

Race

A classification of human beings into different categories on the basis of the way we look, for example, our skin color, head shape, eye color and shape, nose size and shape, and so on.

Racial Discrimination

1. Unfair or abusive treatment of another person based on their perceived or actual race.
2. The unequal treatment of individuals on the basis of their race or perceived race.
3. Discrimination usually refers to negative treatment, but discrimination in favor of particular groups can also occur.

Racial Hierarchy

Structures in society that reward some races or ethnicities more than others based on a belief that some races are more intelligent, physically able, or more capable, and should have more.

Racial Restrictive Covenants

Restrictive covenants are agreements placed on people when they are selling their home. Racially restrictive covenants forbid the seller of a home to sell the house to people of different races, most often African American, Latinos, and Asian Americans. Racially restrictive covenants are illegal and homeowners can get a Restrictive Covenant Modification to have the racially restrictive covenant removed from the property deed.

An agreement between a person selling property and a person buying the property, to restrict the future sale of the property to people of a particular race. Race-restrictive covenants are recorded on property deeds.

Racial Identity

An individual's sense of having their identity defined by belonging to a particular race or ethnic group. The strength of such identity is dependent on how much he or she has processed and internalized the sociological, political and other contextual factors within that group.

Racial Identity Dilemma

Racial Identity Dilemma concerns a person's inability to experience Immersion, Internalization, or Commitment to a racial identity. Rather than experience comfort, realization, and positive sense of one's race, the individual is stuck at a preencounter or an encounter stage where there is a general lack of awareness of the impact of race or an ever-new sense of racial discovery. For nondominant racial groups, the encounter stage is sometimes very negative or hurtful.

Racism

An ideology based on the idea that humans can be separated into distinct racial groups and that these groups can be ranked on a hierarchy of intelligence, ability, morality, and so forth.

Referendum

The submission of a proposed public measure or actual statute to a direct popular vote.

Ramadan

The 9th month of the Islamic year observed as sacred with fasting practiced daily from dawn to sunset.

Refugee

A person who flees to a foreign country or power to escape danger or persecution.

Refugee Assistance Act H.R. 6755

The Indochina Migration and Refugee Assistance Act was passed in 1975 for refugees from Vietnam and Cambodia who were being persecuted or who were in fear of persecution due to race, religion, or political opinion to resettle in the United States.

Refugee Camps

Temporary shelters for people fleeing their home country. The United Nations High Commissioner of Refugees administers camps sheltering a vast population of displaced people. World conflicts often result in scores of refugees around the world seeking shelter in camps. Contrary to popular belief, many of these settlements are far from temporary, and today most of the largest ones are in Africa and South Asia.

Relocation Camps

Another name for internment camps or concentration camps.

Repatriation

To restore or return to the country of origin, allegiance, or citizenship.

Research Question

The primary question guiding someone's research. The research question is usually large enough to have several subquestions within it.

Reservation

A federal Native American Indian Reservation is an area of land reserved for a tribe or tribes under treaty or other agreement with the United States, executive order, or federal statute or administrative action as permanent tribal homelands, and where the federal government holds title to the land in trust for the tribes.

Respect

Willingness to show consideration or appreciation; the state of being regarded with honor or esteem.

Restrictive Covenant (Race Restrictive Covenant)

An agreement to restrict the future sale of property to people of a particular race between a person selling property and a person buying the property.

Right Of First Refusal (RFR)

As it relates to the town of Locke, the RFR is a policy in the bylaws of the Locke Management Association. Conceived of during Locke's revitalization by three of the four Chinese American advocacy group representatives on Sacramento County's Locke Community Advisory Committee. The Right of First Refusal (RFR) requires that any Locke property for sale after the 2004 subdivision and sale of land by the County to then-current building owners would be subject to an RFR granting the Locke Management Association the first opportunity to purchase the property after notifying interested parties that the land was for sale. The intent was for the LMA to act on behalf of Locke's original residents, their descendants, and ascendants, eventually selling the land to these families.

Although the historic wrong of the 1913 Alien Land Act could never be righted, the representatives believed that creating and exercising this RFR would be in the spirit of righting the historic wrong of the Alien Land law. Through the RFR, an original Locke resident, for example, a Chinese American family, or their descendants, could finally own the land of their ancestor's homesteads.

Rock Springs Massacre

An especially brutal anti-Chinese riot in Wyoming, 1885. White coal miners, who scapegoated Chinese American coal miners for their poor working conditions, rioted and massacred 28 Chinese American coal miners, and drove hundreds more out of town. One of the worst examples of anti-Chinese sentiment, which swept up the nation with a racist "The Chinese Must Go!" mentality. "The Chinese must go!" was a slogan of the anti-Chinese labor leader Denis Kearney, a labor leader and central figure in the founding of San Francisco.

In a parallel anti-Asian American murder, showing how little has changed in institutionalized racism in the United States, Vincent Chin was beaten to death with a baseball bat in Detroit, 1982. A White man and his stepson scapegoated the Japanese for losing their auto industry jobs. They mistook Chin for a Japanese and killed him in front of a McDonald's a week before his wedding. Just as in the Vincent Chin murder of 1982, the Rock Spring Massacre murderers never spent a night in prison for their crimes.

Romanized Transliteration

Representing the oral or written language that uses different alphabet symbols in Roman, as with the English language.

Sacramento Committee For Fair Housing Colored (SCFH)

A civil rights organization advocating for fair housing in Sacramento alongside other organizations such as CORE and the National Council for the Advancement of Colored People (NAACP).

Sacred Geography

There are many different types of sacred geography. Some examples include the following:

1. Shrines, vision quest sites, altars, and sweat bath sites that serve as ritual settings.
2. Monumental geographical features that have mythic significance in a group's origins or history. Included are mountains, waterfalls, and unusual geographical formations such as Pilot Knob, Kootenai Falls, Celilo Falls, and Mount Adams.

3. Rock art sites such as pictograph and petroglyph panels.
4. Burial sites and cemeteries.
5. Areas where plants, stones, earth, animals, and other sacred objects are gathered for ritual purposes or where sacred vegetation such as medicine trees serve as objects or center of ritual.
6. Sites of major historical events such as battlefields where group members died.
7. Sites where groups are thought to have originated, emerged, or been created.
8. Pilgrimage or mythic pathways where groups or individuals retrace the journeys and reenact events described in myths and in the lives of mythic and other figures.
9. Lakes, rivers, springs, and water associated with life and the vital forces that sustain it.
10. Areas or sites associated with prophets and teachers like Smohalla, Handsome Lake, Sweet Medicine, and others.

Sacred Geometry

Geometric shapes and solids whose interrelated dimensions allegedly possess mystical or occult properties. The pentagram and the Egyptian pyramid are two commonly cited examples of sacred geometry—both conceal the golden ratio in them.

Sacred Narratives

Myths. Stories about how the world was created, and humans' role in it.

Second Great Migration

The Second Great Migration (1940–1970) is considered by some historians as, essentially, the sequel to its predecessor, the Great Migration (1910–1930). While both had a tremendous impact on the lives of African Americans, the second migration was much larger in scale and dissimilar in character to the initial migration and arguably affected the lives of African Americans much more so than the preceding migration period. Historians will argue that the effects of the second migration precipitated a more enduring transformation of American life, for both Blacks and Whites. However, many of the factors that spurred migration remained the same. The economy, jobs, and racial discrimination remained top factors for Black migration to the North. The advent of World War II contributed to an exodus out of the South, with 1.5 million African Americans leaving during the 1940s; a pattern of migration which would continue at that pace for the next 20 years. The result would be the increased urbanization of the African American population, with fewer Blacks working in agriculture or domestic labor; occupations by which the Black race had previously, and solely, been characterized.

Segregation

1. The act or process of segregating: the state of being segregated.
2. The separation or isolation of a race, class, or ethnic group by enforced or voluntary residence in a restricted area, by barriers to social intercourse, by separate educational facilities, or by other discriminatory means.
3. The separation for special treatment or observation of individuals or items from a larger group—*segregation* of gifted children into accelerated classes.

Self-Determination

The right to live and act without outside oppressive forces acting against one's will.

1. Free choice of one's own acts or states without external compulsion.
2. Determination by the people of a territorial unit of their own future political status.

Servant Leadership

Someone who leads by serving others. In other words, servant leaders place the interests and needs of their followers ahead of their own self-interests and needs. Generally, they value the development of their followers, building their communities, acting authentically, and sharing power.

Sexual Orientation

An enduring sexual attraction toward members of either one's own gender or the other gender.

SIC

A term indicating the preceding quoted word or words is the original writer's wording. Most often used when original wording is incorrect, in spelling/grammar/use of terms; used to confirm it is not the editor's error

Example: Locke was designated a National Historic Landmark for being the ". . .most intact surviving example of an historic rural Chinese-American [*sic*] community." The original writer, in this case the federal government, unwittingly (?) uses the insulting hyphenated term "Chinese-American" instead of the correct "Chinese American" (no hyphen)(see **Chinese American**, above).

Sinocentric

Any **ethnocentric** political **ideology** that regard China to be central or unique relative to other countries. A hierarchical Sinocentric model of international relations, dominated by China, prevailed in East Asia until the weakening of the **Qing Dynasty** and the encroachment of European and Japanese imperialists in the second half of the 19th century.

Slave Trade

The business or process of procuring, transporting, and selling Enslaved people. Slavery is most often associated with the transatlantic slave trade where countries in Europe, the United States and others enslaved Africans for some 400 years, but it has existed all over the world since ancient times and it exists in many forms today.

Slavery

The keeping of enslaved people as a practice or institution.

Slur

An insulting or disparaging remark. Specifically, a racial slur is a racist term used against another person.

Social Construction

A theoretical approach which regard certain aspects of human experience and knowledge as originating within and cultivated by society or a particular social group, rather than existing inherently or naturally.

Social Darwinism

The theory that persons, groups, and races are subject to the same laws of natural selection as Charles Darwin had perceived in plants and animals in nature. According to the theory, which was popular in the late 19th and early 20th centuries, the weak were diminished and their cultures delimited, while the strong grew in power and in cultural influence over the weak. Social Darwinists held that the life of humans in society was a struggle for existence ruled by "survival of the fittest," a phrase proposed by the British philosopher and scientist Herbert Spencer.

Social Scientists

A scientist who studies society and human behavior, such as a historian, economist, or sociologist.

Social Statement

An assertion, teaching or policy that about a social issue, concern or crisis.

Socioeconomic Status

Socioeconomic status is the social standing or class of an individual or group. It is often measured as a combination of education, income, and occupation. Examinations of socioeconomic status often reveal inequities in access to resources, plus issues related to privilege, power, and control.

Sociophonetics

A branch of linguistics studying sociolinguistic aspects of speech sounds; the interaction between sociolinguistics and phonetics.

Sociopolitical

Of or relating to both social and political factors.

Southeast Asia

Southeast Asia consists of a vast territory encompassing 11 countries that reach from eastern India to China and is generally divided into mainland and island zones. Burma, Thailand, Laos, Cambodia, and Vietnam are in the mainland zones. Malaysia, Singapore, Indonesia, and the Philippines are part of the island zone.

Sovereignty

The authority possessed by the governing individual or institution of a society. Sovereign authority is distinct in that it is unrestricted by legal regulation since the sovereign authority is itself the source of all law.

Spanglish

A hybrid language combining words and idioms from both Spanish and English.

Spanish–American War

The war started because the USS Maine sank in Havana Harbor, Cuba, and the Spanish government was blamed by newspapers and "Yellow journalism." These news reports argued that the USS Maine was sunk by a Spanish mine, but later reports and investigations cast doubt this explanation. Still, the United States went to war with Spain based on these rumors. During this war, the United States invaded the Philippines, Guam, and Puerto Rico and made these islands American colonies.

Stereotypes

This term derives from the printing process and refers to a plate made by taking a cast or mold of a surface. A stereotype then is anything which lacks individual marks or identifiers, and instead appears as though made from a cast. In sociology, the stereotype (the plate or cast) is always a social construction, which may have some basis in reality but is a gross generalization (e.g., women like romance novels). To stereotype is to apply these casts, or gross generalization, to people or situations rather than seeing the individual variation.

Storytelling

The act of sharing an event, incident, or sacred narrative for entertainment, social cohesion, spiritual insight, and so on.

Subculture

A culture-within-a-culture; the somewhat distinct norms, values, and behavior of particular groups located within society. The concept of subculture implies some degree of group self-sufficiency such that individuals may interact, find employment, recreation, friends, and mates within the group.

Subgroup Identity

A smaller group within the larger community that shares some aspect of their identity with the larger group, but also shares some uniqueness within the smaller community that sets them apart from the others. For example, within the larger group of African Americans there are Afro-Punk Rockers, Black Christians, Black Muslims, and so forth.

Sugar Plantations

In the mid-seventeenth century, sugar cane was brought into what later became the British West Indies by the Dutch, from Brazil. Upon landing in Barbados and other islands, they quickly urged local growers to change their main crops from cotton and tobacco to sugar cane. With depressed prices of cotton and tobacco, due mainly to stiff competition from the North American colonies, the farmers switched, leading to a boom in the Caribbean economies. Sugar was quickly snapped up by the British, who used it in cakes and to sweeten teas.

During the colonial period, the arrival of sugar culture deeply impacted the society and economy in the Caribbean. It not only dramatically increased the ratio of slaves to free men, but it increased the average size of slave plantations. Early sugar plantations made extensive use of enslaved people because sugar was considered a cash crop that exhibited economies of scale in cultivation; it was most efficiently grown on large plantations with many workers.

Symbiotic Connection

Usually a close connection over a period of time between two different specious—or communities that enjoy a mutual benefit by connecting.

Symbol

Something that represents something else by association, resemblance—a material object used to represent something invisible.

Termination

In 1953, the House of Representatives passed Resolution 108, proposing an end to federal services for 13 tribes deemed ready to handle their own affairs. The same year, Public Law 280 transferred jurisdiction over tribal lands to state and local governments in five states. Within a decade, Congress terminated federal services to more than 60 groups, including the Menominees of Wisconsin and the Klamaths of Oregon, despite intense opposition by Indians. The effects of the laws on the Menominees and the Klamaths were disastrous, forcing many members of the tribes onto public assistance rolls.

The Katipunan

A Philippine revolutionary society founded by anti-Spanish Filipinos in Manila in 1892, whose main goal was independence.

Theories

A belief, policy, or procedure that guides action.

Third World

This way of categorizing societies has lost much of its meaning with the breakup of the Soviet Union and the decline of communism as an economic system. First world countries once referred to the developed, capitalist societies, while the second world identified the developed socialist societies. Third world countries were those large political communities in the initial stages of development while fourth world societies are those that are traditional communities marginalized from economic development and political power. The concept of "fourth world" has been applied to the aboriginal communities of North America.

Third World College

The name given to proposed programs during the strike by students demonstrating for Ethnic Studies classes at UC Berkeley.

Third World Liberation Front

The name given to the students demonstrating for an Ethnic Studies program at UC Berkeley.

Totemic Ancestor

An object (such as an animal or plant) serving as the emblem of a family or clan and often as a reminder of its ancestry.

Trail Of Tears

Several routes over which thousands of Cherokee and other Indian peoples were forced to march and along which many died during the late 1830s to be resettled west of the Mississippi River largely in what is now Oklahoma.

Trauma

A disordered psychic or behavioral state resulting from severe mental or emotional stress or physical injury; an emotional upset.

Transcontinental Railroad

The first railroad uniting the western and eastern United States. Before the Transcontinental Railroad was completed on May 10, 1869, the two "halves" of the United States were "impossibly" far from each other. The western part of the Railroad, the Central Pacific Railroad, was built by Chinese laborers. The eastern part of the Railroad, the Union Pacific, was built largely by Irish American laborers. Both sets of workers were exploited and underpaid for their labor, but especially the Chinese and Chinese American laborers. Its completion in Promontory Summit, Utah, marked an epic milestone in U.S. history, celebrated with fireworks and fanfare across the country.

Transliteration

To represent or spell the characters from an alphabet different from your own.

Transnational Social Movements

A group of people organized, outside of institutions and across more than two countries established for this purpose, so as to bring about political and social change which will satisfy their shared interest or goal. Examples include the environmental movement, the gay rights movement, the women's movement, the labor movement, victim's rights movements, prisoner's rights movements, and movements for drug decriminalization.

Treaty

Unlike other racial-ethnic groups in the United States, the federal government signed treaties as international agreements with Native America tribes. While complex, in general, the act of treaty-making by the United States acknowledges the sovereign status (possessing the inherent right to self-government) of Native American tribes. Although the power of the President to enter into treaties with Native American tribes is rooted in the United States Constitution, treaty-making with Native American tribes ended in 1871 by an act of Congress.

Tribal Governments And Councils

The term "tribal government" is defined as any Indian tribe, band, nation, or other organized group or community, including any Alaska Native village or regional or village corporation as defined in or established pursuant to the Alaska Native Claims Settlement Act (85 Stat. 688; 43 U.S.C. 1601 et seq.), which is recognized as eligible for the special programs and services provided by the United States to Indians because of their special status as Indians. The tribes have their own laws and governments.

Tydings–Mcduffie Act of 1934

A law that

1. Promised independence to the Philippines.
2. Excluded Filipinos from entering the United States by setting a very low yearly quota of 50 immigrants a year. It was a compromise bill between Americans who wanted to exclude Filipino immigration and Filipinos who wanted independence for the Philippines.

Unconscious Bias (Implicit Bias)

Unlike *explicit bias* (which rejects the attitudes or beliefs that one endorses at a conscious level), *implicit bias* is the bias in judgment and/or behavior that results from subtle cognitive processes (e.g., implicit attitudes and implicit stereotypes) that often operate at a level below conscious awareness and without intentional control.

Undocumented

Not documented: such as

1. Not supported by documentary evidence *undocumented* expenditures.
2. Lacking documents required for legal immigration or residence *undocumented* workers.

UNESCO

An agency of the United Nations established in 1945 to promote the exchange of information, ideas, and culture.

Unfree Labor

Indentured servants and enslaved persons.

Universal Declaration Of Human Rights

Following World War II and the horrific experiences of that struggle, many nations set to creating the United Nations. The original Charter of the United Nations contained a general statement on human rights. The need for a more detailed and substantial statement on human rights was seen and a Commission was established to create such a document. This commission wrote the Universal Declaration on Human Rights (drafted largely by a Canadian) which was adopted by General Assembly of the United Nation on December 10, 1948. This document was described as humanity's response to the death camps of the Nazis, the countless refugees and the tortured prisoners-of-war. In 1966, the United Nations adopted two further documents on human rights: the Covenant on Civil and Political Rights and the Covenant on Economic, Social, and Cultural Rights. These covenants contain many of the rights asserted in the Universal Declaration but they differ in that they are legally binding on those nations signing the covenants. The first of these covenants declares that everyone has the right to life; freedom of thought; equal treatment in the courts; freedom of assembly; and no one shall be subject to torture, slavery, or forced labor. The second declares that everyone has the right to the enjoyment of just and favorable work conditions; form trade unions; an adequate standard of living; education; and take part in cultural life and enjoy the progress of science. In 1989, a third covenant was added, the Convention of the Rights of the Child. These four documents together comprise what is called the International Bill of Rights.

United Farm Workers Union

See United Farm Workers Association.

Unratified Treaty

A treaty that has not been confirmed, signed, or acted upon. This term is often used with regard to Native Americans where the ungratified treaty has resulted in a loss of land.

U.S. Census

A periodic counting of all people living in the United States. The census also records information about people's employment, ethnicity, race, gender, and so on.

Utopia

1. An imaginary and indefinitely remote place.
2. A place of ideal perfection especially in laws, government, and social conditions.
3. An impractical scheme for social improvement.

Values

Relatively general cultural prescriptions of what is right, moral, and desirable. Values provide the broad foundations for specific normative regulation of social interaction.

Variation

A speaker's use of different linguistic forms on different occasions, and different speakers of a language expressing the same meanings as others using different forms. Most of this variation is highly systematic: speakers of a language make choices in pronunciation, morphology, word choice, and grammar depending on a number of non-linguistic factors, such as age, race and ethnicity, gender, geography etc..

Vientiane Agreement 1973

A cease-fire agreement between the two warring Lao factions—the monarchial government of Laos and the communists.

Veterans Administration (VA)

The U.S. Department of Veterans Affairs is a government-run military veteran benefit system with Cabinet-level status. The VA provides health, home loan, and education benefits and other services to U.S. military veterans.

Vowels

1. The one most prominent sound in a syllable
2. a letter or other symbol representing a vowel —usually used in English of *a, e, i, o, u,* and sometimes *y.*

War Brides Act Of 1945

Waived visa requirements and provisions of immigration law when they concerned members of the American armed forces who, during World War II, had married nationals of foreign countries.

Wop

A derogatory term for Italian Americans, stemming from the designation "without papers," or illegal Italian American immigrants.

Xenophobia

An individual's irrational and obsessive hatred of people perceived as different and foreign. Related to the concepts of racism and ethnocentrism.

Glossary Sources

American Psychological Association Psychology Topics. Retrieved from http://www.apa.org/topics/socioeconomic-status/

Angel Island Immigration Station Foundation. Retrieved from http://www.aiisf.org/education/station-history

Chinese American Council of Sacramento. Retrieved from http://www.cacsweb.org/2017_02_index.php

Congress of Racial Equity. Retrieved from http://www.core-online.org/History/history.htm

Defense Language Institute Foreign Language Center. Retrieved from http://www.dliflc.edu/about/

Densho Encyclopedia. Retrieved from http://encyclopedia.densho.org/Loyalty_questionnaire/

Duhaime's Law Dictionary. Retrieved from http://www.duhaime.org/LegalDictionary/R/RightofFirstRefusal.aspx

Encyclopedia.com. Retrieved from http://www.encyclopedia.com/social-sciences/applied-and-social-sciences-magazines/ethnic-enclave

Everyculture.com. Retrieved from http://www.everyculture.com/multi/A-Br/Asian-Indian-Americans.html#ixzz4buy3Tszi

Federal Housing Authority. Retrieved from https://portal.hud.gov/hudportal/HUD?src=/program_offices/housing/fhahistory

Global Nonviolent Action. Retrieved from https://nvdatabase.swarthmore.edu/content/nonviolent-action-defined

Ifa-House of Wisdom. Retrieved from http://ifa-houseofwisdom.com/babalawo.html Intercontinental Cry https://intercontinentalcry.org/indigenous-peoples/nahua/

It's About Time Black Panther Party Legacy and Alumni. Retrieved from http://www.itsabout-timebpp.com/index.html

Locke Foundation. Retrieved from http://www.locke-foundation.org

Legal Information Institute Open Access to Law Cornell University Law School. Retrieved from https://www.law.cornell.edu/uscode/text/25/3001#fn002191

MERRIAM-WEBSTER. Retrieved from https://www.merriam-webster.com/dictionary/historiography

National Conference of State Legislators. Retrieved from http://www.ncsl.org/research/state-tribal-institute/list-of-federal-and-state-recognized-tribes.aspx

National Archives. Retrieved from https://www.archives.gov/education/lessons/japanese-relocation

National Center for State Courts. Retrieved from http://www.ncsc.org/~/media/Files/PDF/Topics/Gender%20and%20Racial%20Fairness/Implicit%20Bias%20FAQs%20rev.ashx

Native Hawaiian Organization Association. Retrieved from http://www.nhoassociation.org

Online Dictionary of the Social Sciences. Retrieved from http://bitbucket.icaap.org/dict.pl

Oral History Association. Retrieved from http://www.oralhistory.org/about/principles-and-practices/

Oxford Dictionaries. Retrieved from https://en.oxforddictionaries.com/definition/intersectionality

QAHWA PROJECT. Retrieved from http://qahwaproject.tumblr.com/post/128608599064/multiplex-identity-refers-to-people-who-hold

Racial Equity Tools. Retrieved from http://racialequitytools.org/glossary#diaspora

Sacramento County Clerk. Retrieved from http://www.ccr.saccounty.net/DocumentRecording/Pages/RestrictiveCovenant.aspx

SCHMOOP. Retrieved from http://www.shmoop.com/ethnic-studies/

Teaching Tolerance: Teaching the New Jim Crow. Retrieved from http://www.tolerance.org/sites/default/files/general/Jim%20Crow%20as%20a%20Form%20of%20Racialized%20Social%20Control.pdf

The Encyclopedia of Political Thought —Black Political Thought. Michelle D. Deardorff

Published Online: 15 September 2014

The Free Dictionary. Retrieved from http://www.thefreedictionary.com/kinesthetic

The Root What was Black America's Double War. Retrieved from `http://www.theroot.com/what-was-black-americas-double-war-1790896568

http://www.urbandictionary.com

Biology Online. Retrieved from http://www.biology-online.org/dictionary/Phenotype https://leginfo.legislature.ca.gov/faces/billNavClient.xhtml?bill_id=201520160AB30

Bracero History Archive. Retrieved from http://braceroarchive.org

U.S. Immigration Legislation Online. Retrieved from http://library.uwb.edu/Static/USimmigration/1970s_indochina.html

Veterans Administration. Retrieved from www.va.gov

The Nation. Retrieved from http://nation.com.pk

Index

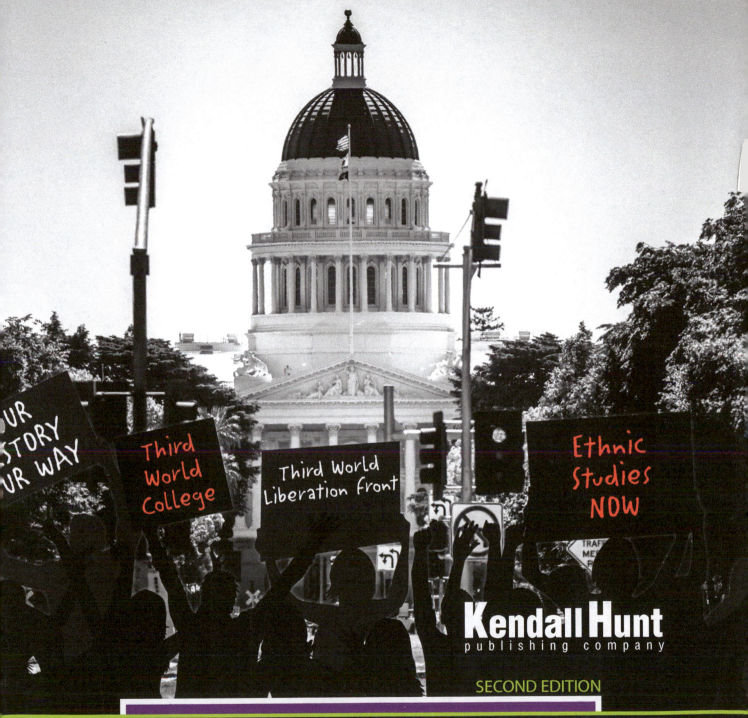

OUR STORY
OUR WAY

Third
World
College

Third World
Liberation Front

Ethnic
Studies
NOW

Kendall Hunt
publishing company

SECOND EDITION

OUR STORIES IN

OUR VOICES

Dale Allender | Gregory Yee Mark

Cover images © Shutterstock, Inc.

Back cover photo of Dale Allender courtesy of Arya Allender West.
Back cover photo of Gregory Yee Mark courtesy of Christina Fa Mark.

Kendall Hunt
publishing company

www.kendallhunt.com
Send all inquiries to:
4050 Westmark Drive
Dubuque, IA 52004-1840

Copyright © 2017, 2019 by Kendall Hunt Publishing Company

ISBN 978-1-5249-6875-5

Published in the United States of America